MOTHERING

An Expert's Guide to Succeeding in Your Most Important Role

Dr. Grace Ketterman

OLIVER
NELSON

THOMAS NELSON PUBLISHERS
Nashville

To All Moms

Copyright © 1991 by Grace Ketterman

Published in Nashville, Tennessee, by Thomas Nelson, Inc.

Scripture quotations are from THE NEW KING JAMES VERSION. Copyright © 1982 Thomas Nelson, Inc. All rights reserved. Used by permission.

Library of Congress Cataloging-in-Publication Data

Ketterman, Grace H.
    Mothering : an expert's guide to succeeding in your most important
role / Grace Ketterman.
       p. cm.
    Includes bibliographical references and index.
    ISBN 0-7852-6648-8 (pb)
    ISBN 0-8407-9101-1 (hc)
    1. Motherhood—United States. 2. Mothers—United States.
    I. Title
HQ759.K48 1991
306.874'3—dc20   90-29993
                                                         CIP

Printed in the United States of America
05 04 03 02 01 PHX 2 3 4 5 6

CONTENTS

Introduction

Like lightning sparking between lowering clouds, anger flashed between mother and daughter. Amber had caused immeasurable anxiety for her parents, and treatment for the family's problems had cost a small fortune. When improvement finally allowed Amber to return home, each family member had high hopes for a new era of harmony. Yet within a month of her homecoming, once again Amber had broken the rules, and her mother believed all their efforts and sacrifices were in vain.

The mother had experienced problems as a child and even now could barely force herself to face the pain of those years. How hard she had tried to create a home that was better than the one she had known! She adored her gorgeous dark-haired baby with sparkling brown eyes that could smolder in rage and twinkle with mischief in equal intensity.

As Amber grew, Mother could see some of her own traits developing in the child. They played, laughed, sang, and cried together as Amber and her little brother grew. Mother could relive her painful past in her child, and this time, everything would come out right. There would be no alcoholism, no poverty, no separation from a mother who worked long hours every day.

Then the hammer blow fell that shattered the idyllic world. Amber's father found that his job alone could not support the family. His retirement plan was inadequate, and he knew the family would need another income. Mother returned to work at his insistence. And she grieved over the loss of her time with Amber and Ray. The picnics, stories, games, and laughter suddenly were gone as she, like her mother before her, spent long hours at a job she hated fiercely. By evening, she was so angry and weary that she yelled at the children she loved and spurned the affection of the husband who demanded such a sacrifice.

Wise and healthy mothering is essential in today's cold, restless world. Many mothers, though, have grown up without the template needed to guide their mothering patterns.

Relentlessly, Mother drove herself to do the tasks she so utterly abhorred, and the price of her resentment had to be paid. The children missed her presence, but even more they grieved over the abrupt change in her. Where were the laughter and the games they had shared? The entire family grieved, and from the anger of that extended grief came the misbehaviors that threatened Amber's life.

As many aspects of family life improved, Mother believed they had turned the corner into a new era of warmth. Yet in one night, Amber had broken every rule they had so painstakingly formulated.

And now Amber and her mother sat confronting each other with all the power of their rage lashing tempestuously across my table. Their old habits of hurting each other with the same pain each felt were getting into motion, and I could well predict the results of such anger released.

Fortunately, I was able to speak above the thunder of their fury and get them to be quiet. After having a short time of silence and regaining some control, I questioned Amber about the events immediately preceding her rebellious acts. What had happened to prompt the dangerous irresponsibility she had demonstrated?

Without hesitation, she told us about a succession of interactions with supposed friends who had snubbed her, leaving her feeling abandoned, helpless, lonely, and sad. As she put words to these tragic emotions, Amber's eyes filled with the genuine tears of her vulnerable emotions. Her anger was completely dissipated.

It was easy then for Mother to take her teenager into her arms, cradling her like the young child she was at that moment. Mother, too, knew pain and tears, but she was equally practiced in covering them with anger. The tenderness of those moments as the tears of mother and daughter mingled brought real healing into both lives.

The story of this mother and daughter will be told in numerous variations in this book. Each case is unique, but all have much in common. Wise and healthy mothering is essential in today's cold, restless world. But like Amber's mom, many mothers have grown up without the template needed to guide their mothering patterns.

Amber's mother had temporarily lost the capacity to react to her troubled behavior with wisdom and gentle strength. She had attempted to deal with problems through the deceptive power of anger. However, she was basically wise, honest, and open to guidance and change.

Many women in the Western world have lost some of their capacity to show genuine tenderness. Several years ago, I briefly observed an interview of a popular TV star. The character she portrays is a hard-driving, cynical, and sophisticated businesswoman. She commented, "I wish in real life I was more like this person I play." Many women echo her wish, and the hard, competitive, unemotional woman has become the idol of too many. With the effort to emulate such personal qualities, there is a loss of tenderness, and the strength of gentleness and the ability to forget oneself in the interests of children are becoming increasingly rare.

It was in the mid-1960s that I was confronted with the idea that human beings could lose the capacity for compassion, protective love, and self-sacrifice in the interest of helping others. Then, I refused to believe such a thing could happen. I believed God-given instincts would prevail, keeping people humane, altruistic, and caring. The conscientious research of a brilliant man taught me I was wrong. Since then, I have learned of other research that verifies the possibility of losing the tender and compassionate interaction between mother and child.

It was also in the 1960s that Dr. Harry Harlow conducted an immensely significant research project at the University of Wisconsin. He realized the need to understand how parenting skills were passed from mother to child. Assuming they were purely instinctive or genetic was not good enough for him.

With the help of students and laboratory staff, Dr. Harlow contrived his techniques. Immediately after birth, baby monkeys were separated from their mothers. They were placed in small groups in comfortable cages and carefully fed and tended. There was even a wire mother monkey figure covered with fur that looked a great deal like an adult monkey.

It is reported that as time elapsed, the researchers were surprised to see that the babies matured on monkey schedule. They ate well, played happily together, and finally mated and bore young. None of this well-adjusted living had been expected. It seemed to negate the vital role of motherhood in the successful maturation of the new generation.

But then the significance of the studies emerged. The new mothers, who had grown up without a mother's presence, seemed to know nothing about baby care. They didn't nurse their young, cuddle them, play with them, or protect them. In one short generation, the animals lost the capacity to be healthy mothers.

Several years ago, I was intrigued by a newspaper article (now lost to me) that described a new type of clinic established in a large midwestern city. A psychologist had discovered that many mothers among her clientele didn't know how to interact with their babies. They weren't providing the stimulation that babies' senses need to grow and develop into intelligent, healthy adults.

This perceptive woman taught the mothers how to cuddle their babies, blow gently on their necks, and tickle them pleasurably. She showed them how to sing and talk to the babies and play with them in various ways that made them laugh, gurgle, and respond lovingly to their mothers.

In nearly five decades of medical training and experience, I have seen only a few children who were severely lacking in mothering; they were tragically damaged individuals. But I have seen a growing number of children and young adults whose parenting was inadequate in some way. Their mothers were not bad people. They simply had not received the kind of treatment they needed to be the mothers they wanted to be.

The horrors of World War II erupted while I was in high school. Most of my classmates and one of my brothers were drafted into the armed forces, as were many young men in countries throughout the world. Millions of people died in that conflict, and more were maimed.

Facing imminent death, the young men felt a desperate need to experience as much life as they could pack into their numbered days. Many of them married young women who were not truly ready for such an adult role, and a great many bore children. The young couples usually lived far from their extended families and were desperately poor, lonely, and scared to death of their futures. Most of the young mothers had to work, finding whatever child care they could. Other young men didn't marry but procreated children whose abandoned single mothers struggled heroically to provide for their needs.

Following the war, the young men who returned were different—they matured into hardened adults through all the experiences they had somehow survived. The couples, so deeply in love a few months or years ago, were strangers. No letters could portray the deep-seated changes war had hammered into their lives. Divorce became increasingly prevalent, leaving mothers alone again to provide for yet other children.

Those years seem to have precipitated an avalanche of troubles that focus more and more clearly on a loss of values, particularly those relating to marriage and the building of strong, safe families. The babies of the 1940s were often hard-pressed to be the parents and partners they wanted to be. The imprint of adequate mothering on their infant lives was missing in some degree. Without that, like the monkeys who grew up with a wire mother, people can lose the basic skills so vital to the next generation.

Fathers, too, have an essential role in parenting. We need to study and learn more about how dads fit into the transgenerational patterns of parenting. Even the abuse of drugs and alcohol is clearly related to inadequate parenting. Alan (not his real name) sat in my office obviously embarrassed by the tears that he could not control. He had abused chemicals for years and finally decided to gain control of his expensive and debilitating habit.

"How do the drugs make you feel?" I questioned.

Alan's face revealed the truth of his words: "I feel relaxed, safe, and happy when I use marijuana."

"And how would you have felt when you were a child if your father had been there to take care of you?" I probed. The truth was clear. Alan's father had not taken time to be with him. He never attended school events and never observed his Little League games. Alan had found in chemicals at least some of the pleasure his father should have provided.

This book cannot broaden its scope to discuss fathering. Perhaps that book needs to be written later. But even more integral to a child's eventual health is the bonding with a loving, devoted mother. The very existence of life depends on her nurturing and protection, particularly in the early months.

Present trends seem to permit mothers to settle for less-than-adequate mothering. It is a grave concern. Can a nanny or a series of day-care workers provide the imprint so necessary to mothering the next generation? I doubt that is possible, but I believe we can turn the tide of social ills and in a while renew the practices of parenting that can still change our world.

Miriam, a wonderful middle-aged woman, bore negative imprints of parenting from her mother. The anguish oppressing her was the result of destructive actions she endured during her growing-up years. Miriam's mother was, and still is, a self-centered, self-pitying woman. She pushed her child, early in life, to be the comfort and reassurance for her many trials and tribulations. But try as hard as she might, Miriam knew she had not once succeeded in bringing peace or joy to her mom's troubled spirit.

It was natural for Miriam to choose as a husband a man who needed her. She was accustomed to feeling her mission in life was taking care of someone. All of her efforts to meet the needs of her husband, however, suffered the same failure she had known with her mother. She couldn't make him happy, and when he became abusive, she finally had to leave him.

At work and in her personal life, Miriam kept playing the role of the rescuer but only with occasional success. She always felt anxious, and she was often deeply depressed because she could not succeed, just as she had not been able to do with her implacable mother.

My prayer for each person who contemplates this book is that you will become a successful mother. I hope that you will learn to love and accept yourself; that you will unconditionally accept your children; that you will work through any difficulties with your husband; and that your children will become a source of joy, pride, and deep love both now and later.

I must clearly state at this point that I haven't been the perfect mother of the year. I've made more than my share of mistakes. And I've learned from them. I've been privileged to observe mistakes and how to correct them. I've read, listened, pondered, and explored. Perhaps something I've learned will help you!

Grace H. Ketterman, M.D.

Preparing

CHAPTER ONE

Thinking About Becoming a Mother?

In today's world, becoming a mother is a choice, not a necessity. In some countries in the Orient, in fact, having more than one child is forbidden, and the cost of breaking that law is steep. How will *you* decide whether or not to become a mother? In this section, we will discuss some ideas that can help you know if you are ready now to become a mother.

Perhaps you have decided never to have children. Several of my friends have struggled with this choice and decided against having a baby. Often their friends and family have criticized them, and they themselves have had second thoughts. Growing older, alone, is depressing and even frightening.

But having a child who is not anticipated and desired is equally painful and may result in lifelong resentments and tensions. So you must reserve the right to decide and then have the courage to live with your decision. I will say that having a child is not easy or convenient. But living with an ever-developing person who is part of you and your husband and all of your ancestors can be an exciting and joy-filled adventure!

HOW MATURE ARE YOU?

You're almost certainly a mother already, or you wouldn't be interested in this book. But perhaps you know some women—your own daughters perhaps—who aren't mothers yet. You may find this section thought-provoking, so feel free to share it with them.

Peggy's blue eyes stormed, her voice boomed, and her rage blustered at Tammy. Her daughter had dared to defy her, saying, "I'm *not* going to clean my room. I'm going over to Sally's to play!" Such emotional storms were commonplace, and mother and daughter were in intense controversy much of the time.

As I watched the storm brewing and heard the devastation as it broke, I could see part of its course. The mother was reacting as childishly as the daughter, arguing and retaliating in a way that escalated rather than resolved issues.

Peggy needed to grow up. Being a mother demands maturity. How mature are you? I've made a list of ten signs of maturity. No doubt you can add some of your own thoughts. Read them carefully, and give yourself an honest and fair evaluation.

TEN SIGNS OF MATURITY

1. Having goals
2. Being flexible
3. Postponing pleasure
4. Coping with crises
5. Exercising self-control
6. Building self-esteem
7. Promoting emotional health
8. Maintaining physical health
9. Striving for interpersonal health
10. Practicing affirming attitudes

SIGNS OF MATURITY

1. Having goals. Mature people are able to set realistic goals, both short- and long-term. Karen, in her early twenties, was caught in a vise. She wanted to stay a dependent, carefree schoolgirl, getting her parents to support and protect her. She was ashamed, however, of her irresponsibility and also wanted a job, an apartment, and independence. She found herself unable to function, trapped in her confusion, and she became deeply depressed. When she set goals, worked to reach them, and had achievements worthy of pride, her depression vanished.

Make yourself do at least one task daily you don't want to do. It may be as small as neatly making your bed in the morning. Just do it. Then survey your accomplishment and let yourself feel proud.

Now, set a goal for the end of the week. Perhaps it's to make that bed every morning. Or it may be something quite different, such as balancing your checkbook.

Next, try a goal one month away: saving a sum of money, cleaning your house or apartment, or visiting a friend you've missed for a while. As you learn to reach your goals, you'll silently stretch your whole being to new levels of maturity.

A mature person is able to postpone present pleasure for future good.

2. Being flexible. In achieving goals, living with others, or functioning at all, you need flexibility. This is especially true in thinking about being a mother. Rigid, compulsive attitudes and behaviors set up needless power struggles and often defeat you in reaching goals. On the other hand, being too laid-back, careless, and inconsistent makes you unpredictable and confusing to persons around you—not a trait of a successful mom.

In setting and reaching goals, therefore, try for flexibility. If you get a phone call or happen to oversleep and can't get that bed made one morning, don't let it defeat you. Get on with your schedule, and decide how you will do it better next time. But follow through with the plan you make.

Practicing flexibility is a key ingredient of good mothering. Knowing when to give a little, yet holding the overall goals and limits firmly, will make sense to a child and will benefit you, too.

3. Postponing pleasure. One of the best single definitions of maturity I've heard is this: "It is the ability to postpone present pleasure for future good."

Rita needed to study for her semester final in history, but her fiancé called and suggested a shopping trip. Without hesitation, she agreed and was off, forgetting her exam until late at night. Her grade suffered. She was not mature.

I'm not suggesting that good moms can have no pleasure. But there are many times when pleasure must be put off in the interest of meeting basic needs (not selfish whims!) of the family. Practice that skill now if you want to be mature enough to be a successful mother.

Postponing pleasure involves the ability to adapt to change and losses. You may have exciting plans for your evening, but you learn you have to work late—a grave loss of fun and a dreary substitute for your fun. Your job success, however, may depend on how graciously you can accept such a necessity. The very existence of that job for you can be determined by your attitude. Being a mature person is important, even if you never become a mother.

4. Coping with crises. Immature persons tend to collapse when a crisis occurs. A run in your hose when you're late for work? It can ruin your day. Stopping to change or having to go by a store and purchase a new pair can be a nuisance. But it's a crisis only if you let it be. I never knew a valued employee to be fired because of a run! Planning better time control and keeping a spare pair of hose are ways of preventing recurring crises of this type.

If you experience crises with regularity, you likely are not very mature. You may be reacting to life instead of being in control.

There are, of course, crises that descend on us, and we may have little or no control over them. Strangely enough, these massive events are often easier to handle than the minor crises like runs or spilled coffee.

Mothering *guarantees* crisis situations. Learning from them, remedying their causes, and refusing to let them make you grouchy or even nervous are great achievements!

5. Exercising self-control. "I'm not going to work today!" Marilyn announced.

"I'm tired, I have a headache, and the boss was mean yesterday." No amount of reasoning made a difference, and Marilyn eventually lost her job. She had not mastered self-control. When demands were difficult and she felt unappreciated, she pouted, spoke rudely, and easily gave up.

For many years, counselors in America have been urging people to be "real" and to express their feelings honestly. But I have seen many people use this well-meant teaching as an excuse to act like two-year-old children.

Self-control, as a matter of fact, is learned at about age two. When toddlers begin to separate from parents, they test their limits: "Do I have to take a nap?" "No, I won't eat my lunch!" When parents don't find a way to break through such miniature power struggles, the child is likely to grow up acting like Marilyn. If she doesn't feel like it, or it's "too hard," she simply won't.

Emotionally healthy people don't react in destructive or hurtful ways—they are reasonably in touch with their feelings and know how to cope with them most of the time.

You can only imagine what sort of mother someone who has inadequate self-control will be. The laundry will be undone, the baby's room will be cluttered, and meal schedules will be fragmented. If you want to be a good mother, develop the willpower to make yourself control your attitude, your tone of voice, and your facial expression—as well as your organization and completion of tasks.

Such control is heroically difficult to achieve, and you may need the help of a friend or counselor. But only you can choose, and that is the secret of change—deciding that you will speak courteously, tackle tough assignments, and tenaciously stick with the job.

6. *Building self-esteem.* If you have grown up with too much giving in and giving up, too much help and rescuing, or too much criticism and blame, you may not feel good about yourself. Your self-respect and self-esteem may be poor. Persons who do not feel good about themselves are likely to do one of two things: they give in and become doormats to others, or they are arrogant and controlling in an effort to compensate.

Loving your neighbor *as* yourself is a wise philosophy. When that love is healthy (tough and tender), it provides the best possible chance for positive relationships. Mothers who feel good about themselves are much more likely to raise children who have healthy self-esteem.

7. Promoting emotional health. By this, I mean that you are aware of your feelings most of the time, don't try to hide them, and can express them appropriately and honestly.

Many people are trained to believe that certain feelings are not acceptable. To them, anger is a sin, and tears are a sign of weakness, so they work very hard to avoid such forbidden emotions.

Emotionally healthy, mature people are reasonably in touch with how they feel and what they need to cope with those feelings most of the time. If they are angry, they know why and decide what to do about it. They don't react in destructive and hurtful ways. This is essential in working with and living with children. When mature people are sad, they find a time and place to express their sadness—alone or with a trusted friend. When they are excited, they share that feeling, and when they are worried or afraid, they admit to needing help.

Mature people rarely show feelings in melodramatic ways. Learning to recognize your feelings and deal with them in constructive ways is another part of maturity.

8. Maintaining physical health. (Equally important is having the ability to cope with pain.) Helen suffered from PMS (premenstrual syndrome). Every month she endured headaches and abdominal discomfort, and she became grouchy and sensitive, weeping at the least annoyance. Her husband and coworkers sighed with relief when those days were past.

Most women can identify with Helen. In mild or more serious degrees, women universally struggle with physical discomforts from various sources. Immature people use their symptoms to gain attention, pamper themselves, or vent bad feelings without concern for those who must live and work with them.

Mature people take care of themselves. They eat a well-balanced diet and organize their time to allow for adequate rest and exercise. They seek medical help for conditions that require it but don't concentrate unduly on transient aches and pains.

Avoiding the extremes of stoicism and hypochondria allows most people a broad middle-of-the-road spectrum of feeling good. In a workshop I attended, a well-known psychiatrist stated that he has learned to choose not to catch a cold. He meant that by taking care of himself, he can, to a great extent, choose to avoid catching the colds so many of us endure. I'm certain that this ability is one not all of us could master, but we could come much closer if we took commonsense care of ourselves.

Being a mother is an everyday and all-the-time role. Cultivate good health, and practice self-control over your discomforts. Don't dump your bad feelings on others.

9. Striving for interpersonal health. Many mother-child conflicts emanate from poor communication, hypersensitivity, and confused emotions.

Sally seemed to be in conflict with her twelve-year-old daughter, Millie, most of the time. Millie was nearly a carbon copy of her grandmother, and Sally had never understood her mother. They, too, clashed most of the time.

Sally felt with Millie the same hurt, angry helplessness she had endured as a child with her mother. To her, Millie's normal adolescent attempts at independence were intolerable rebellion and insulting rudeness.

Many people who are overly sensitive (understandable though that may be) end up in a complex system of retaliation. One mother asked me whether she should do her daughter's laundry if the teenager didn't clean her room. The idea could have merit if it were carried out thoughtfully and consistently. But the mother spoke in a petulant, childish manner that revealed ongoing patterns of getting even with each other. Everyone loses when such behavior occurs.

Mature people work out their disturbed relationships, even if they have to get professional help, and find reasonable self-assurance that prevents unhealthy sensitivity with its constant hurt feelings and tendency to set up retaliatory habits.

10. Practicing affirming attitudes. Although recognizing mistakes and wrongs is important, coping with such negative events in a healing, affirming manner is far more important.

Being a successful mother demands intimacy with your child.

Claire needed to correct her son, who had created a major mess with his toys. She firmly told him what to do and helped him with areas he couldn't handle. When the chaos had returned to order, both she and the wayward child were weary. But she pulled the lad in her lap and said, "Kevin, that was a very hard job, and I know you didn't want to finish it. But you did. And now everything is okay. I'm especially proud of your doing such a big task!" Her hug reinforced Claire's pride with her forgiving love.

Even in the worst of circumstances, you can sift out a redeeming fact—if you practice an affirming attitude. The worst culprit desperately needs hope for himself or herself for tomorrow.

How to Develop an Affirming Attitude

- *Face your faults and mistakes with courage and honesty.* Correct the problems you can, forgive yourself, and live at peace with the inevitable weaknesses you can't change.
- *Separate the deeds from the person.* Your child is not a bad individual because she blunders at times, any more than you are. Accept others unconditionally as you do yourself.
- *Confront others directly and kindly about unacceptable behaviors or attitudes.* (This step is extremely important in successful mothering.) Always have a constructive suggestion about possible corrective action, and offer your help to make these changes.

- *Follow through with your offers of help, encouragement, and affirmation.* An affirming attitude always cheers others on to success. Some people (even mothers) are so insecure that they compete more than they facilitate the success of others. That attitude is certainly childish and endangers the likelihood of being a successful mother.

All of the qualities of a mature person may already be parts of your life, or some may be absent. Enjoy and cultivate the strengths you possess, and work hard to develop those traits that are weak or lacking. When you become a mother, you'll be glad you did. But even if you never are a mother, you'll be a wiser, better person.

ARE YOU CAPABLE OF INTIMACY?

Practitioners of both physical and psychological health are discovering more about the vital process of bonding between mother and child. Without positive attachment, children grow up unable to trust anyone; they are fearful and constantly test the safety or danger of their environment. To be ready for motherhood, then, you need to test your capacity to be appropriately intimate.

Dr. Eric Berne developed a concept of mental health called transactional analysis. Within that framework, it was taught that people progress through stages to the state of intimacy.

STAGES OF INTIMACY

The first stage, which can be repeated at any point, is **withdrawing.** People who prefer privacy or are fearful of others set more or less strict boundaries that distance and protect them from others who might hurt them. All of us, of course, are separated from persons we do not know.

Even the most timid person, however, sooner or later must meet a stranger. There are established rituals in all cultures for such occasions. In the U.S., we introduce ourselves, or a mutual acquaintance brings us face-to-face with a new person. We learn certain phrases to repeat, and often we shake hands with the individual. This second stage is called a **ritual.**

If there is opportunity, we progress from the ritual of meeting a person to *making small talk.* We discuss politics, the weather, current events, or any of a variety of superficial concepts, avoiding any real emotion or serious disagreement. We call this **pastiming.**

The fourth stage is **sharing activities.** In the period of pastiming, one often discovers areas of mutual interest and enjoyment. It becomes possible, then, to invite the new acquaintance to share that activity. Going to a concert, playing tennis, and hiking together are examples.

In the interest of completeness, there is another stage called **game playing.** This sort of game is played unconsciously for the sake of exchanging feelings and gaining attention. The emotions are negative ones, and such games, though extremely common, are not psychologically healthy.

> *Successful mothers find a balance between serving/giving to their children and needing love/help from them.*

If the relationship continues to be positive, the chances are that you will *become friends.* An intimate friend is a treasure to be cherished. With such a person, you can be totally honest; you are able to disagree and challenge, criticize, and question. You may also discover more shared feelings and experiences. You can safely trust such a friend, and you, in turn, are trustworthy. This is **intimacy.**

Obviously, you can't be intimate with everyone, so you need discernment to know whom you can trust. You may know from your first meeting that the stranger will remain distant. And at any point in the progression, you or the other person may stop.

Being a successful mother, however, *demands* intimacy with your child. Children need trust, a safe climate of unconditional acceptance and warmth, and clear pride and approval if they are to become healthy people, capable of good parenting when they reach that point in their lives.

Ingredients of a Mother's Intimacy

1. Enough self-esteem to believe that you are capable of giving love and worthy of receiving it.

2. The vitality to develop a variety of interests and opinions worth sharing with another, and the unselfishness to show genuine interest in that person's life.

3. A sense of good judgment that enables you to keep secrets, detect any lack of integrity in the other person, and set limits on the degree of intimacy you will choose.

4. The capacity for warmth and affection and a healthy sensitivity to your own and the other's comfort zone in exchanging this expression. (This quality becomes extremely significant in mothering older children, who may be uneasy with too much physical affection.)

5. The ability to be profoundly honest in a nonjudgmental manner. Many mother-child conflicts would never develop if moms could master this skill.

What Is Healthy Intimacy?

Healthy intimacy demands the ability to receive and learn as well as to give and teach. Unfortunately, a great many people have misunderstood the statement that "it is more blessed to give than to receive" (Acts 20:35). In fact, it *is* happier (more blessed) to be able to give, because you must first have something in order to be able to give. Admitting that you are poor and needy in certain areas of your life is risky and even painful. But just as you are happier when you give, so are others. And your healthy humility will endear you to those you are able to turn to when you have a need because you trust their love for you.

Mothers who are successful find a balance between serving and giving to their children and genuinely needing love and help from them.

Obviously, children don't always (or even often) want to offer that help. But I have observed that their refusal is frequently the result of mothers' demanding or manipulating rather than honestly admitting needs and requesting aid. That's why you need to understand and practice these ideas *before* you become a mother.

Enduring, healthy intimacy requires you to know who you are and what you have so that you can give it. For many years, I attempted to meet every need of all the people who came to me. I was trying to be all things to all people. Through some painful experiences, I discovered that I couldn't be who I wasn't. For example, several foster children joined our family. I tried to be the mother who was missing in their lives, but both they and I knew I wasn't that biological mother. Our relationship worked much better when I gave up that false expectation and settled for being a friend and adviser instead.

Overextending yourself as a mother or simply as a person is likely to result in fatigue and burnout. Just as you will be bankrupt if you constantly spend more than you earn, so you will become emotionally overdrawn if you try to be and give what is impossible.

The logical sequel to avoiding personal bankruptcy is learning to be sensitive to the resources of others. Expecting of them what they truly cannot be or do is unfair and will lead to bitterness and broken relationships.

My mother wanted and expected me to be perfect in the areas of life important to her, but she set the standards so high, I couldn't reach them. Years of striving for her approval in vain left me bewildered and, finally, angry. Long after her death I at last understood that she set such goals out of her love for me. Yet she was mistaken in her consistently critical, disapproving attitude.

A good mother finds each child's capabilities by exploring, observing, listening, and asking others. Next, she teaches, guides, encourages, and even requires the child to measure up to a personal best. Then she gives genuine approval.

UNHEALTHY INTIMACY

Intimacy is commonly considered in sexual terms. But it is much more than that—and very different. Intimacy is spiritual, emotional, intellectual, and social. Its best physical expression is sexual only in the total commitment of marriage.

Some parents have apparently lost sight of that valued boundary. In a sometimes-desperate search for intimacy they once knew as children, misguided parents may become sexually involved with their children. Such acts are called sexual abuse, yet few parents intend abuse; they simply yearn for closeness and often feel like children themselves. Most, if not all, of these parents were used sexually when they were children, and they carry the long-forgotten imprint of the excitement of their own experiences, now repeated on their children. However we understand incest, it is clearly unacceptable and leaves its scars for the next generation to suffer.

Readiness for motherhood has a great deal to do with the strength of your marriage.

Assess your sexual attitudes. They must be balanced and wholesome if you are to teach your children positive attitudes and values in the context of responsible behaviors.

Unhealthy sexual attitudes include:

- a morbid curiosity that is never satisfied but is evidenced by preoccupation with heavily sexual reading, movies, jokes, and conversation
- a rigidly closed mind that does not tolerate the word *sex* and a frigidity that prevents marital sex from being the joyful expression of total intimacy God designed
- habits of flirtatiousness in social situations that imply sexual interest and may lead to affairs.

One result of problems with sexual attitudes relates to adolescent children. Mothers who have unresolved sexual issues tend to be either too permissive or too rigidly strict with their teenagers, especially their sons.

Several years ago, a young woman asked a newspaper columnist for advice about her eighteen-year-old brother. He was dating a fourteen-year-old girl, and her parents allowed him to sleep overnight in their home. I have known personally of many similar situations, resulting in precocious sexual intimacy and even pregnancy.

At the other extreme, I have seen parents restrict children so severely that they felt they had to rebel to escape. Such extreme rigidity, I have learned, is often the result of sexual problems those parents experienced early in their lives that resulted in the overprotection of their children.

You may well need professional counseling to sort out old experiences, residual feelings, and confused attitudes. Be sure to get such help before you become a mother (or even a wife). And if you're already a mom struggling with unwholesome attitudes or misinformation, seek help as soon as possible. It's never too late to make corrections. Search for a counselor who has wholesome attitudes.

Once you are confident that you have positive, balanced sexual values and attitudes, you are ready to consider the delight of physical affection with others—especially children. I can still recall the goose bumps I felt when I was a very little girl and my grandmother blew on my neck or my father tickled my feet. And I can even feel my mother's warm stroking of my head and scratching of my back as I sat by her while she rocked.

Everyone needs physical touching—the warm and tender, light-hearted and teasing, loving and safe sensations so vital to being really alive. Find a way to enjoy and express your love in such wonderful ways.

IS YOUR MARRIAGE HEALTHY?

Many women, by choice or circumstances, are mothers alone. I have both empathy and respect for their often-heroic management of their myriad tasks. But the majority of mothers are also wives, and this section is for them.

Readiness for motherhood has a great deal to do with the strength of the marriage. A newspaper columnist stated some years ago, "The greatest gift you can give your child is two parents who really love each other." I agree! And in my opinion, he is still right!

How to achieve and maintain a strong marriage is the challenge. No one has the perfect solution, but I'll offer some suggestions that have proved to be of merit.

Be committed. Good marriages are based on meaning those wedding vows "for better for worse, for richer for poorer, in sickness and in health." Couples often change those time-honored words or state them glibly, only to renege when the first quarrel happens or things don't go perfectly.

Larry and Carol had been married only two years when they divorced. A friend asked him what had happened to cause such an early end to what had seemed a romantic relationship. With no evidence of remorse, the young man replied, "Oh, I don't know. I guess it just ran its course."

Quick and seemingly easy separations are all too common and often result from an inadequate degree of maturity and a lack of commitment. If couples will work at it, they will find successive disagreements and storms easier to resolve and to weather. Such work is vital to building families that can produce secure children.

Commitment demands an awareness of the facts. There will be worse times, times of loss, worry, illness, and disenchantment. He may fail to pick up dirty socks or change the lightbulbs; he may work too much or earn too little; and he is almost certain to spend too much money (or too little) and too much time watching TV sports. It's smart to share your feelings and wishes about these faults. But if he doesn't change, focus on his endearing smile, the fact that he goes to work at all, and how handsome he looks when he's dressed up. It's *your* choice to enjoy his good points or become dissatisfied with his imperfections.

Keep a positive attitude. Looking back over my marriage gives me an excellent perspective on my mistakes. Being active in my children's organizations meant contact with lots of other moms. I vividly recall huddling around the campfire after our Scouts were finally asleep. Over hot chocolate and gooey marshmallows, the conversation frequently turned to the faults of husbands. By the time the adults finally went to bed, we were certain that men were hopeless, egotistical slobs and that we wives were the most abused people on earth.

I'm convinced that such "ain't it awful" games train us to dwell on the problems without suggesting answers. This situation promotes self-pity and widens the gap between spouses. Furthermore, such talk is rarely revealed to the husbands, who must be sorely perplexed by the resulting estrangement and outright hostility of their wives.

I experienced a painful reminder of some of my early marriage mistakes. Two relatives of mine, Cheryl and Derek, were visiting in my home, and the talk reverted to household chores. Cheryl was feeling put-upon because of her many duties after work. Her young husband spoke up, "But I do try to help you. I do some laundry."

The response was quick and bitter: "Yes, but you put your blue jeans in with the towels, and they turned everything blue!"

Embarrassed, Derek's gray eyes turned to the floor as he almost pleaded, "But, Cheryl, I washed the dishes just last evening. I try to help!"

Again her retort was harsh: "Yes, and you broke a glass, and I can't find where you put the measuring cup!"

Derek changed the topic because he knew he couldn't win. Cheryl was convinced that he was a bumbling man who couldn't please her. In her innermost being, she felt everything must be done perfectly, but that perfection was so elusive, it could never be attained. Outwardly, Cheryl made demands for such perfection on her husband. Her children would be in for a difficult time if she had any. And her marriage already suffers.

Take a look at yourself—and at your past. Do you try too hard to be exactly right? Who taught you such standards? Perhaps you will discover, as I did, that true perfection belongs only to God, and that you can settle for judging your own best efforts and feeling good about them. Being fair and kind to yourself will help you be more gracious to and accepting of others. Then your marriage will be enriched and will be much more the loving, respecting relationship you want your children to see.

Learn to disagree agreeably. No matter how committed you are or how positive an attitude you develop, there will be times when you and your husband disagree. Many personal and household issues arise that demand decisions. You are sure to discover that you strongly believe one choice is best and he is equally certain that one will never do. How do you solve such problems and still remain friends?

First, keep an open mind. You could be wrong. How embarrassing it would be to hold out so stubbornly that you win an argument only to have the decision turn into disaster! It is much wiser to approach a difference of opinion by collecting information. And gather all you can—not just data that will support your preconceived notion.

After you have enough information, arrange all the facts into pro and con columns. Then discuss the facts with each other, and be certain they are accurate and complete.

Parents who show respect for each other build healthy self-esteem in their children.

Finally, forget *who* is right (who gets his or her way), and concentrate on *what* is best for everyone in the long run. Not only is this a great plan for a successful marriage, but it is also an incomparable asset to avoid power struggles later with a strong-willed child.

Be playful. Life is full of stress, and if you are not alert to it, you may fall for the danger of taking it too seriously. Laugh often and play regularly. Schedule time for sports or games you both enjoy, but beware of letting them become overly competitive instead of fun.

Plan time for play with friends. Develop a social life that will provide contacts for your children when you have them. Look for peers who share your values and interests.

Don't overlook the fun in sexual intimacy. This part of your marriage falls prey easily to resentments and hurt feelings you can allow to stack up. Keep your lovemaking romantic and joyful.

Children thrive on laughter, so maintain a sense of humor. It will enrich your life, strengthen your marriage, and bond you with your children.

Never store resentments. It takes a firm commitment to be free of bad feelings between you and your family. Janet had grown up in a sensitive family whose feelings were easily hurt. She would cry frequently and withdraw from her husband, a direct, even blunt, person. Trying to be strong, she would quickly recover control, but she failed to discuss the problems or confront her husband's intense reactions. Both issues and hurts stacked up on each other to create a wall between them.

Janet realized she could not and would not live in a chronic state of resentment and martyrdom. She resolved to find better methods than tears for expressing her emotions. And she vowed to clear up every misunderstanding of the day before retiring at night. Because her former habits were old, entrenched ones, Janet had a long struggle to break them and still more work to learn to confront honestly and lovingly. But she did it. It's a comfortable and even exciting way to live.

Communicate clearly. In marriage, being poorly understood causes more serious problems than almost any other factor. Without realizing it, you can expect your husband to know what you need without ever telling him—to literally read your mind. Without excellent communication skills to resolve those problems and restore harmony, your relationship will suffer.

SUGGESTIONS FOR IMPROVING YOUR COMMUNICATION

- *Think before you speak.* Are your comments kind, clear, and necessary? If not, revise them. Many times I say things that imply the other person may not know what to do or how to do it. I have no such thoughts or intentions, but over the years I've developed the habit of guiding troubled children and trying to help their parents through difficulties. Without realizing it, I speak to my family and friends with unnecessary bossiness. This is poor communication, and I work hard to correct it. Try to distill your thoughts into a few words that convey clearly what you want to say.

> *To leave a healthy imprint in your children's minds and morals, you must carefully formulate and live out your own value system.*

- *Observe the person who is listening to you.* Does his facial expression match what you are saying? If not, stop talking and ask what he heard you say. This simple step can short-circuit many misunderstandings. Reading body language is a great skill.

- *Listen to your tone of voice, and pay attention to the tight spots in your body.* A knot in your stomach or tension in your neck or arms may be your best clue that you are more intense than you need to be. That could be a serious turnoff to your listener.

- *If you hear any message from your conversational partner that hurts you or seems out of character for him, stop at once.* Chances are, he doesn't intend to hurt you unless someone else hurt him. It's a wonderful gift to say to him, "I know you love me and wouldn't hurt me, but what you just said was an unfair shot. Did you really mean that, or did I hear you incorrectly?"

- *Always make it your goal to complete every conversation with a clear exchange of information and the maintenance or restoration of harmonious, loving feelings.* Can you imagine a world where everybody did?

Show respect. In his scholarly book *The Antecedents of Self-Esteem*, Dr. Stanley Coopersmith explained that parents' evidence of respect for each other was one trait that built healthy self-esteem in children. This is another reason to stop being picky or critical of your husband. Instead, remember the kind and loving things he does and focus on all the positives. Thank him and comment on his good qualities whenever you can.

Where he is less than perfect, try to help him improve and grow. But remember: no one can change anyone else. You can help him change only if he wishes to do so. It is cruel to try to change another person because it clearly labels him as being in need of correction. Unconditional love is as vital to a healthy marriage as it is to good mothering.

Creating and maintaining a loving, healthy marriage requires constant effort. Without that, however, you have nothing to hold to and are likely to be unhappy or even divorced.

FORMULATING A SOLID VALUE SYSTEM

We live in a pagan society, according to some thoughtful theologians of the day. Many people do not attend religious services and rarely think about their spiritual lives. Atheism is the professed philosophy of much of the world.

Schools believe they cannot teach values, and many parents fail to incorporate such teaching into their parenting practices. Who, then, will teach values to the children? And do you know your own values and their priorities?

Three questions have helped me order the importance of my values:

• Will practicing this value help me be a better person?
• Will this value help those around me be better and more comfortable?
• If everyone held this value and lived by it, would this be a better world?

If any value passes the scrutiny of these queries, chances are good that it is one you should adopt.

To leave a healthy imprint in the minds and morals of your children, you must carefully formulate your own value system. To help direct your thinking on this subject, here are some values that are important to me:

Honesty. Some years ago I watched the TV version of *Samson and Delilah,* a magnificent movie based on the biblical story. To my horror, the movie depicted the cruel ritual of stoning to death a woman caught in the act of adultery. I recalled another biblical story of Rahab, a prostitute, who saved the lives of some Israelite spies. God honored this woman for her brave deed, although she made her living by sexual acts, but a law that God had given demanded that an adulterous wife be put to death. I was most perplexed.

I have learned that God's Word is right, so I prayed for understanding of an apparent contradiction. The answer has reordered the priorities of my values. It was simple. The prostitute was honest about who she was. She advertised her trade and was well known. The wife, on the other hand, had promised faithfulness to her husband, but she was living a lie. Pretending to be a faithful wife, she was sneaking around with another man. How could a dishonest woman leave the imprint of basic honesty in the lives of her children? This meditation made me see that honesty must be first on my list. Without it, nothing else is believable.

Spirituality. For people who have no acquaintance with a power beyond their own, life loses its perspective, and they lose the vital source of wisdom, love, and power for living. I have learned that everyone must decide just what to believe and how rapidly to grow spiritually. But to deny this essential aspect of life and not to grow at all is a tragedy.

In developing your spiritual life, there are many avenues to explore. One of my favorites is nature. In sunsets, clouds, mountains, and oceans as well as in the vastness of the planets and the intricacy of the molecules is evidence of the genius of a Creator beyond my comprehension. Learn to look at and listen to the sights and sounds of nature. Let yourself revel in the rich colors of rainbows, the magnificence of thunderstorms, and the gentle unfolding of a flower.

Spiritual life grows also through observing and getting to know people. Infants, as they discover the world with fresh, new senses, always remind me of the wonder of it all. Their every developing stage is a reminder of the endless processes of life, birth, growth, a new generation, and eventually death—the transition to ultimate Life. The eagerness and energy of youth, the tender love of new parents, and the gentle glow of older folks—each stage of life points to its ebb and flow, its eternalness.

I don't deny the negative facets of people. Often they are burdensome, rude, lazy, and irascible. But I choose to believe in transcending the negatives and focusing on an individual's endless potential for good.

Prayer, Bible reading, and thoughtful meditation add options for spiritual strength. So does the constant practice of the presence of God through your day. Knowing that God is an ever-present Source and is accessible can bring you comfort, peace, strength, wisdom, and love.

Commitment. Unfortunately, this has become an era of the "easy out." If he doesn't make you happy, find a man who will. Never mind that you must eventually find happiness within yourself! Let me remind you that there is no perfect person. The choice is yours—to seek and enjoy the good or to bemoan and resent the faults.

Consideration for yourself and others is the basis of respect.

Much of the joy in marriage rests on your decision to be a loving person and to live out that love in tenderness, humor, and tenacious toughness. A secure, committed marriage is a distinct asset if you are to become a good mother. The degree of your commitment to your husband helps assure your commitment to your children as well. Commitment demands a mature sense of altruism and self-control; you must choose what is best for your family, no matter how you may feel.

Material comfort. This value has swung wildly on our cultural pendulum in recent years. Young people have rightly become disgusted with the greed of affluence. "Things" have become too much a preoccupation with many people.

I grew up, however, in a time when the benefits of electricity and other forms of energy were not available. I vividly recall the biting cold of an unheated upstairs room, the inconvenience of kerosene lamps, and the time-consuming effort of cooking on a wood-burning stove.

Although material comforts do not make us happy, I see nothing wrong in wanting a home that is cozy, attractive, and as comfortable as you can make it. Making many of your furnishings and other household items can become a value in itself. Friends of mine have made their bed frames, some of their chairs, most of their curtains and linens, and play equipment for their children.

Young children don't notice the slick finish and colors of factory-made toys. They are enriched by the time and efforts of parents to create a bright environment woven with love.

Whatever your resources, I urge you to carefully consider your child's home. Keep it safe enough to protect him, attractive enough to please her, and simple enough to allow a high degree of freedom.

Creativity. Be creative in all aspects of your life. Practicing this value will enable you to discover and enjoy your uniqueness—your God-given capacity for artistry. People who cultivate their creativity seem to feel better about themselves; they are a part of their environment and can help others to feel a sense of belonging.

Creativity keeps life fresh and delightful, preventing boredom and depression. Being creative demands taking risks. Someone else may not like your taste in color or style. So what? You may change your mind or focus on design. That's okay, too. Part of creativity is the ever-shifting expression of your emerging artistry. As long as the changes don't outstrip your financial resources, let yourself enjoy variety.

I trust that as you practice being creative in material areas, you will learn to apply creativity to all of your life—your thoughts, your play, your relationships, and even your spirituality.

Responsibility. For some people, exhibiting responsible behavior on the job seems too demanding. Having home repairs done is a constant disappointment as the costs increase and the workmanship declines. Supervisors tell me that many employees are far more focused on the time clock than the quality of their work. As a society, people concentrate more on looking forward to weekend fun than being responsible on the job to their employers.

If more people endeavored to be responsible, our economy would reap the benefits. Stealing from employers costs all of us in increased prices to cover losses of stolen tools, office supplies, equipment, and even toilet paper!

To be ready for motherhood, you need to understand and accept your feelings— and know how to express them constructively.

Responsibility toward others would make life much more civil and safe. Careless driving makes roads hazardous. Jostling that occurs in unruly crowds can actually crush people to death, and destruction of public areas and national shrines is a reality. If you value responsibility, you will not only practice it, but you will also teach it to your children.

Our society would improve if people were responsible for their actions; families would benefit from having responsible adults as parents.

Recreation. Remember your most delightful experiences as a child and find ways to re-create them. When did you laugh the most heartily? (And not at the expense of another's good feeling!) What experiences can you recall that energized you and enabled you to face your duties again?

If your life has gotten out of balance and you are fatigued, bored, and burned out, I dare say you need more recreation. Develop a plan for regular rest and relaxation, and you will discover new zest for living. When you become a mother, you will really need to practice healthy recreation!

Respect. Consideration for yourself and others is the basis of respect. Developing and practicing this time-honored value demand an inner attitude, not a superficial set of manners. Self-respect must come from a sense of your worth. You need not be an egomaniac, but do practice the discovery, development, and enjoyment of all your good qualities. Make yourself as attractive as possible by cultivating health, dressing carefully, and grooming neatly. Practice smiling, be friendly, and treat people around you kindly. Learn to do something really well, and allow yourself to feel proud of your achievements. Everyone can be worthy of respect.

Only when you enjoy some degree of self-respect can you honestly respect others. But work at that while your self-respect is growing. Rather than speaking rudely to a snippy salesperson, try a friendly smile and kind comment. Chances are, she's had a hard day and her feet hurt! Respect has many expressions, so you may even find some that are humorous.

On one hand, respect must be earned. If you become a mother, remember that! But on the other hand, it is an inner quality you choose to develop and live out—whether the other person deserves it or not.

Balance. This value has become a driving force in my life. And the more I understand and pursue it, the more I believe in it. Enough rest to restore energy is vital. Too much can deprive one of any sense of achievement.

Recreation is an essential value. But when people pursue it to an extreme, and it becomes an end in itself, it will consume them. They will be deprived of the energy to be productive at work and will neglect other aspects of their lives.

People who get out of balance spiritually can become fanatics or bitter agnostics. Any extreme in life is likely to create discomfort for you and those around you. Early on, I hope you will find your balanced position and stick with it.

You may well have other values that you would include in this list. There are many. The important point is, do you practice them? Or do you only intellectualize about them? If they make you a better person and enhance the lives of others, you are doing a good job!

A HEALTHY EMOTIONAL LIFE

Silence, filled with tension, was palpable in the office. The principal had just described his concern over Tim's behavior. He would hit or kick classmates and teachers alike. The names he called adults were words strictly forbidden in the rule book, and no amount of effort had made even a dent in Tim's armor.

It was obvious by his ten-year-old face that tears were ready to flow down the angry lines on his cheeks. But Tim stubbornly held them back. He couldn't afford to let anyone know that he was capable of tender emotions.

Later, I learned much more about Tim's emotional distress and his mother's part in that. She had grown up with abuse and left home early, seeking in marriage some of the warmth and safety she needed. But her young husband didn't prove much kinder than her family, and soon he left her with Tim, a tiny baby.

Linda (not her real name) decided that life was easier if you simply didn't permit yourself to feel anything. She couldn't totally eliminate the anger that blew up at times like a volcano erupting. But she could prevent the other feelings she once had known—no worry or concern, no joy or excitement, no hope or anticipation, and certainly no love or peace. The numbness of a forced indifference somehow helped her remain sane.

Tim copied his mother's restricted emotional life. He, too, hid every tender feeling and allowed only anger to explode through the walls of his defenses. The core of hurt, loneliness, and need was still reachable but not for much longer. Without the help that Linda willingly accepted, two angry shells of people might have been all that remained.

Like Linda and Tim, many people have been hurt so seriously and repeatedly that they have trained themselves to stop feeling at all. Other people are taught selectively to screen out certain unacceptable emotions. Carrie's father ridiculed her bubbling excitement over her high school's football games. Marie learned from her strict mother that it was sinful to be angry, and Bill's dad made it all too clear that it was "sissy" to cry or show any sadness or fear.

Such parental messages are intended for the good of children who are dearly loved. But they are terribly wrong and create lifelong problems for the children who believe them. Emotions or feelings are not right or wrong, good or bad—they just *are!* They exist at birth and expand in scope and depth as we grow. They become windows into one another's souls and bridges between us. We cannot define joy and comfort unless we understand pain of some sort. Uncomfortable emotions have meaning through the healing of another's concern and help. Healthy human beings experience and learn to cope with all sorts of emotions—negative and positive.

> *Emotional health is not only being aware of your own feelings, but also being sensitive to and caring about others' feelings.*

To be ready for motherhood, you need to understand and accept your feelings. And you must know how to express them constructively. Hiding them from others—even yourself—simply won't work.

There are three main categories of emotions. Two of them are present at birth, but the third must be learned.

1. *Aggression (anger).* Newborn babies arrive skilled at expressing their anger. It is prompted by pain, and its physical expression is identical in all babies all over the world. The eyes close tightly, hands clench, and along with that, the feet are drawn close to the body, then they flail about. Angry babies let loose a piercing cry that is uniformly recognized by mothers as a cry of pain and indignation.

2. *Fear.* A routine part of the physical assessment of every newborn is the discovery of the startle reflex. A sudden jolt of the bassinet or a loud noise will induce in a newborn a typical response that differs from the anger response. Her eyes open wide, the arms and legs extend, and there

is usually a general jerking of the entire body. The cry is different from an angry cry, though the arms and legs will be drawn in quickly toward the body similarly to the anger response. Sensitive parents quickly learn to distinguish these two basic emotional expressions.

3. *Love.* Although babies prompt a great deal of love in parents and grandparents, they show no signs of being loving for many days after birth. Not until several weeks of age do they begin to smile responsively, and it is rare for them to hug or kiss even the most loving parents until they have received such expressions for many months.

All of the aggressive emotions branch out of the inborn anger. These are many and varied, ranging from slight irritation or frustration through rage and fury. Their cause is always some type of pain—experiencing an injustice or being picked on, labeled, ridiculed, robbed, or attacked. Anger is nature's gift for protecting oneself and counterattacking a foe.

Fear is also a life-preserving gift from our Creator. Sudden sounds and motions may signal danger and even late in life are useful in helping us move to safety. Healthy fear is caution and alertness. But in its intensity, fear can become panic or an emotionally crippling phobia. Anxiety and worry branch from fear and may lead to depression.

It is in teaching love that both the greatest opportunity and the gravest danger lie. If love is learned through the early imprint of parents' touch, voices, and total care, a child has a good chance of developing a loving personality. But if not enough time, energy, and credible love are expressed to a baby, she can grow up unable to offer such love to the next genera-tion. Dr. Harlow's studies certainly point to this fact (see Introduction).

LEARN TO LOVE YOUR CHILDREN

Above all else, if you want to be a mother, you must learn how to love. If you have been deprived of love in some degree, the following sugges-tions may help you.

Imagine. If you were to feel truly loved, what would that be like? To answer that question, try to recall your childhood. Perhaps your grand-mother held and hugged you at times. Or maybe you had friends or a teacher who gave you a sense of warmth and fun. A pet or favorite doll or stuffed animal may have served as a confidant and comforter. Whatever you can recall or even imagine, use that to recapture or create a sense of love. Then practice passing on that love to someone else.

Observe. Some people cannot remember any loving experiences in their entire lives. If you happen to be one of them, learn to watch other families at parks, the zoo, or shopping centers. Sit on a bench and watch long enough, and you will see some mothers and children having fun and showing love for one another. As you observe, focus on the type of inter-action that appeals to you. Such expressions will probably seem natural to you. Again, practice these ways of showing love until they become sec-ond nature.

Another source for observations may be television. You'll have far more opportunities to learn violence and seductiveness there, but you may well find a few role models for really effective parenting.

Read. A librarian can probably suggest books that describe family rela-tionships in a wholesome, readable manner. You may discover other resources by reading book reviews in newspapers or parenting magazines. As you read, try to inject yourself into the situations. What would you like if you were sad, scared, angry, or excited? What seems to work out in the story? Can you apply that action to yourself and your relationships?

Meditate (pray). God is far too immense for our finite minds to com-prehend. He may seem to you to be austere, remote, even harsh. But I perceive God as a loving, wise Being who cares about infinitely small things like atoms just as much as incredibly immense things like space, stars, and solar systems. So I know He cares about people. The Judeo-Christian faith teaches that mankind was even made in His likeness, so we must be precious.

Imagine God as a loving, laughing, wise Parent or Grandparent. Allow yourself to soak up that divine love until you are saturated and can then pass it on to others.

Whatever you do to learn to love demands effort and some risk taking. Move slowly in these or other activities to explore love. But don't refuse to try at all. Expect some disappointments and failures, and keep right on trying. A dear friend of mine practiced hugging her pillow, and she found in its softness some of the warm gentleness she had missed in her mother. Just don't settle for doing nothing.

Risk pain. When I commit myself to honestly love anyone, I include in the package the awareness that he or she may hurt me. But I will not give anyone the power to destroy me. The ability to experience pain means that I am alive. And that life can also experience love, joy, and peace. You may well have known more than your share of pain, and for that I grieve. But slowly and watchfully, select yet another person and try again to learn the positive side of love. Avoid inflicting pain, and stay as cautious, yet as positive, in your attitude as possible. You *can* learn to love.

Emotional health is not only an awareness of your feelings; it is sensitivity to and caring about the feelings of others. Children get hurt in many ways, and they need understanding and guidance to transcend the pain and return to comfort.

A good mother must know how to empathize with her child. Empathy means that you feel *with* your child some of whatever she experiences. It is better than sympathy because it is less likely to allow the child to develop the crippling disease of self-pity. Empathy enables you to interpret to a child what you guess he is feeling and find a means for meeting the need accompanying it. Often, in empathy with a child, parents find healing and insight for old wounds from their childhood.

When you are with friends or around complete strangers, observe their faces, posture, and tone of voice. What message does this body language convey? When it's appropriate, find some way to reach out to others—a wink, a smile, a passing touch, or a tender glance can say far more than words. And practicing these habits of kindness will prepare you to be an outstanding mother one day.

RELATIONSHIPS WITH YOUR EXTENDED FAMILY

Night after night, Frances was startled awake by the sounds of anger. Her parents were arguing; that would escalate to yelling and often would explode into physical abuse that filled her with terror. She tried repeatedly to stop those fights, only to be punished and locked out of their bedroom.

Fran could never find a way to get close to her parents or to get them to be nice to each other. She could hardly wait to grow up, get married, and leave that miserable situation. The man she married seemed to be devoted to her, and for the first time in her life, she felt loved and safe.

That is, until Fran realized he was jealous and suspicious of her activities. He listened in on her phone calls and followed her on shopping trips. Before long she was a participant in regular fighting. Her husband was so much like her dad!

Activities consume our time, and enrichment opportunities abound for children. But it's vital to balance busyness with times to communicate, care, and support each other in our families.

Despite the couple's unhappy marriage, two children were born to them. Their daughter inherited the characteristics of Fran's father. She looked very much like him and was extremely fond of her granddad. As the girl learned his manner of talking and copied his attitudes, Fran found it more and more difficult to tolerate her child. She could hardly believe the truth as it finally became clear. She had reconstituted the painful family situation in which she had grown up.

Fran's situation is typical of many families. No family, to my knowledge, is perfect; in any set of relatives there is the likelihood of some ill will and resentment. When you become a mother, who will your husband and child remind you of? Could the resemblance of your first child to a problem relative reinforce an old pattern of resentment? Unless you are most exceptional, the answer is yes.

HOW SHOULD YOU HANDLE DIFFICULT FAMILY MEMBERS?

There is no way to rid yourself of such difficult people. Relatives are for life. And even after death, the memories live on. So I haven't found a way to eliminate that aspect of family trouble.

What I have found useful, however, is to understand those difficult folks and to forgive their hurtfulness. Being an emotionally healthy person requires mastering the art of forgiving. Forgiveness results in a marvelous freedom that will be a major asset in your mothering. (For further reading about learning how to forgive, see the book I coauthored with David Hazard, *When You Can't Say "I Forgive You"* [NavPress, 2000].)

Clarify the actions or attitudes of that difficult person. Distinguish his or her part of the problem from what could be an overreaction on your part. Find out all you can about that individual. Once you know what happened as she grew up or how unfairly he was punished, for example, you may see things very differently.

Open your heart as well as your mind. It is safer to stay irritated with and suspicious of a difficult person than it is to open the possibility of loving him or her. You must be willing to be reconciled.

Allow your information to penetrate your emotions, and take the risk of experiencing insight. Insight is the "Aha! Now I see why she did that!" experience. It doesn't mean the act was okay, but it does explain the motivation, which usually is all right.

Don't worry about the other person. Your insight and forgiveness are all that are needed for the purpose of loving your child unconditionally. You are now free of the old hidden hurts and anger that could negatively influence your mothering. You are no longer likely to unknowingly take out on your child or husband these damaging feelings.

Unconscious expectations are also likely to damage your child. Your son, Lance, may resemble Uncle Howard, who was a football player. That doesn't mean Lance is cut out to play football. He may be, or he may not be. Your job as a mother will be to help Lance explore. Give him the opportunity to play, and encourage him to put every effort into mastering the skills required. But if he never develops a strong interest or has bones that could be unduly at risk in a contact sport, have the common sense and fairness to let him do something else.

Explore with a child what she is really capable of doing. If that happens to be something reminiscent of Grandma Alice's abilities, no doubt the family will be pleased. If not, I hope they, and you, will be equally pleased about whatever that child chooses.

Expecting a child to do something of which he is truly incapable is unfair. It establishes a probability of failure and disappointment deadly to a relationship.

ENMESHED FAMILIES

In the mental health profession, *the enmeshed family* describes family members who are overly involved with one another. One assumes impossible responsibilities for another, just as Frances felt she had to prevent her parents' fights. In enmeshed families, personal boundaries are unclear, and individuals have a difficult time establishing their identities, much less their independence.

Such overinvolvement may stem from various causes. Old family habits that extend across many generations can keep the process active. A lack of balance in tender and tough love and a failure to practice unconditional love may also contribute to enmeshment. So can a sense of guilt in both parents and children. Whatever the cause, I strongly urge you to evaluate your situation before you become a mother (or at any time!). If you are caught in this trap, find your way out. You may be able to extricate yourself, but you may need professional counseling.

Start by recognizing the problem. Be sure that you are enmeshed. Some families are simply loving, caring, and intimate and give one another adequate space and mutual respect. If, however, you feel invaded, condemned, or overpowered much of the time, you may need to make some changes.

Seek to change only yourself. Forget changing others unless they seek your help. If you genuinely change, everyone else in your family system will change in some manner. Gradually establish your opinions, allow yourself to feel your emotions, and identify which problems are yours.

Avoid going to the opposite extreme. To get free from overinvolvement, you may at times resent people and not have any contact with them. Although that may be useful in freeing yourself, you may later find that having a healthy and warm relationship is better than being hostile and estranged.

Practice the golden rule. Discover first what is comfortable for you in family relationships. With individual modification, offer to your family what seems good to you. Chances are, they'll like and benefit from your discoveries.

At any rate, when you have children, you'll give them some excellent advantages you didn't have. You'll be a better mom if you don't enmesh your children. Learn to be open and honest in an affirming and positive manner and you will be well on your way to the potential for a healthy family.

ESTRANGED FAMILIES

Many families are completely opposite from enmeshed ones; they are estranged. People often don't know how to be intimate. For various reasons, they may fear getting close to one another.

The culture in which we live lends itself to remoteness. Activities, both work and play, consume our time as adults. And I often feel that a whirling dervish is controlling the time of children. They are expected to be good at sports, dancing, art, music, gymnastics, and academics. Enrichment opportunities abound. But rarely, if ever, do these activities bring together the entire family. Mother becomes the taxi driver, older sister is the social secretary (since she loves the telephone), and Dad (if there is one) and big brother are working or involved with separate sports teams.

You need to work through past conflicts with your own mother so that you can be a happy, affirming mother.

Families have become, at best, a conglomerate of individuals, each whizzing about in a personal orbit. Once in a while they bump into one another quite by accident and are too surprised to say, "Excuse me!"

It's wonderful to be busy and involved in activities. It's essential that family members share in one another's work and play. And it's vital to balance the busyness with times to communicate, care, and support one another.

Be alert to the possibility that your family, too, can be caught in the maelstrom of frantic activities that separate you. Find and guard the time and means to promote intimacy.

ARE YOU PREPARING FOR MOTHERHOOD ALONE?

"I'm thirty-five, and I don't know a man I would want to marry. But I want so desperately to have a baby. I can support myself and a child well enough, and I may just decide to be a mother alone." In several variations, I have heard these words from young women. Their eyes often stream tears, and their faces vividly portray the deep emotions of anger, sadness, and anxiety.

Life is slipping by. They have traveled widely and secured the success they set out to achieve. But somehow they have missed the one most important experience of all—that of becoming a mother. Who can blame them? And many successful women are choosing to become pregnant by "using" a friend or even a chance acquaintance or by being artificially inseminated. It is increasingly easy to become a mother without a spouse.

For nearly four years, I worked in a home for unwed mothers. There I touched, directly or indirectly, nearly one thousand lives of women who were expecting a child quite by accident. Through loneliness with its need for companionship, rebellion with its consequences, or simply the intensity of sexual passion, these women faced motherhood alone.

One more category of single mothers exists. With startling frequency, couples seem to discover that they cannot stay together through the birth of a child. Perhaps she focuses too much on the child, leaving him feeling unimportant or abandoned. At times he feels overwhelmed by the responsibility of being both husband and father. Often, he has grown up without much fathering and doesn't believe he can be a good one. At any rate, separations occur, leaving her to face motherhood alone.

If you are in any of these three groups, you'll need support. You may be too proud or independent to admit it, but let me assure you, you will find out. I strongly urge you to plan ahead and build around you a significant support system.

Ask a close and committed friend to attend birth classes with you. Seek financial counsel to be certain the costs of medical care and child care after birth are provided. Choose reliable medical providers, and be *very sure* you have included a person to stay with you for a time after the birth of your baby.

If you consider deliberately becoming a mother without making a loving commitment to a husband, *recognize that every child needs to know both parents.* Personal identity and emotional security demand that. It may even be true that a child has the *right* to know his or her father. At any rate, think carefully about the child as well as your natural desires.

Plan out the answers you will be prepared to give. If you were that future child, would those answers satisfy you?

We'll discuss more issues about mothering alone in Section Four.

PREPARING TO BECOME AN ADOPTIVE MOTHER

Deciding whether or not you are ready to be a mother isn't easy, as I hope you now know. Becoming an adoptive mother is even more complex and demands unique thinking and processing.

First, **most people who consider adopting must face the fact of their infertility.** That discovery is always a grief experience. To choose to never have a child is one thing, but to be unable to leave behind a genetic replica of yourself and your spouse is a major tragedy for those who really wish to have a child.

Many infertile couples feel guilty, as if God were punishing them for some real or imagined sin of the past. They may blame their families or each other, and almost always they experience a sense of inferiority.

You can readily see that such painful emotions are powerful. They must be erased if you are to find the energy and peace of mind with which to truly enjoy an adopted child. Without such a resolution of feelings, you may be vulnerable to a great hazard. You may believe that you are inferior to the child's biological parents and unconsciously set up competition with them for your child's respect and loyalty.

Make peace with yourself, your husband, and your families. Finish the grief process, and leave off blame, guilt, resentment, and self-pity. You may very well find that you require professional counseling in order to do this. By all means, seek it out. Whatever it costs in time, emotional energy, or money, you will be more than repaid in the success it will afford in adoptive mothering.

This process *must* include your husband. He, too, will have some of the feelings you experience. You will need each other to get ready to become adoptive parents.

Some grandparents or extended family members may disagree with your decision. I haven't found a way to convince such people to agree with you. You will want to include their possible dissension in your decision making. Usually, they will be won over by the universal charms of the child. If not, be prepared to cope with whatever resentments may exist.

Many children who are candidates for adoption have been neglected or abused by troubled parents in early life—from a few months to some years of age. Many prospective parents believe such children need only plenty of love to thrive.

Unfortunately, that is not true. They need expert treatment to bond with anyone. And they require infinite patience and absolute consistency and persistence. So preparing to become the adoptive mother of an older child takes a special sort of planning and professional help.

There are many parentless children, oftentimes older, who desperately need homes. Perhaps you may find the resources to offer one.

HOW WERE YOU MOTHERED?

Joan nervously paced the floor of the room where we both sat awaiting her performance before a large audience. She was a musician of considerable renown. She could usually face any group with poise and confidently win their acclaim. Yet today she was obviously anxious.

Always the nurturing mother at heart, I attempted to soothe her. My comments soon unlocked a torrent of relief-producing tears. The problem Joan faced was her mother's presence in the auditorium. Through all of the years of her life, Joan stated she had never known the full approval and pride of her mother. Fleeting compliments about her ability were inevitably coupled with criticism. After such harsh words, Joan was left feeling helpless and hopeless that she could ever please her mother. She was surprised by the praise of others and became more confident herself. But the very knowledge of her mother's attendance had the power to counteract her hard-won poise. Joan reverted emotionally to her child-hood status. Mother knew all, was all-powerful, and was always critical.

With variations, Joan's story fits many people. Because of biological factors, imprint, and instinct, Mother is the most powerful being in a child's life. As was discovered with Harlow's monkeys (see Introduction), the impact she exerts for good or ill is lifelong. Yet you need not feel hopelessly caught in the web of pain your mother may have woven about you. Instead, like the caterpillar, you can break out of the restraints of your past and emerge a gorgeous butterfly, ready to soar.

Before you are ready for motherhood, you need to work your way out of your cocoon. You may be able to do this independently, or professional counseling may be required. Whatever it takes, I urge you to follow through with your search for freedom from your mother's power over you.

No matter how intelligent you are or what you could tell someone else, if your life is marred by old mother-child conflicts, you need help. Most children believe they, not their powerful mothers, are at fault. They develop habits of rebellion, or they constantly seek to please others. And many of these struggles carry over into their reactions to their own children. You can take some steps on your own to resolve your struggle.

Try to recall specific events to formulate the pattern of your conflicts. In many cases these are so painful people totally block them out. One excellent way to restore your memory is to review photographs of your childhood. Try to recapture the events that are caught in those pictures and, in a measure, relive them.

Avoid blaming your mother for those difficult times. Doing so will fill your heart with resentment and bitterness. And you will become stuck in a sense of helplessness.

Collect information about your mother's childhood. Strangely enough, she, too, had a childhood influenced by imperfect parents and the problems they inherited from *their* parents.

Margaret was in a group of mothers I once worked with. Because of her daughter's rebellion, she sought guidance and help. As the weeks rolled by, Margaret discovered that some of her child's problems originated in their frequent mother-daughter conflicts.

Furthermore, she learned that their fights were extremely similar to those she participated in as a girl with her mother. Once again, the trans-generational habit took control.

Margaret was still angry with her mother for the hurts caused by her sharp criticism. She repeatedly tried to win at least an occasional round, but her mother seemed always to be the victor. Now, with her own daughter, Margaret could often win. But the price of her winning was her child's rebelling.

Margaret knew what she must do. She chose to make peace with her mother. She wrote her, telephoned her, and tried to recall events from the past. She accumulated as much information as possible about her mother's childhood. At last it was clear. Margaret's mother had grown up in a critical family. The harshness she had experienced was intense, but all the children had become fairly successful adults. Therefore, she assumed that being critical was the way to raise successful children. She was much less harsh than Margaret's grandparents, but she still caused much pain to her family.

The day came in group when Margaret shared her search and discoveries with us. With the tears and smiles of genuine emotions, she spoke of the process of understanding and forgiving her mother. "Only now," she concluded, "am I finally free. I can love my mother *and* my daughter because I know I'm not a bad person. And I know they aren't bad, either." She and her daughter soon learned to successfully work out their differences.

Be willing to forgive and release your old hurts and painful struggles. Many people tend to hang on to them, to stay a bit resentful or downright angry. Such reactions are understandable because in a way they protect you from further hurts and give you an excuse to "lick your wounds" and indulge in self-pity. If you prefer that, no one can help you very much!

But if you'd like to be free to be happy, affirming, and loving with your children, I strongly urge you to let go of that past through practicing forgiveness. When you have accomplished that, you will be a giant step nearer to readiness to be a great mother!

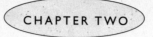
Deciding to Be a Mother

Ginny and Jim had finally decided. Most of their decisions had not been too difficult, and generally they reached agreement quickly. This time was different. This decision would profoundly affect their lives forever. Should they, or should they not, have a child? Frankly, Jim wasn't excited about the new responsibilities a child would bring. He worked hard, but he also liked to play hard. He enjoyed playing golf and hunting, and traveling was part of his job. The cost of having and raising a child was high, and his income was only average. Also, he wasn't sure he could share Ginny with a baby.

Ginny had her own doubts. She had loved teaching, and spending less time with her friends and giving up her income wouldn't be easy. But she had always loved baby-sitting as a teen, and seeing her students learn and grow was a source of great pride. Yes, Ginny really wanted a child. So Jim had agreed, and now she was off all birth control and eagerly awaiting that first missed menstrual period. She assured Jim that she could work as a substitute teacher to help out on expenses and yet be able to enjoy being a mother.

As their lovemaking focused on the desire for conception, it took on new meaning; there was a sense of awe or almost reverence. They realized that this could be the time that new life would begin. Even Jim, the worrier, began to share the excitement of Ginny's anticipation, and he started to imagine the little person who would one day join their family. Actually, it took more than six months for that conception to take place, and they began to worry about infertility.

Perhaps you see yourself and your husband in this picture of Ginny and Jim. There are many things you will want to know. How will you know when you are pregnant? What will that be like? Are those scary stories you've heard really true? What if . . . ? This section is for you. It contains ideas about getting acquainted with your baby before birth and practicing some mothering skills so you can feel really confident after your baby finally arrives.

HOW MANY CHILDREN SHOULD WE HAVE—AND WHEN?

In America we are blessed with the freedom to make choices about most issues. Where we will travel, how we spend our time and even our money (after taxes!), where we attend church, and whether our children will go to college—all are decisions many people in this world cannot make for themselves. And many people in other countries are extremely limited in the number of children they can have. For example, in China an abortion is required if pregnancy occurs after the second child.

We often fail to appreciate our freedoms, and we complain about the laws and regulations we dislike. So use your freedom now to think about your family and how many children to have. Ask yourself the following questions, and be honest in your answers.

THINGS TO CONSIDER IN PLANNING YOUR FAMILY

- *Is my physical health good?* You will enjoy your children more if you feel well and have enough energy to care for them and play with them.
- *Are there serious illnesses in our families that can be inherited?* For example, cystic fibrosis and certain neurological illnesses tend to run in families. If you have a healthy child (or children) already, you may want to avoid the risk of having a child with a serious defect. Most of the families I know, however, who have lived with a child suffering from a birth defect or inherited illness are immensely enriched by the experience. That blessing, of course, is not financial but spiritual and emotional.

> *From a developmental standpoint, a space of three years between children is ideal.*

- *Are we able to provide financially for the basic needs of several children?* Be careful at this point, because ours is a materialistic world and the things you think a child should have may not be necessary. Children need warmth, food, and lots of love. So be conservative in thinking about costs. Many parents, for example, calculate many thousands of dollars for each child's education. By using local schools and junior colleges, that expense can be greatly curtailed. I worked for a great majority of my college expenses and am proud of that fact. Your children can, too!
- *Can I love a second child as much as I love this one?* That was a question I asked myself and have shared with many other mothers of one child. A nurse who was a dear friend of mine reminded me that love is not a limited, measurable entity. In fact, the more love one gives, the more one has to give. Furthermore, she told me, the best gift you can give a child is a brother or sister. Someone to compete with, share with, and play, laugh, and cry with is a wonderful blessing. I know when they argue and fight at times, you will think I know nothing and am totally wrong. If you have siblings, however, I suspect you will discover that the one you struggled with the most eventually became your best friend.

- *Do both my husband and I enjoy children?* If both of you are not reasonably unanimous in this decision, I urge you to wait. Some intense resentments are likely to grow if you insist on one decision or the other. You may even need to visit a counselor at some point to reconcile your differences and come to a fair agreement. Children are greatly torn by basic hostility between their parents.
- *How close together in age should children be?* That is another choice most people can make. Obviously, the best plans are often thwarted for one reason or another, but today's birth control methods are so varied and safe that most couples have the luxury of deciding how far apart they want their children to be.

As a pediatrician for a number of years, I had firsthand experience with poorly planned families. Many times I saw sick babies with an extremely exhausted mother who had tried to care for three or four ill children under the age of five. Much as she loved them, she simply could not find the strength to provide all they needed.

Having studied the developmental stages of children, I am aware of the significance of finishing certain tasks during those crucial time periods. From birth to age two, for example, babies need enough access to Mom to develop a sense of trust. They need to know

Being a mother isn't convenient or easy.

she will come when they cry or are in danger. When Mom is overwhelmed with too many other responsibilities, she simply can't provide all of these needs in a timely manner. (Now, I'm not suggesting a mother must run at every whimper to a spoiled child, indulging or pampering him!)

Between ages two and three, children normally begin to separate from their mother. They become physically and intellectually independent. They still need care and protection, but they seek freedom to climb, run, explore, and experiment. They are committed to defying parents' authority and establishing their own.

Certainly, no two-year-old is capable of making her own decisions, but every child should learn how to choose. The demands on parents during this age are crucial. Two-year-olds need to establish a new balance almost every month between independence and submission.

Two-year-olds are not able to enjoy or play constructively *with* other children. They tend to play in the midst of others but are possessive, aggressive, and really incapable of cooperation at play. They are not mean or bad. They just haven't yet become mature enough to handle other children.

Jill remembers being two when her baby brother was born. She would look at him in his crib and poke at him until he cried. She would then run to her mother, telling her, "Baby cry!" She still recalls her mother's unhappiness at having to leave her work to care for the baby. Jill believed her mother would love her more because the baby was "bad." Mother never discovered Jill's tactics, and a long-term pattern of intense sibling rivalry was established.

Some mothers and many children will survive their being separated by only one or two years, but it is much more difficult than the ideal three-year span. By three, children understand language, and you can explain to them about a baby. They are quite independent and have balanced that with some submission to authority. They are able to cooperate with parents and other children and will be quite interested in and loving toward a new baby.

WHAT YOU NEED TO KNOW ABOUT PREGNANCY

Once you have decided to be a mother, and you know what it takes to become pregnant (more than simply having sexual intercourse!), how will you know when you actually *are* pregnant? There are common early signs of pregnancy.

A missed menstrual period. Unless your monthly periods are most irregular, being at least ten days late for your menstrual period is likely to mean you are pregnant. Many women miss a period or two without being pregnant, so remember this sign alone is not a definite diagnosis. Furthermore, some women have a light period or two after conceiving a child. These female bodies of ours are complex and confusing at times.

A simple event, such as flu, a severe cold, fatigue, or stress, can cause you to miss a period. So can a serious problem, such as an eating disorder. Even an intense desire to have a child can stop your periods, cause a weight gain, and convince you that you are pregnant when you are not. This is called pseudocyesis, or a false pregnancy.

Frequent urination. As the womb prepares for the nurture of a growing baby, it enlarges a little, even early in pregnancy. The size of this growing organ creates pressure on the bladder, which makes you feel like urinating frequently. When you have to get up at night several times, you may wonder if you've made a mistake. Being pregnant is not always a pleasure! Once your womb grows to the point that it moves into the abdomen rather than rests in the pelvis, this particular sensation will disappear for a while.

The trials of pregnancy can be viewed as your opportunity to prepare for the wonderful challenges of motherhood.

A sense of heaviness in the rectum. Just as the enlarging womb exerts pressure on the bladder, so it also may create a feeling of heaviness in the rectum. You will probably feel like moving your bowels only to find the effort unsuccessful. You will believe you are constipated, but probably you're not. Do be careful about taking harsh laxatives because they can stimulate contractions of the uterus. If you've been trying to get pregnant, are late with your period, or have other signs of being pregnant, this sense of rectal discomfort is likely to add to the certainty of your diagnosis.

Tenderness and enlargement of the breasts. Mild or moderate enlargement and discomfort of the breasts occur before and during menstruation. This sign alone is not diagnostic. In pregnancy, however, breast changes are ongoing. There is continuing growth, slowly preparing your breasts to feed your baby after birth. You can often express yellowish white fluid from the nipples during pregnancy. Finally, the skin around the nipples becomes darker than usual. The color ranges from a dark pink in people with light complexions to a dark brown in brunettes. In dark-skinned people, it becomes quite dark.

Nausea and vomiting. In my opinion, the most miserable event of pregnancy is the nausea and/or vomiting. Usually, this is mild and most likely to take place in the morning. Eating a saltine cracker before arising is a time-honored method of alleviating this uncomfortable symptom. For many women, however, nothing seems to help, and they continue to vomit, often throughout the entire day. When it is severe enough, a woman may need intravenous fluids and feedings to prevent dehydration or malnutrition. Such severity, fortunately, is rare. Being pregnant is not for the fainthearted!

Nausea and vomiting usually improve remarkably after three months. At that time, the womb emerges from the pelvis where it has been constricted by the bony structures. Having space for the uterus to expand in the stretchable abdomen seems to have much to do with relieving the nausea and vomiting. Some unfortunate women continue to be nauseous till the very day their babies are born. For you, I have a great deal of compassion. But the child you create can make it worth it all!

Unusual drowsiness. Many women feel unusual energy and vitality during pregnancy. Others, even early on, have difficulty staying awake. I urge all pregnant women to get a little extra rest—or a lot. Your body is going through unprecedented stress. There are many processes, as described above, that disturb sleep. So try to lie down now and then, even for a few minutes, and pamper yourself.

Changes in mucous membranes. The mucous membranes are soft tissues lining the nose, mouth, and vagina. During pregnancy, these tissues become moderately swollen and somewhat reddened and may be uncomfortable.

The discomfort is especially annoying in the nose because you are likely to feel that you have a nine-month cold. Such changes are due to the levels of certain hormones present. Again, let me reassure you, this symptom will disappear after your baby is born.

Less common signs. Some pregnant women first consider that they are carrying a child when they experience dizziness or feel light-headed, and they may faint. Such episodes are uncommon and occur rarely in any given individual.

Constipation is another complication as well as a sign of pregnancy. It may be the result of the nausea and vomiting and the lack of fluids and dietary roughage caused by inability to retain certain foods. Consult your physician for the proper treatment.

If you have been trying to become pregnant or if you are afraid you may be pregnant, you will want to know as soon as possible. Almost every magazine and many TV advertisements will try to sell you a home pregnancy test kit. They are fairly reliable and are harmless to use. They can, however, be erroneous. I urge you to consult a doctor or a clinic where a more reliable test can be done. A blood test will be quite accurate as early as seven to ten days after your first missed period. You need a thorough physical examination early on, and that should be done as soon as you know you are pregnant.

Your doctor will want to be sure that you are free from any infection, that your blood is healthy, and that your body will be able to carry the baby to its delivery. You will be taught in general how to care for yourself and your child, and that includes your need for a healthy diet.

LATER PHYSICAL CHANGES OF PREGNANCY

I hope you will be delighted to know you are going to be a mother. It is, of course, logical that your joy will be mixed with apprehension. You will not like the discomforts and inconveniences of this time in your life. But today's world has promoted a belief that we should gain all the pleasure and avoid all the pain possible. That is a highly deceptive and very wrong philosophy. We grow the most in enduring pain and become mature through transcending difficulties. Being a mother is not convenient or easy. The trials of pregnancy can be your opportunity to adapt to the hard realities of life and to prepare your inner attitudes, your very spirit, if you will, for the wonderful challenges of motherhood.

Skin changes. I have already described the change in color of the skin around the nipples. The skin across your nose and around your eyes may also turn darker. I have noticed this more commonly in the summertime, but it may occur anytime. This condition is called "the mask of pregnancy." You are likely to abhor it, but it will disappear, so just cover it with makeup or wear it proudly as a sign of the wonderful new life you are creating.

On your abdomen, especially if you have a dark complexion, a dark line called the linea nigra will appear. It extends in the center of your tummy from the base of your breastbone (sternum) to the pubic area. This, too, will disappear.

Stretch marks are trademarks of most pregnancies. They are called striae gravidarum, and I hope that knowing their technical name makes you feel better about them. Only rarely does a mother have skin so elastic that it can stretch without causing them. You may never again be comfortable in a bikini, but an ordinary swimsuit will cover them nicely. These marks are caused by the rapid and extensive stretching of skin by the enlarging breasts and abdomen, resulting in some breakdown of tissues in the deeper layer of the skin.

These marks are most often found in the breasts and lower abdomen and over the hips. They are reddish purple in color, and though the color fades with time, they will not disappear. If you tend to be vain, you will try to make them go away. I suggest that instead of being frustrated, you use this experience to learn a new set of values. Your child will be worth every stretch mark and more.

Varicose veins. These enlarged blood vessels occur due to pressure against the large veins in the groin. This pressure slows down the return of blood through the veins from the feet and legs back into the abdomen. The walls of the veins distend and, in a sense, break loose from the tissues holding them deeply within the muscles. They become quite visible under the skin, and they may cause discomfort. Wearing elastic support stockings can minimize the occurrence of these changes and alleviate the discomfort. In the future, you can elect a surgical procedure to remove some of them.

Some preventive measures exist for you. Lie down or sit with your feet up to assist the blood flow. Wear an abdominal support. A maternity girdle can take some of the weight off your lower abdomen. Avoid gaining too much weight, and remember those support hose.

Cramping of legs and feet. During my three pregnancies, at some point I would awaken regularly with severe muscle cramps in either my feet or my legs. My doctor couldn't give me a remedy, so I learned to massage them and focus on relaxing those muscles. Propping your feet up on a pillow may help. A warm (*not* hot) heating pad may relax them.

Walk every day, but don't exercise too strenuously, lest that aggravate the cramps. Wear shoes with low heels.

Heartburn. Heartburn is the passage of some of the stomach's contents into the esophagus (the tube that leads from your throat to your stomach). As your baby grows, the pressure in your abdomen increases. That pressure pushes against your abdominal muscles, bladder, and rectum, and upward against your stomach and diaphragm. It constricts your lungs so that breathing becomes a greater effort, and it simply squeezes the contents of the stomach up into your throat. Since that material contains acids as well as partly digested food, it creates a painful, burning sensation in your mouth.

You can prevent some heartburn by taking a few simple precautions. Don't eat hard-to-digest foods such as spicy, rich, or greasy items. You will discover certain foods that seem to make this happen.

Sleep on two or more pillows to elevate your chest. That posture keeps those stomach contents where they belong.

Eat smaller amounts than usual, and avoid eating a few hours before bedtime, except for a small glass of milk or a light snack.

Heartburn usually occurs only in the latter weeks of pregnancy, so you won't have it very long.

Changes in the uterus and abdomen. As I have already explained, the womb normally rests securely within the sturdy structures of the pelvic bones. As it begins to enlarge, it exerts pressure on the bladder and rectum. As it enlarges even more, it pushes its way into the abdomen where it presses the intestinal tract, then the other abdominal organs (the liver, spleen, pancreas, and stomach) against the diaphragm, ribs, and abdominal wall.

Start early in your pregnancy to exercise your abdominal muscles and those in your perineum (the "floor" of your pelvic area around your rectum, vagina, and urethra, or opening from the bladder). Tighten the muscles that control both bladder and bowels, then relax and tighten again. Raise and lower your legs, turn from side to side, and as much as you can, tighten and relax those muscles in your abdomen. Practice breathing deeply at times to keep those crowded lungs functioning well.

Not only will these exercises keep your pregnant body in better condition, but they will also help you recover your shape more quickly afterward.

Quickening. This ancient term applies to that first palpable motion of your baby. At first you will think it is merely a gas bubble, but very soon you will know it is your baby moving slightly within your womb. This usually takes place between the fourth and fifth months of pregnancy. If you are very sensitive or in a second or later pregnancy, you may experience quickening as early as the end of the third month. Occasionally, mothers are unable to feel the baby's movements until as late as six months. Check with your doctor or nurse if you are concerned about a later quickening than you think is normal, but there's probably no cause for worry.

As your baby grows, you will feel a great deal of movement, and at times that will awaken you at night and may even become uncomfortable. Frankly, I recall the pressure of my developing babies against my ribs and pelvic bones as quite uncomfortable. But I never experienced pain from the babies' movements. It helped me to become acquainted with them. I used to feel sorry for them being cramped into such close quarters. I knew they'd be so pleased to be born into a world where they could move unhindered by limitations of space.

Bone discomfort. Your enlarging womb will create pressure on your bones as well as your muscles and skin. The first area in which I experienced pain was in the center of the pubic bones. A very tough ligament binds the two pubic bones (that form the front of your pelvic structure) together. Those bones bear the increasing weight of your enlarging womb, and a tug is felt by that ligament. As it stretches, most women undergo a period of real discomfort. That is nature's way of enlarging the canal through which your baby must eventually be born. Both your baby and you will have an easier time at delivery because of this stretching.

The next bones to be affected by your pregnancy will be those in the back. Some women even have back pain with the pressure of their menstrual period. You will have backaches off and on during most of your pregnancy. They, too, will pass.

Finally, during the last of the second and all of the third trimesters, your ribs will ache. The top of the womb reaching higher will inevitably cause spreading and stretching of your rib cage. Much as that hurts at times, you can see it is absolutely necessary. If the ribs were unable to expand, how would your lungs be able to help you breathe? By the widening of your ribs, your lungs as well as your stomach, liver, and spleen can find extra space. I'm sorry this is so miserable, but it just is.

Walking will be uncomfortable for you in the late weeks of pregnancy, but you must do so. The more you walk (within the limits your medical consultant recommends), the stronger your bones and muscles will become, and the easier your delivery will be.

It will also be uncomfortable to breathe deeply, but do it anyway. To provide adequate oxygen for your baby and you, you need to practice those deep-breathing exercises you will learn.

Tissue swelling. Some morning you'll step into your comfortable old shoes and discover that you can't quite fit your feet into them. Your rings will be tight, and you may have difficulty removing them. Don't panic! You've reached a noticeable level of tissue swelling called edema, which occurs from three causes: (1) the hormonal levels of pregnancy; (2) the effect of pressure on your circulation by your growing uterus; and (3) the tendency of the body to retain salt and water during pregnancy.

Most women gain some real weight as well as collect fluids. The total of all these factors seems to suddenly catch up with them and create the situation just described. Usually, such swelling is harmless, though annoying, and it's not constant. Normally, this type of edema occurs in the last trimester.

During my first pregnancy, I experienced a more serious type of edema. Not only did I have extensive swelling, but I also developed hypertension (high blood pressure). And I began to lose excessive amounts of an essential body protein called albumin. This condition is given a fancy title called preeclampsia. At that time it was considered fairly serious. Even in the world of advanced medical science, your doctor needs to know about this situation and monitor it closely. That is why you must have your blood pressure checked and your urine specimen examined regularly. Don't worry about this diagnosis whenever your shoes or rings feel tight. It's rare, and your doctor will be very careful to watch for it and tell you if there is any cause for concern.

How Does Your Baby Grow?

Most health professionals divide pregnancy into three three-month periods called trimesters. In the **first trimester,** the fertilized egg attaches to the wall of the womb, and a blood-vessel-rich tissue (called the placenta and amniotic sac) forms there. A protective tissue (amniotic sac) forms around the developing embryo, and from the baby a cord extends and attaches to the placenta. Through this cord course large veins and arteries that carry nutrients to the developing baby and remove waste products. This cord, the umbilical cord, is literally the baby's life line. It must remain functional until the baby is born when it is carefully cut and tied to prevent bleeding or infections. It dries and falls off about a week after birth.

In the first trimester, the uterus (womb) is gradually enlarging, but it stays within the protective framework of the pelvic bones. This gradually enlarging organ creates the pressure that makes you feel like going to the bathroom frequently.

In this period, many women experience morning sickness, described above, which sometimes lasts all day. Occasionally, this sick feeling occurs at other times of the day and often results in severe nausea and vomiting. Your doctor may need to prescribe medication to relieve you, but most people prefer not to medicate. Eating small amounts frequently, getting extra rest, and enduring these early weeks will see you through.

During the **second trimester,** the uterus grows into the larger abdominal cavity out of the pelvis. You will suddenly become aware one day that you don't even feel like vomiting and that you rarely think of urinating. You may be quite sure you are in your fourth month—nearly halfway through this lengthy process.

The second trimester is usually an uneventful time when you must get into those new or borrowed maternity clothes. You begin to feel the baby move—a really quite delightful period for most expectant mothers. Continue to take good care of yourself. Eat carefully and rest well. Get plenty of moderate exercise and fresh air. And enjoy yourself because the next trimester becomes more tedious.

During the **third and last trimester,** the uterus occupies the pelvis, fills the abdomen, and robs the chest of some space. Your normal abdominal contents have to make do with the crowding of the ever-growing baby.

During these months, it isn't easy to sleep comfortably, eat as much as usual, or walk gracefully.

The best thing I can tell you is that the days in this trimester are numbered. By the time you feel you can stand only one more day of it, you will have less than twenty-five days. So count them down, pamper yourself, get your husband or a friend to rub your back now and then, and think ahead.

One of the most unpleasant occurrences of the last couple of months is heartburn. That symptom has been discussed earlier, so I'll just remind you that it becomes especially annoying in the last few weeks.

Those of us who are short usually have more trouble with morning sickness and heartburn. But it can happen to anyone and almost always does.

During each trimester, your doctor will look for specific signs that indicate whether or not you and your child are doing well. And he or she will teach you what to expect and when to be in touch about a potential problem. It's tempting to believe you can handle this process with the help of nature alone. And often people can. But to prevent those rare emergencies or to catch them early, you need to check in regularly with your doctor.

By the end of the first trimester, most babies are about three inches long and weigh about one ounce. Obviously, the size of your baby then doesn't cause all your early discomfort. The growth of the placenta, the many blood vessels it takes to nourish your baby, and the fluid that surrounds and protects that tiny life create your early pressure.

Also, most of us tend to eat more frequently to ease the sick feelings, and we gain weight. Your breasts are enlarging, your body's tissues collect a little extra fluid, and you begin to feel fat. Even by the end of your second month, your belts and waistbands will feel tight and just may not fasten at all. I found that I grew weary of maternity clothes, so I wore my "regular" garments as long as I could with sweaters and jackets to hide my stretching middle.

By the end of the second trimester (twenty-eight weeks or 196 days), your baby has reached about fifteen inches in length and weighs about two and one-half pounds. That is quite an expansion when you consider that it is five times the length at three months and some forty times the weight! Although you may at times *feel* you have gained forty times your weight, if you really did, you would literally weigh about two tons. The growth and the development of your baby are truly amazing!

By the sixth month, your baby's body is well developed, and if he or she were born, the chances of survival would be fair. You can feel and even see some movements through your abdomen. Have your husband feel these tiny parts and their motions so he can become a part of this wonderful process with you.

After forty weeks or 280 days, the end of the third trimester has been reached. By that time most babies are nineteen to twenty-one inches long (depending on the family traits) and weigh seven to eight pounds. They are fully mature and can function outside the womb quite independently if they are cuddled, fed, changed, and loved!

How Long Will This Last?

You have already learned the expected length of your pregnancy. There are, however, many variations. Due to many factors, a pregnancy may end in the first three months. Doctors call this a spontaneous abortion, which is a medical term that has nothing to do with the moral and political controversy.

After the first trimester, the ending of a pregnancy is called a miscarriage. Prior to the end of the sixth month, a baby is usually too undeveloped to live outside the womb. But between the sixth and seventh months, many prematurely born babies survive and do well. There are so many technological gadgets and well-trained medical people that excellent care can make the difference.

A normal pregnancy reaches its full term about forty weeks (280 days) from the first day of your last menstrual period. A full-term baby, however, may be born as early as 240 days or as late as 300 days after that period. Some babies may grow to a larger size earlier, the womb may reach its stretching capacity at a different point, or perhaps conception took place at a different point in the menstrual cycle than usual.

At any rate, I learned through personal difficulty not to count on a given day to expect labor to begin. I was pregnant with our second child during my residency in pediatrics and was eager to be through with the extra weight and awkwardness during long days and nights on my feet.

With a delightful smile of encouragement, my obstetrician said on August 17, "Well, Grace, it could be any day now!" Happily, I returned to work looking eagerly for that telltale contraction. He said the same thing in mid-September. By the end of September, I was more ready for psychiatry than obstetrics. It was not until October 2 that our healthy seven-and-one-half-pound son was born. The best of doctors and the most careful predictions, you see, can be absolutely wrong. So try not to set your mind or heart on a given day.

It is tempting to talk your doctor into inducing labor or doing a Caesarean (or surgical) delivery. I urge you not to do so. If he or she sees signs that require such procedures, you will have them clearly explained and will know that must be done. But don't rush. Nature does know best! Waiting those extra days often gives your child benefits and advantages you would not think of.

WHAT COULD POSSIBLY GO WRONG?

In a TV comedy many years ago, the aging hero would typically set out on a detective's adventure and ask reassuringly of his son, "What could possibly go wrong?" Of course, everything did routinely go wrong.

Considering the amazing intricacies of developing life, it is simply miraculous that things so rarely go wrong. But common complications can occur. I will briefly list the most likely events, and if you are concerned, ask your nurse or doctor for reassurance.

Early delivery. I have already described a spontaneous abortion (first trimester). Early or premature birth may take place anytime during the last trimester.

Early deliveries may be due to defects in the womb, cord, or placenta. They may be caused by abnormal hormone balances. Injury, serious illness, or necessary surgery may cause an early labor and delivery. Rarely, a defect in an ovum or a sperm may result in a baby that is too abnormal to live.

I hope such an event never happens to you, but if it should, please don't blame yourself or anyone else. You are bound to go through grief over this loss. Many people may be unable to comprehend your grief, especially if you lost a baby early on. Don't let such lack of understanding bother you. Most mothers who suffer a loss at any point grieve for that child who never lived and wonder what they did to cause the tragedy. Almost never did they do anything. Bad things just happen sometimes— to the very best people. The ability to accept things we did not cause and cannot change, and to move on in life, is a sign of maturity. I hope you will be able to do this if you ever face such a time.

Here are the symptoms of early labor and delivery (any or all of these may be present):

- severe or recurrent cramping
- bleeding or spotting
- in the last trimester, leaking of fluid
- having back pain that may come and go

Severe vomiting (hyperemesis gravidarum). This condition starts with common morning sickness but graduates to noon, afternoon, and evening sickness. When this condition persists, a trip to the hospital may well be necessary. Intravenous feedings and medication can be given that will prevent serious dehydration and harm to the baby. I have known a few women to struggle with this serious vomiting for an entire pregnancy, but almost everyone recovers when the third month is over.

Placenta previa. In this condition the placenta (the area from which blood containing nutrients flows through the cord into the baby's body) is in a bad position. If it is too close to the cervix or even the lower part of the uterus, pressure and stretching of the uterus can dislodge part of the placenta and cause bleeding. If this is severe enough, the blood flow to the baby may become so poor that the baby's life is at risk. Also, the placenta may cause obstruction in the birth canal, making delivery impossible. Emergency Caesarean surgery usually is required.

Problem with your blood. Until the mid- to late-1960s, a baby whose blood factor differed from the mother's could develop severe anemia. At that time, the only way to save such a baby's life was to do a complete blood exchange, removing the baby's blood and replacing it, a syringeful at a time, with healthy blood. This condition was due to the mother's blood being Rh negative and the baby's Rh positive.

Check with your doctor before taking any medication during pregnancy—even over-the-counter pain relievers.

The inevitable mixing of the mother's Rh-negative blood with the baby's Rh positive set in motion a complex battle that resulted in the breakdown of the baby's red blood cells. When this was severe, a baby might die without a complete blood transfusion.

Because of new procedures and medications, Rh and blood type incompatibilities are now extremely rare. Other blood problems are so rare that you need not worry about them. If there are any indications, your regular examinations will reveal them, and your doctor will let you know and will take the proper precautions.

Excess fluid in the womb (polyhydramnios). This condition occurs in only four cases in a thousand or more pregnancies. It may occur suddenly over one to two weeks or very slowly over several months. It is most common in twin pregnancies.

Too little fluid (oligohydramnios). This is an extremely rare condition, usually due to a slow leakage of amniotic fluid from a small rupture in the tissue. Rarely, it may be associated with an abnormality in the baby, which is especially likely to involve malfunctioning of the baby's kidneys.

Urinary tract infections. Women are exceptionally vulnerable to urinary tract infections, especially bladder infections. With the added stress of the enlarging womb, the bladder is pressed down, and the urethra is stretched and more widely open. Bacteria from the skin or rectum have easy access to the interior where an infection can become established. If you have burning and pain during urination, urgency and frequency, or any blood in the urine, tell your doctor as soon as possible.

TAKE GOOD CARE

Taking good care of yourself is always important, but it's vital when you are carrying a baby. And you can't do it all alone; you must see your doctor regularly. Even though I was a practicing doctor when I was expecting each of my children, I had regular examinations and followed my doctor's instructions carefully.

Most obstetricians like mothers-to-be to visit once a month during the first trimester, twice a month in the second trimester, and once a week in the last trimester or at least the last month. If you have any special problems, you may need to be seen more frequently.

Expect a thorough evaluation by your doctor and nurse. They will ask for a detailed family history, so have the facts handy when you make your first visit. You will need to know if any relatives have diabetes, epilepsy, or other neurological problems. Has there been serious heart or respiratory illness? Are there allergies or deafness? Are there any known hereditary illnesses? Has anyone had cancer or any blood diseases? They will want similar information about the father's family. If you're like me, you won't be able to collect all that information about everyone, but do the best you can.

Next, you'll have a physical examination. You probably have never had such an extensive physical, but I trust you will *try* to relax and cooperate. Knowing the size of your pelvis, for example, is extremely important in predicting the safety of a vaginal delivery or the possibility of a need for a surgical procedure to deliver your baby. All sorts of measurements will be taken, and every one has a reason.

Don't hesitate to ask every question that enters your mind. You and your medical team will become good friends in the next few months, so you need to learn to trust each other. If something concerns you, find out whatever you need to know to be comfortable and secure.

The laboratory tests always include blood tests and a urine analysis. One blood test will determine if you have ever had three-day (German) measles. Unless you are sure that you are not susceptible, stay away from anyone who might have that disease. In the first trimester, German measles is highly likely to cause deafness or other birth defects in your child. Don't take that chance!

Only a decade ago medical people asked mothers-to-be to restrict their weight gain to between twenty-two and thirty-one pounds. Currently, doctors are more permissive about weight gains. Your doctor will tell you just what is best for you and your baby. Limiting weight gain correlates with the lowest incidence of complications.

A well-balanced diet includes the following nutrients. Be certain to have some of each daily.

Dairy products. Milk provides calcium, protein, milk sugar, and vitamins B and D. Dairy products include cheese, yogurt, ice cream, and puddings as well as plain milk. We know that butter and cream are high in cholesterol, so you may use products low in butterfat. Once you get accustomed to skim milk, it isn't too bad.

Minerals. Iron is the best-known example of a mineral required by the body. It is essential in building red blood cells to supply oxygen for both you and your baby. You also need many other traces of minerals, which are found in vegetables, meats, fish, raisins, and prunes, for example.

Protein. Lean beef, fish, poultry, eggs, cheese, dried beans, peas, and nuts are common foods that are rich in protein and vitamins. Avoid excess animal fats, since they are high in cholesterol.

Fruits and vegetables. These foods provide vitamins, some carbohydrates, and much fiber. Yellow-colored foods are rich in vitamins A and C, whereas the green ones furnish more of the B complex. Phosphorus and other trace minerals also come from this group.

Grains (cereals). Whole grains and bran products are the best sources of the fiber necessary for good health. They are also rich in carbohydrates, some minerals, and especially vitamin E.

Fats. Fats contain about twice the amount of calories of either proteins or carbohydrates. In the desire to be fashionably thin as well as really healthy, many young women eliminate this essential food element from their diet. You need some fats daily to keep your body's metabolism in balance. Most TV and magazine advertisements advise you to seek more vegetable oils and less butter. For most young people, some butter and cream can be all right. But again, ask your doctor. If you need to watch your cholesterol level closely, stick with vegetable oils labeled "polyunsaturated." These products contain little, if any, cholesterol. Take time to read the labels on foods; they will list clearly the food elements present.

Vitamins. Although a well-rounded diet will provide most of the vitamins you need, your doctor will recommend prenatal vitamin and mineral tablets as well. I know they sometimes make you burp and the aftertaste is not good, but take them anyway.

Your eating pattern is likely to change during pregnancy. Especially during the first trimester when you feel nauseated, you will learn that nibbling certain foods helps you feel better. You may want to eat small amounts of food frequently rather than large meals at the classic break-fast, lunch, and dinner hours. I recommend a little snack at bedtime so your body will not go without food for an excessively long time. I suggest a protein food and some fruit. In my experience, bland foods (without much seasoning) are less likely to cause heartburn.

Many jokes about pregnancy relate to food cravings. Frankly, I always wished to experience such cravings, but during three full-term pregnancies, I never had one clear-cut craving. If you crave a particular food, your body may be telling you that you need certain food elements. So indulge it—within reasonable limits. I don't recommend sending your husband out at midnight to locate a rare delicacy!

BEND AND STRETCH!

Medical professionals are much more liberal about exercise in all forms during pregnancy than when I was pregnant. We now recommend carrying on all your usual activities. Swimming, running, and even more strenuous athletic endeavors are now permitted.

A word of warning is necessary, however. If you have a history of or any likelihood of a miscarriage, you may need to restrict yourself. If you have a tendency to push yourself excessively, please call a halt to that! Moderate exercise is great, but excessive exercise, like all excesses, can be harmful. The best form of exercise is a brisk walk, and several short walks are better than a very long one.

Most clinics now have brochures that depict exercises designed to prepare you for delivery. A specific exercise I like is this one: with your feet several inches apart, hold on to the back of a sturdy chair. Lower your body until your buttocks rest on your heels. Stay in this position until it becomes uncomfortable. Stand up and go about your activities. Repeat this several times daily. You will feel your pelvic muscles as they stretch and strengthen.

Breathing exercises are also useful. As you have already learned, your lungs get squashed by your expanding tummy, so give them a break and try these procedures.

Abdominal breathing. Inhale slowly to a count of eight. You will be able to feel your diaphragm and abdominal muscles move. Then exhale to a count of eight until your abdominal muscles tighten. This controlled breathing will help you cooperate with labor contractions.

Costal (rib-cage) breathing. This can best be learned by lying flat on your back. Place your hands over your lower ribs, and take a deep breath. Let it out. You can feel your rib cage widen and narrow as you breathe. Remember to breathe deeply at times to keep your oxygen supply adequate.

Sternal (breastbone) breathing. Place your hands on your breastbone. (This is the flat area between your ribs.) As you breathe slowly and deeply, be aware of the rise and fall of this bone. Sensing this motion will help you know if you are breathing deeply enough. Don't get preoccupied with this breathing stuff! You will automatically keep on breathing. But a little extra focus on deeper breathing now and then is useful.

Childbirth classes can teach you all about exercises, breathing, and diet. Find and attend such classes regularly.

LOOK YOUR BEST

Most of us feel fat and ugly during pregnancy. Actually, I think expectant mothers have a unique radiance and beauty, but somehow I never felt that way when I was awaiting childbirth. There are some things you can do to enhance personal hygiene, good health, and appearance.

Most physicians permit pregnant women to *take tub baths,* so enjoy a good soak in bath preparations. They will soften your skin, relax your muscles, and help you feel just a bit pampered. Be careful not to fall, though; some preparations make the tub slick. Showers, of course, are also relaxing and a nice place to give yourself a shampoo.

Many times you will not feel like cleansing your face or shampooing your hair. Raising your arms up for that long may seem like too much to ask. Just do it anyway. You and those around you will be glad to see you shining, neat, and clean.

Avoid douches and tampons. At times you will have a discharge, and you'd like to use a soothing, cleansing douche. I recommend you settle for extra baths or external sponging. The pressure of a douche may be harmful. Ask your doctor if that discharge becomes annoying. He or she may need to determine its cause and prescribe medication.

Gentle, firm rotation and massage will stimulate circulation in the breasts and reduce some pressure of rapid enlargement. Massage the nipples and areola (area around the nipples) to toughen the skin for the baby's nursing, but use a cream to keep tissues soft and elastic.

Visit your dentist. My very first cavity occurred during my first pregnancy. You need to brush, floss, and massage your gums regularly to keep your teeth and mouth healthy. Be sure your dentist knows you're pregnant in case X rays are recommended.

Take good care of your skin and nails. Use a mild soap and plenty of soothing lotion. Baby's skin is tender; rough or jagged fingernails could easily scratch it. The habit of good nail care is important.

JUST SAY NO!

This motto is one we are all familiar with. It's not too difficult to do— unless you're in the habit of indulging.

All medical evidence verifies the damaging effects of tobacco and alcohol on babies. They don't do you any good, either. And of course, drugs are extremely likely to harm your child. I hope your mothering instincts will enable you to completely eliminate tobacco, alcoholic beverages, and unnecessary drugs.

Over-the-counter pain relievers are comforting for daily aches and pains. Even they, however, may not be advisable, so check with your doctor about which and how much of them are permitted. It's surprising to many folks to know they can survive even a severe headache without a single pill now and then. In the good sense, mothers must be tough, so learn to ignore some aches and pains.

Tell your obstetrician about any medication you take. If there are any side effects, he or she needs to know about them.

Monosodium glutamate (MSG) is a commonly used seasoning agent. It is present in many foods and may have allergic or toxic effects on some women.

Most physicians advise against significant amounts of caffeine during pregnancy. I admit, I drank coffee during my pregnancies and know of no negative effects. At least limit your intake of caffeinated beverages—and consider eliminating them. You probably don't need it, so why take a risk?

WHAT ABOUT SEXUAL INTIMACY?

Some pregnant women have increased sexual desire; others couldn't care less. Unless you have some bleeding or a history of miscarriages, it is permissible to enjoy sexual intimacy whenever you like. In fact, I strongly urge you to maintain your romance. This business of mothering is a most demanding job, and you can neglect your husband, focusing too much on the baby, if you aren't careful.

In the last few months, most of us become pretty uncomfortable having intercourse, so be honest about that. But reaffirm your tender love for the father of your child. Include him as much as you can in the baby's growth and development. Without overburdening him, let your husband know how much you need him and how proud you are to be carrying his and your child.

During the weeks when sexual intercourse is not possible, discover the emotional, social, and even spiritual intimacy that far transcends the purely physical.

I Don't Have Anything to Wear!

Most of us have said this many times as we rifle through our crowded closets. You certainly will feel that way during your pregnancy. Few people can indulge in extensive maternity wardrobes for the few months those clothes are needed. Plan ahead, and you will find you can expand your outfits. By selecting proper fabrics and colors, a summer sundress can become a fall jumper (or vice versa).

Many young moms exchange their maternity clothes. This trading demands consideration as well as generosity. You must take care of borrowed items and return them in fine condition. Even if your lender-friend says you need not return the garments, I suggest you do so. After all, who knows if she may need them again?

I recommend investing in good support bras that can double as nursing bras afterward. They are fairly costly but well worth it for the comfort they provide.

I also recommend investing in support maternity panty hose. Worn regularly, they can enhance the circulation in your legs and prevent *some* of the cramping, swelling, and discomfort.

R and R

Many times during my second pregnancy, I became immensely sleepy. I couldn't seem to stay awake. Perhaps that was due to my medical responsibilities, since I worked long hours. But I believe that fatigue just happens to some mothers. I was often able to slip away from duties, find a couch, and take a short nap during my lunch break. Without that, I think I would have been a zombie doctor.

When you are exceptionally tired, try to find a spot to rest. Sleeping for even ten minutes can be a great refresher. Sit relaxed, feet propped up, head supported, and practice your breathing exercises. Or lie flat on your back and put your feet and legs up on a pillow if you can for a short time. Lying down for a brief period, several times a day, is wonderful for both you and the baby. Allow yourself to be conscious of your baby, let some picture of what he or she will be like come into focus for you, and go ahead and feel some tenderness. Giving a little time to getting acquainted with that tiny life inside you will be a great beginning toward the bonding process.

It was difficult, I admit, to get up from my rest period and face the remainder of a grueling day. You, too, may be tempted to stay in bed and rest more and more, neglecting yourself, your home, and your family. So discipline yourself. Work some, exercise a bit, play a lot, and balance activities with rest and relaxation.

Rest and relaxation may involve a trip to a vacation area. Or your job may demand travel. Most pregnant women can tolerate extensive travel with a few commonsense precautions.

When you drive, stop every hour or so, and walk around. Changing position and getting exercise feel good, improve circulation in your abdomen and legs, and help prevent blood clots.

If you must fly, ask for an aisle seat so you can get up and stretch your legs a bit. Now don't ask me how to get around those ubiquitous carts that fill the aisles. You just have to wait and catch your opportunity when you can!

I recommend traveling before the eighth month. I took a short vacation late in one pregnancy, and I was not comfortable. I had to sit it out many times while my friends were doing fun things, and I know I hampered their fun sometimes. Staying close to home during those last several weeks seems wise.

One of my R and R activities was sewing for my children. I can almost hear you groaning that you can't sew, it won't fit, and it's not worth the trouble. Okay! But even a bit of needlework on a bib or kimono can take very little time, can hardly go wrong, and will give you a sense of creative pride. You will be giving your child a unique token of your love, something both of you can cherish.

Fixing up the baby's room is another fun activity. You may live in an apartment and can allot only a corner to the baby. At the very least, you can hang some prints on the wall, arrange a chest and bed, and make that corner charming. On inexpensive plain sheets, you can stencil a colorful design that makes them your own creation.

If money is no problem, having the walls painted or papered and finding bright curtains and wall hangings to match bed linens can occupy your energies.

Perhaps the urge to get ready for the baby is part of that universal nesting instinct. Enjoy it!

WHO WILL MY CHILD BE?

Many people are so busy that they don't find the time to enjoy each day. They may even rush through a nine-month pregnancy without stopping to contemplate the wonder of it all.

Schedule some time every day when nothing else is pressing on your mind. Think about your child. What does she look like? Examine your baby pictures and trace the features you like. Check Dad's pictures, too. Maybe she'll look like him. Will that be okay? This is a good time to reaffirm your love for him.

Your child will be a unique little person, but some of both parents and all of your ancestors will be there, too. I hope you love all of them so you will love your child all the more. Just one caution! Don't set your mind and heart on a certain set of features; be prepared to accept what you are given.

To get acquainted with a new adult friend, you would talk with that person, sharing your ideas, experiences, and feelings. And that, too, is something you can do with your unborn baby. Think about your child's physical proximity. Although he can't talk with you, the tiny motions and nearness communicate something to you. For example, if he could talk, he might say, "I'm so little and helpless. I'd never make it without you, Mom! I can hardly wait to see you. And I like it when you talk to me because I can feel your voice."

Why not respond to your child? Say all the tender or funny loving things you can think of. If you're not a very sentimental person, that's okay. Just say normal things in your usual way. I like to believe such conversations have an impact on babies and their bonding with mothers. But at a practical level, the discussions help you get ready to talk with your child. You recognize your child as a person who deserves your respect.

You may think this idea is foolish, but I also recommend singing to your baby before birth. It makes no difference whether you can carry a tune or not. The softness and rhythm of singing soothe the baby, and once again, the practice is important. Borrow or buy some tapes of Mother Goose rhymes set to music or any simple songs that may appeal to you. Or make up your own.

I used to sing to my grandson, "I love Bryan, yes, I do! I love him, love him, love him true. He's the neatest little boy, and he brings us so much joy." Any notes will do because you are communicating your love, responding to his dear infant ways.

Imagine as you talk and sing that you are finally holding the baby in your arms. Picture the round cheeks, rosy mouth, tiny fingers and toes, and the utter helplessness wrapped in your loving care. Let yourself feel the warmth and tenderness. You will build the bonds that offer your child the security she needs to thrive.

Now that I've pictured the warm, cuddly aspect of your baby-yet-to-be, let's face the harsh reality as well. Imagine your little angel crying at 3:00 A.M. How will that sound? And how will you feel, since you didn't fall asleep until one o'clock? Will you find the strength to show compassion and tenderness? Or will you feel cross and wish you'd never thought of having a baby? Perhaps somewhere between these two extremes, you can marshal your energies and take care of the physical needs gently and lovingly, even if you can't feel so kind. Thinking about those actualities now can help you better prepare for them when they happen.

A valuable quality of a good mother is empathy. Imagine how you would feel as a baby. Thinking of the pain of hunger, wetness, colic, or loneliness will help you find patience with your child's angry-sounding cry. Anger is always prompted by some sort of pain, and remembering that has enabled me to deal with anger much more successfully.

To help you empathize, I suggest that you look over your baby pictures. You aren't likely to have many conscious memories before the age of five or six. But those old family albums are filled with treasures. Look at those who are holding you or playing with you. Select the pictures that most vividly portray the love and pride someone felt for you. What pose or activity brought the brightest smiles to your face? Try to see what stimulated you to the best responses when you were little. Home videos, of course, are even better for such studies. Once you have some clear pictures of yourself and your parents, try to transpose your discoveries to your baby and you. What can you do that is like the pictures? Or how might you choose to be different if your pictures aren't happy? This time *you* are in charge, and you can exercise many choices that can make things better than they were for you.

Empathy is a valuable quality of a good mother.

Perhaps your review of the family album or videos reveals that you missed out on the cuddling and play that babies need. Many people, in my experience, have had to face that fact. To most children, such a discovery means that something is wrong with them. They feel ugly, burdensome, guilty, and often angry at the deprivation. Those feelings are realistic, and to a child, they make sense. As an adult, however, you might find yourself still experiencing those disastrous emotions. Explore why you may have suffered neglect or abuse. Perhaps your parents hadn't settled into a good marriage before you were born. They may have had illness to conquer or financial struggles to surmount. The pressures of *their* lives were the reasons for your pain, not you.

Many of you experienced some degree of inadequate parenting, or even outright neglect or abuse. Rather than harboring bitterness, self-pity, or a sense of inferiority, accept this new opportunity. Decide how you will avoid the most mistakes possible, and do the best job of mothering you can. You are creating not just a baby but a new generation. Put lots of love, firmness, and common sense into it. We'll all be glad you did!

You can already anticipate that having a baby will change your lifestyle. You really discover just how much only after the baby is in the crib. Yet, many new parents vow that their child is not going to run their lives, and they try to live almost as if they didn't have one. One mother told me that just a week after her baby was home, a friend called her to go out for coffee one evening. Only as she sat sipping her drink and chatting with her friend did she remember her baby was home alone.

The baby was fine, but Mom was devastated. I must say, she must have gotten through her delivery with fewer stitches than I. But at any rate, she never again forgot her baby.

The point is, having a baby disrupts your life. And it does so permanently! You will never again be as free or as self-determining as you are now. Even with later children, you will discover additional losses. And all loss results in grief. Grief involves denial, anger, guilt and blame, preoccupation with the problems, and usually self-pity. If all moms could understand the facts about loss and grief and the grieving process, I daresay we'd have fewer instances of postpartum blues and depression. To be sure, some of that depression is physical and time heals that. Getting normal hormonal cycles reestablished and muscles back in shape takes several weeks. The emotional facets seem harder for moms to accept and cope with. They feel guilty because they don't feel 100 percent excited over this tyrant who monopolizes their time, energy, and ingenuity. So they get stuck in the grief process, and a vicious cycle develops and worsens as the days go by.

Planning ahead what you will do when your baby cries will help you be a more confident mom.

Go ahead and admit your frustration; guilt is a normal feeling all of us moms share if we're honest. Paradoxically, honestly admitting those bad feelings will set you free from them more quickly.

By the way, don't forget that your husband will face similar losses. And he also loses a big part of you to his new rival, the baby. Share this insight with him, and you can both get through the grief more quickly. Only then can you fully enjoy being parents.

One of my worst prenatal fears was this: *What if she cries and cries, and I can't ever make her stop?* My real fear was that I couldn't meet her every need. That never happened. Sooner or later, each of my three babies would stop crying, and I egotistically believed I was, indeed, the magic. And so will you!

The child whose parent ignores crying or hovers overprotectively suffers. So find your balance and stick with it.

Here are some insights into your baby's crying:

- Remember that crying is the only means of communication available to a tiny baby. The child will need to cry because of pain, fear, boredom, or loneliness. I suggest you learn the difference in your baby's cries. You will discover the angry outcry of pain is quite different from the startled shriek of fear. A dog's bark or a sudden jolt or jerky motion will cause this frightened cry.
- For the cry of pain, develop a list of things you will do. Planning ahead will help you be a more confident mom.
- Check the diaper and see if the baby is wet and cold. (It seems to me

they always were wet!) Change the diaper, and provide good skin care. A little ointment or lotion will prevent irritation and rashes that create even more discomfort.

• Observe the clock. How long has it been since the baby nursed? And how much did she eat? Currently, almost all doctors recommend frequent feeding to comfort babies. I like that much better than the old watch-the-clock routine. Most crying in tiny babies is due to hunger, so why not feed them?

At first, your nipples may be sore, so pump your breasts, use the medication your doctor can give you to soothe your tissues, or occasionally offer a supplement. I am, of course, assuming you will nurse your baby. I hope you will. For various reasons, you may be unable to nurse your baby. Don't feel guilty about that. Just be sure to hold your baby when you give the bottle and rest assured that the cuddling needs will be met.

• Be sure the baby is not sick. Take the baby's temperature; see if gentle pressure on the ears causes pain (you'll need to wait for a moment of quietness to test that out).

• Observe the stools; the baby could have diarrhea. Notice if he spits up more than a small amount, indicating a stomach upset. If in doubt, do not hesitate to call your doctor. Call your doctor when necessary at any time, but don't wait until 2:00 A.M. to ask about a problem you noticed at noon. He or she will help you become aware of your baby's needs, will distinguish one kind of problem from another, and reassure you so that you can be a relaxed mother.

If there is no illness or wetness and the baby is full but still crying, there are a few more actions to take:

• Pick up the baby, and holding him close, walk or rock. The rhythmic motion is often soothing.

- Sometimes babies settle down best when they are wrapped snugly in a light blanket. It must make them feel as secure as they do before birth, all safe in the womb.
- There is a wonderful invention you may include on your wish list from a special relative or friend. It is a tape that plays the sounds of the mother's body as the baby hears them before birth. It is somewhat expensive but worth the cost. I observed my grandson when such a tape was playing and rarely saw it fail to quiet him.

I recommend practicing these activities if you are a first-time mother. Take a doll or stuffed animal and try various ways of holding, rocking, or soothing it. Or if you prefer, borrow a baby. Store up some favors for later on by offering to baby-sit. You may want to be careful how you phrase your offer. No one wants her baby to become a guinea pig, but she'd surely be glad to have you take a turn at baby-sitting now and then.

Observe other mothers and see how they handle their babies. Some of them will do things you don't feel good about, so you can avoid those methods. You will see other moms handling their babies so expertly you'll know that is exactly right. Copy those ideas in your mind and practice them when your baby arrives.

Unless a baby has colic, time plus one or more of these measures will eventually provide the comfort needed. Sleep will overtake that fretful child and you until the next cycle of discomfort occurs. The best comfort of all is knowing that rest gradually increases and crying decreases.

Actually, this process of the baby's need expressed through crying and your gentle response of comfort best strengthens your bonding. When you realize that you, and you above everyone else, are the source of supply for your child's daily (and nightly!) needs, you will have a sense of worth and strength that few others can equal.

Giving too much attention, anticipating baby's every need, can spoil her. You can become resentful, and that bonding process can be retarded.

He needs to cry a bit to exercise both his lungs and his healthy will.

Too little responsiveness, on the other hand, slows the bonding even more. That slowness makes it difficult for the baby to trust you. And you are deprived of the warm glow of pride in knowing you are a good mother.

The big task, as is true in so much of life, is finding the right balance for both you and your child. You must take care of yourself, so if you've done all you can and your baby continues to cry, he may as well cry on the mattress as on you. Set the soothing-sounds tape in motion, plug your ears, and harden your heart just a tiny bit. Sometimes a little skillful neglect is the best cure for excessive crying.

All of this advice and information will be most useful to you later, when your baby is in the crib. But understanding now how babies make themselves heard and how you can respond (or not!) can prepare you for the sometimes tough times.

Some babies kick strongly and move about a great deal in the womb. These high-energy babies are likely to need more feedings, will cry louder, and often are more sensitive to stimulation such as loud sounds and bright lights than less-energetic babies.

On the other extreme are those gentle babies who move so slightly that you worry about them. They sleep a lot after birth, and nothing seems to rouse them. The loudest thunder or wailing siren is not the least disturbing to these placid little ones.

And of course, there are babies between these extremes. You can't, and needn't try to, change these inborn traits. But you can plan the environment that will help you cope with your special child.

If your baby is the active type, plan the nursery area to be as peaceful as possible. Soft colors, dim lights, and low music will usually calm a high-energy baby. Play actively with the child. Tickle and exercise those arms and legs. Laugh and be boisterous, but gradually reduce the stimulation to the quiet level.

The too-placid baby, on the other hand, needs somewhat brighter lights and colors, louder sounds, and more stimulation. In this case, too, do not go overboard. Allow plenty of time for gentle cuddling and soothing sounds. Just alternate stimulation and soothing to seek the best balance for your child.

HOW MUCH ROOM IS THERE?

You may get so caught up in learning about your baby and your brand-new role that you forget other important people. Dad, especially, needs to be included. Take him with you to your doctor's office now and then. Let him listen to that tiny, fluttering heartbeat, and show him the sonogram. Let him feel the baby's round heel (or elbow) and share the thrill of the baby's movements and quiet times. Let him also sing and talk to the baby. Many dads do, and they don't consider it silly. Be certain he attends Lamaze classes with you and is present at the delivery. Have him help prepare the nursery and learn how to hold, feed, and change the baby. Commend him for his efforts, and if he's a bit unsure of himself, never criticize or ridicule him. You will both make mistakes, so help each other grow.

It feels so good to have your husband rub your back now and then. And somehow a little sympathy and encouragement can see you through some impossible days. (If you are a single mom, find a friend to take on this role.) Asking him to walk or exercise with you can make it easier to go that extra lap! At times, just be comfortable in silence.

Plan ahead for time off for yourself. When Dad is at all willing, leave him in charge and go out for a walk or window-shopping. (Don't buy a lot of new clothes, however, until you're settled into your new figure—whatever that is.)

When Dad has the baby, don't hover over them. I didn't realize how many mothers do that until I saw my niece *not* doing it. She handed the baby, only three months old, to her husband and went blithely off to do her own thing. He never did drop the baby, she learned to love and bond with him, and they became a family. Mothering is magnificent, but "familying" is even more fantastic.

Older children vary a great deal in their curiosity and involvement with a new baby. They must know about the expected birth, but not too soon. Usually about halfway through your pregnancy is soon enough to tell them, depending on their ages.

Make this event as natural and delightful as possible without turning it into something bigger than life. I urge you to help your children understand that because you have loved and enjoyed them so much, you want another child.

When I was wondering how in the world I could love a baby as much as I did my first child, a friend gave me a new idea. She suggested that, next to a good father, the best earthly gift I could give my child was a brother or sister. She was right, but it is so easy to get wrapped up with the new baby that the older one may feel discarded. That is especially true when there are too few months between children and the older one has to surrender a bed or toys to the new member that he never wanted in the first place!

If you must move the older children to a new bed or room, do so as early as possible with pleasure in their advancement. Allow them to keep special security blankets, toys, and familiar pieces of furniture. Teach them how to welcome babies of friends and how to touch them (as well as how *not* to!).

I've learned one big lesson about love: the more of it you give away, the more you get to keep. Remind your family, and yourself, of this fact every day.

What If Your Pregnancy Is Unplanned?

The fifteenth of May came and went; so did the sixteenth, seventeenth, and eighteenth. Della's menstrual cycle was as regular as the calendar, and she was anxious. Dan, her husband, had been acting strangely. He was angry to the point of being almost abusive. He often stayed away for extra nights on his business trips. Della was almost certain he was having an affair. She had taken her birth-control pills faithfully, so she couldn't believe she was pregnant. But indeed she was. Her daughter was almost three, so the spacing was good. But what if Dan left her? How could she manage?

Betty and Kent had intensely wanted children, but it took more than a year and fertility medication before Becky was conceived. When she was only nine months old, Betty and Kent decided they would stop using birth control because they feared another long wait before Betty would become pregnant. You guessed it! She became pregnant the very first month.

Birth control and family planning don't always work as precisely as you wish. Perhaps you, too, are pregnant with an unplanned child. The circumstances, as in Della's case, may be frightening. You may be strongly tempted to terminate the pregnancy.

Please don't give in to that temptation. Seek counseling and find a support system for yourself. Life is precious, and choosing to destroy it is not a decision, I believe, that anyone has a right to make. You have several choices to explore.

No matter how difficult, you *can* make the adjustment and find the resources to see you through. Public welfare assistance may seem unbearable, and it is not really adequate, but many people survive with such help during crises. The way things seem today may not be the way they eventually turn out. Della's husband, for example, stayed with her several more years, though he did eventually leave.

Perhaps, for you, welfare assistance is unavailable. You can't earn enough to survive, and your predicament seems to have no answers and no way out. Find a counseling center and share your problem. The staff may be able to locate resources you haven't thought about. Temporary placement of the baby in excellent foster care can enable you to get back on your feet after your delivery, find a job, and then make a home for your child and yourself. This suggestion assumes you are a single mother with few or no resources of your own.

Painful as it is, adoption is a possible option. In recent years, many women have been unable to bear a child. Numerous families are eager to adopt and provide a loving home for a child. So, in the worst possible case, at least you can give life to a child, love and pray for that person, yet allow someone else to provide what you cannot.

CHAPTER THREE

Trying to Get Pregnant

*A*s you know, not every woman becomes pregnant the first month she tries. Many couples who had been using birth control pills find they must wait several months before pregnancy occurs. In a rare, exceptional case, even though the woman is on the pill, conception takes place.

WHAT YOU NEED TO KNOW

Normally, ovulation occurs once a month. Usually, the tiny egg is released from the ovary sometime during the middle part of the menstrual cycle. Conception rarely takes place the week after or the week before that menstrual period. The egg moves slowly through the fallopian tube and into the uterus, where it remains available to sperm for two or three days. Usually, all the conditions created by hormones are just right for the fertilized egg to plant itself into the wall of the uterus, and the microscopic cells begin to become a baby.

But the *usual* doesn't always happen, and you must be patient. The more anxious and tense you become, the more likely it is that you won't become pregnant. So relax, enjoy your lovemaking, and expect the best. Concentrate the frequency of intercourse during the two weeks in the middle of your monthly menstrual cycle.

If you have been unable to conceive for a few months, start a temperature chart, and take your temperature every morning. At the time of ovulation, your basic temperature will go up about a degree. You will find that a few months as a baseline will help you know your most likely time to conceive.

A commonsense rule is to lie still after intercourse. Many women prefer to use the toilet and even to wash after making love. The semen containing your husband's sperm is a somewhat thick substance. When you stand up, it tends to flow out of the vagina rather than stay in the womb, where it needs to be.

If you haven't become pregnant after six months, see a gynecologist. There may be some easily correctable defect that will, once fixed, enable you to become pregnant promptly. Be sure your husband is prepared to see a doctor, too. Sometimes men are unable to produce healthy sperm, and the doctor needs that information to determine your best course of action.

If you are unable to conceive at all, your doctor may prescribe a medication that promotes ovulation. Such hormonal preparations are safe when properly prescribed. Sometimes they are so effective that twins or even more babies result.

Simpler medical assistance may be the use of a prescribed vaginal douche or suppository. These medications are especially prepared to create just the right degree of acidity or alkalinity and to remove a possible mucous plug in the cervix. Avoid self-medication, however. The proper medicines for you can be determined only after careful studies by persons qualified in the field.

Lorie truly wanted to have a baby. She had enjoyed her younger sisters and loved to baby-sit as a teenager. After many months and extensive medication, she became pregnant. She and Kevin were deliriously happy.

Even the nausea each morning was a pleasure because it reminded Lorie that her dream of having her own baby was about to be fulfilled.

In the middle of the third month, some spotting occurred. Lorie went to bed and called her doctor. He reassured her, but the spotting became bleeding and then cramping. Early that evening, Lorie lost her baby. She grieved. Later, she was able to become pregnant again, but that one, too, resulted in a miscarriage. After the third heartbreaking disappointment, Lorie and Kevin decided they could not bear to go through the loss of another child.

Some couples, after a number of losses, bear healthy children. Each couple must decide what is right for them. The science of obstetrics has advanced light-years in the past few years! Today there are several miraculous techniques that can diagnose infertility and recurrent miscarriages. Furthermore, there are several options available to successfully treat the malfunction.

For Elaine, too, pregnancy was a longtime wish. She believed that having a child would turn her life around from the somewhat selfish pattern she had developed to one of meaning and purpose. The problem was, Elaine was single. She had never found the "right" man for her. *Not to worry,* she thought. *I'll just have artificial insemination. I can do this by myself.*

And so Elaine tried not once but repeatedly to become pregnant. The clinic where she sought help maintained a large sperm bank that could provide the genetic background Elaine wanted for her dream child. In many cases, conception is possible through injecting sperm from a volunteer donor into a woman's "ripe" uterus. That is, the hormone cycle is right, and the walls of the uterus are ready for the fertilized egg to attach and develop. But the procedure didn't work for Elaine.

For some people, it does work. In the case of couples, the husband must explore his feelings carefully. Jackie's husband cannot tolerate the idea of his wife bearing a child who is not theirs, while Jill's husband graciously gives her the choice to have a biological child who is genetically hers. And men like Jill's husband seem to become good fathers, eventually forgetting the child is not biologically theirs.

Both you and your husband must be honest about your feelings regarding artificial insemination. If you cannot reach agreement, one or the other will have to give in. Above all, be honest with each other, avoid being stubborn, and consider other options.

Medical developments have made it possible for the female ovum (egg) to be fertilized by the male sperm in the laboratory. Through a tiny incision, ripe ova are picked from the ovary and kept until active sperm can be placed near them, and fertilization may occur. In some cases, the couple's cells may be used. For example, a woman may have scarred and blocked fallopian tubes, or a man's sperm may be so inactive or so few in number that they cannot reach the ovum in the uterus. Under proper laboratory conditions, however, fertilization may successfully occur. At the right time, the fertile cell can be implanted in the womb, and pregnancy will result.

Cells from other people may be implanted in a woman who can carry through a successful pregnancy. Although this situation would result in a child who is not genetically related to the parents, at least it feels like having one's own baby.

In one friend, three fertile eggs were implanted, all three grew, and the couple had triplets. Another friend had an identical procedure done, but not one cell survived. There are no guarantees, only possibilities.

Some people believe these medical techniques are wrong. They feel that using them is a bit like playing God. And they consider artificial insemination to be an act of adultery. You must decide what is right for you.

One last option for the couple who cannot conceive is that of surrogate mothering. A man's sperm is injected into a woman who is willing to conceive and bear his child, then give that child to him. Some media headlines have revealed all too vividly the complexities of this plan. Laws are being considered and passed that will forbid or regulate surrogate mothering.

Frankly, I think this plan is a poor one and personally recommend that you avoid the heartache it could cause.

There are even newer and more amazing techniques for enabling a couple to become pregnant. They are extremely costly and come with no guarantees. They are also too complex to describe in this book. I recommend that you find a fertility expert and explore all possibilities, if you have the money.

INFERTILITY

If you must face the painful fact of infertility, you will experience grief. You must work through the stages of the grief process, but you can do so. If you need it, seek counseling. Practice your faith. Confide in friends and family, and ask for their comfort.

And then move on! Children with handicapping conditions, babies with AIDS, and babies born to addictive mothers are increasing in number. Perhaps you can be a mother who is able to love these special little ones and provide temporary care for them.

Volunteer to work with abused and neglected children, those placed in institutions, and those with single mothers who have full-time jobs. There is a desperate need for quality child care for parents who have no choice but to work. And some schools are now developing after-school programs for latchkey kids. You can find more outlets for your skills than you have dreamed. So don't let yourself drown in self-pity or bitterness because of what you can't have. Seek and enjoy whatever you *can* do to bless other children!

In the process of trying to get pregnant, whether you succeed or not, you will become well acquainted with your doctor, so seek one with whom you feel confident. Discuss your concerns and your feelings. Lorie (who was discussed earlier) became extremely angry with her doctor. She had carefully researched medical people and chosen him because he was highly respected in the area of fertility problems. In fact, Lorie did get pregnant, but then she miscarried. The second stage of grief is anger, and she needed a target for her rage. Fortunately, her doctor understood that and helped her through it. But some doctors are not so compassionate, and some women can be downright unreasonable when they are angry.

We may never understand why such a normal and intensely desired wish is not fulfilled. But once you complete the grief, keep in touch with your doctor. New discoveries are regularly being made. Perhaps sometime you may achieve pregnancy. Meanwhile, select and enjoy mothering in other ways.

CHAPTER FOUR

Having Your Baby

The delivery of a baby is, to me, the most miraculous and dramatic art in medicine. A human being so totally dependent for life on its mother at one moment is the next discovering how to breathe, cry, and physically function apart from her. Certainly, her nurture and protection are still vital, but what was once a part of her becomes separate.

Despite modern medicine's amazing capacity to make deliveries safe and comfortable, almost every mother has some fears. *What if . . . ?* is a haunting question. Knowing the many types of birth defects made my nightmares especially vivid.

A young friend shared with me her fears about the birth of her child. She had learned that sometimes a baby had a reduced amount of blood flow and oxygen to the brain. In that case, a baby would be likely to expel a stool before birth. This stool, called meconium, stains the mother's amniotic fluid. Gwen was a child psychologist, so she knew a great deal about brain-damaged children. It was understandable that she should pray that such damage not be inflicted on her baby.

Gwen's pregnancy went several days beyond her expected due date, and her doctor felt she needed to try to start labor. Before any medication could be given, however, Gwen's labor contractions began on their own. Because of the doctor's original plan, Gwen was attached to several monitors that recorded her and the baby's vital signs. Thanks to the providence of the heavenly Father, the doctor learned that the umbilical cord was wrapped around the baby's neck. As the womb contracted, pressing the baby's head down into the narrow birth canal, circulation would be greatly reduced, and the baby's heartbeat would slow.

Expert medical care enabled Gwen to deliver her baby after a short labor. But her nightmare became a reality: the amniotic fluid was dark with her baby's meconium stool. After an extremely careful evaluation, the doctor discovered the baby would be perfectly well, and indeed, he was. The grueling experience will not be easy to forget, though.

After Gwen was rested and recovered from her waking nightmare, I sat with her in her hospital room. I asked, "Can you tell me your feelings as you learned of the possible trouble with your baby?"

With the gentlest possible words, Gwen answered, "I just prayed that God would give me the courage to accept whatever child He gave us." I could not imagine a more mature answer. And I hope you have faith in God to help you if you, too, face any difficulties.

The average length of time for labor is about nine hours.

Most women dread the pain of the delivery itself. Over the past few decades, the pendulum has swung far between natural childbirth (with little or no anesthetic) and excessive anesthesia that created some risk for the baby. New types of anesthesia are now available that are both safe for the baby and nearly pain-free for moms.

You need to be forewarned that after delivery, you will have mixed emotions. At first you will feel pure physical relief. You are likely to feel pride and even elation over the tiny being you have created. Then you may experience surprise over his beauty. Or you may think she is ugly—

especially if there are marks from a difficult delivery. You will at some point feel sheer panic and think, *What will I ever do with this tiny, helpless bit of humanity?* If you allow it, you can work yourself into an anxious state. But believe me, you can learn to control those emotions. Arrange for some supportive help for a few days, and try to get sound sleep. Exercise those flabby tummy muscles even when you're resting. Just tighten them and relax them repeatedly several times a day. Begin to do all those things you practiced before the baby arrived, and slowly you'll fit into the mothering habit, your mood swings and panic will subside, and you'll even start to enjoy your new lifestyle.

LAMAZE CLASSES

Most hospitals conduct classes in childbirth that relieve fears and increase confidence. They are established to include expectant fathers, so they serve multiple purposes. A great benefit is their encouragement of the dads' active participation.

If you live in a rural or small town, these classes may not be available. But ask your doctor or county medical society where to find them. Even traveling to a larger city would be worth the effort if you can do that.

In childbirth classes such as the Lamaze course, you will meet other expectant parents. You will not feel so alone in your discomforts and fears through sharing with others. Husbands especially may value the support of the other men and their unique problems.

One of the terms I like in the Lamaze approach is "coach." The father or a trusted friend learns how to count breathing and teach the mother to rest between labor pains, breathe properly during them, and push as the baby is actually being born.

More problems during deliveries are caused by the mother's fears and tension than can be measured. As a senior medical student on obstetrics rotation, I often had the duty of walking with moms in the early stages of labor. It was then the theory that walking helped the baby's head to settle in the pelvis, stimulated healthier contractions, and shortened the length of labor. Some mothers would walk proudly, stopping briefly to get through their contractions, and walk again. No complaining. Just pure courage. But others would complain, try to sit down, and wail loudly as the contractions intensified. We all knew the latter group would have a longer and harder labor.

Although most hospitals no longer require those endless walks, they encourage mothers to be up and about until the actual delivery. The coach becomes the encourager, and the mom doesn't feel so abandoned when nurses' attention is needed elsewhere. The bonding process between the coach and the waiting mother is a very tender one. I believe fathers are more closely entwined with the entire family because of this.

Labor and Delivery

Many young women once approached motherhood terrified of delivery. That was often due to the horror stories of their older relatives, unaware as they competed for the most shocking tales that young ears were listening. Such gossip goes on today just as intensely as it did when I was young. But today's myths can be dispelled in the light of modern science. So enroll in your hospital's classes, and turn on the light! First, let me explain that you *will* know labor. Genuine contractions may resemble the false labor we call Braxton Hicks contractions, which are relatively painless. In real labor, however, pains build in intensity and recur regularly. You can soon time them as accurately as your clock works. Every ten minutes, then eight, six, five, and so on. Most doctors want moms in the hospital at least by the two- or three-minute interval. If there are special concerns or you have a long way to drive, you may need to go earlier. Be sure to have this plan cleared with your doctor long before your due date.

Sometimes the bag of waters, in which your baby has floated for some nine months, will break before labor pains start. Be sure this is not urine before you rush to the phone. As you know, baby's motions can be quite strong and may squeeze out a substantial amount of urine. Amniotic fluid is a bit sticky, smells different from urine, and continues to flow as the baby moves or contractions occur. Most, if not all, doctors like to see mothers quite soon after the water breaks. You may not go into labor right away, maybe not for some hours or even days. But you must avoid any infection or the few complications associated with the early rupture of those waters.

There usually is a discharge of slightly blood-tinged mucus. This mucous plug has protected the cervix (the opening into the womb) from infections during pregnancy. If you can't identify this substance, don't worry. So much will be happening in the next few hours, it's easy to overlook some events.

The length of labor varies greatly, but the average time is about nine hours. Carefully established criteria enable doctors to know if the birth will proceed naturally or if a surgical delivery will be necessary. Caesarean deliveries used to be done only 4 percent of the time; that figure has now risen to 18 to 20 percent.

Just as your pregnancy is divided into three trimesters, so delivery is defined in three stages. The first stage lasts from the first contraction to the point of complete dilation of the cervix, the second stage goes from this point of time to the actual delivery of the baby, and the third stage is from birth to the delivery of the placenta and tissues that have held the baby. The first stage lasts about eight hours for later deliveries. The second stage averages fifty minutes for first-timers and about twenty minutes for second or later deliveries. The third stage is very brief, perhaps half a minute, and painless in most cases. Rarely, the placenta may create a problem by failing to separate from the uterus. As the womb continues to contract, however, that tends to complete the separation, and delivery is over.

The advent of many mechanical devices has made deliveries immensely safer than some years ago. Monitors observe the mother's physical functions as well as the baby's. Warning signals permit medical staffs to recognize early any dangers and respond quickly. You can feel quite secure in the expert care available to you in almost any hospital in this country.

Although complications are possible, problems are actually rare. The major signs to remember are (1) bleeding of any significant amount, (2) early breaking of your water without prompt beginning of labor, and (3) any change in your baby's usual movements.

The pain of labor contractions is quite bearable because they last for only a measurable period of time. You feel so good between them, and you are so glad this process is going to be over soon, that you can bear them. In the last few minutes when the baby's head is being delivered, your doctor will give you a mild anesthetic. You may even have a local anesthetic so that you can handle the last few pains quite comfortably.

I realize many women are still reluctant to accept an anesthetic during labor. While I respect your right to choose what is good for you, I recommend accepting some pain relief. Doctors are extremely cautious. They will give you only those amounts of thoroughly researched medications that are safe for you and your baby. So I hope you'll accept that help and not become exhausted through needless discomfort and pain.

When my grandson was born twelve years ago, I was delighted at the changes in obstetrics that had taken place from even ten years before that. The birthing room looked a lot like a living room. The grandparents, father, and mother were exuberant over the new baby, who was passed around to all of us after his mother held him. The doctor was still repairing the episiotomy, and the nurse was cleaning the baby as we all tried to decide whom Bryan resembled. Precautions were taken to avoid any sort of infection, but the sterile, forbidding atmosphere of my training days was gone. It really is fun to have a baby these days.

GOING HOME

Because of pressure from many health insurance carriers, hospital stays are greatly curtailed. In many cases, the push to return home early is most unfortunate. Tired, insecure new mothers are literally forced to assume total responsibility when they are hardly able to do so. In a few cases, it may be really risky to be at home and responsible for a new baby, perhaps older children, and the management of a household. If you are an over-burdened mom, consider these ideas.

- Seek the help of a relative, friend, or neighbor for at least a few days. Even a few hours a day can provide moral support and physical help. If you are a single mother, this assistance is especially necessary.
- Even during the day or two you are in the hospital, get all the rest you can.
- Plan ahead for the first few days at home. You must eat, use the bathroom, and sleep a little bit. All other tasks can wait.
- Think about when you can straighten up your home to make it orderly and pleasant, wash dishes, prepare some meals, and do whatever other duties you want done. Plan these tasks when you feel more rested and energetic.
- Above all else, try not to do so much that nothing is completed, you get frustrated, and the new baby, sensing your fatigue, becomes irritable. Take plenty of time with your baby; master the art of nursing and cud-dling. Most other things can wait.

BONDING

Bonding is the process by which a new baby and mother become securely attached to each other. It demands plenty of time to hold, play with, and admire that new person. It also requires a loving, protective attitude in the mother. Many new moms expect a sudden rush of strong maternal emotion as soon as the baby is placed in their arms. When that doesn't happen (and it rarely does!), they fear something is wrong with them. The more concerned they become, the more that anxiety is communicated to the baby, who becomes irritable and has a hard time relaxing and cuddling. Moms become convinced something is wrong with them, or even worse, they fear that the child just doesn't like them.

Prebirth classes, hospital staffs, and pediatricians all recognize the importance of bonding and do everything possible to facilitate it. That concern accounts for making changes in delivery rooms and encouraging the presence of fathers and grandparents. And in some hospitals older children are permitted to be in the mother's room. Having the mother hold the baby immediately after birth and even nurse a little is another practice that enhances the bonding process.

Breast-feeding also adds to bonding. Realizing that Mom is the source of life and health to her baby has a physical, emotional, and psychological impact that no other areas of child care can duplicate. I strongly recommend breast-feeding when it is at all possible. And with patient endurance, it usually is.

If you don't have a miraculous surge of maternal feelings right away, please don't get uptight! Just as some mothers crave dill pickles during pregnancy and others never have a craving, so some mothers just don't experience bonding as a mystical, sudden event. For you, the process will be slower, gradual, and almost imperceptible. As you feel more sure of yourself, concentrate at times on the helplessness and tiny perfection of your baby's physical being. Stick your finger into the grip of that little hand. Touch the little toes and stroke the foot. Stroke the head gently and feel the softness of those dimpled cheeks. Hold the baby close, and snuggle the head in your neck. Place the baby on your lap and gently rock him awake or asleep; try different positions, on either side, back, or abdomen. You will learn the way the baby becomes most comfortable.

As you discover the impact you can have to soothe, nurture, and gain responses from your child, you will sense your importance to her, and bonding will grow. Maybe you missed out on great bonding. You can at least give your child more than you had. Try to imagine yourself as a baby. Let yourself enjoy the warm, gentle touches you give your baby. Try to picture a person who loves you very much caressing you as a child in a very maternal way. You will be able to give that kind of tenderness to your baby even more effectively as you strengthen your emotional patterns. Remember, Dr. Harlow's studies showed that even play with other baby monkeys created healthier adults. You can help turn the tide of inadequate mothering that concerns many people.

Bonding takes time. If you don't have a surge of maternal feelings right away, don't get uptight.

ADJUSTING

I warned you that being a parent is not convenient, let alone pleasurable, at times. If you have let yourself believe that everything in life should be easy and fun, you will be frustrated and resentful much of the time, even toward your child. It is urgent, then, that you examine your beliefs and values. Try to see that life is composed of cycles of work, rest, and play.

Periods of pain alternate with times of peace and happiness. When you can accept these facts, you will be much more able to really enjoy your baby. You *will* make it through dirty diapers, spitting up, and nocturnal crying because you will remember that once cleaned up and comforted, your baby will cuddle as if to say, "Thanks, Mom!" and will smell good until the next round.

Intense feelings of anxiety, fear, and inadequacy can result in depression. When you give in to such negative emotions, you can feel helpless and may become so tense that your baby absorbs your concern and becomes tense or irritable, too.

If you live far away from your families, are afraid to seek help from others, or are a single mom, you may become exhausted trying to meet your baby's needs. And absolute fatigue can slow down the bonding process.

Here are some ideas to help you correct or make up for these potential handicaps:

- *Find and observe other mothers and babies.* Copy what you see them doing when you find actions that seem to fit well.

- *Explore, reconsider, and, if necessary, change some of your values and beliefs.* Reassessments are a good practice anyway, but at this time, you especially need to be aware of lasting values, courage, and self-discipline rather than searching for the easy way out. Such a reevaluation may mean giving up a career that is too demanding. If succeeding at your job means that you must sacrifice the time and energy your child needs, I urge you to consider your values carefully. Most women can reenter the job market and move ahead in a career at any time. True, you may have to back up and start over, but that can be done. However, you can never return a child to those crucial early months and provide what was needed so badly at that time. No job is as important as raising a secure and healthy child.

- *Be prepared for your peers to disagree.* For the last twenty years or so, the trend has been for young women to believe they can have it all and do it all. Those who have chosen to sacrifice careers for motherhood are often ridiculed. If you decide to be a stay-at-home mom, don't let that attitude influence you. Do what your intuition and heart dictate.

  If you feel you must work or your situation demands that you earn money, plan how to do that, yet keep priorities in order. We'll discuss that later on.

- *Seek an older, wise woman as a friend.* This person could be your mother, another relative, or a retired person who has raised a family. Since so many families are widely separated by distance, borrow a mother. She will be blessed by your friendship and can be most supportive in many ways.

- *Build a support system.* Not only do you need a mother or substitute mom, but you are likely to need several other helpful people in your life when your children are young. Don't forget a church community as a source of support.

Babies need to see the glow of your joy in their existence. They respond to the energy of smiles and laughter and tend to become sad when they fail to experience adequate stimulation. Keep searching until you find a neighbor or friend who will offer you encouragement and help. Both your child and you will benefit from the support.

Responsibilities

CHAPTER FIVE

Getting Settled

*H*aving your baby is such a relief that you're likely to feel that you can manage the whole world after that experience. Let me forewarn you, that feeling may be short-lived!

YOU'RE HOME!

I will never forget the birth of my first baby. She was so tiny and yet so perfect, so helpless and yet so demanding. When we arrived home from the hospital, I was weary, having had some serious complications. My husband and I felt we had planned for everything, so I was horrified to discover when it was time for her first feeding that we had forgotten her formula. While he rushed out for her special formula, I sterilized her bottles. The poor baby was exhausted by the time we could feed her, and so was I.

Be more organized than I was! And I hope you can breast-feed your baby because that is much more convenient, once you establish the nursing technique. Have the crib made up, the temperature set, clean diapers and bath and skin care materials handy, and a comfortable spot for yourself arranged.

When my grandson was born, the nurses recommended that he be placed on a small section of lamb's wool. It was comfortable, not too warm or too cool, and he would settle into it with ease. Babies can survive without the "lambie," but it was an asset in his care.

You need to decide beforehand whether you will take advantage of the time-honored custom of having your mother or mother-in-law stay with you. Some couples prefer to make things work alone, while others prefer the help of a relative. Frankly, I suspect that my daughters invited me to stay in order to pamper *me!* I loved being with them, and I have enjoyed really close relationships with my grandchildren.

Sadly, some young mothers have very strained relationships with their mothers. If you are one of those, I suggest you find other help. Tension, worry, or disappointments can take a toll on your energy, and you need all you can muster to adjust to this big change in your life and lifestyle.

If your husband can be at home, you may well manage with no additional help. Or you may ask a neighbor to pop in now and then to see how you are doing. Don't be afraid to ask her to take over for an hour or so while you relax and catch a nap.

BALANCING AND JUGGLING

The first few days and even weeks of your life with a baby, you'll feel like a juggler as you try to keep everything going. The ability to balance rest, work, and recreation is totally elusive. You'll believe that never again in your life will you feel rested. But you can achieve a semblance of calm and order within a surprisingly short time.

First, tune your mind into a new way of thinking and prioritizing. You can now put into action the plans and concepts you anticipated in Section One. Obviously, the baby's needs come first. Everything else can wait until you establish the feeding, diapering, and sleeping routines and you will manage to do that.

Most household tasks can wait or can be done quickly. If you are a fastidious housekeeper, you may be reluctant to leave corners and closets untouched, but I learned that you can actually get used to doing a lot of skillful neglecting. And this is the time to learn to keep your children and husband ahead of any other duty.

Other family members are important, especially older children. Even the baby may bear a little bit of neglect while you acquaint older siblings with their new rival for your attention. Extra time and effort early on can prevent much heartache later. Help them learn how to touch the baby, and encourage them to participate in some way at bath time. All children will experience some fear that the baby will replace them in your heart. Just remind them and show them how much you love them. Demonstrate through the new baby how they looked and acted as infants and how much you enjoyed them. Reassure them that you love them even more now.

You'll need your husband's help, but be very clear about what you need, and be thoughtful in how you ask. He is not a servant to be ordered but a friend to be considered. Above all, do not criticize his best efforts. Show your appreciation.

I hope you are blessed with many visitors, but even more, I hope they will be thoughtful enough to wait a few days and to call before they drop by. If not, call them and let them know when you would like to receive visitors. I've not seen this done, but I suggest a brief note on the birth announcements you probably will send out. Add a simple statement such as, "We'd love you to come and visit us after the baby is a week old," or whatever date you may choose.

When visitors arrive, how about having an older child show them the baby? The big brother or sister can conduct them to the baby's bed and tell them the name and whatever information he or she wants to reveal. Children make some fascinating observations.

Now, let's consider your needs. If you fail to take care of yourself, you'll be unable to care for your family. Here are some tips for your comfort:

- Apply warm, moist packs to your tender breasts and a heat lamp to your breasts and your stitches. A heat lamp is an ordinary lightbulb held a few inches from tender areas or painful nipples. It creates an amazing sense of comfort while your tissues are healing and the nipples are toughening.
- A shower or a soak in a nice warm bath can make you feel almost like a new person.
- Remember that it will be difficult for you to get long periods of sleep for several days or longer after the baby is born. If you will take advantage of short rest periods, you can adapt to less sleep than you would think possible. When the baby sleeps, lie down and relax; try to catch a nap. Many new mothers have trouble doing that because of the instinctive need to stay alert to their baby. But after a while the nervousness subsides, and sleep comes more easily.
- Learn to be a procrastinator. Many duties will wait while you are establishing your new routine. Doing this waiting for some tasks is simple; feeling good about it isn't so easy. But if you remember who is really important, you can adjust your attitude.
- Work efficiently—"smarter, not harder" is a great motto. While you prop up your feet and rest, make a mental list of duties you would most like to accomplish. Plan how you can do them with the least effort, then follow through whenever you have a few minutes.
- Again, ask for help when you reach that point of need. Later you can pay back people who respond to your needs by helping them.

REMEMBER YOUR HUSBAND

One more ball to toss into your juggling act is your husband. He will have his own set of anxieties. He, too, must assume a new set of responsibilities. He may fear you will no longer have time for him or desire sexual intimacy. He will feel sad over giving up some of his freedom and having more expenses.

- Don't be afraid to talk with him about his concerns, and offer all the reassurance you can. Caring about each other's concerns and working and planning together can make the two of you an unbeatable team.

- Include your husband in caring for and enjoying the new baby. Keep in mind the demands of his job and other responsibilities and don't overburden him, but let him know how important he is.

- Keep your romance alive. Romance is far more than sex; be attractive, gentle, sensitive, and basically loving within the realm of the possible.

> *Take care of yourself so you will able to care for your family. When baby is sleeping, lie down and try to take a nap instead of trying to catch up on household tasks.*

- Trust his parenting values and instincts as you become more familiar with your own. Discuss together the dreams, wishes, and plans each of you has for your child.

- Avoid criticizing him. If he is too loud or a bit awkward, the baby's response will tell him. A suggestion now and then usually will be helpful, but most men do not respond well to disapproval any more than women do.

- As soon as you regain your physical strength, and when you are ready, plan some special times for just the two of you. Budget, if you must, for child care while the two of you keep close through sharing some activities you most enjoy.

- Show your confidence in him by leaving the baby alone with him now and then. I suggest that for both your sakes, you try this for only a short time, say a half hour or less at first.

- At all times express your appreciation of his help, your pride in his fathering, and your primary love of him.

YOUR PHYSICAL RECOVERY

Doctors call the first seven weeks after your baby's birth the puerperium. Don't try to pronounce it; just feel smart because you know it is the time your body takes to return to its relatively normal state.

The most urgent change I recall desiring was healing of my perineum. The perineum is the area around your vagina that was stretched, torn, or cut and repaired at the time of delivery. Rest, heat, and patience will see you through this healing stage in about a week to ten days. Be sure the nurse explains how to take proper care of this area before you leave the hospital.

Painful breasts are a major source of distress for a week or two. The La Leche League has excellent literature and people who are qualified to guide you through this. (Their Web site is www.lalecheleague.org.) Once nursing is well-established, you will experience discomfort only when the baby sleeps too long. Keep a breast pump handy if you are too uncomfortable, but your body will establish its own balance.

Most hospitals have nurses who are well-trained in teaching moms how to successfully nurse their babies. If you are a first-time mom, or if you had problems with another baby, take advantage of this help. Nursing should be a happy process, not a frustrating one.

Many new mothers feel very weak and tired for several weeks; others seem to experience very little fatigue. You should get up and walk as well as do some tasks every day. But balance activities with enough rest.

For several days you will menstruate. The color of the flow will gradually change from red to darker red or brown and then a yellowish to clear discharge. This flow may last from a few days to a week or more. While you are in the hospital, a nurse will show you how to massage your uterus. Do that regularly for the first week or more because that gentle pressure, through the abdomen, helps your womb return to its normal size more quickly. It may take several months before your menstrual cycle is reestablished. If you nurse your baby, you may have no periods for a number of months, but that doesn't mean you can't get pregnant.

Bladder and bowel functions will be uncomfortable for several days. As your perineum heals, that pain will disappear. You must drink plenty of water, and you may need a mild laxative just as you did before your baby's birth.

Your diet needs to continue to be balanced and healthy. You may be able to tolerate some foods now that you couldn't tolerate during pregnancy. Foods that are too rich in fats may create milk that is too rich for your baby. If she starts spitting up or has stools that are too loose, you must cut down on the desserts and increase your intake of fruits and vegetables. You may lose a few pounds while you nurse your baby. If you need to lose weight, diet minimally and lose slowly. Your figure's restoration is not as important as your baby's good nutrition. But with care you can do both.

When you feel ready, begin exercising. Even when you are recovering from delivery, you can tighten and relax those flabby abdominal muscles. Walking, twisting, and exercising arms and legs are all means of increasing your circulation, burning up excess fat, and getting back in shape. Your doctor and nurse can advise you of special restrictions.

Resume sexual intimacy cautiously. Your pain level will guide you as to when you are ready for this. Discuss it with your doctor when you are likely to be ready. You may be more prone to bladder infections after delivery anyway, and intercourse may aggravate that possibility. Use common sense, but do remember to keep your marriage and romance alive and well. You are likely to have less sex drive than was normal for you, but that, too, will return, so don't let your husband panic.

Use some form of birth control at once. You are not likely to get pregnant soon after delivery, but conception can take place very early. And your body and your family need time to adjust to this child before another one arrives.

THOSE TROUBLESOME EMOTIONS

If you are an emotionally intense person, you may fluctuate from depression to anger to excitement in a short time. Such rapid mood changes can worry you and are exhausting, to say the least.

Some of these feelings are normal and universal. More than one mom has confessed that she went from adoring her baby to fearing she might harm her child in five minutes. Some of these intense emotions are related to your physical state and the hormonal changes taking place. Some are aggravated by fatigue and the grief process over the loss of your freedom we discussed earlier.

Be patient with yourself if you are having wild swings in your emotions. If you honestly can't regain control, call your doctor.

Be particularly patient with yourself regarding these emotional storms. They will pass. Meanwhile, use this opportunity to practice self-control and increase your maturity. A great many people rely on medication to control their moods. Certainly, there is a place for well-prescribed pills. But there is a healthy power in learning to think positively and take charge of your attitudes and actions; then your feelings will usually come into line. If you honestly can't regain control, call your doctor for help.

As usual, I have some practical steps for you to take.

DEALING WITH YOUR EMOTIONS

- Get your mind back in control by thinking of a concise name for the emotion you are experiencing.
- Try to understand why you are feeling this emotion. When did it start? What were you doing or thinking at that time? When have you felt this way before? Consider what you can do about the situation or thoughts that precipitated such uneasy feelings. Most uncomfortable emotions

gain power from a sense of helplessness, but you are not helpless. You have power over your thoughts, and you still have considerable control over your actions. Call a sitter for a little while, and go for a walk. Even making simple choices can demonstrate to you that you are not really helpless.

- Every day do something for yourself.
- Keep in touch with other new mothers. As you discover that they share your experiences, you won't feel so alone or guilty. And you can learn from one another what works or doesn't work with a newborn.
- Express your feelings verbally with healthy control. You can choose to be in charge, even though it isn't easy to do so. Being in control doesn't mean hiding or denying emotions and then acting them out; it means expressing them appropriately, with control.

BECOMING FRIENDS WITH YOUR BABY

Now, at last, you can become acquainted with this little person you have carried so long! It is pure pleasure for me to see a new mother holding and just looking at her baby. Have fun doing that. Memorize his features and marvel at his perfection. Cuddle and hug, let the soft breathing tickle your neck, and rock to your heart's content. You have carried this child nine months, so you can't spoil him by continuing such closeness. When both you and your baby will have enough of this cuddling, you'll find it gradually decreases.

As you get to know your baby, avoid trying to decide whom she resembles. Relatives will do enough of that for you. Instead, think of her as an individual, separate and unique. There are some of your genes in her and some of her father's as well. But she is her very own person, entrusted to your care until she is able to make it on her own. Babies are not possessions.

Think happily about your child, even when he cries. Crying is a new baby's only language for a while until he learns to coo and gurgle, so don't let crying make you tense and anxious. Carefully attend to a crying baby with milk, a dry diaper, cuddling and rocking, but then let him cry to himself for a while. Overly tense, tired mothers make babies more tense and fretful, so take care of yourself.

During pregnancy, I recommended that you practice talking and singing to your baby. Now you can put those skills to work. Your baby listened to your heartbeat before birth, so keep her close to your heart now. After nursing and while soothing the baby, place that little head against your heart. The rhythm of your heartbeat can be very soothing.

Sudden or jerky motions may frighten your baby. Move in gentle and deliberate ways that will not startle him. Loud noises also tend to over-stimulate babies. You may enjoy loud music, but for a few weeks, turn it down! Babies don't need intense stimulation, and I believe that too much noise and overly intense handling can cause some of the hyperactivity that handicaps many children. A calm, soothing environment will be good for the whole family.

Several years ago, I spent an evening with some very special parents. They were meeting together because every one of them had a child with a defect. Many of them appeared to be perfect but hidden was a more or less serious handicapping condition. All of them were obtaining help, and most of them could describe progress as they worked heroically to overcome those problems.

You, too, may discover a defect as you get to know your child. It may be as minimal as a nose or ears that seem too big or too small. It may be as serious as paralysis or a severe learning disorder. Whatever the problem, learn to love and accept your child unconditionally. Seek sound medical evaluations, and get all the help you can. Make the most of your child's assets, and don't allow the problems to rob you of the enriching experience of mothering a special child.

CHAPTER SIX

Affirming Your Child

*B*eing a mother was far from easy when I was born, about seventy-five years ago. My mother is a prime example of that fact. She bore seven children from two to five years apart. All of us were born at home. She had no anesthetic, no pain pills, no monitors, and no white-uniformed nurse to whisk away the new baby and let her rest a bit.

Yet, repeatedly, my mother affirmed that each of us was a wanted child. She made many mistakes, as I have, and as every mother has. But she lived out her responsibilities in mothering. She loved us and wanted us to be good (even perfect!) and to find the best in life.

CREATING A HOME

The birthing of seven healthy babies certainly crowned my mother's creativity. She took the best possible care of herself and of us. Never did she hint that we were a burden, though I know we were; nor did she indicate that she wished she had never had us, though surely, at times, she must have!

Mother's creativity became apparent in many ways that have enriched my life. She had a great nesting instinct and made our old farmhouse as attractive as possible. Flowered wallpaper adorned every room. There were always clean sheer curtains on the windows that were carefully mended. I can still see the picture on the wall of a lone wolf howling across the snow at a dimly lit cottage. And I felt that I was the sleeping child guarded faithfully by a huge watching dog. Every room held a motto quoting some wisdom from the Bible, reminding us of God's care over us.

Our beds were warm even in the howling cold Kansas winters because of the quilts my mother made. They may have been pieced together from the rough fabric of my father's worn-out suits, but they were lined with soft flannel and knotted with bright yarn. Many an exquisitely quilted bedspread cost her weeks of labor and arthritic fingers, but they still stand as symbols of love and ingenuity.

During the economic depression of the 1930s, our pillowcases and even sheets were made out of coarse muslin from the sacks of flour we used. But we felt we were rich because their borders were decorated with embroidered birds and flowers Mother drew and stitched on them.

Even in her cooking, Mother was creative. Her pies were works of art, with the edges evenly fluted and designs carved into the top crust.

At times, Mother was irritated by my restlessness during the long church services on Sundays. But when she realized I simply could not tolerate another minute, she would, at times, draw for me on her tablet. It seemed magical to me as I saw, on the margins of her notes on the sermon, a chicken, bird, or flower emerge.

Mother was also a creative storyteller. She could make me almost hear the roar of lions in the den where Daniel was thrown. In the dusk of a summer evening on the front porch Mother told how God Himself walked with Adam and Eve in the Garden in the cool of the day, and I could imagine the three of them walking along our front lawn under the pines. The lessons of her stories, biblical and secular, remain engraved in my memories and my life.

You, too, are gifted in many ways. You have only to discover and put those gifts to work. It takes very little money, though you can spend a great deal, to make your home clean, bright, and attractive. You, too, can create games, stories, appealing foods, and pleasant mealtimes. Try turning off your radio and sing together. Leave the TV unplugged, and make up skits or plays. Try to remember what was fun when you were seven. Your creativity will enrich your life as well as your child's.

NURTURING

Most of my brothers and sisters are living testimonies of our mother's good nutrition. Within the knowledge then available, we had well-balanced and delicious meals three times every day. My grandmother lived with us for many years, and we were blessed with various relatives, hired help, or needy friends often for weeks. Cooking for ten to fifteen people regularly was a huge task. Yet I never recall Mother complaining about it.

Furthermore, we grew vegetables and raised chickens. So Mother had to dig the potatoes and carrots, wash them, and then prepare them. The chicken had to be caught and killed, plucked and drawn, and cut up before cooking.

Nurturing was not easy! But Mother's nurturing was not limited to food. She nurtured our minds. Though she had little formal schooling, she taught us spelling and helped us learn arithmetic. I can still add accurately because I visualize those white dots on the black dominoes we played with.

We were well-nurtured socially. Because of the isolation of farm life, we commonly had guests for Sunday dinner. There were usually children who came to play in the hay barn or hike to the creek in the pasture. Mother made certain we passed the food properly, ate with our mouths closed, and generally practiced good manners.

Spiritually, we were well-fed. Not only did we attend church faithfully, but we were also taught our Sunday school lessons on Saturday nights. And every day we participated in family prayers and thanksgiving for every meal.

There are many ways in which we all need to be nurtured physically, intellectually, socially, and spiritually. By creative thinking, you can find means by which to feed your children. And I trust you, too, will be nurtured.

PROTECTING

My father fulfilled the role of physical protector more than my mother. Nevertheless, Mother performed this service most memorably in the spiritual and moral aspects. In fact, I believe she overdid it.

No books or magazines were allowed in our house that were less than totally moral and uplifting or at least informative of social issues. I read most of Charles Dickens's books, *Pilgrim's Progress,* and books upholding animals' rights and decrying the past injustices to minorities.

Mother abhorred advertisements promoting alcohol consumption and the use of tobacco. The use of drugs never even occurred to her, but the very idea would have been relegated to the opium dens of "heathen" countries.

Mother never used a swear word, and even slang was foreign to her vocabulary. I cannot recall her ever gossiping, but she was clearly critical of anyone who lived a less-than-exemplary life.

Since Mother wouldn't allow us to attend events she considered unwholesome, we didn't see movies, and we never went to a school dance or the skating rink. Any public entertainment was limited to interscholastic sports and the rare event of a U.S. Navy band or a classical music concert.

Fighting, name-calling, and rudeness were not tolerated in our home, at least not in Mom's presence. She did her best to protect us from becoming hurtful people and taught us to be kind and courteous. I would not have you believe we were always perfect, but Mother endeavored to rear children who would not turn into obnoxious adults.

In the world of my childhood, many dangers did not exist that have become commonplace today. Not long ago a grandmother came to me with a tragic story. Her daughter, a single mother, had just discovered that her preschooler had been sexually molested by another child at the day-care center. The attendant there was a capable woman who provided a lovely well-supervised environment. In spite of her watchfulness, the two children found moments alone, and the older one taught this innocent youngster far too much sexual information. Regularly, sensational news items relate to sexually inappropriate treatment and even exploitation of little children.

A number of people have been started in precocious sexual habits by curious and poorly informed baby-sitters. And young baby-sitters have, more than rarely, been sexually involved with a family member where they sit. Ours is a highly sexualized world. Protecting children from premature sexual knowledge and experiences is a major responsibility of every mother.

Another source of child sexual abuse is a boyfriend of the mother, a stepfather, or even a father or other relative. Mothers are usually unaware of these activities and often refuse to believe the child's revelation. They may even blame the child for initiating the sexual activity and punish the victim.

According to a study several years ago by Search Institute in Minnesota, young people believe that cheating, lying, and even stealing are acceptable as long as they don't get caught. You, Mother, are most likely to be the one who can protect your children from a loss of healthy moral values. It's up to you to be the example as well as the teacher of right and wrong.

Don't allow your children to sexually arouse and tease their friends by provocative behaviors and attire. There are so many years for exploring and enjoying healthy sex in marriage. Help your youngsters learn to postpone some pleasures now for their future good. You can hardly start too soon. Puberty starts early, if not in your own children, certainly in some of their friends.

Protect your children from becoming TV zombies. The habit of vege-
tating in front of various amoral and immoral programs is widespread. It
is deadly for the creative, energetic part of life. So turn on TV only for
well-chosen programs. Help your children judge and select beneficial
shows from the many bad ones. Teach them to be critical in analyzing
advertisements as well as programs, and you may protect them from
wasting a large segment of life because they lose a sense of discrimina-
tion and individuality.

EDUCATING

Let me startle you at once by urging you *to avoid academic teaching of
preschoolers.* Many child-care centers advertise their unique methods of
teaching toddlers how to do kindergarten-type activities. In fact, so many
children have had so much exposure to formal learning that they are
bored when they finally reach the actual school setting.

The preschool years are necessary for children's learning about themselves, their world, and their families. At ages two, three, and four, a child
needs to run, climb, take turns, and throw big balls. He or she loves to
color with big crayons on paper, and the feel of clay is intriguing.
However, conforming to a class activity is not useful.

My mother taught me to make mud pies, build castles in a sandbox,
and make playhouses out of string, wood, and discarded household
items. I was quite a big girl before I realized you could buy valentines or
Christmas cards. We had a large green hatbox full of old cards, ribbons,
lace, and pieces of bright paper. From that exciting collection of stuff, we
made greeting cards and gifts for one another and our friends.

Walking along the roadside and exploring in the woods were excursions into a world of magic. Wildflowers, colored leaves, bright blue-jay
feathers, hedge apples, and black walnuts were all to be had by simply
picking them up. At regular intervals, there were cloud-soft baby chicks

to feel against my cheeks. The almost imperceptible tickle of an inch-worm marching up my bare arm still delights my senses. I watched colonies of ants clearing intricate mazes underground and hid as bees swarmed to a new hive. The wobbly legs of baby colts and calves seemed totally unable to support the bulky bodies they somehow kept erect.

Farm life offered a wealth of material for exploring and learning. But I missed visiting a fire station, large library, and art gallery. Wherever you live, there are countless resources for educating your children.

Expose them to as much stimulation of the physical senses—sight, hearing, smell, touch, taste, and motion—as possible. While they are still babies, take them outside, and from then until they will no longer go with you, go for walks. Point out the blue sky and marshmallow white clouds. Show them the chirping birds, the hopping rabbits, and the chattering squir-rels. Have them touch satiny flower petals and rough leaves. Introduce them to the scent of roses and the smell of an onion. When they are ready for regular foods, let them taste the batter from a cake and the juice from a pickle. Blow on her neck and kiss her toes. Hug him tight, and twirl him in a circle until you both sit down a bit dizzy.

> *Avoid academic teaching of preschoolers. Instead, expose them to as much stimulation of the five senses as possible.*

So many children miss the exquisite joy of these gems of nature. All too soon, they become supersaturated with and overstimulated by the rau-cous sounds of rock music, and they never notice the chirp of a cricket or the call of a cardinal. Unless you point them out, your children may never see the stars or revel in a rainbow or sunset. They may fear rather than marvel at the thunder and lightning of a summer storm and may never watch a plant grow, blossom, and bear fruit.

It's up to you, Mom, to teach your children about baby kittens or pup-pies and how they grow to mate and give birth to their own babies.

Help them discover the amazing order and meaning of nature. By showing your children the exact position of the Big Dipper and North Star, you can reveal the genius of the Creator. As they can comprehend, you can discuss the increasing complexity of the animal world, from simple insects to the habits of fish, birds, and raccoons.

One day, I discovered a baby blue jay dead in my backyard, prey to a neighborhood cat. Soon an adult jay also discovered the tragedy. I was surprised to hear, in a short time, a loud cacophony of blue jay grief as the word spread that junior had died. If you observe and listen, you will discover much to share with your children that will encourage them to have sympathy for hurt animals and to recognize the many facets of life we humans share with all of God's creatures.

Instill a sense of awe and wonder in your children. You can accomplish this best by modeling these qualities yourself. When he was only four, I spent an evening with my grandson. He lived on the edge of a large pasture and small woods. We played and walked through the tall grass and bike trails until it grew dark. Then we sat and just listened to the night sounds. There was the mystical hoot of an owl in the woods after the mournful turtledoves went to bed. The raspy chirp of crickets and the hoarse croak of a bullfrog in the tiny pond all blended in a wondrous symphony of nature. A small wild animal rustled through the weeds. My voice became a whisper as I described to Andy the beauty we were sharing. I will never forget his reflecting my awe as he crept from his seat beside me into my lap. As I cuddled him, we both reveled in the wonder of God's world. Even though you live in the heart of a large city, you can find and make opportunities to help your children experience nature.

Develop in your children a sense of curiosity. Most four-year-olds are naturally curious. They exhaust you with their questions of why, how, and what if. Take time to discuss their interests; you needn't have four thousand scientific answers. You mostly need to reflect those questions back to the child: "Jimmy, what do you imagine happens to pets that die?"

"How far away do you think the moon is?" "How do you think the moon keeps following us as we drive along?"

Go to the library or a bookstore to obtain resources for answering many questions, and show your children how to use the dictionary and an encyclopedia as early as possible. But concentrate on getting them to question, wonder why, and seek out information. Respect their questions and strange-sounding ideas. If you don't agree with the suggestions, offer your ideas, but give them the right to explore and express their own.

At five, Kelley may believe the sky is green. You might say, "Most people use the word *blue* to describe the sky. Let's see whether your green crayon or your blue one matches the sky." Help your child draw a picture with green grass, a blue sky, and a yellow sun. But avoid trying to prove you are right and he is wrong. Such power struggles squelch communication and curiosity.

Instill a sense of awe and wonder in your children. Develop their curiosity.

However, moral issues and values must be handled differently. When those issues are at stake, you must explain right from wrong and put the proper consequences into effect.

Share your discoveries with your children. To do that, you must develop an exploring, inquisitive nature. And it necessitates finding an opportunity to talk with each other. Keep your senses alert. Describe a sunrise you saw, or better yet, have your children get up and see one with you. If you're like me, a sunset is easier, but if you are excited by the blaze of color, your children are more than likely to catch that spirit. Have some watercolors and paper handy. Sit on the grass and paint the sunset with your children. Who cares if it is a work of art for framing? You are capturing the joy and wonder of creation! Perhaps you have seen an act of dishonesty or rudeness. Explain why the conduct is reprehensible. If someone cheated or insulted you or a member of your family, your indignation will be genuine. You can then teach a lesson in the art of considerate and honest living. Use daily events to give mini-lessons in living.

A vital area in the basic education of your children is helping them determine right from wrong. You can use some guidelines and pose some questions to help in this endeavor.

Mother, you are most likely to be the one who can protect your children from a loss of healthy moral values.

You may consider the Bible your ultimate authority for right and wrong, and I agree with you. Many current issues, however, are not specifically addressed in it. The fundamental guidelines are there; know them and practice them. Many people have a gift of common sense. That is the ability to apply good judgment, healthy self-control, and practical wisdom to everyday affairs.

Here are some questions that may help you evaluate whether something is right or wrong:

- *Will doing this act or refusing to do it harm me?* If so, it is wrong. You are a unique and worthwhile person, so you don't have the right to hurt your health, physically, mentally, or spiritually. Abusing alcohol, drugs, or tobacco is an example of a harmful practice that endangers your health and values.

- *Will this decision limit my growth or effectiveness?* If so, it is wrong. Whenever you choose the easy way in life over a more challenging, disciplined habit, you weaken your character. Avoiding college or some additional skill training when such opportunities are available to you will seriously limit your professional or job potential. Taking the easy course in life to avoid hard work and self-denial may be very wrong.

- *Will my decision or action hurt or limit someone else?* Ours is an extremely competitive world, and many individuals drive themselves to win, no matter how they damage other people. This attitude is extremely wrong. No one has a right to damage or hurt another person.

Teach your children to be team members, furthering the good of others as they strive for excellence. By practicing this philosophy, you will provide the best teaching model.

- *If everyone in the world practiced the lifestyle I'm considering, would it be a better place?* If not, why would you plan to do such actions or evidence such attitudes?

SHARING AND BONDING

We have discussed the need for infants to connect with mothers through that somewhat mystical bonding process. Although the early hours and days of life are essential in initiating that process, bonding is lifelong and requires constant encouragement.

A vital area in your children's education is helping them learn right from wrong—and what makes it right.

My mother was a master at organizing teamwork. Seasonal housecleaning was a family affair. My brothers carried the mattresses and carpets into the yard and beat out the dust that had collected. Mother and my older sister washed and ironed the curtains and linens while my younger sisters and I scrubbed the floors and windows and polished the furniture. My father was there, too, painting or wallpapering where those repairs were needed. As we worked, we joked, and laughter was often the melody of the day. Whether we cleaned house, planted gardens, tended the animals, or did the weekly laundry, it was a family activity.

During the long winter evenings, we often played together with similar enthusiasm. We had our own version of "Authors" that used the names of all the books in the Bible. As we slyly traded First Chronicles for Judges, we learned to remember who had which card as well as how to pronounce and spell those difficult scriptural names. There were, of course, plenty of titles for all of us to use.

Nearly always on the game nights there was a dishpan full of fluffy popcorn in the center of the table. We had all shared in planting it, harvesting it on cool autumn evenings, shelling it, and fanning away the chaff. We could relish every kernel, knowing the teamwork that had been necessary to produce it.

Your family can also work and play together without any significant cost. A young mom once complained to me that her family couldn't really have fun because everything cost so much. I enjoyed suggesting that her family plant some seeds in planters, watch them sprout, and then transplant them in a corner of the backyard in the springtime.

Even if you live in an apartment, I'll bet you can find a spot somewhere that would be beautified by flowers or a few tomato plants. A large clay pot in a sunny area of the house will produce some plants. Be creative. Both work and play can become fun to share and will result in knitting together a loving family.

Sharing and bonding include emotional issues as well as the physical aspects of work and play. There are few days, indeed, when a family member has no joys or sorrows that need to be communicated. In high school, Wendy tried out for the school play. Despite heroic efforts, she was given only a minor role, and she was dramatically devastated. Her parents and brother heard her wails of disappointment and then entered into enjoying the bit part she did have. Her mother made her the best costume on stage. The night of the final dress rehearsal came, and Wendy's brother crowned the event. When she climbed the stairs to her bedroom, with mixed emotions of elation and sadness, she found the entire hallway covered with his homemade banner that proclaimed, "Wendy, You Are Our Star!" On her table was a small bouquet celebrating her success.

Whatever the emotion, pain, sorrow, joy, excitement, frustration, or fear, it is enhanced or relieved by the caring hearts of family members. Mother, you must set the stage, teach the concepts, and encourage the intimacy of hearts and lives bonded in love.

RELEASING

World War II was under way when I was in high school. Most items were rationed, even in this country, because of the immense consumption of products by the world's armies. We couldn't buy the tires or gasoline that would allow the fifteen-mile daily drive to and from school. Quitting school, of course, was unthinkable. There was only one answer. My sister and I would have to stay in an apartment in town.

When I was only fourteen and my sister was seventeen, we literally left home to live on our own. We had a small but comfortable apartment upstairs in the home of some acquaintances of our parents. The temptations and opportunities to do foolish or risky things were rampant. But my mother had the courage to release us. I know her prayers guarded us daily and tucked us in at night.

One day a neighbor reported having seen a man standing on the fire escape, trying to open a bedroom window. But we were never harmed because Mother had released us directly to the One who held us, safely sheltered, in the palm of His mighty hand! I'm not at all sure, looking back, how Mother was able to release us at such an early age to such a degree of independence.

One Saturday morning, when my older daughter was a senior in high school, I was changing the bed linens. Without conscious effort to think about the future, this knowledge invaded my mind, *At this time next fall, Kathy will be away at college!* The certainty of the loss of my child hammered at my heart, and I buried my face in her pillow and wept. Not for the world would I have held her back from completing the education she needed. I just hated losing her as my little girl. And lose her I did. She went away to college, returning only during vacation times. And then she married, so she really left home.

When the bonds are tightly knit, cutting them hurts a lot. But like the proverbial handful of sand, you get to keep a lot more when you don't squeeze too tightly.

The way to successfully release your children is to do so in tiny increments. Fortunately, most children help us do that by being difficult and unpleasant at times. Let me explain.

Carol was overjoyed at the birth of her first baby, Ryan. As she nursed him, she observed in awe the perfection of his cuddly little body. When he slept, she often held him in her lap, soaking up the features of his tiny face, his little fingers, and his auburn hair.

By the time Ryan was nine months old, however, he had become restless and a bit irritable. It was apparent he wanted freedom. Carol was ready to encourage his freedom because she was weary of his weight and frustrated by his grouchiness. Soon Ryan was safely roaming his child-proofed house, quite content with his adventures, and Carol could sometimes complete a load of laundry without his interruptions. Ryan got some independence, and Mom got back a little freedom. Yes, there were some pangs of awareness that Ryan was growing up, but the eventual time of leaving was remote, so Carol could postpone thinking of that time.

> *The way to successfully release your children is to do so a little at a time.*

The process of releasing continues relentlessly. Off to Mother's Day Out, preschool, or day care they go. Then the real world of public school opens its doors. At only ten or eleven they are in middle school with its grown-up scheduling; and all too soon, it's high school with more opportunities and responsibilities than you can measure.

At each stage of development, you must remember five things:

1. You've done the best job of parenting you possibly could. Now trust your good work.

2. Your child is capable of more than you probably know. Trust your child to do right. Children tend to do what we adults expect them to do.

3. Keep a watchful eye open to verify that your child is staying out of trouble. Even the strongest young person may yield to temptation at times, so catch him or her promptly and short-circuit mischief before it becomes a habit.

4. Work methodically to replace your parenting role with an intimate friendship.

5. Remember the powerful function of prayer. God loves our children far more than we ever could. I don't know how it works, but I know prayer and faith in God will protect, guide, and empower our children when we no longer can do so.

Practice letting go of your children a tiny bit at a time, and by the time they are really ready to leave home, you'll be ready, too.

STABILIZING

Going to medical school, starting a marriage and a medical practice, and having three children added up to a complicated life for me. Many weeks I was exhausted, and it wasn't easy to cope with the demands of my pediatric patients and their parents as well as my own family.

My old farm home was my stabilizer during those stressful times. Whenever we could get away for a brief weekend, we would travel there. I always knew three things would happen as we drove up to the house. Mother would be watching from the kitchen window and would greet us with her smile and waving hand; Dad would walk from the barn or back porch to see if we had any trouble on the trip; and Collie, our special pet, would bark circles around the car as we unloaded our bags and children.

When we would leave, our car would be overloaded with fresh vegetables from the garden or beef from the freezer. But above all, we took home with us the certainty of changeless people and their values in our changing world.

My mother died in 1956. Several years ago, I drove by the farm. The house, barn, and most of the other buildings were gone. A new and elegant brick house stands where our white frame house should have been. I pulled into the churchyard nearby and visited my parents' graves in the little cemetery. I sat and cried for a while. It was a sad moment. But my grief was comforted by those indelible memories.

The simplicity, generosity, honesty, and unconditional love were still there, deeply rooted in the very fiber of my being. And they will never change.

See to it that you live in such a way as to build an anchoring spot for your family. They need, as I did and you do, a haven from the heartless world. You can create a safe place for returning when they need you.

Techniques

CHAPTER SEVEN

Establishing Your Child's Temperament

I have had the privilege of discussing children and their needs with the best researchers of our day. Dr. Burton White from Harvard, Dr. Ed Zieglar of Yale, and Dr. Foster Cline from Idaho are a few of them. They are men of brilliance and evident integrity. Each one has reiterated the significance of the early months of life.

By eighteen months, rudiments of a personality are set, and by three years, the child is basically the sort of person she or he will be. That is not to say that habits and ideas cannot change. But the child's temperament is established by then. Let's consider some categories so that you can get your child off to a good start.

CULTURAL HERITAGE

America's melting-pot heritage offers a rich set of resources for understanding and respecting much of the world. When it comes to any individual family, however, the varying expectations of different national backgrounds can be most confusing.

Pete believed that his son, Larry, should behave in very prescribed ways. He needed to keep his room neat, tools he used were to be cleaned and put away, homework was to be done between 7:00 and 8:30 each evening, and it had better be correct. Larry was expected to say, "No, sir," or "Yes, ma'am," and use every known phrase of courtesy. Pete was almost like a naval officer barking out orders as he tried to get Larry "shaped up." These ideas and practices might have worked, but they didn't!

Larry's mother, Carmen, believed that childhood was a time for fun, games, and plenty of hugs and kisses. She chided Pete for expecting too much and being too harsh. Larry learned to run to Mother for protection and comfort, gradually seeing Dad as "mean."

Actually, these parents could have provided a perfect balance in teaching Larry responsibility and fun. But sadly enough, they set up a competition instead. Pete's deeply ingrained Nordic heritage told him exactly how his son ought to be. Carmen's southern European background was rich in laughter and outspoken emotions of all kinds. The cultural differences became a battleground rather than a broadening experience. And Larry paid the price.

What is your national and cultural heritage? Rich or poor, lenient or strict, happy-go-lucky or enterprising, how can you find the healthiest balance for your child? Observe other families and learn to respect the differences between you and your spouse. Chances are, like Pete and Carmen, you were attracted to each other because of your differences. If you will sift out the good qualities each of you is seeking to give your child, they will be a fine mix. Your emotionality can be balanced by his intellectuality to give your child control but warmth. Just as your child is made physically healthy by a combination of your genes and chromosomes, so she will be strong in other ways by your mutual respect for each other's cultural background and collaboration in teaching the best of both worlds.

Whether your differences are ethnic, economic, or educational, don't allow them to create problems. One of your vital roles as a mother is to help your children respect their heritages and incorporate them into their lives.

WAYS TO TEACH YOUR CHILDREN ABOUT THEIR HERITAGES

1. *Respect your own and your husband's background values.* You may need to read about the history and cultural contributions of your country of origin.

2. *Teach your children about their grandparents and great-grandparents.* Tell them all the anecdotes you can collect—funny, serious, sad, and even bad stories will help them know themselves and their personal history. As a fringe benefit, you may stimulate curiosity in them that will motivate them to study more as they grow older.

3. *Cook some of the special foods your ancestors relished.* Whether they are Italian, Scandinavian, German, French, African-American, Native American, Oriental, or Spanish, you can learn to prepare some dishes your great-grandmother served. However, you may want to present these foods as a curiosity because your family may not enjoy them.

4. *Search for old family treasures.* When my family's farm home was being dismantled, I grabbed every item I could that no one else wanted. A wooden kitchen cupboard, a pie safe, and a rotting wagon seat, all repaired and restored, now grace my memory room. There, too, are the iron skates, the rusting orange lunch pail, and utensils so old we have difficulty identifying them. You may not be so fortunate as to acquire the actual pieces your ancestors used, but you may find similar items in secondhand stores, rural farm auctions, or antique shops. Family photographs will remind you of things you had forgotten. With a lot of time and some ingenuity you can piece a quilt or carve a bench that will somewhat resemble your grandmother's.

5. *On special holidays, bring together as many family traditions as possible.* These occasions enable you to focus your teaching in ways that are fun without the risk of becoming tedious.

Physical Actions

I remember my grandmother stimulating my sense of closeness in physical ways. She could blow in my ear or down my neck in a delightfully tickling way that still gives me goose bumps. And she always knew when to stop so I didn't become frustrated. I can barely recall Mother holding me, but she touched me as I sat by her chair on my little wooden bench.

We have already discussed the importance of stimulating all of the body's neurological senses—sight, hearing, smell, taste, touch, and motion (proprioceptive). The latter helps us learn our position in relationship with the rest of the world.

Most tiny babies like to be wrapped snugly and held close to your body. I recommend a gradual loosening process, especially if you have a high-strung, sensitive child. By that I mean that you take the baby's hands and arms out of the blanket. Stretch the tiny fingers and then let them grasp your fingers.

Move the arms slowly up and out, stretching them gently. Later, unwrap the feet and legs, scratch the soles of the baby's feet and pull the legs out straight, then double them back. Do these motions gently and only a few times each day. After these exercises, wrap up the baby and hold her close as you rock her.

As your baby grows, you will want to move him about more and more. Put him on a blanket on the floor and have fun moving arms, legs, head, and the entire body. Avoid being mechanical. Talk, smile, and just enjoy the process. At frequent intervals, pick up your baby and hug her tightly but not too tightly. With a four-week-old, you may have two or three exercise times, one in the morning, one following the afternoon nap, and one during the evening bath.

Plenty of kisses and gentle blowing on the baby's tummy, neck, feet, and toes usually bring on smiles and gurgles of delight. These early expressions of affection imprint deeply your wee one's awareness of tenderness, fun, and healthy intimacy.

I feel I need to warn you against undue focusing on a baby's genitals. It is unfair and unwise to stimulate the clitoris or penis.

On the other hand, simply changing his diaper may create an erection for a baby boy. He will touch his penis and find that touch feels good just as some babies discover that it feels good to suck their thumbs. Don't be horrified, and above all, don't punish the baby. Ignore it, and as soon as his diaper is back on, he'll be interested in something else.

The only cases I have known in which masturbation becomes a problem are these: when the child does not have enough interaction with other people and stimulation from activities; the child has been precociously sexually stimulated by others; and/or the child has been severely punished for playing with the genitals.

So play with your children; tickle, hug, gently wrestle, cuddle, and kiss them. Teach them to taste, touch, hear, and smell every appropriate item in their world. The physical area of mothering is enriching and fun for both you and them.

SOCIAL SKILLS

Jerry's smile was contagious, his sensitivity to another's tears was touching, but his explosive anger was frightening. Jerry was large for his nine years, and when he kicked or hit a classmate or teacher, it was likely he could inflict serious damage. Jerry had not learned to take turns or to accept correction. When another student asked him to do anything different from what he wanted, Jerry would lash out at that person. Needless to say, Jerry's social skills were sadly lacking.

Whether the problem is physical aggression, excessive shyness, or controlling bossiness, children instinctively avoid a playmate who makes them feel uncomfortable. Some parents I've known tend to view social problems as being caused by rudeness from others, always taking their child's side. Such overprotectiveness prevents the child's learning to overcome poor social skills.

Other parents want their child to be so well-liked, they consistently teach that child to adapt to everyone, becoming a "people-pleaser." Without intending to, these critical parents find fault with their child, damaging the self-respect essential to a healthy personality.

Again, let me remind you of the balances crucial to successful adjustments in life. Observe your child at play. Try to look at him as you would a stranger. Is he too controlling? Is he too withdrawn or shy? Does he always let others have their way? Or can he be assertive at times but able to give in fairly for both sides? Once you have a fairly balanced perspective, talk privately with your child.

Let her know the actions of which you are really proud, and tell her where she needs to develop a new habit. Make clear the basic facts that friends are not for hurting or bossing, but they should not treat her with disrespect, either.

Children tend to live up to expectations—so expect mainly the best.

Teach her how to handle disagreements and to stand up for herself in a firm but polite way. You may need to practice several different approaches to find a suitable one.

Whenever possible, be near your children and their playmates so you can tell how well they are solving problems and when they may need adult intervention.

HOW TO TEACH CHILDREN APPROPRIATE SOCIAL SKILLS

1. Be clear about your observations and interpretations of each child's skills and weaknesses in relating with friends.

2. Be equally clear about the specific changes that must be made.

3. Be positive regarding corrective measures and kind, not condemning, about the mistakes.

4. Never embarrass your child by correcting him in front of friends. Graciously excuse your child and go somewhere you can speak frankly and privately.

5. Always commend your child's efforts to improve, and remind her when she backslides.

6. Follow through with your responsibilities to help completely break the old, negative habits and form new ones.

Social skills vary immensely with the ages of children. Up to eight or nine months, a baby smiles at everyone and wiggles with delight when someone talks with him or touches him. Parents usually are proud of their tiny tot's social skills.

Many parents, however, are unprepared for the abrupt change at nine to ten months of age. Almost overnight, the delighted baby becomes shy and fearful of strangers. Instead of smiling and reaching out, she hides her head in mother's neck and may even cry or hit at the approaching stranger. Your baby has not suddenly become a recluse. She has simply reached the point of realizing that others are not you or Daddy. Children early on recognize features, but they all look a lot alike. By about ten months, they clearly know who is Mom and who isn't. And they're not so sure about someone who isn't Mom or Dad. Given time, encouragement, and understanding, your child will become friendly again.

This shyness and reserve will continue off and on until about age three. The best advice you can offer relatives and friends is this: allow the child to approach you, and then respond very gently and gradually. A little smile or motion of your hands is as much outreach as a toddler will usually tolerate. If you patiently await his curiosity to make him look at you and then come nearer, you may be rewarded with his trust and eventual friendship. By the way, that's not a bad philosophy to practice with lots of people.

By age two, and even before, some children become downright aggressive. They are grabby, selfish, stubborn, and generally obnoxious unless you understand them. They are trying their wings, so to speak. They need to learn what they can get into and what is off-limits; how far they can climb and how it feels to tumble down; what they will eat and what they won't; what they can say and what you won't allow. They are so busy discovering their capabilities and their limits that they truly cannot socialize. So don't expect your two-year-old to play amiably with others. You will need to protect his environment from him as well as to protect him from the risks he cannot comprehend.

Your three-year-old will more readily get along with playmates. Try to locate friends who are about the same age or a little older, so they won't overwhelm your child. Play with them at first, and guide both your child and the friends in sharing, taking turns, communicating, and being generally kind human beings. Once such positive habits are formed, you can go about your activities for periods of time. It pays, however, to check up on youngsters at regular intervals to be certain they practice what you have taught them. All of us need refresher courses at times.

EMOTIONAL CONCERNS

Most of the adults I know have two mistaken concepts about feelings.

First, they believe that certain emotions are absolutely unacceptable. Most commonly, they believe that fears are weak and cowardly and that anger is a sin.

Second, many people mistake ideas for feelings. In a counseling session, a husband said to his wife, "Even the children can't stand your housekeeping!" When I asked how she felt in response to his hurtful attack, she replied, "I feel like he's just trying to blame me so he won't have to change." Although her reply was not altogether mistaken, she had adroitly sidestepped the issue of her feelings of hurt, guilt, and anger.

The basic emotions we all experience are fear, anger (aggression), and love. Each has many variations, and each variation becomes mixed at some point with one or more other emotions. Fear, for example, may be caution, panic, anxiety, or just plain fright. Anger may be indignation, irritation, frustration, rage, or fury. Love may be companionship, friendship, romance, protection, or passion.

When you love someone very tenderly and that person mistreats you or takes some risky action, you can see how love causes pain, anger, fear, or worry. Emotions, thus, are extremely complex. Above all, you need to recognize they are God-created and serve useful functions; it is the way people express their feelings that is good or bad.

Fear, for example, can be lifesaving. It can prompt a person to take proper precautions and avoid needless risks. These are protective measures, not cowardice. On the other hand, someone may allow fear to become panic, and that intense feeling often "freezes" the individual, preventing appropriate action.

Most people cope poorly with anger. They dread the anger of others, and they explode or try to hide their own anger. Anger is a powerful energizer that stimulates the body to either run or fight. That energy needs to be recognized, focused, and directed to make right the situation that produced the anger.

In our often undisciplined culture, many children are allowed to take out their anger on others in painfully destructive ways. Children who are afraid may give in to their fear, never learning to face challenging situations. They may, on the other extreme, deny their fears, becoming daredevils who take foolish, dangerous risks. Some children we call accident-prone fail to practice healthy caution.

Helping Children Understand and Express Emotions

Teaching children to understand and express their emotions in a constructive and healthy way is not difficult. It does mean that you first discover and master these basic principles:

- Accept the fact that all emotions are acceptable and God-given and serve a useful purpose.
- Identify emotions accurately. It's not enough to say or think, *I'm mad!* Are you irritated, indignant, enraged, or furious? The secret is getting your mind back in control of the emotion. Even thinking of the most descriptive term for an emotion starts to put you in charge.
- If your child is experiencing the feeling, use this opportunity to teach her the vocabulary of emotions. By reading her facial expression, you can quite accurately see what your child is experiencing.

  To a young child, say, "Cindy, your face looks worried, and I think there are tears in your eyes. Are you afraid?" An older child may respond to the sincere invitation, "Honey, it's okay to tell me what you feel now. Maybe we can solve your problems together."
- Move as soon as you can from the feeling to whatever is causing it. This step helps to put your mind in control. And this will be more evident as you teach your children to think about problems as clearly as they identify emotions.
- Formulate a plan to resolve the situation that prompted the feeling. Young children may need to be given some options from which to choose. With assistance children who are four or older can usually formulate a plan of their own. The more initiative children take in problem solving, the better. Teaching them this process guides them in smart decisions and good judgment and promotes healthy independence and self-confidence.

There are times when children, and adults as well, prefer to scream, hit, or throw things instead of practicing these steps toward self-control. Don't overreact or lay on a guilt trip when that happens. With a small child, I recommend that you pick her up, kindly but firmly, and hold her until she gets back in control. I suggest you sit in a rocking chair, your arms around your child's arms and chest, your legs wrapped around her legs. Allow a little wriggling but no hurting, and rock gently, not saying a word until control is reestablished.

I have used this method successfully for many years, and so have a great many parents to whom I have recommended it. Adults who have experienced such strong, loving controls when they were young tell me they felt comforted and secure. It won't work if you are too angry or if you give in before control is established. I have even seen this "magic" work on older youngsters, but it takes more than one person to provide the strength to win the struggle.

Once you conquer the emotional battles, you'll be ready to revel in honest, open, trusting expression of the wealth of feelings of which we all are capable. You can't truly value peace unless you've been through a storm.

And real joy finds its greatest meaning in the midst of trouble. A great psalm says, "Weeping may endure for a night, but joy comes in the morning" (Psalm 30:5). Enjoy your legacy of feelings and teach your children, also.

INTELLECTUAL FACTORS

Preschools are abundant in which toddlers are supposedly being stimulated mentally. It's true that three-year-olds can learn to read. But unless they are exceptionally gifted, those who learned to read at age three are no better readers by the third grade than those who began to read in the first grade.

More and more, consensus is being reached on this point. Do not practice, and do not allow, any major emphasis on academics until kindergarten. And I really believe that academics in any degree should wait for the first grade. These early, impressionable years are urgently needed for other functions. Let's think about some constructive activities.

Birth to one year. Babies need lots of loving, cuddling, tickling, playing, and laughing. My grandson loved to knock down the block towers I built. I would sing, "London Bridge is falling down" as he did so. Then as I rebuilt, I sang, "Build it up with iron and stones." We laughed and I picked him up and squeezed him tightly. Usually, he would pamper me by holding very still so I could squeeze him several times. (A squeeze is a short, tight hug!) Bryan could add a block to my stack and even do a couple on his own. For that I would clap and say, "Hooray for Bryan." I think that's the first stage of building as well as tearing down, and both are normal and okay.

At about a year, children love to touch leaves and flowers, smell them, roll in the grass and autumn leaves, slide down a small slippery slide, and ride slowly on a merry-go-round, especially if you hold them.

They also love to put items into and take them out of containers. Toys, vegetables, and any safe items they can handle will keep them busy for some moments. It's good to catch them on the "in" cycle, praise them for picking things up, and whisk them off to another activity.

One-year-olds have enough fun with a wooden spoon and an old pan or lid that you can almost prepare a quick meal while they play. Bright plastic cups or measuring spoons make great toys reserved for the kitchen and meal preparation or cleanups. You can sing to the rhythm of the lid drum and use your child's name in the songs.

I often ironed several items while my grandson put toys into the empty dryer. But believe me, I watched him closely and made certain that every item was out of the dryer and Bryan couldn't open the dryer unless I was there. Balance the adventures of exploratory play with close supervision and protection.

One to two years. At about a year, or even younger for many tots, children are ready for books. If you value books and reading, you may try to get your toddler to listen as you read. With rare exceptions, there's no better way to defeat yourself. At one to two years, tots love pages with one or two basic pictures. I like alphabet books with *A* for apple, *B* for ball, *C* for cat, and so on to *Z* for zoo. Many of the children's books I see are overloaded with too many characters or even frightening animals. Bryan loves to hear that ducks go "quack, quack," lambs go "baa," and calves go "moo." Keep pictures, words, and sounds simple and single.

By a year, most children have a receptive vocabulary—they understand very well when you say "cookie" or "bye-bye." They usually can say several words, but only their mothers understand them. Begin saying the names of objects you hand a child: "This is your spoon." "Here is your cup." "Would you like an apple?" Repeat the name of the object once or twice, but don't get pushy. Some mothers can hardly wait for children to talk, and ironically, they resist when efforts are too persistent or intense. Just invite talk by teaching sounds through repetition.

If you can't find the sort of book you want, make one. Plain paper and crayons, felt-tip pens, or pictures cut out of a magazine make wonderful ABC picture books. My daughter and I did a number book using as many different textures of materials as we could find. Velvet, corduroy, sandpaper, muslin, and a favorite wallpaper sample formed the basic numbers from one to ten. Remember your creativity? Put it to work! Continue all the play activities of the last section, but add more.

Playing in sand is great, though at this age they mainly scoop it into and dump it out of a pail. They can use slides, swings, and merry-go-rounds more independently but still need close observation. In play activities, teach the words for swing, slide, twirl, climb, and run. Again, say the words casually. Don't try to make your child repeat them. She will talk when she is ready.

When you look at books with several objects on a page, take your child's little finger in your hand. Point to each of the puppies or balloons and count, "One, two, three." I learned that Bryan (at fifteen months) lost interest after three or four. Observe your child. He has no way to tell you in words, but if you are sensitive, you will clearly hear him plead, "Mommy, don't go too fast! I'm so little, and I can only do as much as I can!" Later, you can nudge and urge but not yet. Just explore, observe, and enjoy learning together.

By age two, and often by eighteen months, children can talk quite well. If adults have not talked baby talk to them, their words will be quite intelligible. True, they major on "No!" and "I won't," but usually they are experimenting with the language they've been hearing.

Read short stories to your child, only a few words to a page full of pictures. You can teach him to build simple bridges or houses with blocks; children can identify two items or activities in sequence. "Get your ball and bring it here so we can play!" is likely to result in cooperation.

By age two (and, again, younger), your child will benefit from *Sesame Street* and perhaps a few other TV programs. Many local TV stations have some kids' programs and cartoons that encourage positive social skills. Many widely syndicated cartoons, however, are quite violent and otherwise antisocial. Parents must be vigilant and screen out all TV shows that do not promote the best interests of children!

When my older grandson was only two, he and I were making cookies. I would pour in ingredients as he stirred or vice versa. We were having a really fun time.

Andy looked up at me with his sparkling brown eyes and said, "Gwandma, dis is coopewation!" Matter-of-factly, he added, "From *Sesame Street!*" At two, children are much more cooperative when they are encouraged and invited into learning experiences: taking long walks, playing at a park or any safe outdoor area, or drawing with big crayons curled up on an old blanket under a tree. You can teach your child to draw a flower, a bird, or the sky by having her work among the models nature provides.

As you walk, look for tiny items that will interest your child. Stop for a minute to touch the soft moss growing in the shade, watch an ant colony at work, and try to catch a butterfly. Pick up a rough, symmetrical pinecone or examine a sparkling rock. As you touch and stretch your bodies, stretch your mind, also. Describe the blue sky, the flashing bird, and the darting squirrels. Listen to the sounds; follow the tracks. And on the way home, go to the library and find some books about the things you saw. Ask questions you can't answer; it will humble you and arouse the curiosity of your child.

The awakened interest and curiosity of a child motivate the desire to learn. And teaching that books and other people can help us discover more and more offers the resources we all need to grow intellectually.

Learning, early in life, takes place through the senses and emotions, so become excited and delighted about your child and all of your shared experiences. The love of learning and these feelings are contagious. Catch them and pass them on.

Three and four years. Children at these ages are naturally eager to learn. They create and imagine wonderful things, and you can feed their intellects by encouraging them. My children and I had elegant tea parties. A cardboard box with a tea towel for a tablecloth was our luncheon table. We had tiny pieces of cookies served on doll dishes. The children dressed up in old clothes, and we spoke with the exaggerated politeness children are so good at.

> *There will be days when you feel like screaming because of the endless chains of How? Why? and Why not? Let other duties and demands wait while you focus on your child's intellectual explosion.*

You can combine teaching social skills with having fun and being creative while you show your preschoolers how to talk about ideas. Bring up a topic all children would be interested in, such as new equipment for the local playground or a trip to the library. On little issues, help them learn to think and express their ideas. Listen to them with respect and guide them to think clearly and accurately. You are helping them learn wisdom.

There will be days when you feel like screaming because of the endless chains of How? Why? and Why not? Keep your priorities straight. Let other duties and demands wait while you focus on your child's intellectual explosion; it lasts only a few months. Fostering curiosity, searching for some answers, and even more important, helping your child accept the fact that we can't always find answers at a specific time will have a major impact on your child's developing mind.

Listen well and reflect some questions back to your child. Ask him what he thinks is the answer. Offer ideas you have considered, and find books that discuss possible answers. Exact information is not the real issue. Cultivating thoughtfulness, showing respect, and working on open and honest communications with each other are the lasting values you can build.

Kindergarten and elementary-school age. I hope by now you understand that each age, its needs, and the answers build on the past. So don't stop the activities you have already shared; adapt them to the more mature child who is developing. Then add to them the new ideas, more advanced communications, and additional activities of working and playing together.

In elementary school, children build their academic foundations for life. Basic reading skills should be mastered by the end of third grade. Arithmetic facts should certainly be well-learned about the same time. The role of your child's teacher becomes more and more important. But do not believe for one moment that you can heave a sigh of relief and turn over to that teacher your child's intellectual development.

Your responsibility is even more far-reaching during elementary-school years. You must fulfill certain roles and address certain issues if your child is to reach maximum potential.

SHOW THAT YOU VALUE LEARNING

My parents' value of learning steered my academic course. In addition, even while I was in college and medical school, my mother prayed for me. I know her prayers channeled God's power and wisdom to me repeatedly as well as giving me the tenacity to simply hang in there when the going was tough.

Your example in mastering academic knowledge will say more to your child than a thousand lectures. Read thoughtful books and articles, and discuss them briefly during dinner or whenever you can get the children to sit still long enough to communicate. If you know only about the latest episode of soap operas or *The Simpsons,* your children are likely to question whether it's worthwhile to study algebra.

TEAM UP WITH YOUR CHILD'S TEACHERS

Having worked for some twenty years as a school consultant, I know the destructiveness of the adversarial attitudes that can develop between mothers and teachers. Both of you want your child to behave properly and learn successfully. But each of you often blames the other for failures. Don't do that! Visit with your child's teacher enough that you get to really know each other.

Share with him or her your concerns, your child's interests, and some of your dreams. Ask the teacher's help in areas where you have some difficulty, and share what works for you in achieving cooperation and motivation.

Discover how your child's teacher conducts class. Almost all children complain about their teachers at times. If you are to avoid taking sides against the teacher unfairly, you need to know the truth. Always support the teacher, but also interpret unpleasant behaviors or practices to your child.

If the teacher is grouchy, for example, help your child understand that she may be overburdened by problems. Teach your child to try to help her by studying hard and acting in a kind and positive manner. Knowing she can be helpful to someone as powerful as her teacher can build in any child a sense of healthy importance.

Certainly, there are times when a teacher will be unfair to your child. That is no excuse to pity your child and attack the teacher or the school. I have seen many parents do those very things, and the result is the child's growing sense of unhealthy power. Children quickly learn they can get by with almost anything by making the teacher look bad. Instead of taking sides, visit the teacher with a friendly and open attitude, and discuss the problem. Hear all sides of the issue with equal objectivity, and then seek the course of action that will work. Include your child in this process so he will see where he may have been at fault. Help your child correct that fault as best you can.

ESTABLISH A GOOD STUDY CLIMATE

I believe in structuring a daily study time for children as early as first grade. This time may be only fifteen or twenty minutes in first or second grade, but it needs to grow to two hours during high school.

Never ask your child if she has homework. Almost all youngsters will deny that they do so they can play or do something else. You know that children cannot possibly learn everything they need to know in class. It's up to you to establish what I call a climate for learning.

Decide with your child the best time and place for study hall. Make certain, however, that it's a time when you can be there to supervise. Usually children need to run and play for a while after a long day in school. By then it may be dinnertime. And all children must have some family duties to perform. Schedule your child's study time among these other priorities when it is good for everyone.

If you have several children, this time may include all of them. And I strongly urge you to have some academic pursuit of your own. It may be writing letters or reading a book or magazine, but doing some activity similar to your children's will enable them to see study as a normal pattern for life. They will be less likely to feel sorry for themselves because their friends don't have to study and most of them won't. But don't let that fact deter you from your plan.

Part of a good study climate is a lack of distractions. That means, no matter what your kids claim, the TV is off. No one can watch the exciting *Adventures of Adrian the Asiatic Monster* (or whatever your child's favorite show is) and concentrate on spelling or higher mathematics. Even radio music that is too loud may be distracting. Low-level sounds to muffle outside noises, proper lighting, and some private seating, along with your role modeling, can create the atmosphere you're looking for. Once established, maintain these conditions as rigidly as possible; even one or two evenings of giving in to no study time will multiply the difficulty in reorganizing it.

Admittedly, studying is less fun than riding bikes, playing ball, or watching TV. So you need to build in some system of rewards. Most important are your commendation and smiles of approval. But also I found my children loved an occasional, "Now that you've worked so hard for an hour, let's have a game of Monopoly and some popcorn." A small treat now and then is a tangible reward for doing a job they'd really rather avoid.

With children in early adolescence, you may encounter some teenage rebellion about study time. I won't forget the evening I was trying to be diplomatic with my oldest child. Recognizing that her favorite TV show was nearly over, I caught a few seconds during a commercial and gently reminded her, "Kathy, as soon as this program is over, it's study time."

She taught me a few things in her instant and perceptive retort! "Mother," she stated, "don't talk to me like I'm a child! I always study, and you couldn't make me, even if I didn't. Yeah, you can make me sit there in front of my books (at least she acceded a little power to me!), but you ought to know you can't make me learn that stuff!"

I hated to face the truth of her angry comments. In adolescence, learning becomes a personal matter. Indeed I could help her study, but I could no longer make her learn. Kathy and I negotiated that night and saved the day for both of us. I would no longer remind her of study time—at least not until her first report card. If her grades represented her usual capabilities, she would continue to monitor her own study time. If they dropped, we'd have to renegotiate.

She continued to want me to hear her vocabulary words, quiz her on history facts, and review her English papers. And I continued to show my pride in her scholarship and enjoy the development of her fine mind.

In so many ways, teens become adults. They need to be treated with adult respect and expected to perform responsibly on their own most of the time. True, they won't always behave maturely, and there will be times when you have to revert to treating them temporarily like the children they again become. But children tend to live up to expectations, so expect mainly the best! I trust that as your children grow intellectually, you will keep pace with them. No matter how wise and knowledgeable you are, the process of continued growth can be an infinitely exciting adventure.

SPIRITUAL DEVELOPMENT AND TRAINING

Techniques for spiritual aspects of mothering do not vary as much with the age of the child as with the spiritual health of the mother. Your beliefs about yourself, the world in which you function, and God influence what you impart to your children.

For most of us, the spiritual level of life deals with the awareness of a source of wisdom, energy for living, and love beyond our own. To Jewish believers, that Source is Jehovah or God; Christians look to the Trinity (one God: the Father, the Son, and the Holy Spirit). The Jewish Old Testament and the Christian Bible are historic sources of spiritual knowledge. If you are a member of any other religious group, you most likely own a textbook that outlines beliefs and practices you are to follow. To impart spiritual information to your children, you need to know what you believe and what you want your children to know.

In addition to knowing your religious reference book, you need to learn from other thinkers about your beliefs. And I urge you to study other belief systems as well. Eternal truth is not to be feared but to be learned. And I, for one, trust God's Spirit to teach you His truth and facilitate your teaching it to your children.

Another resource for your spiritual growth, as well as that of your children, is the universe. Whether you study the solar system and space or the electrons and protons in atoms, there are amazing perfection and pre-dictability about them. The same is true for all the orders of animals and plants. The wonder of nature is a never-failing source of spiritual insight and strength.

As I was writing this section, I was sitting in an airport in the East. Flights from all over the United States were delayed from one to several hours. My delay, risking a loss of my connecting flight home, was nearly three hours. The woman at the computer where I checked in was phe-nomenal. Disgruntled passengers cursed and stormed at her, displacing their wrath at the weather and God to the airlines in general and to her in particular. This amazing woman never retorted unkindly. She was remarkably thorough and efficient as she searched for alternate flights or substitute routes. When I complimented her on her gracious demeanor, our conversation revealed that she is a woman who prays. It became clear to me that God's love and grace are often apparent in such unsung followers as this won-derful woman.

> *Teaching your child about God is your most important task and privilege.*

Look for a little bit of God in the people you meet and in those you know so well you may overlook that Presence in them. Even when your children are not at their best, you can see the perfection of the Creator.

You may be the parent of a child who may not be so perfect. Perhaps your child was born with a handicapping condition or was marred by an accident. You must wonder at times where God was to allow such imper-fections with their limitations and frustrations. Frankly, I can't answer that query. But I have seen the miraculous courage, tenderness, and patience that families develop as they care for a child with problems. To me, such transcendence over limitations and losses is more convincing of the Power beyond one's own than initial perfection would be.

Finally, my inner sense of awe and reverence in response to the grandeur of nature or the smile and grace of troubled people convinces me of spiritual truth. That same capacity lies within everyone I know. Some folks are more aware of it and cultivate it better than others. I hope you maximize your spirituality. As you do, you cannot help communicating it to your children.

You will do this through the radiance of a sunset or rainbow reflected in your eyes; through the patience and gentleness as you quiet a tired child; through the clear, firm way you guide and teach your children to become decent people. So cultivate and benefit from your spiritual resources as you mother your children.

This book is intended for people of all religions. But I must write this section on teaching spiritual values from my perspective—that of a Christian woman. My mother could literally make the Bible come alive as she told its ages-old stories to me. She and my father taught me to respect our Jewish religious roots almost to the point of hero worship. So I cherish the stories of Adam and Eve, Abraham and Sarah, David and Saul; the wisdom of Solomon; the integrity and miraculous courage of Daniel; and the faith of Hannah as well as her ability to turn Samuel over to God's work as a child.

The heroes of the New Testament are no less loved. Luke the physician, Peter the tempestuous fisherman, and Paul the concise and convincing preacher all taught me about God and my faith.

How you teach your children about God and your faith determines much of their journey in faith. Here are some of the ways my mother taught me and a few I have discovered.

STORIES FROM GOD'S WORD

Rather than read the concise stories about heroes of faith, study them until you can translate them into language children can understand. Tell them, one by one, as soon as the child can sit still and understand. That is usually from three to seven or eight years old. During those years, the imagination is so active it can make your stories come alive in living color. What fun you can have painting word pictures of the arrogant giant, Goliath, as young David with only a slingshot came against him and killed him. You may need to create a slingshot to help your child understand what an effective weapon it was. (And then teach him not to hurt anything with it!)

PRAYER

I can never remember going to bed without kneeling and praying, "Now I lay me down to sleep. I pray Thee, Lord, my soul to keep. If I should die before I wake, I pray Thee, Lord, my soul to take." Over the years, that prayer became merely a ritual, and I found myself mixing it up with my multiplication tables or a poem I might memorize for school.

Nonetheless, a time came when I really wanted God to know I loved Him, and I wanted to know that I was His child. For many weeks I did everything I could think of to make myself good enough to be God's child. But I had no certainty, no awareness, that I was acceptable to Him. One evening, for the first time in my life, I added my own words to that familiar and comforting prayer. "Dear God," I prayed, "You must know that I've done everything I know to do to become Your child. I just want You to know that's all I want." I fell asleep peacefully, feeling and knowing nothing different from all the days and nights before. In the morning, however, I experienced a new phenomenon. Just as I awoke, a thought pierced my consciousness: You are a child of God! With that awareness, a very private sense of elation permeated my entire nine-year-old being. The whole of nature seemed more colorful and indescribably glorious than I had ever before seen it. The birds sang with ecstasy, and even the chickens and geese made joyful sounds.

At that time, I was a very private child, so I told no one of my unique and personal experience. Yet its glow has never left me. I know I am a child of God not because of my heroic efforts to be good but because He is my Father and He loves me completely—just as I was and am!

It seems possible that such an experience could come about only because my mother taught me about God and His love, about prayer and how it touches the heavenly Father, and about Christ and how much He loves me. You may believe your teaching won't penetrate your child's mind, much less her heart, but you can't always see the slow-growing seed sprout. It takes time, tending, and patience.

You may try to teach your children to pray in a conversational manner. Some children, however, seem unusually sensitive to the greatness of God, and they are unable to say their own prayers. If your children have that difficulty, help them memorize a simple prayer and let it become a ritual. Rituals have a marvelous way of turning thoughts and souls toward their focus. When Jesus Christ is that focus, His Spirit will make Him real to your children in due time.

NATURE

The apostle Paul wrote to the Christians in Rome, "For since the creation of the world His invisible attributes are clearly seen, being understood by the things that are made" (Romans 1:20). Many people see God most clearly, as Paul stated, through His creation.

Teaching your children to absorb the sounds, sights, scents, tastes, and touches of nature helps them recognize the God who made the senses and the rich array of stimuli that create such joyful sensations. Share your joy, and teach your children to cherish these sensations. There surely would be less desire for the earsplitting raucous noise of some of today's music if children appreciated the gentle sounds of rain falling, a rabbit rustling in the bushes, or a mockingbird singing in the stillness of the night.

Your children will become curious about the stars and planets. Find an easy-to-use guide on astronomy. Go outside some clear evening, and explore the various star patterns. Every time you see these formations they will be exactly the same, though their positions in the heavens will move a bit with the seasons. Tell your children the preciseness and order could occur only by the design of the Master Creator.

Still later, your children will learn about chemistry and physics or other sciences. The orbits of the electrons around the nucleus of an atom are no less exact than those of the planets about the sun. Discovering other evidence of such masterwork will unfold more information about this great Being we call God.

The beauty of leaves and flowers and the sameness of each species of bird or insect reveal the wonder of God. As you teach, I hope the certainty of God's power and perfection will grow in your heart as well.

OTHER PEOPLE

Talking with Sherman, I could hardly believe we were sitting in the visiting room at a state penitentiary. Sherman was an inmate there serving a fifteen-year minimum sentence for murder. He had grown up on the streets of a large city. He was the only son of loving parents who had taught him right from wrong but often failed to require the right. They rescued him from the consequences of the wrong so he grew up believing he could do just about anything he pleased.

Sherman became involved fairly early in his teens with drugs. They made him feel even better than his usual carefree lifestyle did. More and more, he lived for drugs. To support his habit, he began to write bad checks and, at last, to steal. During a robbery, an accident occurred in which a person was killed. Sherman was so high on drugs that he didn't actually know what happened, and it was all too easy for his "friends" to make him the scapegoat.

He displayed no anger and made no excuses as he related some of his life story to me. Instead, his dark eyes glowed warmly and brimmed with tears as he told me of his encounter with Jesus Christ. After the horrible wreck, he finally awoke in jail. Suffering drug withdrawal was painful, and realizing some of the tragic events of the previous night, he lay in agony on the hard bunk. There, however, in the cold, noisy, ugly cell he remembered the Savior. He had no other recourse, just as I, an innocent child, had no more good deeds to make myself worthy to be God's child. Sherman turned over his life to Christ and started down a new path from which he has not strayed.

I knew that day that before Christ we all are alike—Sherman, a prisoner; I, a physician; his inmate friends; and my professional friends all must reach the end of our resources if we are ever to reach out for His. This truth must be the core of spiritual health.

When I admitted that I needed a Father and Sherman knew he needed a Savior, we both found freedom and joy that are the symbols of intimacy, as best we humans can know it, with the God of the universe. The profoundness of that interaction—I in Christ and He in me—is beyond words. Jesus Christ said it best: "Whoever loses his life for My sake will find it" (Matthew 16:25).

You can see strong evidence of God in babies, in developing children, in mature adults, and perhaps best of all in the elderly. Those who have experienced His forgiveness, guidance, protection, and wisdom in their life's journey can witness most clearly to His presence.

However you experience God will influence how you teach. The techniques of teaching emanate from your inner beliefs. You actually teach by talking about those convictions, by indicating your certainty about biblical truth, by offering sincere prayers, and above all else, by living an honest life. If you join me in belief in Life after life, you will agree that teaching your children to know God is by far your most important task and privilege.

Challenges

CHAPTER EIGHT

Meeting Challenges

J was giving Lyndon his bottle and enjoying his tiny perfection, totally engrossed in mothering him. *What a miracle babies are!* I thought. But even as I was feeling the elation and realizing how blessed I was to have a son, I heard a little voice beside me.

Four-year-old Kathy was mourning her new position as big sister. "Mommy, you just aren't paying me any attention at all!" And for the moment, she was right. I had purchased a baby doll for her to mother as I mothered the new baby. She had her baby, its bottle, and wet diaper, and she was rocking right beside me in her small chair. But it wasn't enough! I will not forget my sadness at realizing there would always be times, from then on, that I simply could not meet the needs of all my children at the same time. But the good aspect of that dilemma was the necessity of the older children to learn to take turns and to wait a bit. And the love we shared grew as they developed.

This section of the book will deal with some challenges most mothers face. I'm sure I've left out something you wanted to hear about. But I hope you will find many answers that will help you be the mother you want to be.

Philosophically, the points you must remember are these:

1. *Believe in yourself.* You have this child, and you have within you, someplace, all the resources to raise her or him. If you remember that, you will not be as anxious during difficult times.

2. *Believe in your child.* The Creator has implanted in every life a will to survive. In some children and adults, that survival instinct is stronger than in others. But it is there, and you can count on it in most instances.

3. *Develop a positive attitude.* Babies are so sensitive that they soak up our attitudes more than most people believe. If you develop a confident, relaxed, and positive attitude, your baby will usually feel more relaxed and will be a happier child.

THE COLICKY CHILD

Having just given you such great assurance, I must immediately tell you there is an exception: the colicky baby. Colic is bound to be as old as the human race. Colic is often designated by its expected duration. There may be six-week colic or three- or six-month colic, or it may last longer. A friend told me one of her children slept only a few minutes at a time for over a year. I don't see how she maintained her sanity.

The symptoms of colic are well-known, and the most annoying is crying. Colicky babies cry hard and loudly! And they cry for extended times. Generally, babies with colic draw up their knees and then kick their feet; they clench their fists and wave their arms. You are certain to believe they are in agony and must need emergency medical care. That is not the case, and for most infants, there is no demonstrable cause for such crying. Breast- and bottle-fed babies suffer similarly. Changing mothers' diets and babies' formulas rarely helps except temporarily. Walking the floor, rocking, and crooning may relieve the crying for brief moments. So may helping the baby burp, expel gas, or have a bowel movement. But these methods do not significantly relieve the crying.

One is tempted to think colic is due to the vicious cycle of anxiety and tenseness shared between mother and child. And I'm sure that understandable tension is a factor. But many mothers awaken at that magical six-week or three- or six-month anniversary to realize the baby has slept gloriously for four hours, more or less. They can't think of anything in their household that has changed, but suddenly they can enjoy the baby who was a tyrant only a day or so before.

First, get your doctor to confirm there is nothing seriously wrong with your child. Then, the treatment begins with your awareness that you are not a bad mom and your child is not deliberately mean or bad. Pay plenty of attention to your baby; cuddle, carry, and croon to him. But then lay him down, tuck him snugly in his blanket, and get a bit of rest for yourself. Use earplugs, or hold a pillow over your ears. Set an alarm if you fear sleeping too soundly, but the more rest you can sneak in, the better you'll make it through the tough times.

Save enough money to hire someone to give you a night's relief now and then. Or beg a friend or relative to provide a respite. If you can look forward to a half day once a week to get the crying sound out of your ears, so to speak, you'll maintain your poise more easily.

Pediatricians now know very little more about colic than we did decades ago. Some babies with colic have allergies to ingredients in mother's milk or to various formulas. But most pediatricians believe that colic is related to tired, tense, and overburdened conditions in mothers. They try to use as little medication as possible, but in extreme cases, prescriptions can help.

Many young mothers are reluctant to administer medication for excessive crying, and I basically agree with them. To break the vicious cycle of crying and tension, however, it may be the very best solution. If it is indicated, try medicine for at least one week to relieve the colic and to give you and your baby some rest, and then gradually stop it.

SINGLE MOTHERS

Being a mother is the greatest experience of my life, but it has never been easy. Being a single mother is a heroic task! I have a young friend, Julie, who at the time this book was written had been a single mother for four years. I asked her to share some issues that have been particularly trying to her. She far exceeded my request and wrote the following about the knotty problems she had encountered:

I believe that some of the issues I am experiencing with single parenting are complicated by the fact that I have a child of the opposite sex than myself. When my son was born, I tried to decide what he would actually be needing and how many of those needs I, myself, could meet or how many I would need help with. One of the biggest things I knew he would need was time with a man, someone who would simply be in his life for a very long time. The person I chose was my brother-in-law, as he was a member of the family and willing to spend time with my son. Tyler gets a great deal of information from his Uncle Jim that he doesn't usually even think to ask me. He asks him if he will have a beard when he grows up, and he has asked Jim if he will show him how to shave when it's time. Once he asked him what kind of underwear men wear, simply because he had never had the opportunity to see men's underwear. He once asked Jim if men's bathrooms look the same as women's, so Jim took him to a man's bathroom. It never dawned on me that he knew he always went into the women's bathroom in public and that there was a men's room he had never been in.

I try to always be aware that I am Tyler's role model and that, like any child, he wants to do what he sees me do. For that reason I am very careful not to allow Tyler in the bathroom with me or in my bedroom while I dress. I didn't think a lot about that until one day when he was two, he was playing with a Popsicle stick and pretending to be shaving his legs. He had actually gotten that idea from TV, but I realized that if he constantly stands and watches me put my makeup on every morning, that is how he will imagine himself as a "grownup." He desperately wanted to wear my perfume, to the point of sneaking and putting it on. I talked to him about the fact that perfume was for girls, but that there was a kind of perfume for boys. I asked Jim to talk with him about that; Jim took him in his bathroom and got out the aftershave, showed Tyler how to put it on and let him try it. Now, Tyler is very proud of the fact that boys "have their own perfume" and that Jim lets him wear it sometimes. Using his uncle for information and showing him how men sometimes do some things differently than women is the only way I have found to actually show him that there is a difference in how I am and how he will be when he grows up.

> *All children are gifts—to be cherished, cared for, and trained well. They are not possessions.*

I also know that I have to constantly be aware that Tyler is my son and not my spouse. We spend so much time together, talking and taking care of the house, that it is sometimes easy to get into conversations that should not involve him. For example, if I am feeling hurt over a relationship I am having, I tell him I am feeling hurt or angry about whatever happened, but I am careful not to discuss the details of that incident and get his opinion. I have adult friends that I can process all of that with, not a four-year-old. This is not always as easy as it might sound, and there are many times I have found myself in conversations with Tyler that I had no business discussing with him, simply because he was there to listen. At any rate, Tyler and I spend a lot of time talking, and there are plenty of things to discuss that won't cause him undue worry or concern.

Since I work full time, my time with Tyler is very limited. I try to think of things that Tyler and I can do together, things that have to be done, and ways to spend time alone. There are numerous ways Tyler and I spend good quality time together while he makes a salad or whips the potatoes. I make it a point to always have as many meals as possible with him. It's easy to get into the habit of feeding him quickly and "getting that out of the way," but we are a family and it helps to eat as a family. He helps with doing dishes and laundry because he's still at the age where he thinks that's fun and it's something we do together. By the end of the evening, we have taken care of all that needs to be done, and we've spent good time together. When things happen that way, I can put him to bed without feeling like I've pushed him aside all evening to get stuff done, and he's not as resistant to bedtime because he hasn't had enough time with me.

> *True strength is always gentle. Real gentleness is always strong!*

As far as making sure I have enough time for me, that gets to be tricky sometimes, especially with working full time. I have made sure that I have a couple of good dependable baby-sitters to call on when I need them. I ask family members to watch Tyler sometimes while I simply stay home and do what I want, or go out. I make the best of my time before Tyler wakes up in the morning, which is usually just a quiet cup of coffee before the morning rush starts. I also value my time after he goes to bed at night, and both of those "quiet times" really help with dealing with busy days. Tyler has things that he can enjoy alone, and I try not to get caught up in making sure he is always entertained. I have purchased videos that he enjoys; while I don't think it's wise to use the TV as a baby-sitter, we have already viewed these videos together and I think it's fine for him to sit and watch them alone while I have time to myself.

If things are really busy and I don't have time to spend with him, I try to make it a point to tell him I'm busy and let him know exactly when I will be able to stop and be with him. If I tell him "not right now," I know he will continue to try for my attention, but if I tell him "I have to finish doing this, then I have to do that, and when I am done I will color with you," he accepts that rather well. Sometimes that means bedtime is a little later, or the dishes don't get done, but I try to be with him when I tell him I will be.

As far as discipline, it is harder as a single parent and I have found no way around the obvious traps involved. I find discipline exhausting, as I'm sure most people do. The very best advice I ever got was when I was told to pick one of Tyler's misbehaviors and focus on that one thing that was bothering me. That works so well for me, especially when I am on "overload" and Tyler is misbehaving. I have shared that with a lot of my friends when they say their kids are "driving them crazy" and they always are amazed at the results. One trap I found myself in was comparing my situation with other families that had both a mother and a father. Single parenting has just as many joys and rewards as any other type of family. There have been times when I have caught myself feeling guilty about the situation, but I realize that if I believe things would be better if Tyler had two parents, he will soon take on the same belief and feel something is wrong because his father does not live at home. There is nothing wrong with our family; it is simply a different situation. When I do feel guilty, or sorry for Tyler because his father isn't living with him, I think about the traumas we have endured together and how wonderfully we have survived each of them.

Financially, things are usually strained due to the fact that we have one income and the high cost of day care. Because of that, we simply make alterations in what we want, and that usually turns out to be better than we imagined. Many times we make gifts rather than purchase them; we go fishing rather than go to a movie; and when possible, Tyler goes along with me rather than my hiring a baby-sitter.

Things somehow always turn out better when using your imagination rather than your money.

When Tyler was an infant, I did explore what was available to me as a single parent, and was surprised to find so many resources. There are support groups, such as Parents Without Partners, who are always willing to help or offer suggestions. I found out what was available to me through the state programs and found financial help with day care and health care. Most churches I visited had ministries for single parents. I talked with my employer about certain demands on my time that may interfere with my work day and made arrangements to be able to make up time on weekends when Tyler was sick or off from school. When I came to my present job, I talked this over with the director; I have always been grateful that most employers will work with you when they know your situation.

When Tyler was tiny, I felt so guilty about taking off work that one day I took Tyler to day care while he was very sick. I quit that job and found one that would work with me on these things and that makes it much easier.

About all this mother has left unsaid is her grief over the abandonment she and almost all single mothers feel. She has not harbored bitterness and tries to give her son positive messages about his father. Like most single moms, she has developed great strength and courage that have matured her into a gracious lady.

Women who choose to have children without marrying do not experience the grieving process of women who lose a relationship with the child's father. But they still must cope with the many challenges of mothering alone.

A single mother has no intimate, significant partner with whom to share a child's first tooth, first steps, first words, or any of the other firsts. Joy is enhanced through sharing.

There is no built-in backup. Having someone available to take over when you feel exhausted and confused in parenting is a great advantage. Without that person, you may make more mistakes and certainly will become more fatigued. Being consistent in discipline is easier with that readily available reinforcer.

Julie listed financial problems as a struggle. She has worked around this issue in a positive way, but you may have a more difficult time.

Finding adequate child care is a major concern. One young mother has an income adequate to hire a trained nanny. Yet, in her child's first year and a half of life, she had to change nannies three times. Such changes are not easy for babies in their early months. The fear of neglect and abuse in child care by others lurks in the mind of nearly every mother.

Having a social life as a young single mother is complicated. Not every man who might be fond of her is willing to be involved with her child. Often she must choose to let go of a relationship in the interests of her child.

Perhaps your child's father abandoned you. You may have a special problem if the baby resembles him. The daily reminder of him and the pain you associate with him may make it difficult to love your child wholeheartedly.

When you try to appropriately train and discipline your child, you may lose your perspective and become overly emotional at times. Having someone for emotional support can help.

The loneliness and craving for personal intimacy can cause periods of depression. Here are some practical steps to help you recover:

- Work your way through the stages of grief about losing your child's father—denial, anger/blame, depression, resignation, and recovery. Any good counselor can help you reach recovery when you are ready.
- Find your own joy through being creative, looking for the positives, and finding new friends.
- Remember how much God loves you and wants you to know Him and use His resources.

- Know that God made you a *whole* person. You can create a good life for yourself and your child, even without a husband.

THE ADOPTED CHILD

I will give a brief review of the challenges of adoptive mothering. Be certain, first of all, that you have finished the grief over your inability to bear a biological child. Grief is a painful process, and you will be tempted to deny it rather than fight your way through it. To avoid completing that process, however, leaves you at risk to feel angry or be self-pitying at times. So just get through that and put it to rest.

Make peace within yourself with your adopted child's biological parents. You may well experience gratitude for their going through having this child and then giving her up for adoption. None of that is easy, and you will recognize and appreciate the treasure they made available to you.

There will also probably be times when the adopted child, like most biological children, acts like a monster. At such times, you may blame those "other" parents for passing such awful genes to your child. Or you may discover some genetic problem in your child that came from the birth parents. If you fail to get over the resentment you feel toward them, you could unconsciously take it out on your child. Being aware of such a possibility may be all you need to guard against it. But at times, you would do well to visit a family counselor. Getting a little help along the way can prevent big problems later on.

Many adoptive parents have their own biological children as well as an adopted child. Most parents tell me they feel no differently toward one or the other. But sometimes parents have warmer feelings toward biological children. And occasionally, I have seen the opposite to be true. Once again, the awareness of possible variations in your attitude can help you prevent their becoming a problem.

At some point, explore your reasons for adopting. If those reasons include an attempt to strengthen your marriage, provide companionship for your periods of loneliness, or compete with your sister for family attention, you may have problems. Children need to be loved, wanted, and accepted for themselves. And that philosophy applies to biological children as well as adopted ones. It's not likely that you have only ulterior motives for wanting to adopt a child, but if they are mixed up with your altruistic positive motives, sort them out and get rid of them.

All children are gifts to be cherished, cared for, and trained well. They are *not* possessions. Adoptive mothers and biological mothers will be successful if they remember that.

THE CHILD WITH A HANDICAPPING CONDITION

Thanks to modern medicine and technology, the incidence of birth defects has declined greatly. For example, the advent of measles vaccine means that no baby needs to be born deaf or blind due to a mother's having rubella in the first trimester of her pregnancy. Rhogam, a vaccine to prevent mothers from building the substance that once caused severe anemia in Rh babies, has virtually eliminated that problem. The list could go on.

Despite these advances in medicine, too many babies still are born with defects. Fortunately, many birth defects can be corrected or minimized. The daughter of a friend is ready to graduate from high school along with many other young people. But Ellyn has struggled through nearly thirteen years of school with braces, crutches, and canes. She was born with spina bifida, which in her case was severe enough to partially paralyze her from the waist down. I recall how dismayed her parents were when they learned the facts of her condition. Their grief was intense, but their courage was even stronger. Over the years they have spent immense amounts of time and money to help Ellyn walk. They have found the strength to trust her slow progress toward independence and rejoice in her success. Ellyn has found areas of strength that enabled her to compensate for her weaknesses and has schooled herself to achieve a level of optimism far superior to my own.

I have worked with children and their families who face life-threatening conditions. Parents of children with cystic fibrosis and certain neurological disorders or cancer know they will not live long. And most of the children are aware that they face untimely deaths. There is a gentle, profound, and often silent strength in these individuals that moves me beyond expression. I grope for words to describe this courageous sort of inner steel that bends with the force of their stress, yet does not break. These folks remind all of us that avoiding pain may weaken character.

Grief has its own timetable. Don't let anyone tell you when you should lay aside your grief.

Learning to integrate and transcend hurts and disappointments makes giants out of ordinary people.

Whatever your child's limitation or condition, **obtain as many opinions and consultations as you need to get an accurate diagnosis.** Read everything about the diagnosis you can find and understand. The Internet offers rich resources of information. Through such personal research, one friend pinpointed the cause of her child's condition when it had eluded medical practitioners. The doctors agreed with her and were big enough to appreciate her help in discovering and diagnosing a rare but somewhat limiting syndrome. Then they were able to provide help and hope.

Focus your energies on completing the tasks of grieving. Remember that grief includes a strong desire to deny the facts. It moves on to anger and blame. During this stage, even God is the target of helpless, blind rage that can cause rifts between people if it is not understood. Grief progresses to extended periods of preoccupation with the facts and feelings that can sometimes be overwhelming. You will need all your energy just to cope with this agonizing stage. Often there is a sense of guilt, and there is a temptation to pity oneself or be bitter. You can survive the grief and move on to healing if you will allow God's peace to reoccupy your mind.

Next, *focus your energies on getting a thorough assessment.* Find out what your child can expect to accomplish in daily functioning and in a set of long-range goals. Be realistic about this process, and again, seek more than one opinion. Try to expect the most and the best possible, but learn to live within reality.

Establish a plan for achieving your goals and helping your child reach his. You are only the facilitator; your child must do his own work.

Avoid self-pity for yourself and your child. Pity can be even more crippling than the condition itself. Whenever you feel too sorry for someone, you tend to make excuses for her and rescue her. It is more beneficial to encourage and challenge her to reach the goals that are possible.

Use appropriate discipline. I have often seen families protect a child with a handicapping condition rather than push him. A child with a low IQ will need extra time to learn many facts, but failing to require the mastery of knowledge that can be gained is wrong. Keep the possibilities clear, but train and teach your child to measure up to the best possible successes.

Be proud of your child. If your child's problem is visible, thoughtless people will tend to stare, make inappropriate comments, or ask difficult questions. Try not to respond to the ignorance and rudeness of such people, and find the strength to reply to their comments or questions with dignity and poise. Perhaps you can inspire some of them to learn more compassion and common sense. You and your child deserve all the opportunities you can pursue. Don't let people embarrass or deter you.

Enjoy every day to the fullest. No one has a guarantee about tomorrow. We all need to learn the secret of living one day at a time. Mothers of children with handicapping conditions are forced to master this lesson well.

Seek support and help. Many self-help groups exist already. If you can't find one to precisely match your child's condition, join the one that seems to fit your child's needs best. Or you may be inclined to begin one of your own. Some national organizations can furnish information and assistance to guide you in that effort.

Don't forget your other children. It's possible to be so committed to working against your child's handicapping condition that it becomes a Cause. In the process, you may unwittingly neglect the rest of your family. You may even marshal their energies to join yours in the big Cause. Although it takes every member of any family to create the strength and health required to survive, be careful that you not ask too big a self-sacrifice of anyone.

Draw upon your faith. There is a Power beyond our own. Even if you doubt this or you are angry that God should allow such pain, don't ignore the help that is there for you. However weak, exercise your faith.

Explore resources. Much of the care and progress depends on you, but many professionals can help. In education, medicine, electronics, and all sorts of scientific discoveries, new territory is being explored. Perhaps today, a researcher is working on the very project that could help your child next year. Be realistic, but develop your faith, too!

THE DEATH OF A CHILD

Many years ago an extremely thought-provoking movie was widely seen. It was titled *Ordinary People*. The movie depicted a family whose two sons had a sailing accident and one drowned. The one who survived blamed himself and struggled with guilt. The mother made her lost son a hero, and his room became a shrine. The father seemed helpless in his efforts to cope with grief and relieve the pain of his wife and son. Eventually, the mother left home in search of some recovery and hope.

My brother was suddenly killed at age twenty-three in an accident, leaving behind a wife and unborn daughter. All of us suffered the indescribable anguish of the untimely loss of this wonderful man. The first time I ever saw my powerful father cry was during the period of our grief.

But my mother's faith remained staunch. She grieved, too, but she held out to all of us the certainty of Life after life and the hope that somewhere in the years ahead, we might discover some answers to our endless whys.

If you have lost a child through death, I know you, too, will endure the tragedy. You will fare much better if you seek help, however. For example, a group called The Compassionate Friends is a worldwide organization of parents who have survived the loss of a child. It takes someone who has been where you are to guide you along the path of your pain, and there are many such people. To find a chapter located near you, see The Compassionate Friends Web site, www.compassionatefriends.org, or call their toll-free number, (877) 969-0010. They have regular meetings where they share their grief, seek and offer help and hope, and even plan some social events. They will explain why your best friends stay away after the funeral. They will let you cry or yell or just be silent. But they will be there for you.

Surviving siblings experience unique turbulence. They are often told by well-meaning others, "Now don't cry! You must be strong for your mother!" When even their best strength can't heal or comfort you, they feel guilty. They believe they have no one to whom they can turn for help. Be aware of their emotions. Avoid playing the game of "hide your feelings." Talk about your loss, and urge your children to also verbalize their thoughts and feelings. When you need comfort, it's okay to go to your children and talk or ask for a hug. In turn, offer these healing processes to them. If you don't know how to do or say it right, don't worry. Grief has few rights or wrongs; the only wrong is distance. Allow your loss to be the magnet that draws your family into a closeness that perhaps nothing else could have created.

Mothers who lose a child through miscarriage also grieve, in spite of some people's belief that you can't really grieve the loss of a child you didn't know. Sometimes the mother does not have a chance to hold or even see that lost premature child. The Compassionate Friends organization recommends that you ask to see and hold your child. Unless there is the sort of trauma that could give you nightmares, I urge you to ask your doctor to allow you a chance to deal with your loss in the way you intuitively feel will help you most. You may want to memorize its features and imagine who that tiny one might have become.

Listen to whatever your heart dictates. You will recover more completely if you grieve in your own way and time.

Don't let anyone tell you precisely when you should lay aside or finish your grief. Grief has its own timing and will end when it is over, not before. So don't rush it.

On the other hand, it's possible to get stuck on one of the detours of grief. You may use your grief as an excuse to feel sorry for yourself and to gain sympathy from others. These detours prolong the long, arduous journey back to comfort, so watch out for them.

Funerals can be painful, but I see them as a healthy ceremonious stage in the grief process. The funeral offers the bereaved a time to mourn and weep, to remember and laugh, to feel tenderly, and to absorb the condolences of loved ones. At one memorial service I attended, songs that the bereaved widower had shared with his wife were played. At your child's service, you may use a favorite lullaby or song you enjoyed singing. Make the service a summary of your child's life.

A little bit of eternal life is that part of us we leave behind in the lives of those we love. Any child who dies so prematurely leaves an impact on those close to her or him. You may find comfort in knowing that you, and all those who loved your child, may live out a bit of that life, multiplying it many times.

During your grief, find comfort in others, especially your remaining children. Don't consider having another child right away to fill the emptiness in your life. If later you choose to have a child, carefully discipline your mind and heart not to make that child a replacement for your lost one. Is she a new person, whole and unique? Or only an image of the child who died? Grief is a process I wish we all could avoid, but it isn't possible. It is, however, a process we can grow through and transcend.

THE SICK CHILD

Some of my warmest memories of my childhood are related to my frequent illnesses. Antibiotics weren't discovered until I was in my teens, so treatment for strep throat or other infections did not exist. And I frequently suffered from tonsillitis and its complications.

The treatment that our wonderful family doctor recommended was followed explicitly. It included getting bed rest, drinking plenty of liquids, and staying warm. I recall spending those long sick days in the southwest bedroom of our house.

Mother would bring my meals on a tray, and she would make them as delicious and attractive as possible. She carried them up the stairs when her feet must have been aching and managed to sit with me, encouraging me to eat just one more bite. My throat was burning with such misery that it was excruciatingly painful to swallow at all. But she managed to serve soup just warm enough to be soothing, so I did my best for her.

During the interminable afternoons and evenings, she read to me or told me stories in her charming manner. I don't recall her showing any impatience or grouchiness. It was no wonder, then, that I didn't mind too much being sick. There were compensations, and having Mother's undivided attention was one of them.

Illnesses today are rarely as extensive or worrisome as they were in those days. Antibiotics abound and quickly cure the many infections to which children may succumb. When children are really sick, as I was with nephritis one summer, they go to a hospital.

Nevertheless, there are hours and days when your child must stay in bed or at least on the sofa. Television often replaces the delightfully creative art of storytelling. And you can almost glide through those childhood illnesses.

Let me suggest instead that you seize these opportunities to strengthen your bonds with your child. Don't make the experiences so wonderful that your child learns to become a hypochondriac, but discover the warm delight of being, for a while, the strong protector and warm nurturer of your sick child.

To accomplish such services and even find pleasure in doing so, you must rearrange your daily schedule. Take time off from your job, let other household tasks wait, and devote yourself to your child. Copy my mother's routine, and add to it your own touches. A big cardboard box can be cut to make a useful tray table that will fit over your child's body and hold her meals.

A colorful tea towel or even paper towels make a tablecloth that will dress up the occasions of meals in bed. A little favor on the tray will entertain your child for a while, and your presence in the room will enhance a lagging appetite. Keep your attitude positive, and cover your worry with a smile of encouragement for your child. Find an excuse to keep TV off and read to your child. Tell stories that will teach your child to imagine the scenes you describe. Play quiet games, or find some craft project to do. Cutting pictures from old magazines and making scrapbooks or a collage can occupy hours that would otherwise drag into utter boredom.

Giving medication can be a major challenge for parents of young children who can't swallow pills. All sorts of clever devices are available to help you accomplish this task, but probably none is better than the spoonful of sugar that Mary Poppins recommended. Coat the bottom of the spoon or outside of the medicine dropper with jelly or honey. That part touches the taste buds on your child's tongue, and your child is less likely to fight the procedure. I'm aware this doesn't always work!

At times you may have to resort to a basic principle: you are the parent, and you alone know what is best for your child and must see that it is done. Here is the best technique I've found for giving medicine to babies and toddlers: have the medicine measured and ready to give in a dropper with a squeezable rubber top and plastic tip. Hold your child's head and body firmly against you with her right arm behind your body. Hold her left hand firmly in yours and pull the left arm up against her head, which is cradled against your arm. You have thus immobilized your child's head so she cannot jerk and hurt herself or spill the often-expensive medicine. Now your right hand is free to put the medicine in the dropper and squeeze it along the side of the tongue and in the back of the mouth between the tongue and cheek. She won't taste it as much and is not so likely to choke and gag. Gently hold her mouth shut so she can't spit it out, and the job is done. If she does spit some out, have a spoon handy to scoop it back in. Prescription doses are carefully calculated; your child needs to get most of it. If you are left-handed, reverse this holding technique. The less nervous and tense you can be, the more efficiently you can accomplish this task, but I know very few people who are flawless at giving medicine to toddlers.

Use your child's illnesses as an opportunity to strengthen your bond with her. However, don't make the experience so wonderful that she becomes a hypochondriac!

If your child is old enough to understand language, explain to him what you will need to do, and tell him you expect his cooperation. Always be honest. Never tell a child that the medicine really tastes fine when, in fact, it is horribly bitter. When a child must have an injection, tell him that it will hurt but that you expect him to be brave. Let him know you are proud of whatever efforts he makes in showing that attitude.

To be sure your child does not learn to enjoy being sick, show her as much happy attention as you reasonably can when she is well. It is tempting to enjoy the chance to cuddle a child who is ill. A child quickly becomes active and independent, and you may miss the rocking and closeness that you enjoyed when she was younger. So go ahead and enjoy that as you nurse her back to health, but avoid encouraging an "invalid" complex.

THE TROUBLED CHILD

Some principles we discussed in "The Child with a Handicapping Condition" will also be useful here. But by troubled, I am referring to emotional and psychological illnesses that assail children.

First, don't automatically assume you need psychiatric help. If you believe your child is mentally or emotionally ill, ask a relative, friend, or teacher to observe him and share impressions. With television advertisements as they are, I see many parents becoming too "suggestible." That is, the ad depicts a dejected child as suicidal. Almost all children go through grief, moodiness, and disappointments, but you can imagine your child is just like the one on TV and run to the nearest emergency room. Keep your common sense, seek input from others, and if the symptoms persist, consult a mental health expert.

On the other hand, don't take lightly signs of serious trouble. When I was practicing pediatrics, Monica brought in her two-year-old son. I hadn't seen him for some months, but I remembered him as a handsome, energetic child who sometimes failed to be very loving and could act destructively. Monica had become convinced that he could not hear. He was unresponsive much of the time and had attacks of rage.

After careful evaluation and extensive consultations, we learned the boy was severely autistic. Autism is a neurological affliction medical science still does not understand. No one knows what causes it; no areas of abnormal tissue can be identified, and no known laboratory or physical assessment reveals abnormal functioning. Despite the sparsity of demonstrable medical evidence, autistic children have classic behavior patterns. They act as if they don't hear mothers (or others), but they respond to many sounds, and they aren't deaf. Research is actively being done, and we hope in the near future to know much more about autism.

Language is extremely difficult for them to learn, yet at times they seem to understand words. They often develop repetitive motions such as rocking or head banging. At times they seem retarded, but often they can learn remarkably, in some specific areas.

Autistic children are extremely difficult to treat and to handle. As they grow, they can become so violent that parents cannot manage them at home, and some must be institutionalized. Many, however, with an extremely structured and consistent environment and firm authority seem to get better. Some of them learn to talk and may become reasonably independent.

The list of diagnoses for troubled children is long and far beyond the scope of this book, so I'll note just a few:

- Childhood schizophrenia is a painful diagnosis because it is so chronic and so hard to treat, and a child who suffers from it becomes so isolated due to his "differences."
- Attention deficit hyperactivity disorder (ADHD) is a common diagnosis these days and describes children who have difficulty sitting still and concentrating. The problem is most troublesome in school; most of these ADHD children can watch TV or play video games with reasonably good attention for long periods.
- Children with various learning disorders are immensely worrisome to parents who know the importance of education.
- Children may evidence anxiety disorders and some degree of chronic depression. They may show, in early adolescence and beyond, serious conduct disorders. We used to call these young people delinquent and sought help from juvenile courts to bring them back under healthy authority.
- Tragically, many young people are seriously addicted to drugs or alcohol. Most of them are depressed, and some are suicidal.

Whatever problem your child may have, you need to know some signs to decide how serious it is.

Evidence of Emotional or Mental Illness

- Any major change from usual behaviors that lasts at least two weeks.
- Moodiness and withdrawn behavior that persists longer than a day or two without some explanation.
- Overeating or refusing to eat, or the inducing of vomiting or diarrhea after eating.
- A change in sleep patterns—either insomnia or excessive sleep.
- A change in attire, hygiene, and grooming. Depressed teenagers tend to wear black or dark colors, become careless about bathing, and neglect their hair or makeup. They may seek bizarre styles.
- A change in study habits and school attitudes. Rarely this may be a heroic effort to catch up by a depressed child. If she or he is unable to improve, it may signal a suicide attempt. Usually, troubled children let schoolwork slide, fail to turn in papers, daydream and dawdle in class, and often become a class clown or troublemaker.
- An alteration in social habits. A withdrawn, quiet child may heroically change into a socially busy one, though all too often his contacts are with other troubled youth.

If you find that you are the mother of a troubled child, first of all, *avoid panic or blame.* You may be tempted to yell at a troubled child, "Why did you do this to us?" Few children intend to do any bad thing to their parents, and when they do, it is in retaliation for hurts they feel they have suffered. Try to find a degree of calm.

Seek input from a few others, especially from your child. If you believe there is definitely some serious trouble, seek a reliable family counselor. No child is troubled alone; she affects the entire family as the family does her. You need help from someone skilled in family dynamics to decide if there is a real problem, to determine the exact type of difficulty, and to recommend a course of action.

If you doubt the evaluation of the first person you see, by all means seek a second opinion. If the two concur, you may be reasonably sure they are correct. If they disagree, go with the one you believe is most in tune with your child. You may, of course, seek a third opinion. Any consultations beyond three, I feel, will make you more confused. I have learned that at some point, parents must accept the facts, choose the best available help, and stick with it until the solution is reached.

Part of getting help for your child is stopping your own feeling of guilt. Almost all mothers blame themselves for their children's troubles. Although all of us make mistakes, sometimes even serious ones, we do the very best we can, a day at a time. The important steps now are to admit your faults, change the negative habits, and forgive yourself. Put the past to rest, and form new habits that will correct problems. At the very worst, all the fault is not yours. Share the responsibility with those who also need to work out solutions.

> *Encouragement and compliments are far more effective motivators than punishment and condemnation.*

Don't forget the good things. In focusing on problems, it's very easy to lose your perspective. Remember the behaviors, achievements, and events that have been positive or even joyful. They often far outweigh the troubles and may give you a handle for working on the corrections.

Many troubles improve with time. Even the severity of some learning disabilities tends to lessen during early adolescence. The insecurities of junior-high-age youth decrease after they turn sixteen. Sometimes your main task is to hold the course, be patient, and wait for time to become your best ally. You must get sound consultation before you take this position, however, to be certain your child's trouble is not life threatening.

What about medication? Many children with attention deficit disorders are put on medication, as are depressed or explosively enraged children. Your doctor or a child psychiatrist will prescribe the right one for your child. In many kids, medicine is most helpful when it is used carefully to establish new behavioral patterns. It is, however, most important that you have a thorough evaluation of your child. Many children carry worries and anxiety inside that you may not have suspected. Sometimes they react to inconsistencies in your training or discipline practices. A great many hyperactive children settle down remarkably with loving but clear and firm discipline. Excellent counseling and medical help are available in most communities. Call your family doctor or county medical society for referrals.

My best recommendation is to **work with your doctor.** Try the prescription he or she offers, but also review your family rules, their consequences, and how positively and consistently you enforce them.

In most cases, your troubled child will improve with such good help. You will one day look back and be grateful that you hung in there and helped your child through these difficulties.

MOTHERING A SON

We need to restore for our children some guidelines and role models for being female and male. Surely we can do this with the carefully interwoven patterns of mutual respect for differences and the teaching of each gender complementing the other.

To mother your son really well, you need most of all to **respect masculinity and males in general.** If you had an abusive father or brother and married an alcoholic man who beat you at times, such respect will not be easy for you. It is, however, possible to correct your old, inaccurate information.

Look around you for male role models. At work, in your neighborhood, in your church or synagogue, you will discover good men. Perhaps they will be few and far from perfect, but they will have some admirable qualities that you would like your son to emulate. Study these men in a quiet way and then teach your son about these qualities.

How would you like your son to be at ten, at sixteen, and at twenty-five? You'd probably like him to be honest, open, successful, capable of warmth and intimacy, respectful, and kind. You will certainly think of other characteristics he should manifest.

Now, consider how you can help him acquire these traits. If your son is still a baby, you are fortunate. He needs great love and tenderness if he is to be capable of warmth. Rock him and hold him closely. Sing to him, and say things to him that communicate how gorgeous and wonderful he is. This practice is the very cornerstone of self-confidence.

As he grows, tickle him, exercise with him, and play hard with him. He will need the physical strength that will result from these activities.

Set clear boundaries for your son. Include him in this process. But within these boundaries allow him as much freedom as is reasonable. Don't overprotect him, creating a "Mama's boy" complex that both he and his peers will resent!

When you need to correct him, do so clearly, privately, and gently. Boys often cover their sensitivity with a bravado that is deceptive. They will act as if nothing you do or say affects them one bit. But inside, harsh discipline sears their very souls. Your son's masculinity must be encouraged, but harsh punishment is not the way to make him masculine.

Honesty can grow only in an environment of trust. Your son cannot trust you if your angry emotions are overwhelmingly intense or if you are inconsistent. You will be angry when he is mischievous or tardy at meals, but control your anger. Tell your son how you feel when he delays coming to the dinner table, and then figure out a plan to help him change his habit of tardiness. For example, you may decide to call him only once, and if he is late, he may have only a small dinner or may have to wait until his bedtime snack. Or perhaps for every minute he is late, he must go to bed a minute earlier. Don't get compulsive in measuring seconds, but consistently enforce your plan. You'll be surprised at how friendly you can stay—how unangry you'll feel—when you have a well-formed plan to put into action.

Don't stop being affectionate with your son too early. I will always love my son's second-grade teacher, who told me he needed a little more rocking and cuddling. I had mistakenly assumed that our rowdy, all-boy person would not need such treatment at seven. But he did. And I loved giving it to him. Watch your child, and let his face and actions guide that gradual progress toward independence.

Teach your son the little courtesies. Have him open doors for you, carry in grocery sacks, and help you with heavy-duty tasks that demand strength. Then compliment him on the help and his strength and thoughtfulness. Your pride and pleasure in his boyish manliness will help him develop strength and kindness.

Review Julie's account of raising her son alone (see "Single Mothers" earlier in this chapter). She had to stop his copying of her applying makeup, shaving her legs, and wearing perfume. She found a male role model for her son, and so must you if you are a single mom. Perhaps a good dad on TV or in books will be all you can call on. Perhaps you can make up some stories. But teach your son how to walk, talk, work, play, and act like a boy.

If you are a divorced mother, you may be full of hurt and resentment toward your son's father. At any cost, get through those negative emotions. Without even realizing it, you may displace those on your son. If he looks or acts like his dad, you may panic and fear he will end up being as bad as his father. The more you think such negative thoughts, the more likely you will communicate that fateful, self-fulfilling prophecy. Get through your grief, and then find all the good qualities you can about that man. Learn about his childhood, and share any and all of these good traits with your son. By helping him understand his dad's childhood, you may enable your son to understand and forgive his father's faults. And the process can hasten your own healing as well.

All children are part of both parents, and they need to know as much about each of you as possible. They can learn to copy your strong points and avoid your faults if they know about them. Be honest with your son about the reasons for your divorce, but don't tell him unnecessary, bitter details. And teach him how to get beyond the faults to forgiving and unconditional love. But don't let these positive processes convey to him that any bad habits are okay. Forgiving does not mean condoning, and even children are quick to understand that truth.

Your son will probably go through a phase of wanting you to never touch him: no more hugs or kisses, no tousling his hair, and no hand-holding. In public, he will spot a schoolmate before you can, and he will probably walk ahead of or lag behind you. Respect this stage without being personally offended. Your son must establish his independence and earn the respect of his peers. I assure you, he will outgrow this stage and will return for your hugs and touch.

At bedtime, or when he is tired, upset, or ill, he will accept your affection. Keep it clearly maternal. As your son develops into manhood, he will have sexual feelings and fantasies. If you are the least bit seductive or sexual with him, he may withdraw out of confused feelings and even anxiety. Boys are amazingly blatant in their comments about one another's mothers. Be sensitive to that fact, and stay gentle, warm, affectionate, and highly maternal. You will maintain such a position best by simply remembering that you are his mother.

When he starts dating, you have an immense responsibility. Your son must learn the quality of respect for girls. Be very clear with him regarding sexual impulses and how they are aroused. Remind him that he may be tempted to be too "touchy" with a girl or she with him. He needs to know how difficult it is to "cool it" once a person is sexually aroused. Teach your son to plan dates to include activities that are around other people and free of sexual stimulation. Make sure he knows sex is not bad; it's so good that he needs to wait for the right person and marriage for sexual fulfillment. He needs to know the risks of pregnancy, venereal diseases, and AIDS not to scare him but to make him aware of these real tragedies that have spoiled the lives of many teens.

Observe your son for some indication of aptitude that may direct his choice of a career. If he loves animals, he could be a veterinarian, a farmer, or a pet store owner. If he is good at math, perhaps he will go into engineering. Artistic skills along with excellence in geometry might suggest architecture. Men have opportunities in mechanics, construction, baking and food services, and tailoring, to name a few. One benefit of the push for sexual equality is the opening of a variety of jobs to both men and women.

Early on, help your son learn that he was born for a purpose. There is a job he can do best that can make his section of this world a better place. Finding that place is one of his primary duties. And you can help him by reflecting your pride in his accomplishments throughout his life.

Many young males lack gentleness. Boys are unsure of themselves and their masculinity, and they often guard their "macho" image in bizarre ways. As early in his life as you can begin, **teach your son the strength of real gentleness.** Only when he is confident of his strength can he risk the seeming weakness of being gentle. Find all the role models and information you can to understand this concept, and then teach it well. Someday your son's wife will love you for it.

When it comes to his choosing a girlfriend, and later a wife, you can also be helpful. In our Western culture you can't make that selection for your son, but you can offer ideas. First of all, avoid criticizing his choice. Doing so will often set up his opposition to you rather than teach him her unsuitability. If, however, he comments on problem areas, you need to help him see these clearly. Most young people in love see each other's faults, but they convince themselves that somehow, magically, these will disappear. You may remind him that personality traits and the clashes they cause will not disappear. He must decide if these qualities are traits with which he can live the rest of his life. If not, he should make a different choice while he can.

Teach your son sexual responsibility. Sexual activity is incredibly condoned and practiced by today's teens. This is not a wise practice until marriage. Teach your son to be the one to set boundaries—not the one who pushes them to his date's limits. Dating is a time to explore mutual interests and to test compatibilities. Sex needs to wait. Teach the values of morality and broad-spectrum intimacy before pursuing intense, sexual relationships.

Teach your son how to evaluate relationships. For example, do he and his girlfriend share similar values and priorities in life? Do they enjoy thinking together? Can they negotiate decisions without frequently getting angry with each other? Is each able to give consideration and compassion to the other? Or does one demand a great deal of pampering? Is she warm and affectionate? And is he? Can they understand and accept each other's feelings and share them? Do they know how to play together? Do they share a similar spiritual level? In those issues on which they disagree, can they find mature tolerance and respect for those differences? If your son can answer most of these questions affirmatively, he may have found the right girl. Hope and pray that she can see in him the right answers as well. Then be as supportive as possible, but don't become pushy or meddlesome.

You may be reluctant to think any girl is just right for such a wonderful man as your son! Being a good mother-in-law can seem like an impossible mission. It's not easy to hear a daughter-in-law criticize your son. Nor is it easy to see her neglect his care as you believe that should be given. If you have ironed his shirts and fixed a hot breakfast for him, you will expect her to do likewise. Try not to place any expectations on her. Reflect to your son all the good qualities you see in his chosen wife, and be quiet about her faults. Avoid giving either of them advice unless they ask. And then be sure it is given as a suggestion. Don't be tempted to boss or control them.

Make friends with your son's wife. Take her to lunch; go shopping with her; invite her to share your family traditions; love her, encourage her, and ask her occasionally if you can be of help. Remember, she has a family, too, and you will need to share your son with them. You can be the best mother-in-law ever!

MOTHERING A DAUGHTER

Many suggestions about mothering a son apply to your daughter as well. But she will need to have some qualities in abundance. To become a good mother herself someday, she will need to develop healthy maturity, a loving heart, a spirit of playfulness, and a clear mind. You can help her develop these qualities.

Babies need strong imprinting if they are to grow up with the traits just described. So, to **teach gentleness** to your daughter, give her plenty of it from birth. Hold, rock, and cuddle her gently, with a bit less of the roughness you might use with a son. Do, however, be playful with her. Somehow, I think instinctively, most people handle girls a bit more delicately than boys. Frankly, I think if we handled boys more gently, they might develop that quality more readily.

Giving plenty of time, attention, and love to your daughter is the way to create the bonds that will hold you together during the storms that may arise later. Between ages two and five, you especially need to have time together because those are the years in which your daughter's feminine identity is being molded. It seems much faster and easier to do household tasks by yourself. But at ages two and three, your daughter wants to help you. She will love standing on a stool and helping you wash dishes, make a cake, or do whatever you do. Plan your time and activities to allow for that help. Give her a dust cloth, show her how to polish a chair, and enjoy the unique companionship of working together.

Then **find time to play together.** Teach her how to play with dolls (by the way, boys also need to play with dolls if they are to become good fathers!). And I urge you to use the baby and child dolls in preference to the glitzy, sexy adult dolls as long as possible. The dolls that take bottles and wet their diapers are ideal to teach basic mothering skills.

There are so many ways to play together that you may choose the modes best suited to your interests and capabilities. Choose an activity you honestly enjoy. You will be able to put more positive energy into the play if it's genuinely fun for you. And that fact generally will ensure that your daughter will enjoy the activities, too.

Many women have told me of estrangement from their mothers. I feel we must think together about how and why such distances or outright enmity occur. Power struggles start early and must be handled properly.

Conflicts between mothers and daughters are transgenerational. More than likely you grew up at odds with your mother. If your daughter resembles her in any way, it is probable that you will unconsciously resent your mom's traits in her and will show that irritation to your child. She, in turn, will be hurt, angry, and confused about why you seem to dislike her, so she will act negatively with you, which will convince you that she is like your mom. Such vicious cycles are common, and they operate just below a conscious level so you'll have a hard time understanding the dynamics.

Perhaps you haven't yet learned to love yourself unconditionally. If you see in your daughter the traits you loathe in yourself, you are likely to focus a lot of hostile energy on trying to weed out those undesirable qualities. You probably are not half so bad as you fear, and your daughter is even less bad than that. So *watch out for negative, critical thinking that can be destructive to loving relationships.* See your daughter as a whole person, and value her good points. Teach her how to overcome any weaknesses and learn to accept the things she cannot change.

My daughter and I have decided that some mother-daughter conflicts are exactly that. How dare my adolescent girl be so aglow with youth and vitality, while I am growing wrinkled and older every day! And how dare her father dote on her so when it seems he has little time for me! The ultimate beauty is what is etched in our faces by love that transcends pain and grows with the wisdom of experience. God has unique blessings and benefits for all stages of life so you really need not feel jealous. Your cute daughter would be blessed if she had just a bit of your maturity.

If you are a divorced mother, and your daughter resembles her father in some way, you are likely to feel some unconscious resentment about that resemblance. Or you may experience concern and worry. If your child turns out to be like that difficult spouse, how will you cope with her? Your anxiety can be so upsetting to her that she feels rejected by you. Children, like adults, do not handle rejection very well, so your daughter is likely to withdraw from you and cause you even more concern, which she may feel is rejection. This is another vicious cycle that can result in heartbreak. Don't let yourself think such negative thoughts. Children tend to live out our expectations and predictions. Predict only the best, expect the best, and you are more than likely to experience the best.

Rather than compete with your daughter, explore the riches of your maturity, and when you know these values, ceremoniously **invite your adolescent daughter to become your friend.** You will always be her mom, but increasingly she needs an adult friend to show her the way healthy adults function.

The role of friend is an enjoyable facet of parenting. Plan a few social times when you go to lunch or sit over a soft drink and discuss life. Tell her the ideas you ponder, the memories you cherish, and the dreams you still hope to fulfill. Don't get carried away with your chatter; listen to her, too. Ask thought-provoking questions, but don't get invasive. You can carefully slip into the conversation many of the values she needs to think about. And she will mull over your ideas, probably privately, so don't spoil these events by pushing to the point of arguing and getting angry.

For whatever reasons, it seems easy for mothers to be too critical. Many researchers have found that encouragement and compliments are far more effective motivators than punishment and condemnation. Avoid put-downs, name-calling, or dire predictions; always be affirming in your attitude.

Most girls go through a stage, just as their brothers do, when they shrink from a parent's touch. Respect that in front of her friends. But at bedtime or whenever you have some privacy, show the warmth you feel. Do so in your own way and in a manner that is comfortable for her. Most teenagers enjoy a neck massage, a manicure, or a back scratch. Express your maternal affection regularly.

As your daughter reaches dating age, be very open with her about sexual and social issues. Teach her about the dignity as well as the fun of sex when she is ready for marriage and a mature commitment. Help her understand the risks of sexual intimacy before that time, however. Encourage her to think of positive, delightful activities to do on dates and how to avoid teasing and setting up unwholesome situations. Sex is to be shared with a life partner.

Help your daughter think about the kind of man she wants to marry. She can have romantic fantasies, but she needs to realize such wild wishes may never materialize. Help her establish some realistic expectations. It's better to be single all her life than to wish daily that she was free of an abusive husband. Remind her that she needs only one husband and it's smart to wait for the right one.

Many girls I know imagine that their dream man will be wealthy and provide for them to live in luxury all their lives. Such dreams are rare indeed. On the contrary, she may be left to fend for herself and her children alone. At best, an income from both her and her husband may be required to make it at all.

Work with your daughter to choose a career that will be fulfilling, will pay a livable salary, and will allow her to be a good mother as well. A tall order? Yes, but some positions can come close. (I didn't say, "Get rich!")

Teach your daughter about birth control. I'm not advocating sexual intimacy before marriage, but I do strongly advocate family planning.

Whatever your religious persuasion, there are acceptable modes of birth control that will give your daughter time to adjust in her marriage before she has a baby. She can allow enough space between babies to regain her strength and meet the most urgent needs of her baby before another one comes along.

Being a mother-in-law to your daughter's husband can also be a major challenge. If he doesn't seem to merit your approval, be as positive and considerate as possible. He will love your child the best when you show him respect and believe in him. Many men these days, as there always have been, are irresponsible and even abusive. If your daughter marries such a man, do everything you can to help him get straightened out. If he refuses, however, encourage your daughter to receive counseling and then support her course of action, whatever that may be.

Once your children are grown and married, it is no longer up to you to run their lives. Support, guidance, suggestions, and resources for help—all of these you may offer. But you are likely to hit the proverbial brick wall and be battered if you are too controlling.

How I hope you will find and enjoy the friendship of your adult children!

CHAPTER NINE

Meeting More Challenges

We've touched on several challenges in the previous chapter, but here are a few more.

SIBLING RIVALRY

Sibling rivalry challenges most mothers of two or more children. There are good and bad rivalries among brothers and sisters. The good focuses on motivation. Children who compete in a healthy way spur one another on to achievement.

When we were in high school, my sister and I, though two years apart, became rivals for the top grade in biology class. After a quiz I would always look for the grin on Mr. Griswold's face and see where he aimed it. If the grin was directed at me, I would know I had gotten the better grade, but if it was at her, I could tell she'd won. We helped each other, but the competition made us even more eager to do well.

In games, sports, work, and study, you can use healthy competition to have fun and to get accomplishments completed. I recommend this as a good mothering technique if you are equal in your praise and value of all your children.

Bad or destructive sibling rivalry is another matter. In this situation, one child feels inferior to another. I have observed several reasons for its development.

WHY DESTRUCTIVE RIVALRY DEVELOPS

- One child is exceptionally gifted in a certain area. Children in the family who are not equally gifted in this activity will clearly see they cannot do as well.

- The area of one child's special successes happens to have unique value to the family, and to you, the mother. If you value physical skills and your daughter happens to be good at ballet or gymnastics, you will show your pleasure and pride in her achievements without even thinking. If another child, however, is not so gifted or is not outstanding in any special area, he may not receive the evidence of your pride. You love both the same, but one does not merit as much praise.

- Other significant people may show outright favoritism to one child. One child may have a personality that others find easy to like. The other child may be more honest and have integrity the first may never have, but may not be as easy to enjoy. One child may remind grandparents of one of their children who brought them great joy, so they relive their pleasure in him, never realizing how left out a sibling may feel.

- One child is underhanded in making mischief, while the other is up front and gets caught and punished. The sneaky child—the apparently good child who started the trouble—may go undiscovered for a long time. Understandably, the child who bears the brunt of the disapproval will feel inferior and resentful and may try to get even by hurting that brother or sister—a wonderful excuse for the "good" child to tattle and get the other in even more trouble.

- Occasionally, one child will suffer constant disapproval for the reasons discussed here. He or she may have the misfortune of being like some family member who was a problem to the entire system of relatives. Such resemblances and the unconscious resentments they create are so subtle that it may take some effort to discover them and even more to work them out. Basically, remember your child is an individual, unique, valuable, and full of great potential. Keep working at that unconditional love, give plenty of deserved compliments, and avoid intense anger.

CORRECTING DESTRUCTIVE RIVALRY

What you can do to correct destructive sibling rivalry depends on the cause.

When one child is exceptionally gifted in an area, look for a different gift in other children. Often each has a unique quality just as worthy of commendation as the one who seems to stand out. Furthermore, each gift carries with it the responsibility to develop and use it well, so don't overreact to any child's talents. Enjoy them, teach him or her to be responsible about them, and then divide your pride and praise fairly among all your children. If they know you value them equally, they can learn to be proud of their sibling instead of resentful.

If you unwittingly feel more pride in one area of achievement than another, simply become aware of that fact. By recognizing your potential to value one child's talent (but not the actual child) more than another, you can correct that. Explain to your children what you have done and clarify that does not mean you love one child more. Then set about changing your values to include the areas in which each child excels.

If your parents show favoritism to one of your children, explain why this might be and that it is just a little fault in the grandparents, not a sign of unworthiness in a child. Also try to show the grandparents (or whoever they may be) that they are hurting the other children. Offer suggestions for correcting their partiality, and insist on fairly equal gifts and attention. Some grandparents are happy for such information and will work at changing; others won't. Your ultimate solution may be to interpret them to your children and teach them to forgive those people. Don't make too big an issue of it, and your children will be able to let go of their hurts more easily.

For that sneaky, "good" child situation, be more observant and less hasty in blaming or punishing one child. It may be wise to announce that you want no more tattling and that the children are to settle their own problems most of the time. Be prepared for a few major battles, but once they establish who is going to win, most of the fighting will stop.

If you experience unreasonable resentments toward one child, think about why that is so. Of whom does she or he remind you? What trait is evident that you most dislike in yourself or others? Keep clear in your heart just who each child is. He is not a reincarnation of Uncle Herbert. She is not totally like you, even if she does have your quick temper. Focus on the good qualities, and gently, consistently, help the child correct the faults that can be changed. Communicating your love will make a difference. Children are motivated to change far more by profound love than by the best behavior modification in the world!

PEER PRESSURE

Peer pressure can affect children as early as the second grade. Marvin was acting very strangely during the first part of his second-grade year. He moped about and was on the phone frequently. He no longer had fun playing with the neighborhood children.

One day his mother overheard his telephone conversation and was horrified to learn that he was talking to a girlfriend. Their talk was not the carefree conversation of innocent children but intense comments about kissing and being in love. When she discussed the situation with Marvin, she learned that all the boys had girlfriends, and his big worry was the possibility that Betsy might like another boy better than him! Mother firmly explained that it would be ten years at least before he needed to worry about such grown-up concerns, and that he was not to make or take any more phone calls. Marvin pouted for about five minutes, then with a sudden spurt of energy, he was off to the neighbor's to play catch. Great boundary setting!

How Children Experience Peer Pressure

1. *Social conduct.* Children are pressured to talk, play, gesture, and act like one another. Having certain friends and excluding others is typical of the preadolescent years and beyond. But it is not uncommon in younger children.

2. *Clothing.* Having the "right" emblems and brand names has been a compulsion among children for some years. Currently what is "right" depends on the group with whom one identifies. The preppy attire of those who plan to attend college is almost a uniform. The "skaters" enjoy the shock effect of weird hairstyles, multiple earrings, and even rings in the nose. The "jocks" are noted for their heavily medaled sports jackets and the cheerleaders for their "cutesy" styles. A few healthy individuals and some isolated ones don't seem to care what they wear, but the common fad is to join a clan of some type.

3. *Recreational activities.* Drug and alcohol abuse has become a passkey to some groups. Others are known for sexual expressions; still others hang out at shopping malls or game stores. Many still hike, run, or ride bikes together. In my city, large crowds of teens gather in public parking lots, sit on cars, and talk or fight. Some groups go to parks or cemeteries and stay until almost dawn. More than a few party at one another's homes, especially if the parents are away. When asked what their parents think of these activities, a group of teens interviewed in a TV documentary replied, "I don't know. They never ask!" Parents, they need you to ask, to know you care!

Few parents seem to know how to help their children plan wholesome, fun parties. And even more tragic is the report that no one would come to such a party anyway. I'm not certain I believe that, but so I'm told by many parents.

4. *Academic standings.* For some individuals and a few groups, excelling in schoolwork is a major goal. Others, however, frown upon such achievements, considered concessions to the establishment. In the addictive groups, academic achievements decline due to the chemical effects.

5. *Positive peer pressure.* I'm excited to say that in many communities, school staffs and parents are working for improvements. Some schools are aware that a student with problems is most likely to tell another student. These schools are training concerned students to help troubled peers. Usually, such help involves going together to a trusted teacher or counselor. Sometimes, just listening and caring are enough. These programs must involve training, strong support, and careful supervision, however. Youths cannot handle in-depth problems, but they can provide information about an acceptable adult helper. Teach your children how to be caring and supportive of peers who are troubled but never try to be responsible for them. Your example, open communication, and trust between you and your children will be the most effective ways of accomplishing this.

How to Guard Against Negative Peer Pressure

1. *Maintain a healthy mother-child relationship* so that the love and respect between you will always outweigh the pressure from peers.

2. *Build an open communication system* so your children can feel confident in coming to you. That means you learn to listen even better than you speak, and your words are wise, not condemning or lecturing sessions.

3. *Never act shocked,* and if you feel angry about peer pressure episodes, keep it controlled.

4. *Help your children distinguish positive from negative peer pressure.* (This distinction is as clear with peers as is sibling rivalry!) Be sure that they exert and respond only to positive pressures.

5. *Give your children clear guidelines about right and wrong, and train them to choose the right.* For example, will this activity help your children and their peers to be better and healthier people? Will it damage them or their environment in any way?

6. *Teach your children wisdom in decision making.* When you see them about to make a dangerous choice, stop them whenever you can. Help them learn from their mistakes when you can't prevent them. Here is a concise outline to teach wise decision making:

- **S** — *Size up the situation.* Clearly define and focus the issue.
- **O** — *What are the options* for solving the problem? (There are always several.)
- **C** — *What consequences* does each option carry? What will the outcome most likely be?
- **C** — *Make the choice* that ensures the best possible outcome.

7. *Encourage your children to balance their relationships with peers by developing more and more into independent, clearheaded, stable individuals.* Discuss ideas and news events with them in a way that will require creative thinking.

8. *Remind your children of the ultimate wisdom of God,* who wants to impart that wisdom to them.

ENTERTAINMENT ISSUES

From the first ABC book of infancy to the last high-school prom, you will have many opportunities to evaluate your children's entertainment choices. Let me give you an example.

When my children were young, there was a series of **books** about a family of bears. The first one described some events in which the baby bear's father was a really clumsy, egotistical oaf. I laughed with my children as he bungled his way through the book while baby bear looked on in wonder, waiting until he could do the job right.

I realized that the final message in the story was that dads are stupid and children know better. I'm certain few authors of children's books would intend to teach disrespect, but that book did so.

Currently, toy manufacturers build a huge enterprise from the sales of **toys** resembling horrifying monsters and grotesquely distorted people. I suspect this monster-toy era is designed to make children less fearful of a monster-filled world of crime and abuse, but there are better ways to work against fear.

Now, don't panic and eliminate all of your children's games, books, and toys. But read and examine each one to determine the answers to these questions:

- Will this item in any commonsense way harm my children's values and ideals?
- Will it teach them something positive and constructive?
- Will it mislead them about important family members?
- Will it help them, ultimately, to have wholesome fun, learn constructive ideas, and be better persons?

You may add your own criteria for judging your children's play items.

Music is a universal expression of feelings. Teach it to your children, beginning with the music of nature. It is all around us if we just recognize and hear it. Take your children to a quiet place and get them to listen to the birds, insects, and wind.

I've already shared with you the value of singing to your children. If you have a musical instrument, play it for them. Even the simplest musical toy can teach them the magic of notes, tones, and sounds.

There are so many kinds of music it is bewildering. But expose your children to most of them—folk songs, country music, cowboy ballads, hymns, gospel songs and spirituals, and even classical music from various periods. Guide their perceptions as they decide which rhythms and words are most significant to them. I see little, if any, value in the extreme beat and heavy sounds of hard rock music. Admittedly, that is my bias, but many of the performers are far from exemplary role models, and the words they express often promote negative values.

From my perch on my father's broad shoulders, I heard my first band concert. When I was only seven, the U.S. Marine band stopped in our town and performed a rousing concert of patriotic music. The local gymnasium was filled to overflowing, so we stood all evening to enjoy the musical treat. When your children are young, you can build into them a love of good music by exposing them to it. If at all possible, take them to hear a really great band or orchestra. Attend the concerts of a college musical group and help your children focus on the thrill of the music, even when amateurs perform it.

Many families feud over music. Parents and teens enter into power struggles no one wins. To avoid those incidents, try this approach with your children. Help them find out what is wrong with the messages that are truly destructive. If you read the words together, it becomes clear that many songs promote drug and alcohol use, sexual promiscuity, and even suicide. Let your children know that such ideas are not to be tolerated, and you believe that many young people will agree with you.

Allow some rock music if the words are not destructive. Encourage your children to balance their interest in current fad music with other types. Keep recordings of good quality music readily available, and listen to them yourself. You may be surprised to learn that when the power struggle is removed, your children will begin to prefer the more enduring music.

Television is a never-ending source of both amazement and concern. Most families own two or more sets, and many children have a TV in their rooms. Just as with nearly every other issue, TV has its bad and good sides. On the good side is the speed of news and information transmission around the world. Documentaries can be reviewed and may even teach us to think about our beliefs regarding the topics discussed. Wholesome comedies can enable families to laugh together, which serves a healthy function. TV can be a teaching tool if parents will use it well. Watch programs together, and comment on them or ask questions that can guide your children to decide what values, good or bad, are being shown.

The negative aspects of TV are often blatant, but sometimes they are so subtle you can miss them, yet be unconsciously influenced by them. On the bad side of TV is the promotion of damaging values. Violence on TV is an inarguable danger, and many TV programs today contain casual sex between unmarried persons or sexual innuendos, as well as portraying gay and lesbian couples. Recent studies reveal major concerns about violence and "free" sex. Parents, be informed and set boundaries!

> *TV can be a teaching tool if you use it well. Watch programs together and discuss what values are being shown—and how they differ from yours.*

In many programs, drinking alcoholic beverages is glamorized. Though still portrayed, smoking has become less popular since the knowledge of its deadly physical effects is so widespread.

Advertising conveys many concepts that most parents do not really like. Sexy legs in sheer hose, seductive bodies in tight jeans, and the ultra-important "value" of fashionable designer brands of expensive clothing are just a few examples. Also the promotion of so many foods and beverages can be confusing. Is oat bran really healthier than wheat? Yesterday, it was; today, it isn't. Does one brand of soft drink really taste better than another? Mothers may be bombarded by requests for a certain brand of cereal because children simply must have the toy inside, not because they'll benefit nutritionally.

Use these negative influences as teaching tools. Point out the deceptiveness of the ads for those plastic, totally destructible toys that appear both durable and desirable on TV but really are neither. It may cost a bit to give your children a chance to discover these facts for themselves, but it's worth it.

Teach your children to think, challenge, doubt, and question what they see and hear on TV. You will be giving them tools to sharpen their discernment for all of their lives.

I don't recommend that you junk your TV, though I respect families who have done so. But I strongly urge you to limit the number of sets you allow, teach negotiation skills through program choices, and watch the programs with your children. Avoid moralizing and lecturing, but logically and clearly help your family discern good from downright evil.

THE ONLY CHILD

After a lecture I gave several years ago, a mother wanted some time to discuss her problems in raising an only child. Her questions were well-phrased and revealed serious consideration.

Is it easy, she asked, to focus too much attention on an only child? Can parents not only pamper or indulge him but also expect too much of that child? When there is only one, he must fulfill parental wishes in so many areas that he is overburdened.

How does an only child learn to compete, share, and take turns? By the time he reaches school or even preschool, he has established habits of doing as he pleases much of the time.

What about the loneliness of a child who grows up without a brother or sister as a dear friend or happy opponent, or even as a fighting, mean one? There are certain pressures on parents of an only child. What can they do to keep from spoiling him a bit out of pity for that loneliness?

Of course, there are advantages to being an only child, and the concerned mother and I talked about them, too. There's no sibling rivalry to arbitrate. Parents may be able to provide extra material advantages for one child that they couldn't afford with a larger family. And they don't have to divide their energy and loyalty into as many parcels.

SUCCESSFUL MOTHERING OF AN ONLY CHILD

- *Avoid feeling sorry for the child or guilty about the situation.* If you have chosen to have only one child or if you are unable to have more, accept the fact and put that behind you.
- *Find ways to compensate for a lack of siblings.* You can act a little bit like a sister if you do so wisely. Go ahead and compete to a limited extent with your child. Require her to share her candy with you, and take turns choosing games, TV programs, and meals. Discover a special friend or two for your child. Encourage him to participate in kids' groups such as Sunday school, Scouts, or sports teams. Allow him to spend nights, take trips, or share activities with these special friends.

  My youngest child was like an only child for some years, and I will always love the family who adopted her frequently. She adored spending time with the six children, parents, and grandmother who so enriched her life. And Susan, her friend, and that entire family became dear to me over the years.

- *Explore with your child her natural talents and interests.* Help her develop them to the best level possible, and then be proud of those accomplishments. Don't allow yourself to expect too much. Your child's teacher and your relatives can be helpful to you in clarifying how you're doing if you really don't know.

TWINS (OR MORE!)

A mother was concerned about but also delighted by the close bond between her twins. If they were separated even briefly, they would cry inconsolably. Although in a way that was both tender and cute, their behavior troubled me. Neither twin will likely reach maximum potential if that dependence remains or intensifies. Human beings must become, to some degree, persons who are independent and capable of standing on their own two feet, not four!

I urge you to think of your twins as separate people who happened to be conceived and born at the same time. Refrain from dressing them alike. If at all possible, have separate beds and, later, separate rooms. Talk with them, observe them, and respond to them as if they had been born years apart as much as you can.

When they start school, I suggest they be placed in different classrooms. Work with their teachers and principal to help them treat each child as an individual.

At some point in life, each person must learn to be whole, self-confident, reliable, and useful. Help your twins achieve this status because it will be more difficult for them to make that transition than if they were not twins. Allow them and enjoy with them the unique friendship and closeness that only twins can know.

DISCIPLINE AND PUNISHMENT

During a seminar on parenting, a soft-spoken mother wanted to know how to be consistent with her two-year-old. She could get him to go to bed and to treat relatives considerately at times. At other times, he became a monster, refusing to go to bed and hitting or biting the cousins who visited. She began to recognize that her inconsistency was at fault instead of his being a miniature Dr. Jekyll and Mr. Hyde.

For many years our society has promoted a permissive attitude, lax disciplinary actions, and an emphasis on children's rights. Too little has been taught regarding children's respect for others and their sense of responsibility. The rebellion of the 1960s and 1970s resulted in so many young people running away and showing open defiance that parents became afraid to discipline children. Rather than risk the loss of a child through running away or through drug abuse, parents reversed their role of healthy authority. Unfortunately, this thinking has continued right into the twenty-first century. In some ways it has become worse!

Brent, a fifteen-year-old who had long tested his parents' authority, wanted to attend a party one Friday evening. His parents knew that both alcohol and pot would be available and suspected there would be little, if any, adult supervision. They forbade him to go and explained their concerns clearly. Brent's reply was typical of many adolescents: "Well, let me tell you, I'm going, and you can't stop me. And if you even try to, I'll not be home at all!" Knowing how many of his friends had extended stays away from home, his parents gave in. They had always practiced leniency, giving in to maintain peace and try to keep their relationship intact and communications open. But their pattern of giving in kept Brent's boundaries so elastic that he never knew where they were. He did know that if he pushed hard enough, he could always move the limits.

Children are more secure and have better self-esteem when they know their limits—whatever their age or stage.

RESPECT OR INVADE KIDS' PRIVACY?

Above, I referred to a recent TV documentary revealing teenagers whose risky behaviors went unchallenged. Their parents, the kids said, simply never asked where they'd been or with whom.

Many parents argue with me that it is not fair, even that it's disrespectful to check their child's room or read notes left lying about. I strongly disagree with them. My lifetime of working as a physician with countless kids and families is the evidence. Most kids at best are ambivalent about invasive parents. Yes, they want and need some privacy, but they have repeatedly told me how relieved they felt when Mom found their pot paraphernalia. They knew Dad's discovery of notes left "accidentally" about would result in helping them out of big-time trouble.

Again and again our nation has been horrified by shootings of kids by their young peers. Let's list some of the known reasons:

- The aggressors lived in dysfunctional homes caught in the cross fire of angry, divorced parents.
- The aggressors' parents were not there for them, giving them excessive freedom, failing "to ask." The bombs used in Littleton, Colorado, were made in a teen's home garage!
- The aggressors lived with a parent who abused them—a big bully at home.
- The aggressors were taught to be bullies with unlimited power without consequences.
- The aggressors were shy and suffered low self-esteem. They were waiting victims for school and peer bullies, who taunted them to the breaking point.
- Rarely, an aggressor suffered from mental illness such as schizophrenia. They heard internal voices telling them to commit violence.
- Our American history is replete with both private violence and participation in horrible wars. In a way, violent offenders are heroes to some of us.

Obviously, no offender fits all of these categories, but each can be found in one or more of them. We must teach you, parents, to regain your proper, protective authority. So *do* check your child's closets, drawers, and pockets. Read those poems and prose your child leaves lying out. And respond in tough, fair, logical love. If you do, you can usually save your child from tragedy.

BOUNDARIES HELP THEM FEEL SAFE

Children are more secure and exhibit the healthiest self-esteem when they know their limits. Whatever the age or stage of development, count on that fact. A child's boundaries should expand as he matures and shows a sense of genuine responsibility. But to have no limits or to change them inconsistently and unpredictably only sets the stage for serious misbehavior. Children constantly test parents' restrictions, and that testing is a sign of growth toward independence. It is your job to determine if that testing is backed up by solid evidence of sound judgment, self-control, and the ability to handle greater freedom responsibly. The child may be testing to see if you really mean what you say and are strong, wise, and caring enough to make your rules stick.

Putting the basic principles of successful discipline into practice and sticking with them require diligence. The risk of losing your children's momentary happiness and putting up with their moodiness is a small price to pay for necessary protection from some of today's dangerous rebellion.

What Is Effective Discipline?

Discipline always teaches a lesson that will be useful as long as your children live. Showing consideration for others, completing tasks, doing quality work, and being honest are all examples of character traits that come about only through good discipline.

Discipline is best done with the fewest words and the greatest action. My father demonstrated that more than my mother. If I failed to do my chores reasonably on time and well, he would take my hand, lead me to the unfinished task, and point a finger. His eyes, always kind, would look stern, and I knew I'd better do the job. His look of genuine approval was my adequate reward. I would have attempted any task for him.

Effective discipline must be built on genuine, unconditional love, love that is strong enough to be tough when it must be.

Effective discipline is a fine balance between rigidity and flexibility. Too much rigidity prompts rebellion. Too much flexibility creates the likelihood that limits will be tested.

It takes teamwork to make discipline work. Both parents and caregivers must expect and enforce reasonably similar rules and consequences.

Good discipline is not based on fear. Respect is healthy, but fear results in either withdrawal or rebellion. Neither extreme will result in a well-adjusted, mature adult, and that is the goal of good discipline.

Discipline is a masterpiece when it is redemptive. Children frequently do some disastrous things. They must learn to stop such actions and understand the basic tenets of good judgment and self-control in order to do so. At the same time they must keep some sense of their worth and some hope for their future.

When I was six, I took part in my very first stage performance at Christmastime. What an unparalleled evening that was! Our community had a new rural schoolhouse. It had electricity, so the Christmas tree was gorgeous with its electric lights and tinsel. Most people in the early 1930s did not have such a luxury, so all of us were excited.

We had practiced for weeks to put on a pretty sophisticated program to launch the Christmas vacation, and all of our families and friends were there to applaud our performance. All of us were dressed in our very best Sunday clothes, which were usually hand-me-downs in those difficult times. But my only classmate came to school that evening looking like a living doll. Her blonde curls shone, and her blue eyes accented her rosy cheeks. She wore a new outfit like none I had seen outside the thick Sears and Roebuck catalog.

Patsy wore a brown pleated skirt and a golden yellow sweater with a brown collar that matched the skirt. At the neck was a bow made out of the brown yarn, and at the ends of the cords were two fuzzy brown balls. They bounced as she walked, and I was fascinated with them.

Part of our program featured carol singing. All of the children in the eight grades of our one-room school filed onto the stage to perform. Since we were first graders, Patsy and I were on the front row. Singing blissfully, I eyed those soft yarn balls. At last I just reached over and touched them gently, feeling their fluffiness and knowing how elegant they truly were. It was a delightful experience!

The next morning at breakfast, though, I discovered that my mother did not see it as delightful. In fact, she lectured me about my dreadful behavior in great detail. She had been terribly embarrassed as people around her laughed at my action. It seemed to me that her scolding lasted an eternity, but finally I was excused.

The lights of Christmas and its sparkle went out for me. There was no joy, and my exhilaration from the night before was dissipated. I found a corner behind the kitchen stove where I sat, head on my knees and tears in my eyes.

Later I felt, rather than heard, a presence near me. I looked through my tears and saw a pair of worn brown work shoes. My gaze slowly rose from the floor to faded blue overalls and a coarse blue shirt to my father's warm brown eyes. Without a word, he reached down and picked me up, hugging me in his muscular arms.

At last he spoke a few magic words: "Gracie, it's okay. I didn't think what you did was so bad. In fact, it was kind of cute!" If my dad had never done another nice thing, I would love him forever for that morning! He restored my dignity and gave me hope. He turned back on the lights of Christmas and the light by which I still live. My father's actions made my heavenly Father live for me.

Such a response to even worse misdemeanors motivates children to change. It is not easy to give up the freedom and pleasures of childhood at best. But being understanding, loving, and positive can make children's efforts to grow up worthwhile.

COMPONENTS OF GOOD DISCIPLINE

The mechanics of good discipline demand some effective equipment to function smoothly:

- **Clear expectations.** You need to formulate policies clearly in your own mind and explain them to your children. Begin this even before a child can talk so you will be well-practiced.

- **Realistic requirements.** You must know your child if you are to understand what he is capable of doing at a given time. Because his older sister could make her bed at age four doesn't necessarily mean your son can do so. But if he can, it is part of your job description to see to it that he forms the habit of doing so.

- **Consistent follow-through.** You must stay in charge of your time if your children are to form good habits. If you oversleep and rush to get the children on the school bus, neither you nor they will be able to get into the habit of making beds, for example. Your creativity in assuring their job completion helps them become responsible. That reliability doesn't just happen.

- **Natural consequences.** Let's stick with the bed-making example. If that is part of the morning routine, and you have allowed for the time, but your child has chosen to dawdle, there may be trouble. That bus will arrive eventually, and she will not be ready. The child has a choice: leave the bed unmade and catch the bus, or fulfill that responsibility and walk to school.

  The distance and age of your child may be such that walking is not feasible, but I trust that you get the point.

  Consequences are most effective when they are established before a rule is broken—and when children know there is a rule.

  To break the habit and do the job for your child, or even to take her to school, will teach her that she can be irresponsible.

- **Your consequences.** For many policies you set, there may not be any natural consequences, so you may need to find some.

  One mother loved to play her piano. Her children loved to watch TV.

They couldn't hear well due to her playing, so they turned up the volume. Mother couldn't hear her playing, so she played louder. At last she became irritated, turned off the TV set, and yelled, "There will be no TV for the next month. You children are so selfish, I'll teach you to be more considerate." Of course, what she really taught them was unreasonableness and bad temper.

Consequences are most effective when they are established before a rule is broken and when the children know there is a rule. What if the mother had thought for a minute, waited for the end of the TV program, and then talked with her girls? She could have said, "You know, we've just had a battle over volume, haven't we? You couldn't hear, and neither could I. The neighbors must have thought we'd gone deaf! What are you both willing to do so we won't have such a problem again?"

After listening to their ideas, she could have continued, "I'm willing to play the piano when your favorite program isn't on if you will then keep the sound down for half an hour so I can play in peace." If they fail to follow the agreed-upon plan, she can make it clear and fair: "If either of us fails to live up to our agreement, TV goes off for the rest of the day, or I don't get to play my piano till tomorrow! Okay?" Such humor, thoughtfulness, respect, and willingness to model taking turns can be nothing but good. Effective discipline is loving, logical, and fair.

• *Praise.* When you least feel like it, your child may most need the reward of your compliments. You may have struggled with your son all evening to complete his homework. By bedtime, you are angry and exhausted, and the work is not as good as it should have been. You don't even want to look at your young rascal.

Put yourself in his shoes. He wanted so much to play ball, watch TV, or work on his model. Instead he had to listen to your nagging and do junk he hated. None of his friends had to waste an entire evening studying! So, Mom, go to his room and explain how you believe he feels. Tell him you know it's not easy to put up with such a demanding mother, and let him know about your pride in what he actually accomplished. Even if he doesn't smother you with a hug, you can know you've blessed your son. And if you will practice praise consistently, sooner or later, he will hug you.

- **Least extreme consequences.** In nearly every lecture I give about discipline, someone asks about spankings. I have learned to strongly urge parents to avoid such physical punishment. In today's stress-filled world, even the most controlled parent may reach her breaking point. So many children are abused by parents hitting harder or being angrier than they intended that I absolutely believe we can find better, less risky methods for giving consequences for misbehaving.

In many audiences, a parent will remind me of the proverb that says, "He who spares his rod hates his son" (Proverbs 13:24). A similar statement reads, "The rod and rebuke give wisdom, but a child left to himself brings shame to his mother" (Proverbs 29:15). After much study and prayer for guidance, I recalled one of my best-loved parts of Psalm 23: "Your rod and Your staff, they comfort me" (Psalm 23:4).

When I was a girl, I often was able to watch my father's sheep in a small pasture. Near the grass they could nibble freely was an alfalfa field. Had they eaten that tasty crop, they would have very likely died because they could not digest it. My task was to dream and think anything I liked as long as I kept the sheep where they were safe.

Interestingly enough, the sheep never ran away; they slowly, gradually, strayed away. To keep them safe, I had to watch them constantly, and I needed to poke or prod them gently but firmly when they neared the border of the good grass. Turning them back was not hard.

Useful consequences include time-out and grounding, physical restraint for preschoolers, loss of privileges and/or allowances, and your loving, firm disapproval. Know your child and what best motivates compliance. But love him unconditionally and you will have found that!

If you follow these two principles with your children from their birth, you can forget most of the rest of this chapter. The wisdom of Proverbs 29:15 bears repeating and rephrasing: "Wisdom is the result of reproof" and that prodding of the rod to get your lamb back on course. Never leave a young child to himself, or he will bring shame to your heart. Love, pay attention to him, and correct him, but never abuse him.

SPECIAL OCCASIONS

VACATIONS

For many families, leaving schedules, work, and the demands of daily living behind for vacations is pure pleasure. Without pursuing so many directions at once, both mothers and children can relax and even at times enjoy one another. At times, however, even vacations can become so difficult that you wonder if they are worth the effort. Let me reassure you, they are, or they can be with some careful planning.

First, an exciting vacation is probably not possible with a very young child. For children under age three, I suggest short trips where you can stay for a few days in the same motel or a cabin. If you have relatives who can accommodate you, visiting family can work. Just avoid staying too long or leaving your small child in their care.

After the age of two or three, most children can handle vacations quite well, but there are conditions to be met.

If possible, travel by car. Doing so allows you to stop, stretch cramped legs, let the children run off energy, and enjoy new scenery.

Having a picnic lunch is better than stopping at a restaurant. When you do eat out, find a place that offers quick service, simple, inexpensive menus, and adequate booster chairs. Teach your children good manners in a quiet and relaxed mode, and be firm but have fun with them as well.

Pack carefully! It's easier to have each child's daily necessities in his or her own bag. You might even sew a bright duffel bag for each one to carry.

Put little surprises among the pajamas: an inexpensive toy, a few crayons and coloring book, or a little book to "read." Each day, add the items your child discovers in the bag to a toy box that you keep in the car. Items in that box should be inexpensive, interesting, and innovative; for example, plain white paper and brightly colored construction paper, crayons that can be wiped off, notebook ring reinforcers, tape, blunt scissors, and plenty of colorful magazines. Small toys that can fit into a child's pocket and little games that older children may play will all fit into such a box.

You may also have cardboard boxes that can be cut out on the ends to fit over a child's legs. These make great worktables that are safe and disposable. Help your children create collages, scrapbooks, or portfolios. Let them pick up rocks or pinecones along the way to add to their box. If you are traveling across several states, check to be certain you can transport any questionable plants across state lines.

Always remember pillows and light blankets. Even the most energetic child will get sleepy in the car and need a comfortable nap. The cardboard "tables" make great footstools, so children can stretch out a bit and sleep better.

The adults on vacation need some fun, too. Have a variety of events planned for each day, but don't be compulsive. You may have to change schedules, and by all means allow flexible time to relax or take in something that just came up. Have you noticed I refer to balance a great deal? Here's another place to seek it. Make enough plans to avoid an empty day in which one might become bored; but be free enough to be spontaneous and find some excitement.

Both fathers and mothers need to take care of themselves so they don't give in to grouchiness or yelling at the children. If you are in a hotel, see if they have reliable child-care people available. Once in a while, you can enjoy some time together free of responsibilities. You will have greater pleasure in your children if you get a break now and then.

If the children become unruly or irritating, I suggest you not hit or lecture them. Instead, pull off the road at the first safe stop, and tell the children that this vacation will go no further until they agree to show respect and kindness to one another. Be prepared to wait for a while. Even if you lose several hours, you will convey an important lesson that could be learned from that day on. Such a method keeps you in a healthy position of being the ultimate guardian and authority, but it also gives children some choice in when they will settle down and how courteous and considerate they can decide to be.

In an extremely rare situation, if children refuse to cooperate and keep testing the limits you have set, you may cut short the vacation and return home. Children need the security of knowing that you mean business. It's better to shorten one vacation, thereby teaching a valuable lesson, than to be miserable on a trip and find your children form habits of aggressiveness and selfishness that could spoil their lives—and yours!

SPECIAL DAYS

Holidays, birthdays, religious festivals, and various anniversaries deserve special attention from mothers. Usually you have the privilege of establishing and maintaining the traditions and nuances that transform ordinary days into cherished memories. You are forging a chain of customs that links each generation to the last and offers a secure sense of belonging.

It's nice if you have memories of Thanksgiving Day feasts and birthday celebrations. If you always had a picnic with homemade ice cream on the Fourth of July, you'll know just what to plan with your family. But if you grew up with no such reference points, don't despair. You can start your very own celebrations.

Try to remember what you wanted to do on special days when you were a little girl. Think of friends and how their families observed Christmas or Hanukkah. Observe your neighbors and your children's friends. What do they do? Read some books and catch some quick glimpses of TV scenes. Out of all these resources, pull together foods, rituals, and customs that seem most desirable to you and your husband.

Practice them, and adjust them year by year until they are just right. Then, even when you might prefer to forget them just this year, keep them up.

It takes years to build traditions. They are a valuable and stabilizing force for your children, and they will continue to serve that function for years to come.

Don't let these special days become too costly. Celebrations can focus too much on giving gifts. Keep gifts simple and thoughtful, and be sure they are something the recipient would like.

Keep food preparations as simple as possible. In trying to maintain my family's Christmas baking traditions, I was often stuck in the kitchen. I missed much of the joy, warmth, and peace of that season by having too little free time with my loved ones.

Encourage input from the family. Offering ideas and helping work out the preparations can be fun if everyone helps. I would have been less stuck if I had insisted that my children join me in that kitchen! Occasionally share your day with people who are not in your family. Our Thanksgiving Days for years were enriched by the presence of local college students from other countries. I hope their memories of our turkey dinners are half as warm as mine! When your children marry and establish homes, give them freedom. It's tempt-ing to yearn for adult children to return for hol-

> *Traditions are a valuable and stabilizing force for children.*

iday fests. I see nothing wrong in their doing so, unless they feel a need to begin their own traditions. In that case, you have a choice: you can be hurt and angry, you can enter into their celebrations, or you can modify yours to fit the new situation.

Finally, *discover some means of conveying the special significance of the day to your children.* Recalling brief memories of their birth or infancy on chil-dren's birthdays helps them form a strong self-image. Stories of loved ones who served in various wars can renew a commitment to peace on Veterans Day. And for each holiday, a memory, a prayer of thanksgiving, and an explanation of the meaning of the day will establish its place in the children's hearts and memory banks. Enjoy celebrating your special days.

MOTHERING THROUGH LOSS AND GRIEF

For many years, I have been aware that our Western culture expends great energy protecting children from the pain of loss and the processes of grief.

One day I encountered a friend who was out with her daughter and one of her young friends. We chatted for a moment, and I noticed smiles on the girls' faces as they discussed plans to attend an amusement park that very day.

As the children went off to play, my friend confided that the little girl's father had died of a heart attack that morning. The bereaved family had suggested the trip to the park to distract the nine-year-old from her sadness.

No one likes pain, but most people will become heroes rather than see a child suffer. I wonder if we have considered just how children will learn about grieving and coping with loss, however. It seems far wiser to guide and support children through this process than to protect them from it.

Judy was having serious problems adjusting in her new school. She seemed sullen and worked far below the capacity of her excellent intelligence. As I sat facing her angry eyes and sometimes-impudent manner, I was able to help her talk out the anguish she had stored up for several months. Her family had moved some distance to a nicer home and a better job. They had new furniture and a comfortable family car. Her parents were so pleased with their gains that they failed to recognize Judy's losses. But she felt them!

She had lost her lifetime friends, her familiar school, and all the teachers she could revisit each year. Gone was the library where she had spent summer afternoons reading. She could no longer walk to the ice-cream shop, and she didn't even know where the post office was in her new neighborhood. Worst of all, her battered but comfortable old furniture was gone, replaced with new pieces she could hardly touch; and her worn old teddy bear had joined her other well-used treasures in the trash bin. Judy was angry over many losses, but perhaps angriest of all because no one understood.

Fortunately, her mother learned to understand, and she cared deeply about her child and her problems. Judy recovered and has become a lovely young woman.

Many children never recover because they learn to hide their grief or disguise it so well that no one can discover it and help them through. Losses important to children are often overlooked, but they need to be recognized and dealt with.

LOSSES CHILDREN DEAL WITH

The loss of dependency was discussed earlier. It's no fun taking on more and more responsibility and giving up one's freedom.

The loss of a period of time is particularly noticeable at the end of each school year but is especially intense when a child moves to a new school building. The seriousness of these losses is modified by the attachment to the teacher, plans for summer vacation, and anticipation of an exciting program next year. But there is always a bit of sadness mixed with the relief at having put another year behind one.

The loss of friends is a frequent occurrence in our mobile society. Moving across the city, to a small child, is almost like moving across the state.

The loss of pets or favorite toys can be almost as grievous to a child as the loss of a relative to an adult.

The loss of a relationship is especially traumatic to teenagers who are dating. Breaking up with a boyfriend or girlfriend can seem like the end of the world.

The loss of a dream or of success is another grief-producing experience to adolescents. Not making the cheerleading squad or being cut from the debate competition can seem like total failure.

The loss of a loved one through death is not that unusual. Accidents and suicide claim so many young lives each year that hardly a teenager exists who does not personally know someone who has met an untimely death. Grandparents and other loved ones die, and tragically, even parents or siblings may be lost in death.

HELPING CHILDREN COPE WITH A MAJOR LOSS

One of the most difficult tasks you may ever face is helping your child through a major and permanent loss. Your ability to do so depends on your stability and your philosophy of life, death, and their meaning in the endless cycles through which generations come and go.

- *Don't try to protect your children from reality.* Whatever their loss, explain it, and tell them you know it hurts and you care that they hurt. Tell them that all of us must learn to survive losses and grief and that you will help them to do so.
- *Try to help your children express their pain over a loss.* Tell them it's normal to be angry and to cry. Encourage them to talk about the experience, and listen to them when they do. It's useless to try to comfort anyone while in the stages of anger and pain. So listen, care, and be available but not invasive.
- *After the acuteness of the grief, offer hope of healing.* Sharing some of your own experiences may help teach that there is such hope. Helping them see the small comfort zones that reappear and grow even in the midst of the pain is also reassuring.
- *Help your children deal with guilt involved in the loss.* Often children feel guilty about a loss, even death, but usually they have not done any wrong. Sometimes, though, they have been at fault. Carelessly leaving a bicycle out in the yard can result in its theft. Failing to care for a pet may result in its dying or running away. If a child imagines guilt, sound information can eliminate it. If she or he is actually guilty, you need to

teach the process of forgiveness. That process involves honestly admitting one's faults, learning a lifetime lesson from the experience, and then letting go of the guilt. You, too, must let go of it. Unless the lesson needs a refresher course, don't remind your child of old mistakes or wrongdoing. Help him or her believe in God's forgiveness and, even more, in His ability to provide wisdom and courage for facing the future.

- *Avoid trite clichés about losses.* Telling a teen that the loss of his girlfriend must be God's will makes no sense. It may be God's tough love to prevent a destructive dating relationship through that breakup. But the peak of his sadness and damage to his self-esteem is not the time to say such things. You will benefit your child more by simply acknowledging that we do not always know why sad and bad things happen. Sometimes we discover some insights later. But we can find the courage to face life and the patience to wait for healing. Remind him that you and all who love him will be there for him; you will listen, love, and always care. Together you can make it.

- *Once your child is finished with the grief process, you may replace the lost pet, girlfriend, or toy,* but the child needs to earn that replacement. You can also offer the comfort that was impossible to believe earlier on. And you can help fix in your child's mind and heart the mellowing lessons only grief can teach.

BLENDED FAMILIES

Half of all marriages in the United States end in divorce. In some areas, this may reach 60 percent or more. I hope you will not have to endure the heartache of that process, but by the law of averages, many of you already have or will do so at some point. Equally likely is the fact that you will remarry. And the possibility of needing to learn to cope with a blended family is very high indeed.

Marge and Bill came to me with problems relating to their heroic attempts to blend her two and his three children. Some of these young people were in their teens, well along in their search for independence, and they could not really adapt to a new mother or father. Even the younger ones struggled with divided loyalties, guilt, and anger. This family (and many others) taught me some lessons.

Children usually maintain a fierce loyalty to both biological parents. They desperately hold on to a wish or a fantasy that someday, magically, their own two parents will get back together. They often actively seek to sabotage a parent's second marriage to facilitate such a reunion. Stepparents seem to threaten the children's dream of a reunited family. They often believe, sometimes accurately, that the stepparent caused their mom's and dad's divorce.

Old familiar patterns of living are changed. The new stepparent has very different tastes and habits that do not fit the children's expectations. These changes are confusing and even distasteful. New parental rules and demands cause resentment.

Children who have lived with a single mother have an especially trying time. They may have shouldered extra duties, but they learned to like having Mom all to themselves. Sharing her with a new father creates jealousy and resentment that are truly difficult to overcome.

Children commonly hold a major sense of loyalty to a deceased parent. To them, a remarriage is an insult to that absent parent, and they resent the new "intruder." "How dare he try to take my father's place?" is the common reaction of children.

If there are stepbrothers or stepsisters, there is usually extreme competition against them. Jealousy grows rampant.

Many disciplinary problems arise. A child says to the new parent, "I don't have to obey you! You're not my dad!" A mother may prefer that the new husband stay away from disciplinary issues to gain the children's favor. At the same time, she needs some help! When there are major disagreements about rules and changes in lifestyle, a parent may wish to be single again. Another divorce could result.

There are varying policies in the home of the other parent. His children will say, "Mom doesn't make us go to bed this early!" And yours may exclaim, "When we're at Dad's, he lets us have all the ice cream we want!" It's not easy to create order out of such chaos and still maintain some semblance of goodwill.

Often the new husband shows many of the problem traits of the old one. You may face discouragement or even despair.

Before you give up, however, consider some of the positives. Bill and Marge loved each other enough to outlast their children's problems. As they left home for college or their own lives, the parents began to enjoy an entirely new dimension in a loving marriage.

SURVIVAL TIPS FOR STEPMOMS

- There is no perfect marriage, and you won't find anyone who can make you happy. You must seek joy within yourself and in your faith in God.
- Consider the strong points in your marriage. What attracted you to him? How can you recapture that idealism and build on it? How can you ensure that you will stay lovable and attractive, avoiding divisiveness and bitterness? Give up trying to get his children to accept you as their mother. They have a mom; help them see the good in her rather than compete for their loyalty.
- Work mainly to understand the stepchildren and love them as a friend. They may reject your offer of friendship, but it's easier for them to accept that role than another mother.
- Look for the good things about his children and your own. Compliments and praise go much further than scolding and criticism to build a loving family.
- Learn to love all your children unconditionally and be more concerned about how much you love them than whether they like you.
- Sift through the values, manners, or actions you expect from your stepchildren to see if these can wait to be instilled while you build a

warm relationship. For example, an elegant and immaculate house can be created after the children grow up. A nice home, but a comfortable one, may allow the children to feel more at ease with you. And exquisite table manners are less vital to your home's atmosphere than passable ones with pleasant mealtimes.

- If the children have trouble with prompt obedience because they're used to more relaxed expectations, patiently earn their respect and provide the warmth that will motivate obedience.
- Make a genuine commitment to your whole family. If you hint at leaving them, they may try all the harder to break up your marriage.
- Develop communication skills. Be clear and definite without being angry or controlling. Learn to negotiate and compromise on decisions but not on values. You can't very well demand values; you can beautifully demonstrate them.
- Forge a strong relationship with your new husband. When the two of you become a team, the children can learn to be good players.
- Avoid comparisons with your prior marriage and home. The tendency is to block out the old pain and recall the better times. Doing so can make you discontented and keep you from really working on this family.
- Know where to turn for assistance. Your clergyperson can be most helpful. Sometimes he or she is not, however, quite right for you, so find a qualified counselor. Do practice the faith you are taught, and allow that to grow through your struggles.

If you are blessed with an objective friend who won't take sides, talk with that person. An outsider can see both sides of an issue much more clearly than you, who are caught in the emotions and hassles of the new adjustments. Try to perceive your own errors; it's much easier to work on them than to convince your husband of his faults and make him change.

If problems seem to be worsening and you don't see the direction to take, you may want to consult a marriage and family counselor. Don't be either too hasty or too reluctant to seek such help. Accepting help beyond yourself does not mean that you are stupid or weak. It means that you are a committed and caring mother who wants the best for herself and her blended family.

PLANNING FOR THE FUTURE

My father taught me to set goals by regularly giving me a smart slap across the shoulders and asking, "Gracie, do you think you'll ever amount to anything?" He always had a mix of serious-ness with a twinkle in his dear brown eyes. I knew he thought I might amount to something and that I would have his complete support.

My mother quietly prayed about my future. She never urged me to enter any certain career, but she encouraged me to be the best I could be. Both parents provided books and discus-sions about a variety of professions. Despite the poverty of my growing-up years and my par-ents' limited opportunities, they never let any of us doubt that we could do whatever God had created us to do.

> *Tell your children and a few others about their good qualities and achievements. It's okay to be proud— children thrive on your approval.*

In working with many young people, I find a great lack of such prospects. Seldom do these youths show confidence in their playing a sig-nificant role in life. I'm certain there are many teens I do not know who have such dreams and aspirations. I hope your children are among them. Certainly, you can do some things to encourage their vision of a bright future.

ENCOURAGING CHILDREN TO ENVISION A BRIGHT FUTURE

- *From early on, regularly tell them all the good qualities you see in them.* Give them examples so they'll know you're honest.

- *Avoid overprotecting or rescuing your children from difficult assignments.* Encourage and help them; in crisis times guide them. But always help them discover how much and how well they can do on their own. Tell them and a few others of their successes. All too often mothers share their concerns, and children who overhear them may fear they are really hopeless. Reverse that tendency, Mom, and tell Dad and the grandparents of your children's achievements. It's okay to be proud. They thrive on your approval.

- *With your children read books, take field trips, and meet people in a variety of careers.* Without getting pushy, focus their attention at intervals on the future. As you notice aptitudes, interests, and skills emerging, let your children know you are delighted about their giftedness. Try to provide opportunities to increase those interests and develop those skills, whatever they may be.

- *As you share your work and your early dreams with your children, let them in on the sacrifice and hard work it took to realize your dream.* Tell the good things about your job so they know it was worthwhile to endure the difficult times. Let them know, however, that there is no perfect career. In anything one does, there are boring, taxing, or unpleasant aspects.

- *As your children learn responsibilities around the house or in schoolwork, make certain that they complete tasks with as high a degree of excellence as possible.* Self-esteem, so essential in future success, is not built from careless and half-completed work. Instill the value of excellence by your example, your teaching, and your training. It's a hard assignment, but the payoff is good!

MOTHERING YOUR PARENTS

It wasn't so long ago that I've forgotten. You never forget sadness over the aging process and the loss of your parents.

During my second pregnancy, my mother suffered a sudden stroke. I was only thirty years old, and I had looked forward to seeing her enjoy the new baby. She did enjoy babies, and after raising seven of them, she knew a great deal about doing so.

As I hurriedly drove nearly two hundred miles to be with her, I wondered if she could recover. She had never seemed healthy or strong, and I felt she might not survive. It was good to be with her, holding her hand, praying a prayer, remembering our good times and those not-so-good experiences.

Some years later, my father developed Alzheimer's disease. His fine mind and sparkling humor faded into memories as his brain deteriorated, slowly at first, but with alarming acceleration later on. My family determined to help him stay at home as long as possible, so we all scheduled ourselves into shifts to take care of him during long, restless nights and frustrating days when his confusion became a routine nightmare. It was a privilege to take my turn on the weekends when I could get away, drive to my old farm home, and care for my father as he had so long before cared for me.

Mothering our parents can be a privilege, and I trust you will see it as that. Perhaps you did not have the blessing of such wonderful parents as mine, and the hurts you endured will make the privilege an unhappy duty. You may, in fact, delegate that responsibility to others. Sometimes that is necessary when care demands skill and equipment you do not have. But as long as possible, and as tenderly as you can, I hope you choose to mother your parents.

There are several areas of care they will need, sooner or later.

- *They will need a safe environment.* The elderly are happier and survive longer with a better quality of life in their own familiar homes. Helping with shopping, cleaning, and upkeep will take time and energy, but I feel it is well-invested.
- *They may at some point require medical and nursing care.* My father-in-law

was a very strong-willed man, and he hated to have anyone telling him what to do. But he refused to get the medical attention he needed. It became our privilege to lovingly but firmly require him to see his doctor and take the medicines he needed.

When bad becomes worse, they may need twenty-four-hour care. Few people can manage this in their homes and still have time for themselves or their children. You may need to practice tough love with your parents, just as you do with your children.

- *Financial management becomes urgent.* The cost of care for senior citizens who need nursing attention becomes exorbitant. So you must plan for the financial needs of your parents. Some senior citizens seem to lose the capacity to care for their own money. They are easy prey to charlatans and may pay bills several times or forget to pay them at all. Be sensitive in this area because older people panic at the possibility of being out of money. Help them manage but discuss their affairs regularly and reassure them of your care.

- *They need to be occupied and busy at something.* Many communities have senior citizen centers, where trained people plan activities and know how to get elderly folks to participate. Require your parents, if you must, to stay as active as they can as long as they can. Seek the advice of their doctor regarding their actual capacity to function.

- *They need plenty of touching.* It's not always easy to hug or even to touch the elderly. Often they become careless of their hygiene, and as they may deteriorate, it seems as if they become strangers. But stroke their heads, gently massage their shoulders, and give them plenty of hugs and kisses. They need loving touches just as we all do! They need to talk with someone who will listen, and most of them have much to say. My sister-in-law made some tape recordings of events her mother discussed. They are precious memories to relive and enjoy. Someday our children will be blessed by them.

- *Whenever possible, take even somewhat incapacitated parents on outings.* A short shopping trip or lunch out is a treat. Of course, you must walk slowly and stop to rest often. Do it anyway! There will be only a limited number of times you can do so, but you'll be glad you did.

A few months before her death, my mother-in-law hesitantly asked a very special favor. I took a day off, and she and I drove some distance to the scenes of her childhood. We saw the schoolhouse where she first taught and tracked the road where she nearly was lost in a blizzard as she returned home after teaching one day. We found many of the old familiar places, now in ruins but alive with memories for her. It was a long day, and I marveled at the energy of this octogenarian. It was the last trip she ever took, and I have been so grateful that I was able to mother her in such a special way.

Preparing special foods, inviting your parents for meals, shopping for warm slippers or new pajamas, finding a delicacy you know they'll relish, remembering to telephone now and then, and sending mementos your children have made—these are just a few ways you can mother your parents. I hope your children will learn from your example.

Self-Care for Mothers

CHAPTER TEN

Honoring Your Personhood

If you are to be the mother you want to be, you must first become the person you can respect and feel good about. And that can be a monumental task.

I grew up in a loving but critical environment. It was not easy to work quickly enough or to do any job quite well enough. Furthermore, I was next to the youngest of seven children. Many of my teachers from junior high on would say, "Oh! You're one of the Horst children. You have a lot to live up to!" To make matters even more difficult, I had an inner yearning to do a terrific job on my assignment, whatever that was. Seldom did I measure up adequately.

Over the first forty years of my life, I exerted relentless energy to try to prove my worth. On professional and social levels as well as in my roles as wife and mother or my place in the church, I tried to do everything I was asked. You can imagine the exhaustion I began to experience! For a while I was clearly depressed. In struggling my way out of that fatigue and depression I learned many things, and I want to share some of them with you in this section.

During my life span of some seven and a half decades, I have observed and experienced many changes in women. We have moved from an era in which many women felt, and were, sorely oppressed to a time of immense freedom. This change has taken place through intensely aggressive work by leaders in the women's movement of the 1960s and beyond. Despite the vast improvements in job opportunities, better pay, and some maternity and child-care benefits, many women feel frustrated and confused by society's expectations but even more by their inner ambivalence.

YOUR WORTH AS A PERSON

As I worked my way painfully through my conflicts, I mastered several lessons. The first involved recognizing that my worth is intrinsic (within me) and is independent of the work I do. I am a being, planned and created by God. What could be a greater endorsement than that?

My peace of mind and joy in living come from inside me, not what others see or how they perceive me to be. Therefore, I no longer had to do whatever people asked of me. I could stop being a people pleaser.

My good feelings no longer depended on others' reaction to me. I no longer found myself saying, "You make me so angry (sad, worried, or whatever)!" People can't make us feel any way we choose not to feel.

A whole new era of creativity, spontaneity, and achievement opened to me. I was rarely afraid to try some new venture, even if it failed. I found that even the hard work and the risks of writing are fun. A new sense of comfort with all types of people grew in me. Since anyone's worth, like my own, depends on the inner being, I no longer stood in awe of the rich and famous, was unafraid of the angry and aggressive, and could even identify with the down-and-out. What a comfortable way to live!

Decision-making became relatively simple because I could choose what was right for me. Previously, I had looked at how my choices or actions would seem to so many people that I was often in a quandary. I simply couldn't please everyone, and the blessed truth was, I no longer needed to try! Paradoxically, I didn't have to become callous or rude, riding roughly over other people, either. Doing the really right thing is usually best for others anyway in the long run.

The mistakes I made and still make, though not to be condoned, are forgivable. Learning from them, correcting the faults as best I can, and forgiving myself enable me to accept and forgive others. My relationships with most people, therefore, are open, positive, and delightful.

Stop being a people pleaser!

Several years ago, I was feeling the pressure of four tasks, each with its unique stress. For a time, I was feeling sorry for myself until it occurred to me that I was most blessed. I couldn't think of another seventy-four-year-old who had my opportunities for service and growth. And none of these would have been possible for me if I hadn't learned to care for myself.

To all the younger mothers, I would love to give a genuine hug and a big share of my hard-earned insights. When a person, book, or magazine article urges you to get out there and prove to the world what you, a woman, can do, tune it out! Think gently for yourself. *Why do you have to prove anything?* Instead, keep looking within yourself. What exciting, lovely traits fill your whole being that you are unaware of? Discover yourself—your emotions, your interests, your capabilities, your weaknesses, your secret yearnings. Accept and love every aspect, even the faults and hurts.

Often in counseling people, I find that they want to get rid of a part of themselves, some ugly, not-so-lovable piece. Once I would have tried to eradicate such undesirable traits. One day, however, I had an unusual experience. As a patient was describing how bad he was, I recalled my son. He regularly tore his jeans, scraped his knees, and became exceedingly dirty. Instead of locking him outside and rejecting his worn, soiled condition, I would pick him up, hug and kiss him, clean him up, and bandage his scrapes. (I wish I had done this every time!) That is a picture of how I try to help people who are torn, bloodied, and aching. Now I try to teach people to love themselves, accept their scars, learn from their mistakes, and integrate all the facets of their lives. And that is what every mother especially needs to do.

I really wish all mothers could see the challenge of child rearing as more vital and rewarding than any other activity in the world. I wish they could all afford to be home with those children, enjoying, guiding, and protecting them. How nice it would be if they could provide for all the basic needs of their children and not have to go to work. But in today's world that is just not the case.

Some women are full of creative energy and need an outlet for what seems significant. These mothers really love their children, but for various reasons, they feel trapped and irritable when they get "stuck" at home too much. They nag and nudge their children, establishing resentments, guilt, and poor bonding. Many of these women are transformed into champion moms when they can work even part-time. Perhaps they need more self-discovery, but maybe they have discovered that some inner part of themselves just has to be expressed outside the home. I can't argue with becoming a better mother through more of that sort of living out of oneself.

One conscientious mother shared an altruistic reason for being away from her children while working at a really demanding job. As they planned for the advent of their first child, her husband offered to take a higher-paying job. It would have enabled her to be at home full-time, but it would have demanded that he be away nearly full-time.

This considerate wife wanted her husband to share in the joys of parenting, so she insisted he keep a job that would allow him to spend time with the children. Their work is planned so that he gets a couple of hours of time with their children before she gets home. Few children in my experience have such a loving and thoughtful set of parents.

ACTIVITIES OUTSIDE THE HOME

Some mothers are so self-centered that it makes you wonder why they chose to have children. Perhaps it was to create the picture-perfect family and gratify their old age. Fortunately, these are not a majority of mothers, but there are enough of them. They look for excuses to find sitters, involve themselves in seemingly glamorous activities, and seem to accept their children only when they are perfect. One cannot imagine them soiling their flawless grooming by picking up a muddy little boy.

Whether your children suffer damage from your activities or working outside the home, then, depends on several factors:

- *Why are you working?* To provide the necessities of life? To allow your husband to be less burdened and therefore more a part of the family? To express the overwhelmingly strong creative urges within you? To avoid the drudgery and monotony of staying at home with children who have multiple needs? So you can dress up, look great, and successfully compete in the workplace? Perhaps only you can tell, but I'll bet your children know. And they can forgive and even respect you for all but the latter reasons. They simply cannot tolerate Mother's working to avoid the inconvenience of mothering.

- *What is your foremost priority?* I was an extremely busy pediatrician when my children were preschoolers. Some days I could control my time and take an active part in their lives. Many days I had no such control and was away for long hours. I was a conscientious doctor, but the high point of my days was always the time spent with my children. I believe they knew that I loved them more than all the rest of the world. That inner commitment goes a long way in compensating for not having all of one's time devoted to them.

  Nevertheless, if I could do it over, there is only one change I would make in my life. I would have left most of my time free for my children (and husband) while they were preschoolers. I feel that the demands on my time robbed me of some of the exquisite joy each of them brought to my life.

- *How guilty do you feel?* Let's review the destructive impact of maternal guilt. If you feel guilty about working and being away from your children too much, you are more than likely to undo your good discipline. In your attempts to make up for being away, you may overspend your energy cooking, doing housework, and acting as if you were a full-time mother. You may be afraid to solicit your children's help so they can be carefree, happy kids.

  Actually, a benefit of the mother's working is the necessity for everyone to help. Being useful in the family is a great boost to a child's self-esteem. Don't let guilt feelings damage your mothering skills. We'll discuss guilt more later.

- *How well can you organize your at-home time?* You can learn to keep a neat house that is comfortable without spending large amounts of time on it. Children can do many household chores well enough. Simple meals can be shared in a happy mood much more easily than gourmet meals that leave you too tired to smile. Keep your household duties to a minimum.

Schedule time to play, read, and just talk or be quiet together. The genuineness of your love will be felt even with few words. Don't forget, though, that everyone needs to be told, "I love you" frequently, with a big hug and a warm smile.

Using a daily calendar for your housekeeping duties may be helpful. Write into each hour some activity that must be done or that you simply want to do. Include time for yourself as well.

Try to limit your children's activities. Many children have special classes or group activities several evenings a week. Whether you're a working mom or not, I urge you to limit those to one or two a week.

Having family time is far more valuable than participating in lots of busy work. The family should share in the activities your children choose. Many depressed children have told me they are sad because Dad doesn't attend their functions, or at times, even Mom doesn't show up. Children often perceive their parents' failure to "be there" for them as a message that they are not important.

Certainly, there will be times when you just can't get to some event. Let the child know how much you'd like to, and show your interest by asking about it and all that happened.

KEEPING PRIORITIES IN ORDER

Using your common sense, keeping your priorities in order, genuinely expressing your love and pride—all of these can enable you to raise well-rounded kids, even if you are a working mom.

I haven't always taken the best care of myself, but I'm learning to do that. So I'm telling you, start now!

Acknowledge that you are worth taking care of. As a child of God, you really are, so believe that, and act like it. Remember, your worth is based on who you are inside, not on your weight, what brand of clothes you wear, your status in your community, or the size of your bank account.

HOW TO TAKE CARE OF YOURSELF

If you were telling a friend or your child to take care of herself, where would you start? I suggest these specific steps:

- Find some humor and laugh every day.
- Do something creative every day, such as needlework, a new recipe, a change in your furniture arrangement, or a new hairstyle. Make this a project you enjoy.
- Do something for yourself. Relax, take a bubble bath, sit in the sun,

read a few pages, or mellow out in front of a TV or with some good music. Only a few minutes of doing something just for yourself can remind you that you really are important.

- Decide how you want to look, and work toward that goal. You may need to gain or lose weight, change your style of dressing or makeup, or cut your hair. Don't be afraid to try some changes, though I generally suggest doing them gradually.
- Hire a baby-sitter now and then. Time off alone or with your husband, sister, friend, or mother can rejuvenate you.
- Begin to take charge of your life. Your time, your emotions, your budget, and your attitudes are much more controllable than you may believe. I have yet to find total control possible because of the unexpected, but you will like every area that begins to come into balance with the whole of your life.
- You are a spiritual being. Find ways to refresh that spiritual aspect. Knowing that God loves you and He will provide for your every need can be the most comforting and strengthening thought of your day.
- Get enough rest and exercise. Each person requires different amounts of rest and different types of exercise. Decide what your needs are and discipline yourself to take care of them.
- Eat properly. There are many books and articles on healthy nutrition. Most people know the basic foods needed; it's a matter of self-control to adhere to healthy diets.

Love God; love yourself; take care of yourself; and love others, especially your children and husband. Let yourself receive love from others. Don't try to follow everyone else's ideas or agree necessarily with their opinions. Think clearly and deeply, and with God's guidance, make choices that are good for you.

Fathers

CHAPTER ELEVEN

Respecting Your Children's Father

Because this book is written primarily about mothering, I have emphasized the relationship with your children. Nevertheless, your relationship with your children's father is also of immense importance. Your opinion of him, your respect for him, and your commitment to him affect the whole family.

Some excellent studies have now been done regarding the vital importance of fathers. Psychologist John Snarey from Emory University published a forty-year-old study of some 250 dads in the Boston area. He found that sons were more successful academically when their dads stayed involved through adolescence. Daughters who had their dads' support were more successful in athletic achievements.

Throughout the recorded history of the Old Testament, fathers were noted for offering guidance, passing on the family inheritance, and maintaining the security of the extended family. Modern research is just now catching up with God's wisdom.

In earlier times, fathers' and mothers' roles were clearly defined, if not always followed. In fact, the cunning device of Rachel, the wife of the

Jewish patriarch Isaac, tells of the historic power of women. Jacob, the second-born twin, was her favored child. And when it was time for Isaac to confer the blessing or legacy on the elder son, she found a clever way to foil this age-old tradition. Rachel disguised Jacob to feel and smell like Esau, the rightful heir, and so she obtained for him his blind father's inheritance. She also set up conditions for a lifelong feud between the twin brothers.

That biblical illustration indicates the pain that can be caused by parental disagreement. Children are extremely quick to figure out which parent will give in, pamper, and indulge them. They are so set on getting their way that they will take advantage of your weakness and those conflicts with your husband to further their selfish interests.

Therefore, your major task as a mother is to get in tandem with your children's father. If you are currently married to him, you need to keep your communication and your basic relationship up to par every day. That means you work through disagreements to a negotiated harmony before bedtime. Avoid thinking, *If he doesn't do things the way I want, I'll just leave him. He'll really have to pay then.* And men must heed this same information. Be committed to each other and the family. Stick together closely enough that your children will not be able to become a wedge between you.

When I was young, we used wood to heat the rooms of our farm home. Often the chunks my father sawed from a huge log were too big to get into the heating stove. Sometimes my task was to split those chunks. I used a heavy iron wedge, sharp on one side and blunt on the other. A blow on the blunt side with a sledgehammer sent that wedge into the wood. A few more blows and the wood fell apart in the right-sized pieces. Whenever I think of parents allowing children to separate them, I see that picture. A solid piece can be broken with constant pounding against it.

The tragedy for the children lies in the price tag of guilt. Although they want their way and are willing to manipulate to get it, they don't feel right about this splitting process. They'd really rather their parents would get together, establish some ground rules, and create law and order. However, since their parents are divisible, and they also want their way, they seem compelled to pursue their bad habits. You can stop them by refusing to accept that very first hammer blow. Stick together firmly and consistently.

Creating and maintaining a strong marriage demands total commitment to some clear, basic principles. And it certainly requires daily, loving, and honest communication. It also is improved by the magic of X-ray vision. If you can see below the surface behaviors to the needs and feelings underneath, you will handle tense moments and grouchy moods with less sensitivity and avoid the wish to escape.

HONEYMOON VERSUS REALITY

In Western society, we have a romantic concept of marriage. In much of the rest of the world, marriages are arranged for convenience, economic reasons, or family traditions. Sometimes I wonder if these philosophies are wiser, but that could be another book!

At any rate, the fantasies and wishes of courtship are not likely to last long in most real marriages. Those faults you could overlook when you were dating become daily frictions. The idea that he will magically change after marriage or that you can make him change is soon realized to be false. His personality is set, as is yours. Now let me hasten to say: habits can change, understanding each other's needs and weaknesses can make adjustment easier, but nothing is likely to make your marriage perfect. So don't expect it, and you won't be disappointed.

EXPLORE, DON'T EXPECT

Once you settle down to the reality rather than the impossible dreams you once held, you have some challenging work to do. I call that work exploring. I hope you have some memories of exploring in the woods or on the seashore. I love to walk along the beach after high tide. You just don't know what treasures may be lurking under the next ripple of sand.

Exploring your husband and your marriage can be like that—exciting and fun discoveries are there. You just have to expend some energy, practice some optimism and faith, and keep your expectations positive. I try to keep my expectations few because often reality does not correspond to expectations.

> *Your major task as a mother is to get in tandem with your children's father.*

My son-in-law taught me a weakness in this philosophy, though. He believes that every husband and wife should have some "bottom-line" expectations. For example, each should expect loyalty, support, teamwork, and faithfulness. Expecting too little, he says, can give each other permission to do things that are good neither for each other nor for the couple. Once again, it's a matter of balance.

Back to exploring. Try to discover all you can about your husband. Find out details about his parents and their parents and the entire family tree. Ask about his childhood. Did he like school? What were his friends like? Did he ever suffer punishments? What were those events like? What did he do to merit correction, and did he learn from the experiences he endured? Try to avoid being judgmental about the goodness or badness of the information you acquire, but weave together all the facts to help you know, understand, and love more completely the man you married.

I advise you to gain your information slowly so you can incorporate it wisely. A question here or a listening ear there is a better source of knowledge than a lengthy interrogation session. If you inquire too intensely, you may look nosy or invasive, and your husband could resent that. Above all, never use the information you collect against your husband. A good wife, says Proverbs 31, will do only good to her husband all of her days.

ACCEPT HIM UNCONDITIONALLY

I hate to admit it, but I was one of those wives who thought her love could change her husband. I am enthralled by nature. A golden dawn or a brilliant red sunset puts me in a state of wonder and awe. So does the grand show of power as a thunderstorm reverberates through the mountains. The ocean holds unending fascination for me.

I was certain that I could teach my husband to revel in and philosophize over nature just as I did. He is the sort of person who says of those majestic mountains, "If you've seen one, Honey, you've seen 'em all. Why do you want to see any more mountains?" Nevertheless, I tried. I tried for years!

One year our family took an exotic vacation to the Hawaiian Islands. We loved the shops and beaches and admired Diamond Head. We could imagine a big volcanic eruption on the island of Hawaii. But on one of the smaller islands, I had to face the Big Truth.

This particular island had been left largely primal as it had been since it grew up out of the ocean by God's designing hand. The foliage was lush, and the palm trees perfectly trimmed the lone hotel on the beach. After the children were asleep, I strolled out on the white sand beach. It was still warm from the tropical sun, but a cool breeze kept me comfortable. A full moon smiled down benignly, and the orchestra played melancholy island music, it seemed, just for me.

As I dug my bare toes in the sand and shivered with the exquisite beauty in which I was immersed, I felt I had to share so much joy! Shaking the sand out of my sandals, I slipped them on and returned to our room. There was my husband, reading the latest issue of his coin collector's magazine. You see, he loves art, collecting, and all sorts of man-made beauty. I tried to describe the indescribable beauty waiting just outside our hotel and invited him to join me.

Deeply engrossed in what he was reading, he politely declined my invitation. I couldn't believe he really meant that, so I asked again, but this time I knew he was serious. Almost without conscious thought, both of us realized it was time for me to quit trying to change my husband.

Alone, and feeling lonely, I trudged back to my place in the sand. The beauty there was unchanged, silent and magnificent. But I was changing. I sat and cried for a long time over the final loss of my dream. My husband could not experience the same insatiable thirst for nature that I'd had since childhood. *I* was the one who must change. I realized the tears in my eyes were clouding my joy, so I wiped them away.

That night I made a major decision: I would no longer try to make my husband different from what he was. I would accept him unconditionally, but I also resolved that I would not let him or my own sadness deprive me of the joy I could feel. Since that time, more than four decades have come and gone. I'm still growing in understanding unconditional love, but that was my turning point.

One facet of this discovery is the awareness of a vast difference between *can't* and *won't*. A wife is tempted to believe that a husband who is not changing is simply stubborn: "He just won't change!" What I faced that night on the beach was much more accurate. He could not change. His values and interests had been cultivated from early childhood, just as mine had been. They were different, that was all.

Once I recovered from the grief of that loss of a big dream, I once again explored. What were the interests we could find and share? There were many, and we are still exploring and discovering.

See Your Children As They Are

A few years ago I sat with a young mother of a troubled child, exploring how the child's problems had occurred and what we could do to help. As I questioned and listened, she gave me some insights.

Her father had made life frightening for her. He worked hard, but he also drank hard, and when he drank, he became explosively angry. She learned to tiptoe around him and gave in to his slightest command to avoid his anger.

Looking back, this mother could see that the subservience she had practiced had set her up for a tragic marriage. Her husband drank and abused drugs, and when he was drunk, he had an abusive temper. Fortunately, she finally escaped that situation and had recently married a truly fine, loving man. She feared that her new husband might become like the other two men in her life.

Understand that each person is not an unavoidable force who can control you.

She loved her son and wanted to see him mature happily, developing his potential. But the lad was beginning to act like his father. He was becoming manipulative and controlling. And his mother was beginning to allow him to control her exactly as her father and her first husband did. She could see the pattern being repeated, and she was wise and strong enough to stop it. She had real hope for constructive changes.

Perhaps your father abused or neglected you. He may have indulged and spoiled you, keeping you dependent on his making you happy. Those early imprints on your developing personality can be very hard to erase, but keep working. You can eventually discover your strength, your child can be a child, not a carbon copy of one of your parents, and you can even work things out better with your husband in some cases. The secret is this: understand that each person is not an unavoidable force who can control you.

BELIEVE THAT YOUR HUSBAND LOVES YOUR CHILDREN

If you were fortunate enough to have a wise and loving father, count your blessings. The chances of your husband's being just like your father, however, are quite small. When he is more intense and harsh than your father was or than you feel is good, you may fear that he does not love his children. And you may instinctively try to protect them from his anger. Doing this is damaging in distinct ways. It sets up their father to be mean and frightening, a man to be avoided. It makes the children feel powerless and may encourage them to hide behind you. It keeps children from ever really resolving issues with Dad and discovering that he has their best interests at heart. It estranges you from your husband as you grow more and more resentful of his methods.

Your husband is his own person, and you must respect that. If he is too harsh, tell him that later on, after you two are alone, or have your children tell him how frightened they feel when he yells too loudly. Believe that every dad wants to be a good father.

Many do not know very well how to be great fathers, but they mean to be! So expect the best; interpret to your children that Daddy really wants them to grow up to be well-rounded people, and if they respect him and are obedient and cooperative, he won't feel he has to be so intense. As you support him more, you will see problems getting solved.

What About the Bad Guy You Divorced?

Perhaps nothing besides abuse is so distressing to a child as divorce. Even the spouse who initiates a divorce in many cases goes through great turmoil and grief in the process of that separation.

Some months ago I listened to a class of gifted high schoolers discuss the issue of divorce. One exceptionally thoughtful young man stated, "After going through seven years of my parents' being divorced, I can say it would have been easier if one of them had died!" He went on to describe the divided loyalty, the parents' constant bickering, and his feeling caught between them.

It seems to me that getting a divorce gives husbands and wives a license to stay angry and to fight as long as they live. And their fights enlist recruits from their entire families and their friends. Obviously, any divorce evolves from pain, misunderstandings, and personal blind spots. Most partners do not enter into marriage intending such misery. Instead, they lack the ability to look beyond their hurts to the pain of the spouse. They rarely can see what they have done to contribute to that pain, though each can clearly see what the other has done! Furthermore, divorcing couples have immense communication gaps, so clearing up misunderstandings becomes rare.

Children are amazingly perceptive about their parents' difficulties. Matt is an example. His grades had been slipping. He was moody and fought with his sister more frequently than usual. As he talked with me, sadness exuded from his posture, his face, and his voice. The core of his trouble was the fear that his parents were going to get a divorce. Later I talked with his parents, and they seemed genuinely puzzled as to why Matt would imagine such a thing.

But just a few months later, Matt's mother called me in tears. The couple were, in fact, in the midst of divorce. "How did he know?" Matt's mother asked. He knew because he wasn't caught in their intense emotions and power struggles. He could see those telltale signs both of them missed.

Children certainly can't manage families or counsel parents, but if you will listen, they have a certain wise intuition that can give you a clearer picture of your problems than you may be able to see alone. Don't lay a burden of responsibility to solve your problems on your children. But talk with them and think seriously about their comments.

As a mother in a divorce, you are likely to have primary, or at least equal, custody of your children. They are likely to spend the major part of their time with you. Furthermore, I think mothers have some intuition that tips them off about the issues and children's needs and feelings connected with them. I urge you, then, to finish your divorce, if you must have one, emotionally.

Many, if not most, divorces are completed legally with some speed. They can be remarkably easy. What does not happen with such rapidity is the emotional divorce. As long as you remain hurt, angry, or vindictive or try to get even, you cannot be emotionally separate.

First of all, avoid divorce if at all possible. Only for serious abuse or neglect do I see a good reason for separation, and some people can convincingly argue against any reason being valid for breaking up a family. Only you can decide about your situation, but think carefully and unselfishly before you take such action.

Next, be extremely thoughtful about severing your emotional ties to your husband before you begin legal action. Doing so is a process that demands understanding of both partners. You need to know why he has done the things (or neglected to do them) that have hurt you. It helps if you can admit the actions you have done (or failed to do) that have fed into the cycle of trouble. If there is any hope of mending a broken relationship, it is at this point of awareness that you, too, have faults.

Third, if mending is still impossible, seek a loving divorce. I know that sounds unrealistic, but it is possible if you understand tough love. Divorce attorneys are likely to make this action difficult. In trying to protect your interests, they often raise doubts you would not have considered. Their questions can resurrect old resentments that you had forgotten. So take time, think for yourself, and stay committed to keeping the process of divorce as constructive, fair, and positive for the children as possible.

This process of understanding, forgiving, and relinquishing is absolutely essential if your children are to be free to love and forgive their father.

Furthermore, all children know they are blessed with some of their dad's traits as well as yours. They need to see some good in him if they are to feel good about themselves. You can teach your children to arrest the development of bad characteristics in their personalities. Whether undesirable qualities are learned from Dad or from you, help your children overcome them as much as possible before they become too habitual.

If their father is not absolutely damaging to them, urge him to attend their school and sporting events. Remind him of their birthdays or other holidays that he might forget. Try to expect the best of him and encourage that habit in your children. If he fails to keep his visiting times with them or is late, help your children understand that is not because they are unimportant or he doesn't love them. He is simply involved in a different life and can't always make things fit. This suggestion is aimed not at making Dad look better than he is but at helping children maintain their self-esteem.

Here are some common pitfalls to avoid if you are a divorced mother:

- Don't make Dad look like a mean monster. Explain his faults that made the divorce take place. It's wise to include your role as well.
- Don't use the children as messengers to carry information back and forth.
- Don't allow your children to become spies to discover and report Dad's business.
- Don't compete to prove who is the better parent.
- Don't use manipulation to keep your children away from their dad. If there is danger of his abusing or neglecting them, seek legal help to curtail visits or arrange for supervised visits.
- Don't exclude your children from their dad's family, unless they could in some way damage the children. Grandparents are a link to the children's past and are extremely important in their identity. If you disapprove of some of their father's actions or values, teach your children what you see is wrong about them. Avoid any attacks on Dad's character.
- Avoid labels and name-calling. Keep child support and other responsibility issues between you and their dad. Children are quick to judge and condemn or take sides over any disagreement, especially regarding money.

Not long ago, a friend of mine attended a baseball game in which her grandson was a star. She was delighted that both his father and his stepfather were coaching that team, with the full support and encouragement of his mother. The boy did not need to feel anxious, because the two men were working together for his good. If you can create an environment in which that sort of teamwork can take place, you can avoid most of the destructive impact on your children that is so typical of divorce.

Stages

CHAPTER TWELVE

Pregnancy, Birth, and Infants

*E*ach developmental stage has unique tasks to be accomplished and goals to be reached. Unless these are successfully done, the succeeding levels of growth and development will be weakened, and the ultimate personality will be less healthy than it might have been. Build these foundations well by understanding each stage in a child's life.

PRENATAL

In Section One, I discussed your pregnancy and what you need to do to establish the rudiments of the bonding process. Here I'll briefly summarize your functions in the prenatal period.

Control the amount of stress to which you subject yourself. There are always stress factors over which you have little control, but learn to avoid worry and anxiety as much as possible. Resist any burdens that you do not have to assume. For example, if you are pressured to the maximum, don't accept any volunteer assignments, and don't begin any big projects such as redecorating your home or starting a new job.

Stress causes your endocrine glands to secrete many chemicals called hormones into your body. Some people believe these hormones may stimulate your baby to become more tense or hyperactive even before birth. It certainly seems likely that such a possibility exists.

To cope with the stress that you cannot avoid, try the following simple but useful steps:

- Think clearly about the cause of the stress, and be sure you understand the source of the pressures.
- Make a definite plan for managing the issues or problems. In this plan include a realistic timetable and a list of people or other resources to help you if you need them.
- Take action to carry out those steps until they are completed and the stress is over. This step is essential. It is easy to procrastinate, so the plan won't work and even more stress stacks up.
- Be sure to think about your baby. Imagine him or her as a real little person, living intimately within you, but already a separate human being.

PHYSICAL CARE

You need only a reminder here to balance rest and exercise, healthy eating and weight control, good grooming and attractive dressing. Avoid taking pain relievers and tranquilizers. Use only the chemicals your doctor prescribes. Stay away from crowds and sick friends for the first three months. Viral infections are not very treatable and may affect your baby's health, so anything you can do to avoid them will be to your advantage.

Preparing for your baby's arrival is a wonderful experience. I urge you to sew something for the baby. If you can read, you can follow pattern instructions, and using a sewing machine is not really too big a challenge. There is something basic about creating at least part of the baby's layette; it makes you aware of your active role in protecting and warming your baby. If you just cannot sew, at least add a ribbon or a bit of lace to articles you buy to make them uniquely your own.

Include your baby's father in as many functions as possible. Be certain he, too, becomes part of the bonding process. Let him share your excitements, concerns, and discomforts, but try not to complain constantly to him.

It is possible during the many uncomfortable times that you may feel sorry for yourself. You may very well wonder why you ever began this process of becoming a mother and wish you had never thought of it. These times offer you an opportunity to give in and be childish (a poor practice if you want to be a good mother) or to learn the maturing process of patience, transcending the pain, looking to the future, and learning how to become a wise and wonderful mother.

Remember, it is not easy or convenient to be a mom. You need practice now to put others' needs ahead of your own; to postpone present pleasure or even comfort for future good; to adapt to change with growing commitment; to organize and prioritize demands and responsibilities. Build into these processes of anticipation and personal growth the habit of seeking help.

Our culture promotes being strong and independent, and when we must function independently, it is good to be able to do so. But babies and new mothers need plenty of help, so don't be reluctant to ask for it. From now on, there will be many times that you will be enriched and your mothering enhanced by seeking many kinds of help.

BIRTH PROCESS

One of the most dramatic times of need is during the birth process itself. Every expectant mother has some anxiety that some complication may arise to make delivery a nightmare. Be certain someone is with you. Ideally, it should be your baby's father.

For a variety of reasons, he may not be able to be with you, though.

Instead of feeling angry or sorry, look for a stand-in. A friend or relative may be honored and delighted to be with you. Let someone know you need that presence!

Be sure you talk with your doctor enough to really get to know him. Tell him your lurking fears and how much you dread the pains. He can reassure you and describe the processes of labor and delivery in a way that can relieve most of your fears.

If you go to a clinic where there are several doctors, it is more difficult to build that basic confidence. Do whatever you can to select one physician and request appointments with her as often as possible.

For a while it was fashionable for mothers to have natural childbirth, avoiding any anesthesia to relieve pain. I have also seen obstetricians use too much anesthesia, and frankly, I believe that practice creates unnecessary risks. But avoiding all pain relief seems equally deplorable.

Having a mild local anesthetic to make the last stages of labor and delivery more bearable is wise. You will relax and get through labor more safely and regain your strength more promptly if you are not utterly exhausted from a difficult labor.

You are also more likely to bond well with your baby if you have had some relief from the pain of childbirth. The almost mystical process of bonding enables a mother to totally accept the baby she has in her arms into her heart. Bonded mothers enjoy holding and gazing at their babies.

In a postgraduate course I attended several years ago, the lecturer quoted a study of bonding. He stated that if a mother had extended periods of gazing into the eyes of her baby during the first six weeks of life, that child would not have serious emotional or mental illness as an adult. Being unable to locate the studies behind that statement, I can only philosophize. But surely that eye contact, with the physical closeness it demands, must be a major function of bonding.

So hold your infant, gaze into those eyes, and allow them to penetrate to your very soul. Feed, rock, cuddle, coo, and talk with your child. Take plenty of time away, as well, to replenish your energy. Bonding will enrich your life experience and lay the foundation for your child's health.

I don't want you to believe that the bonding process ends at six weeks. It goes on in its many variations throughout life. The closeness obviously changes, and the quality will differ with age. But I can assure you, I am still bonded with my mother and grandmother in many meaningful ways. And I am also bonded with my adult children and grandchildren. Bonding begins a lifelong pattern of security and warmth in all relationships.

INFANTS

I hope you will be able to hold your baby as soon as he is born. Even before the cleaning procedures, you can hold and focus on that tiny human being who has just entered the world outside your body. The wonder of it all can best be grasped when he is brand-new. If this experience is denied you, you are most likely to see your baby first all bundled up in a cap, shirt, diaper, and blanket—a neat little package.

I'm embarrassed to admit it, but that was my experience as a new mom. I was intimidated by the starchy, efficient nurses and their tightly wrapped little bundle who was my child. I'll always love the diminutive English nurse who brought my first baby to me the day we went home. She casually but lovingly tossed her tiny frame onto my bed. She unwrapped the baby and pointed out the long, graceful fingers. "She'll be a great piano player someday!" that nurse, now my dear friend, prophesied. Her casual, relaxed, and kindly manner was the first bit of ease and comfort I had felt.

When you are handed your baby, take off the blanket and examine those fingers and toes. Inspect the little ears and button nose. Take off the cap for a minute and feel the incredibly soft hair (if there is any). Trace the face with your finger and feel the soft skin of the tummy and little legs and arms. This is your baby. Enjoy her! Touching, seeing, hearing, and even smelling that tiny person are the ways you become acquainted.

When you nurse your baby, take time and ask for help. Most babies need a little encouragement, and all new mothers need a lot of it. Your breasts become swollen and tender, and the nipples get cracked and painful. Follow the advice of your nurse and doctor, and don't give up. Nursing your baby is a great experience, once you master it. Your milk is baby's ideal food and offers some protection against infections.

Perhaps the greatest blessing of nursing, however, has to do with bonding. In no other way, I believe, can you recognize your total importance to your child and her utter dependence on you. Anyone can feed a bottle to any baby. But only a mother can nurse her own baby, offering life, growth, and health from her body.

The Major Goal of Infancy

The purpose of bonding with your baby and learning how to meet his many needs is to teach trust. The consistency with which you respond to the baby's hunger, discomforts, or loneliness determines the strength of that trust. It will take some time to find the right balance. Crying for five or ten minutes at a stretch is not going to hurt any baby. But go to him before the crying starts at times, so he won't believe that you care only when he cries.

Always try to handle your baby with strength. If you, a new mother, are as nervous and intimidated as I was, you may have difficulty. When you are shaky and tense, your baby will feel tense, also, and crying is likely to result. Take time to be calm, think about how big you are and how tiny she is, and I think you can establish the confidence both you and your baby will thrive on. It's better for your baby to cry alone for a while so you can rest and regain your strength than for you to become too exhausted.

To maintain your strength, you need to have help. Don't hesitate to ask a friend or relative to watch your baby for an hour now and then. Take a walk, go shopping, or just relax. Your independence is not totally lost. Allow all but the most urgent household tasks to wait for the baby's first few months. You will have time to catch up later.

As your baby grows, you will discover some new reasons for his crying and the needs that sound expresses. The sudden bang of a door, a dog's barking, or any loud noise can frighten a baby. Fear is always expressed through a shrill cry accompanied by a look of surprise that quickly becomes an expression of terror. A frightened or even startled child needs reassurance and comfort. Hold a fearful child, rock him gently, speak to him softly, and explore the source of the stimulus that prompted the fear. Even if your child does not talk, he can understand a great deal. Show your child the dog that barked, and if possible, pet the dog. Explain the siren, the bell, or even the noise of your vacuum or lawn mower. Encourage your child to touch the equipment when and where it is safe to do so. Your calmness and instruction will relieve the immediate fear and will build the confidence in your child that only knowledge and experience bring.

The purpose of bonding with your baby and learning to meet his needs is to teach trust.

Babies become angry when they are in pain or when they cannot have what they want. I have felt the angry hitting of eighteen-month-olds, and that really smarts. Being hit makes one instinctively feel like striking back, and I often see mothers do exactly that. That response is a big mistake because it puts you on the child's level.

Here is what I have learned to do instead. I pick up an angry child, if necessary restraining the flailing arms. Looking the angry child carefully in the eyes, I firmly say, "You may not hit! It hurts when you slap me, and I don't allow such actions." I try to get my facial expression to match my tone of voice, and I really do mean what I say. Then I tell the child what is acceptable to do when anger assails. She may hit a pounding board, a sofa, or a pillow, but people are not for hitting. When such a message becomes clear and is consistently taught at this early age, you are likely to have a much better behaved and wiser two-year-old.

CONSISTENCY

The way you respond to your child's needs helps build trust. You must be predictable. Many mothers think consistency means being totally patient, kind, and soft-spoken, no matter what the situation. Let me correct that fallacy. Not only is such a maternal response inadvisable, it is also impossible!

Perhaps the most important aspect of discipline is the careful formulation of a plan.

If your child is about to deliberately spill a bowl of cereal and milk on your clean kitchen floor, you need to act firmly and quickly to prevent that. A decisive "Don't spill your cereal!" may well avert a small disaster. Such a clear, firm order should help your child understand that food is not for playing and that you mean what you say. Of course, you need to take that bowl and restore it to its rightful place on the high chair or in the kitchen sink. (Usually, a child's playing with food or eating utensils indicates she is through eating, so leftovers should be removed.)

You do not ever need to speak in a rude or mean manner to your child. But you do need to be clear, firm, and no-nonsense with him. I am increasingly aware that mothers must avoid hitting or slapping children. Instead use firmness, gentle restraint, and absolute follow-through.

Read each situation involving your child accurately and clearly and respond appropriately:

- If the child is in danger, act quickly and decisively to protect your child and her environment.

- If the child exhibits defiance or rebellion, take time to work through such resistance. (Often the best approach is simply waiting for obedience.)
- If the child is trying to charm or be clever in behavior or play, show pride and pleasure.
- If the child is in pain or fearful, offer comfort or reassurance.
- If the child is lonely or bored, offer your presence and some change in activity.
- If the child is excited over a new discovery (such as a squirrel or bird or Dad's new garden tools), share that excitement and express your joy and pleasure.
- If the child has a smile and a hug just for you, return them warmly and delightedly. And initiate such love frequently.
- If the child is angry, look for the pain that prompted it, and find ways to heal it.

Consistency means that in similar situations you react the same, day in and day out. It equally means that in each different situation, you will react quite differently from all others. I hope this explanation will make it easier for you to respond to your child with appropriate and loving consistency.

ATTITUDES

The way you feel inside and the beliefs you hold combine to form your attitudes. If you feel worried and you believe that worrying proves you care about people, your attitude will be one of deep concern and even anxiety. If you feel angry and you believe that mothers should be stern disciplinarians, you are likely to have a critical or harsh attitude.

A dear friend of mine told me this moving story about her baby. He was just a year old when he experienced his first earache. He was awake and crying most of the night but fell asleep just before dawn. My friend finally went to sleep when he grew quiet. In only an hour, however, when the sun came up, he awakened, all smiles, feeling just fine.

He loudly called out for his mother. She awoke so tired, she felt and acted grouchy. She stomped into the child's room to try to meet his needs, but only when she saw his bright morning smiles evaporate into somberness did she realize what her attitude did to her son. She wept as she described his response. "No mother," she said, "has the right to rob her child of a smile!"

At stress points like this episode, the critical importance of your maturity becomes clear. If you can postpone the pleasure of your needed rest to lovingly and patiently meet the needs of a sick child, you are indeed a mature mother.

But if you allow yourself to become easily frustrated, maintaining an attitude of impatience and domination, you are likely to make some tragic mistakes. You may create a climate of fear in which your child draws away from you. And you put yourself at risk for abusing your child. Don't take such a risk. Instead, make yourself think clearly, respond slowly, taking time to control your feelings, and then handle situations with the gentleness of real strength.

Without realizing it, many mothers have high expectations of themselves and their children. They feel let down and even angry when those goals are not achieved. It seems better, to me, that we open our minds to the possibilities of each child. Of what is he or she really capable? How can those possibilities be translated into actualities? What can we do to facilitate such a process? Such an open and positive attitude can hardly fail.

EARLY DISCIPLINE

Many parents ask me when they should start training and disciplining their children. Actually, you start that at birth and even before. Your attitudes are formed from your beliefs about what children should do and how to make them do those things. Your attitudes and beliefs will also mold your mothering practices.

Indulgence is a very dangerous practice. When I talked with several friends about current mothering issues, we all agreed that too many mothers are overly anxious about children's crying. They give in to children's whims and tantrums if they cry loudly or pitifully long enough.

Trying to always keep children smiling and happy is a huge mistake. Happiness is natural when children are loved, corrected, and protected. We all enjoy a smiling, loving child, but we have reason to fear the child who smiles because she is a tyrant and has acquired absolute subservience from her mother.

> *Trying to always keep children smiling and happy is a mistake. If you are tempted to give in to your child against your good judgment and her best interests, don't!*

If you are even tempted to give in to your child against your good judgment and her best interests, quickly avoid that temptation.

Babies are *not* spoiled by tickling, singing, talking, cuddling, and attention, given freely. They are spoiled when mothers give such attentions in a servile response to their whining demands. An eighteen-month-old child who wants a cookie before dinner will not be likely to eat a good meal if he is given that cookie. He is likely to cry and have a little fit if he is not given it.

It's easier to give him the sweet than to deal with his frustration. But look ahead a dozen years. Will you still be giving in to his demands for getting his way when that could risk his safety in really big ways? It's so much easier now to win the struggle for self-control and boundary setting.

I have a technique for coping with the demands of babies. First, be clear in your thinking about the privileges and activities that are in her best interest. Explain to her what you will or will not allow. If she throws a fit, gently but firmly hold her in your arms until the tantrum is over.

Then with good eye contact, tell her you are sorry she was disappointed at not getting her way, but screaming and kicking will not work. When you, her mother, set a limit, nothing she does will change your mind. Then let her know you love her and tell her what she can have or can do. After a few struggles, your child will give up those tantrums. Then you can really enjoy and love each other.

Perhaps the most important aspect of discipline is the formulation of a careful plan. Refuse to impulsively react to your child. Instead, build a philosophy of child rearing that will result in a positive relationship for a lifetime.

Not long ago I attended a college graduation party for a friend. As I talked with her mother, I learned that many years earlier, she and her daughter had become friends. On the basis of that relationship, training and discipline had become easier, and their success was evident.

As soon as you have the time and energy, begin to think and talk about the essential goals you will set for your children. You can't determine their future, nor should you choose their eventual careers. But you can consider what you want your children to believe, how they will behave, and, simply, who they will be. Let me offer you some ideas.

GOALS OF DISCIPLINE

- *One goal is to have a child who is respectful.* Your task now is to show respect to him and to your spouse.
- *You want your child to show respect for authority by being obedient.* Ask compliance of your child regarding simple tasks. Help her to do as you ask every time. At this age, patiently work with her and show her how to do the tasks.
- *You may want your child to be assertive or to stand up for herself.* Teach her to express her needs, feelings, and wishes. Don't give in to her too easily, and don't give in at all if she wants things she shouldn't have.

- *You want your child to develop physical skills.* Then you must exercise that little body and patiently encourage the creeping, standing, and playing that teach skills. Observe your baby and encourage him only within the boundaries of his readiness. Never compare him with another child—only with himself.

- *Perhaps you would like your child to love music or even perform musically.* Although she may not have the innate skills to make that possible, you can encourage her interests. Sing to her, play recordings of simple tunes, and expose her to many types of music.

- *Reading and intellectual pursuits may be your goal.* Then read to your child. Expose him to all the events of childhood that could arouse healthy curiosity, and when he can talk and comprehend, talk with him. As early as seven or eight months, babies can enjoy simple, bright pictures. Now don't go so far as trying to teach him to read. Just arouse his interest in books.

  My grandson's great-grandmother and I shared in making for him cloth books containing the alphabet and numbers. Each page has only one letter or number, and every one is a different color or texture. These were made from scraps and cost almost nothing, but they are full of love.

- *Social skills may be of great value to you.* Early on, find opportunities to be with people. As soon as possible, teach your child to smile and wave at others. Sorry, but these days, you must also practice some caution about reaching out too much to strangers.

Undergirding your teaching these qualities to your child must be the ongoing building of the bonds of love and trust between her and you. Love becomes the ultimate motivator to give up a child's natural selfishness to become someone worthwhile.

(For more information, see "Discipline and Punishment" in Chapter 9.)

PHYSICAL EXPECTATIONS

Perfectly normal children are vastly different from one another. This variation is true in every aspect of life. But in the first two years, it is especially true of *physical development.*

My niece began walking alone at seven months of age, my children walked at about a year, and the average age for first steps is about thirteen months. The age at which a child sits, stands, and walks depends on the child, so don't worry and don't compare. Do go to your pediatrician or family physician for regular checkups. He or she will let you know if there is any serious delay and what to do about it. Many mothers become overly anxious about these developmental stages.

Help your baby crawl if she does not do so naturally. Most babies crawl by pushing and pulling up from lying on their tummies. They push their knees under their abdomen and then raise their shoulders by pulling their arms (elbows) under them. Gradually, they discover how to move one limb after the other to get close to a toy or to you. Encourage this because a neurological development seems to progress better from the alternate motion of front-to-back and side-to-side coordination that takes place during creeping.

A few months after children begin to walk, they can learn to manage stairs. Enclose any steps your child may try. Falling off the edge of an open staircase can cause serious injury, but tumbling down stairs is less likely to do so. Babies rarely stiffen their bodies and tend to roll or bounce down a step at a time. Do not, however, take any chances! Be within reach of your child during the months of learning physical prowess. And keep a protective gate across any opening through which your child could possibly fall.

When you have time, take her to a carpeted or padded set of stairs. Three are enough to practice on. Place your child on the top step on her tummy. Show her how to stretch her legs to the next step down and then to slide her body down. Next to the third step, and then to the floor. Reverse the process in teaching how to climb upstairs, pulling herself up with her arms and then drawing up her knees. Practice until she is ready for more steps. Always be there until you know she can safely manage those steps.

Keep steps free of any objects. They can trip up even the most agile child. The way you protect your child while encouraging her to explore and develop is a mark of good mothering.

Sleep habits concern many parents. Moving from sleeping twenty hours or more at birth to only about twelve hours a day by twelve months is a major change. Most mothers, however, welcome the change from awakening at night to sleeping through, even if that means a short nap during the day.

I recommend that you teach your child to sleep through the night by at least six months. For most children, this means only a bit of skillful neglect. If she awakens and fusses, be very quiet. After a few whimpers, she will probably go back to sleep. Even a creak of the floor may offer hope of a nocturnal frolic. Most babies can do without that fun, and so can all the parents I know.

If your baby is strong-willed, he may cry until you are convinced he is quite ill. As you drag your weary self to his bed, he will switch on the charm or pitifully snuggle into your tired arms, convincing you that he will be emotionally scarred for life if you fail to get up with him. Check with your doctor, but most babies and mothers will be vastly better off if you let them "cry it out" for a night or two. I can hardly remember a child's crying more than forty-five minutes. Usually, it's about thirty minutes the first night you try it; ten, the second; and on the third night, he sleeps through. I have never seen a child suffer emotional trauma from such a procedure. But I have seen resentment build and the quality of care suffer when a mother becomes exhausted by the tyrannical demands of an indulged child. Good mothers need to be tough at times.

Too many parents are anxious about children's **eating patterns**. I was among them, even though I knew I needn't worry. Children are created with a gauge that tells them when they're hungry and even what sort of food they need. Eating time is not to be confused with playtime. I strongly urge you not to zoom the feeding spoon like a toy airplane and, please, never say, "Just one bite for Mommy! And now one for Daddy!" If you think about this process, you will readily see how futile it can be. Children must learn to eat for their own health, not yours. And they certainly need to distinguish playtime from time for nourishment.

Your doctor will advise you about scheduling strained and solid foods for your baby. Trust her or him, and avoid an absolutely unnecessary power struggle. In eating, as in the rest of her life, encourage your child to become independent as early or late as she is ready. Even if she spills some, she can learn to handle her spoon and become self-reliant.

I highly recommend putting a large plastic protector under the baby's chair. It can be rinsed after meals, and you won't have to mop the floor three times a day.

Playing with your child enhances physical development. Push him in his swing; crawl about with him; tickle, touch, kiss, and hug him; whisper in his ear. Go for walks, touch the leaves, blow dandelion seeds into the breeze, and watch the squirrels and birds. As soon as possible, find or build a sandbox and play in it with your child. Physical play develops your child's body in many ways, but most of all, it develops the strong cords of love that bond you together forever.

Decide carefully what you consider abuse of your child. To me, abuse is any action or neglect that leaves scars—emotional or physical—on your child. Hitting in strong anger, yelling on a regular basis, calling names, failing to respond to a genuine need (not every whim), refusing to smile, laugh, cuddle, and interact with your child—all are examples of abuse. Don't do anything that will damage your unique and precious child.

A word about sexual abuse: Many mothers fail to understand that undue handling of a child's genitals can initiate sexual arousal and feelings that no child can understand or deal with. Treat your son's penis and scrotum or your daughter's labia, clitoris, and vagina as you treat the hands or legs. All are parts of the whole body to be kept clean and free of injury or harm but otherwise to be ignored. Be aware of others who conceivably could focus on or use your child's body for their own perverse pleasure. Protect your child's sexuality by knowing those who provide care when you can't and making certain your child is safe with them. As soon as your child can talk, ask him what the sitter did to entertain him. Return home unexpectedly and check the atmosphere of your home. Take nothing for granted until you develop absolute trust in a sitter.

Building a solid base for your infant is of the utmost importance. In no area is that importance greater than in your child's developing personhood.

CHAPTER THIRTEEN

Toddlers and Preschoolers

TODDLERS

The ultimate goal for a two-year-old is the basic separation from the mother and the establishment of rudimentary independence. The long journey to successful maturity begins in earnest at age two. As you enable your child to separate from you, yet maintain your protection, guidance, and nurturing, you will lay a strong foundation for personality building. Find for each child the best boundaries within which to develop and become a healthy adult.

Typically, two-year-olds search for ways to get exactly what they want. They are notorious for their vocabulary. "No!" is prominent, and it always is expressed with an exclamation mark.

Furthermore, two-year-olds experience repeated losses, which means they will go through some grief. Researchers who have studied grief agree that anger is a universal component of it. Let me give you an example. Brent is not quite two, but already he has lost his mother's breast-feeding, his bottle, and his pacifier. He has lost the pleasure of being carried frequently in his parents' arms, close, warm, and high enough to see everything. He is about to be deprived of having a warm diaper in favor of using the potty-chair. He used to be fed by Mom or Dad, and now he has to feed himself. The list could go on.

Brent wants to run, play, climb, and explore, but he also wants to be picked up so he can see things again. He yearns for the old comfort of suckling, cuddling, and total dependency. But the healthy desire to be a separate individual is also growing. When he tries to build with his blocks, they fall down, and he can't make toys work as he wishes them to.

When the mixed emotions and confused desires become too much for Brent, he will understandably become frustrated. And that frustration will often be explosively expressed in temper tantrums.

DEALING WITH THOSE TEMPER TANTRUMS

Many mothers do not understand the intense, vulnerable feelings of two-year-olds that are translated into anger. So they spank, yell, or jerk these hurting little ones in their attempt to curb such behaviors.

The anger of your two-year-old is strictly a cover-up for and a disguised expression of pain over the problems of growing up. That fact does not mean you should give in to his explosive outbursts, indulging and pampering him.

Observe and study your child to determine strengths and weaknesses. What does she enjoy doing? What is most frustrating or difficult for him? What causes the tears or anger that she expresses? Watch your child at play, at rest, during good events and bad. Notice the facial expression, the tone of voice, the movements of that staunch body. All of your powers of observation are needed to help you understand this unique human being.

As you watch your child, try to step back and see how you react to her. There are sure to be some actions or attitudes that will irritate you. You may see in your daughter certain traits and mannerisms that you couldn't tolerate in your mother or even in yourself. She doesn't practice these behaviors just to annoy you, even though it seems so at times. She is just being herself, as you used to try to be yourself. The more you can love yourself and all of your relatives, the easier it is to react positively to the child who resembles them, and the easier it becomes to determine how you can effectively deal with her.

If you don't like the way you respond, change! A well-meaning father told me that he sends his four children to their rooms when they fight with one another. If they resume fighting later, he whips them with his belt. He couldn't understand why they continue to fight! Of course, his example of violent anger taught them how to hit when they become angry. He fortunately realized that he needed to change before he lost his children completely.

> *A two-year-old's major developmental task is to begin to separate from Mother and establish some independence.*

Your emotional reaction to your child will help create a cycle of action and reaction that can be helpful and positive or destructive and negative. As you feel about and toward your child, so will others react. If you see him behaving in obnoxious ways that irritate you, you may know you must take action to produce changes in that behavior. Knowing your child and yourself will guide your actions, making them loving, firm, and successful.

Focus clearly on the lessons your child needs to learn. Since a two-year-old's major task is to develop some independence, decide how to help her do so. The boundaries within which she can function must be clear: "You may play with these toys but not with Daddy's tools." "Play as hard as you like in our yard, but don't leave the yard." "In five minutes, it will be bedtime. Be sure your toys are picked up when the timer goes off."

Follow through and check on your child's compliance. All children prefer to get by with the most play and the least work. You must see to it that they learn some balance in responsibility and fun, so be sure the cooperation is consistently there. When it is, give your child a warm hug and say, "I really appreciate your help in picking up the toys. Now we have time for a story before you go to bed!"

When cooperation is not forthcoming, your task is to correct the resistance. I suggest that you lovingly and firmly take your child to the assigned job site, prepared to wait with her until it is done. Do not remind and nag her. Simply and clearly state, "Neither of us leaves here until you pick up these toys [or whatever the task is]! And since you wasted so much time by refusing, there will not be time for a bedtime story!"

Challenge your two-year-old to new adventures. It is very easy to become totally exhausted running after an energetic toddler. He can get into so many forbidden areas that you seem to constantly say, "No! Don't!"

Instead, take your child to places with the least possible restrictions and the most opportunities for safe activities. In your garage, basement, fenced-in yard, or local park or school playground, your toddler can get messy, climb, and be active without serious damage. You must, of course, be certain no serious falls are likely and no permanent damage is done to the house or your child.

No matter how safe you make your child's environment, there is no substitute for your presence. You need to be near enough to your child to be able to hear sounds that might alert you to either danger or misbehaviors. Misbehavior is often suggested by silence. When any child is too quiet for any length of time, it indicates illness, boredom, or mischief. Learn to listen well!

WHAT TODDLERS CAN DO

By age two, most children can feed themselves, though they still spill a lot. Encourage as much self-help as your child can handle. Since he is establishing independence, he needs to learn to make certain choices. Ask him if he prefers orange or grape juice. Does he want a whole sandwich or a half? Meals can provide a number of lessons. Not only can he decide how much and what he would like to eat, but he can also learn the consequences of poor choices: "You asked for a whole sandwich, but you ate only half. Next time, we'll start with a half, and then you may ask for more."

Such a response will teach your child—if you remember next time to give him only the half. This approach is much more effective than angrily saying, "You asked for a whole sandwich, and you are going to sit in that chair until you eat it all! Even if you sit there till bedtime!"

As your child gives up nursing to become self-sufficient, compensate for the loss of you, and encourage self-confidence in her. You can do this through complimenting her progress, but be aware of the need, now and then, for brief times of extra holding and cuddling. We all would like to be little now and then. Two-year-olds need to play "seesaw"—being little and then being big. That balance stabilizes their development.

SPEECH

Talking with a toddler is a delightful experience. Language develops best when it is live, and that means when someone talks with a child. Plan times through the day to talk actively with your son. Sit with him so you both have good eye contact; talk about his day and yours; speak of happy things, sad experiences, and frustrations. Let your face, tone of voice, and words all fit, saying the same thing. Ask her questions and encourage her to elaborate: "Tell me more!" When she lacks the words, help her find them, but don't do so in a way that results in her feeling inadequate.

Conversation with any toddler can be encouraged by use of a play telephone or puppets. Somehow the object protects the child against feeling inferior to this big, wise, all-knowing adult. It is good for you to be on a child's level at times. Life takes on an entirely new perspective from a two-year-old's level.

Toilet Training

I'm sorry so many mothers get hung up on toilet training. Many feel they must begin this rather complex process at least by age two. And yet we know that only a few youngsters are neurologically able to control bladder and bowel functions before age three.

Observe your child. If she stays dry for a couple of hours, you may try to sit her on a potty-chair for a while, offer her a drink, and allow water to run nearby. If she is ready to relax the muscles that release the urine flow, she will do so in a few minutes. If she can't, wait a few weeks and try again.

Allow your daughter to see you using the toilet. And many a boy has decided to use the potty after seeing how Daddy does it. Just as with eating, avoid turning toilet training into a power struggle no one wins. Such battles create the rudiments of lifelong estrangement and even downright enmity.

A New Baby

You may be excited about the prospects of a new baby, but your two-year-old is not! He is not really able to understand what it will be like having a baby around, and he is most likely to try to damage the new arrival as soon as he can. No matter how you try to prepare her, she will not welcome a baby brother. Your two-year-old is still technically a baby, still struggling over whether or not to separate from you. A new baby immediately comes between you and him, and he is certain to resent that.

If you can space your children three years apart, you will find an amazing difference in adjustment to a baby. By age three, a child has accepted separation and is ready to be quite independent. He may even enjoy a new baby and see her as an animated new toy. True, a three-year-old still resents Mommy's unavailability, but he can handle it much better than a two-year-old can.

You may not have the choice, however, if you are already pregnant. You may even have the new baby in your arms. But you can make the best of the situation. Above all, in every way possible, help your two-year-old know she is still precious. Find time to hold her, play with her, and talk to her. You will have to neglect your new baby just a bit, but in the long run, it will pay.

Allow someone to help you in whatever areas possible to find time and energy for your toddler. Explain to your child about the advent of the expected baby, and read books to him about new babies. Your local library will have several. Try to visit someone with an infant so she will have an idea of what to expect. Though he won't understand all about the changes in your family a baby will create, he will know you are understanding of and sensitive to his situation.

Do not push your two-year-old out of his crib or his room to accommodate the baby. He is certain to feel displaced and will dislike the one who takes his place. The new baby will not have her own familiar place anyway, so she can adjust to a spot in a bassinet anywhere for a while. Once your toddler has adjusted to the facts of this new life and is closer to three, he can much more easily move to a big bed and accept a roommate if necessary.

If you have them, show photographs to your toddler of her infancy. Let her see your pride and pleasure in her and tell her you love her even more now that you have had her longer and she can talk with you and help you now and then. Find her old baby clothes and blankets and help her see how tiny she once was and how much more fun she can enjoy as a big girl who can run, talk, and play.

If you have a new baby, I urge you not to make any other changes in the life of your two-year-old. Now is not the time to toilet train, change eating habits, or begin day care. Handling a competitor is enough for a while. When the adjustment is made, and your toddler settles into a routine again and is not trying to get rid of the baby any longer, you may gradually resume whatever training measures you feel he can handle.

MOTHER'S AMBIVALENCE

No matter how mature and altruistic you are, you are almost certain to experience days when you wish you could give your two-year-old away— at least for a few days! Even when you understand your child's struggles and have some empathy, you will wish you no longer had to deal with them.

You will find yourself screaming, "No! Don't!" when you wish you could patiently say, "Okay, Sweetheart!" And many a night and day you will feel guilty because of these perfectly normal emotions.

My best words to you are these: Every mother goes through some negative feelings, balanced by short intervals of intense love and adoration. When you see that angelic face sleeping so peacefully, you will wonder how you could have felt so frustrated only a few hours ago. I can tell you it's because you are human. And even the most tolerant human gets weary of the seesaw world. So be kind to yourself. Try to look ahead. Sometime after the third birthday, things *will* get better, and you can again enjoy your child—well, most of the time.

TEN RULES FOR MOTHERING A TWO-YEAR-OLD

1. Challenge him to explore, play, and be constructively creative. Be the guide.

2. When she whines and acts babyish, don't scold or tell her to grow up. Give her some babying. She has no better way to let you know she needs just that.

3. Spend more time and energy finding activities he can do and less telling him to "Stop!"

4. Keep your rules few and simple, focused on structuring her days. Enforce them firmly and kindly on a consistent basis.

5. Give only simple choices, but allow your child to make some decisions. Ask, "Do you want a big glass of milk or a small one?"

6. Avoid dishonesty. Threats you will not enforce or questions for which you already have the answers are dishonest. Never ask, "Don't you want to put away your toys now and take a nap?" No self-respecting toddler will say, "Of course, Mommy!" And don't say, "If you tip over your glass, I'll never give you a drink again!" It's tempting but not true.

7. When your child throws a tantrum, don't react with an even bigger one. Simply take charge. Hold your child firmly and lovingly until he regains control.

8. Watch your child frequently. When she starts getting frustrated at play or evidences fatigue, go to her and help her over the hump or decide it's naptime. Don't help so much that she believes she can do nothing without you, however.

9. Plan for her seesaw life. Challenge her to be even more independent than she demands when she is in that mode. With equal sincerity, cuddle, rock, and baby her when she reverts to needing to be little for a while. As a senior citizen, I still wish I could be little once in a while!

10. Capture the child's curiosity, and use it to encourage exploring, learning, and sharing adventure.

TIPS FOR DISCIPLINING TWO-YEAR-OLDS

- Keep your basic relationship friendly. On a daily basis, reflect on the lovely attributes of your child, and remember the faults will be overcome by your loving correction.
- Be firm, clear, and kind when telling her what must be done.
- Maintain affirming eye contact when you are with your child. Your eyes reveal your soul to him; make sure he never sees so much anger that he becomes afraid of you.
- Find the balance between fear and respect. Sooner or later, too much fear will prompt rebellion. When your child loses control, don't lose yours. Instead, sit down with your arms around her arms and chest, your legs wrapped around hers, and assure her you will release her

only when she regains control. This method will work only if you are strong but not angry, firm but not rigid, and persistent without fail. It's better than spanking any day.

COMMON MISTAKES

Parents make some common mistakes that defeat their otherwise good training and discipline:

Inconsistency. When a child is required to do a job or behave in a certain way one day but not the next, he becomes confused. In such a situation, he will test his parents to see if they mean business. This testing looks like rebellion, so it prompts some anger in the parents. The anger will make most parents react even more harshly on bad days and probably will feed into their sense of guilt and a tendency to "rescue" the child the next day.

Letting them charm you. Some children are born charmers. They can do dreadful things with a masterful look of mischievous innocence. It takes a truly wise parent to resist such charm. Many times I have seen parents scold such a child with grins on their faces. The child can't be blamed entirely for his choice of believing the grin. Resist a charmer when he has seriously erred and be congruent—that means make your face, words, and feelings all say the same thing.

Rigidity. Situations sometimes warrant your being flexible, which makes balance tough to find. Being unbending eventually causes real rebellion, but being too flexible results in the confusion of inconsistency.

The best image to convey this idea is that of enlarging the enclosure of a young colt. As he grows, his fences must be pushed back, or he will break them down. So know how your child is growing and decrease the limits as he demonstrates his ability to be responsible.

Permissiveness. In a well-intended attempt to show respect to children and to allow them to grow up uninhibited, a generation of very easy going parents has arisen. They have ended up with the tail of a monster.

In a scholarly series of studies, Dr. Stanley Coopersmith of the University of California at Davis has shown that children of strict, consistent parents evidenced significantly greater self-esteem and general success than children of permissive parents. Children have neither the experience nor the abstract reasoning ability to make many decisions until their teens. They need limited and guided choices early in life—a few decisions to make independently by age seven or eight, with gradually increasing freedom until the early teens. By adolescence, most young people make many of their own choices.

Lack of clarity about rules. Mothers may allow privileges that fathers refuse, or vice versa. Sometimes rules are too detailed, creating constant hassles, or they may be too vague. Good discipline demands clear-cut principles that cover lots of details. For example, "You are not to hurt your brother or sister physically or with words!" That means no biting, hitting, scratching, name-calling, and so on. You do not need to list those and then find that you forgot "no kicking."

Excessive gentleness and patience. That may surprise you. But children do not understand or respond well to infinite patience. At some point you, the parent, should take no more.

The child needs to believe that you mean what you say, and you can practice firmness without guilt. The Bible clearly says that a father corrects those whom he loves (see Proverbs 3:12). That also goes for a mother. You aren't likely to correct if you don't lose patience. However, the Bible speaks of an appropriate anger: "'Be angry, and do not sin': do not let the sun go down on your wrath" (Ephesians 4:26).

Here, again, are the three steps to deal constructively with your anger:

1. Label your feeling precisely. This gets your thinking in control of your anger.
2. Focus clearly on what has caused your anger or rage.
3. Think creatively about what you can and will do about the cause of your anger, and then do it.

Failure to follow through. You may be ever so clear, congruent, and balanced in your strictness and leniency, but if you fail to follow through, the game may be lost. After you tell your child to do something and he doesn't do it, punish him according to your plans and policies. That will let him know you mean what you say. But don't forget, the punishment becomes discipline only when the child does what he was supposed to do and begins to do so regularly.

PRESCHOOLERS

For most moms, mothering a three- or four-year-old is a breeze after weathering the turbulent twos. Preschoolers are capable of much more independence and are noted for a marvelous sense of imagination. If they have not been pampered early on, they are quite adaptive and cooperative. Unlike younger children, they can play successfully with other children and are able to take turns and give and take very well. Because of their greater level of self-awareness and security, they can adjust to a new baby with relative ease.

The development of language is usually quite advanced in preschoolers. Communication, therefore, is much improved, and mothers are more at ease when they have some idea of what goes on in their children's minds.

The developmental task of a preschooler is to develop creativity. She needs to be encouraged to use her hard-won sense of independence to initiate tasks. Beginning a project seems to happen quite spontaneously. Completing it, however, does not seem to be as easy, so Mom needs to stand by and watch. If your child shows a tendency to stop a task, either at work or at play, prior to completion, step in with some encouragement. Do not take over and do the job for your child, but see to it that most of the time, she finishes it. A word of warning! Don't be so rigid and demanding that you impair your child's enthusiasm.

The great enjoyment of your three-year-old will probably be marred at the ripe old age of four. Then children suddenly become curious about strange and unanswerable topics. "Do dogs go to heaven when they die?" "Where is heaven?" "Do angels really have wings?" "Why can't we see God?" These and countless other queries come from the minds of children. And they hate to hear an "I really don't know!" answer.

Make an effort to answer your child. Try to look up the answers in books, and ask other people who may know. Often it is not the exactness of information that satisfies a child's searching mind. Instead, your taking him seriously and trying to satisfy his curiosity are enough. At this stage you have an unparalleled opportunity to encourage that thirst for knowledge. So be patient, persevering, but also honest. It's a great idea to refer your child's question back to him. While he's considering his answer, you can begin searching for yours.

Avoid Common Mistakes

One mistake in child rearing *is becoming so relaxed in enjoying a happy child that you forget the training and discipline factors.* At age three even the most reluctant child can use the toilet, feed himself without too great a mess, and even partially dress himself. If you especially enjoy taking care of your child, you may do too many things for her too long.

> *A major developmental task of the preschooler is to develop creativity.*

At the other extreme is the mother who believes in independence for her child. You may expect too much of him, thereby *setting a climate for his feeling inept.* Observe your child. See what she can do and encourage her in that, but avoid trying to push her beyond her capabilities. A child naturally reaches for new heights. Pushing can actually discourage her and defeat your ambitions.

Some mothers *worry about their preschooler's imagination.* They fear that fantasy is wrong and will lead to lying. Be reassured! Lying relates to mistakes in discipline or may result from neglect and serve as an attention getter. Your child's fantasy life is his way of exploring all sorts of frontiers and will help him become self-confident and interested in life. As he sees himself conquering monsters or playing with imaginary friends, he can be totally in control, making any event turn out to his liking. You can readily see how such efforts will enable your child to become more confident in the real world if he is not confronted with insurmountable odds, such as abuse.

Do be careful, as you play with your child, that you and she know this is a pretend world. Have fun with that pretense and even add to it from your experiences. But don't try to extend the fantasies into reality. Just enjoy them and let them be. The Creator has instilled wonderful checks and balances into children, and we need not interfere very much. Your child will grow out of this stage of imagination all too soon. Use your child's creativity as a reminder of your own. Dust it off and renew the unique expression of your early pretend life. It will enrich you and draw you close to your child. You see, mothering is a two-way street. Your preschooler can teach a refresher course to you from which you may profit immensely.

PROVIDE THE RAW MATERIALS

To be creative, a child needs patterns, ideas, and raw materials as well as creativity. Materials don't have to be costly. They may be scraps of fabric left over from a sewing project, pieces of wood that are sanded enough to prevent getting slivers in little fingers, and cardboard milk cartons wrapped with bright paper that is securely taped on. Nature hikes can yield a wealth of materials—wildflowers to be pressed and dried, pinecones, brightly colored leaves, rocks, or shells (if you live near an ocean). A few pine needles glued to a piece of plain paper can frame a unique note card.

The greatest joy of creating with a preschooler is the permission to make mistakes. Many mothers are inhibited about being creative because they fear the criticism of others if the end product is less than perfect.

Whatever you do in playing with your child, be relaxed and remember the chance to try, explore, experiment, and experience is what really counts. Don't tell your child what to make or do. Suggest, try different ideas yourself, and then let him work independently.

Be prepared for the inevitable. Sooner or later, she will bring a drawing to you and ask you to guess what it is. You may try your hardest, but you just won't know and you will fear that her feelings will be hurt. If you handle such a situation right, however, it can be an ego builder. Make the best guess you can and when it's incorrect, you can tell her how very clever she is to make something even Mommy can't identify. Then, of course, tell her you like the color, shape, or whatever you think of that is commendable.

> *The chance to try, explore, experiment, and experience is what counts. Don't tell your child what to make or do.*

Preschoolers need to explore on their own much of the time. Your constant presence can communicate to your child that he is incapable of functioning independently. Once again, balance is crucial. Enough of your presence is needed to inspire and encourage, but when you sense your child is becoming too dependent on you, find a reason to get busy nearby. You can look on without intruding, enjoy without controlling, and encourage healthy independence.

Your refrigerator is probably the best display area for your preschooler's creativity. A strip of sticky tape or a magnet can attach a work of art where you will enjoy it, grandparents will compliment it, and your child will recognize the value of her efforts. Again, don't be so enthusiastic your child may consider you a phony. If you overrespond to a small product, how will you increase the caliber of praise when she does something truly great? I recommend simple, sincere phrases: "The colors you used in drawing that rainbow are so bright. I feel good when I look at it!" Or you could say, "The shapes you made with your blocks are really interesting. I'd like to see more of your ideas!"

If you are blessed with a good husband, be sure he, too, notices your child's crafts. Encourage your son to show the garage he made from milk-carton building blocks to his dad. And I hope that Dad will help him park his toy cars neatly inside it.

READING AND STORYTELLING

Reading well is a skill that many Americans never acquire. A personnel manager of a national corporation told me a sad fact. She said the firm has a large workforce of conscientious people, and the supervisors would like to promote a number of them. But, she stated, they have discovered that many employees cannot read well enough to follow the manuals or study guides that train them for new positions. They simply cannot promote some who would be excellent workers, except for their illiteracy.

Be certain your child is not one of those people when she grows up. You can prevent such a tragedy by teaching your child the magic of books and stories. Find books that appeal to your child with lots of colorful pictures, not too many words, and plenty of humor. As you read, use your best dramatic manner. Expression, both facial and vocal, can make a story come alive.

Practice reading and telling stories to your child. Stop at intervals to ask questions or seek responses. That involvement will slowly teach your child to pay attention, increase his concentration, and ensure comprehension.

Please don't try to get your child to learn to read. Certainly, she may copy the sounds of the alphabet and know words that start with certain letters, such as, "*Apple* starts with an *a, ball* with a *b,* and *cat* with a *c.*" Preschoolers have much to learn about adapting to the complex world in which they live. Don't overload them with academic materials they will learn later.

Spend as much time outdoors as possible. Go for walks; plan picnics in your yard or a local park. Sit still at intervals, and see how many different sounds you can count from the environment. (Cars and sirens don't count!) Describe to your child the warmth of the sun, the coolness of a breeze, the infinitely light sensation of a dandelion seed ball or a delicate caterpillar. Teach your child to respect nature by being careful not to destroy wild plants or leave litter lying about.

BE RESPONSIBLE

Whether it's picking up litter at the park or in the woods or picking up toys or dirty clothes, now is the time to teach some sense of order and responsibility. Frankly, it takes more time to let your child help than to do a task by yourself. But remember, it's not easy or convenient to be a mother.

Your preschooler will probably want to be with you much of the time, so encourage him to help with the cleaning, laundry, and dishes. He will love to do many small tasks. And you will love the glow of pride in his eyes when you tell him how well he did the job and how much that helped you.

When your child starts to school, she will need to be responsible. Laying the foundations for that developmental task now will enable your child to get off to a good start in school.

Another excellent tool for building responsibility is teaching your child to make wise choices. Once again, it's much easier for you to regulate and dictate than to teach. But now is the time when your child will listen to you as you help her learn to think. Here are a few examples of teaching decision-making:

"It's a warm day, Jill. Would you like to wear your pink shorts and white shirt or this blue-and-red playsuit?" With a four-year-old, you may even say, "Sam, here are several outfits. Can you pick out things to wear today that will be comfortable and look good?"

Setting aside time for a nap or rest is wise. But instead of saying at your convenience, "Jill, get in here right now for your nap!" try this approach.

At lunch, outline some afternoon activities, then ask, "Would you rather rest now while I clean the closet or later after you pick up all the toys?"

You can teach sharing and choosing simultaneously. "Sam, your friend Tim is coming to play with you today. Remember, he can be a little bit hard on toys. How about putting away your special truck so he can't break it. Decide which toys you can share with him and which ones you don't dare risk having broken. If you're not sure about some things, just ask me and we'll decide together."

Giving your child information, focusing on limited choices, and then kindly offering the feedback about how the choice worked are parts of the simple formula you need. Your child will learn now, when he is still highly teachable, how to think. The need to choose by facts and logic rather than impulse or feeling is profound. When your child is a teenager, she will be much more likely to choose against drugs, for example, if this process has been practiced.

Teaching logical thinking and decision-making takes time. Logic comes from a series of questions, each built on the last bit of information. When your four-year-old pesters you to the limits of your endurance, be grateful. Find the time, patience, and resources to answer. Don't be content with answers, but challenge her to think beyond her questions. Ask her what she thinks, and never belittle her answers. Encourage ever-more-profound wondering and imagining as well as thinking and understanding.

PLAY

Despite their preoccupation with imaginary play, their efforts to help you work, and their many questions, preschoolers need you to play with them. Wrestling, tickling, blowing on their necks, and tousling their hair are all examples of physical touching that is so vital to the ongoing bonding process. Observe your child, though. When rough play is no longer fun for either you or your child, it's best to stop.

Danny's father roughhoused with him. His mother enjoyed their wrestling and watched her son becoming strong and adept through their play. With great frequency, however, she observed Danny's frustration as his father pinned him too tightly and too long. Often Danny would cry and scream out his rage at his dad's overpowering manner.

You must help such excesses to stop. The way you go about the process is crucial. At almost all costs, avoid implying that Dad is mean or your child must have your protection to survive. Most fathers are sensitive and want to be good dads. They also want their children to be tough and strong. So don't be critical in a harsh, condemning manner.

Privately, you might try an approach like this: "Honey, have you noticed that Danny often gets upset when you play with him? I love your spending time with him, and he really needs you to toughen him up a bit. Would you be willing to try a shorter time period and take it a bit easier? I hate for him to think you are mean and to become so frustrated. I don't want to come between you, so what do you think?" My experience tells me that a constructive, loving approach has a good chance of bringing about the changes you want to see.

SHARE HUGS AND KISSES

Preschoolers give and love lots of bear hugs. Sometimes they like kisses as well. My son was an exuberant child. It was pure joy to return home to his football-tackle hugs. Take time out for lots of hugs, but also find time to hold and cuddle your children. Sitting close together as you tell a story or read a book communicates as much as the words you express. And my ever-present reminder of the tenderness and warmth of holding and rocking your child must be given again!

Some time ago I held an adult patient in my arms as she cried out her hurts and disappointments. I unwittingly placed my hand on the back of her head. Immensely comforted by my maternal act, she stated, "Feeling your hand on my head reminded me of being a little girl. My grandmother used to hold me just like that." You may underestimate the immense value of your tender touch. Give it whenever you can.

GROW IN INDEPENDENCE

Your two-year-old had the task of beginning to separate from you, to become independent. Your preschooler must create, imagine, and initiate activities. She also needs to become increasingly independent. Developmental stages never really end. Once they begin, they merge into one another almost imperceptibly, and the focus of each one becomes more clear, precise, and effective as time goes on.

Encourage your child's independence by believing she is capable and trusting her abilities. Your child requires your ongoing guidance and supervision, however. You must help him to master self-control and then teach interpersonal skills.

Model self-control to your child. Remember, control does not mean denial. If you are angry, sad, or elated, express those feelings honestly but without such intensity that your child becomes afraid or anxious. Explain why you feel as you do and especially make clear what you will do about those issues.

Teach your child appropriate words to express her emotions. Help her master a vocabulary of emotions. As you leaf through magazines, find pictures of faces that register a range of feelings. Cut them out and put them in a scrapbook, labeling each one appropriately. Read your scrapbooks to your child regularly. As he recognizes fear, sadness, excitement, and anger, he will learn to sense them in himself. When he can put them into words, he will be on the way to controlling himself.

Preschoolers, like adults, sometimes need to express strong emotions physically. Provide a big pillow, a pounding toy, or some safe object to hit.

The permission to cry or even yell a bit will help your child release strong feelings safely.

Expression of anger is not enough, though. Solutions must be found. Once your child is calm enough to allow it, help her find the answer to the problem that upset her. Furthermore, help her establish a plan to prevent that situation from occurring again, if possible.

As you work out your differences and discipline your child, you will be showing him how to deal with his friends and someday with his spouse. Make your words, attitudes, and emotions so clear and loving that you will enjoy getting them back one day.

DISCIPLINE

Perhaps never again will your child be as close to you and teachable as she is in these two or three years. Capitalize on that fact, and spend more time teaching and training than punishing. Much research verifies that more learning occurs through encouragement and praise than ever happens from criticism and punishment. As my friend Ed Christopherson says, "Catch 'em being good!" Let your child know how much you appreciate that.

A friend told me about a method that worked successfully with preschoolers. One summer day she had a severe headache. Her four-year-old son was playing with four friends in the backyard. In spite of her pleas for them to enter the house only when they absolutely had to and then to close the door quietly, they failed to cooperate. Their loud voices and constant door banging became an excruciating accompaniment to her throbbing pain. Her reminders were useless. At last one child remembered to be quiet and closed the door very gently. This wise lady gave her a hug and a small cookie. When that child returned to play, she explained why she had received the treat. For the rest of the afternoon, the other children became considerate and careful when they needed to enter the house. She caught 'em being good, and it became contagious.

Because of the very gift of the imagination, a preschooler requires very direct and concise discipline. Let her know exactly what she has done that is out of line, what she must do instead, and what you plan to do to help her accomplish that. Don't be too angry. When you become too intense, your child's imagination makes you a monster to be feared and avoided. You can't be the great mom you want to be when your child considers you mean and threatening. Respect is great, but fear is not, and terror becomes crippling.

My daughter described another facet of misunderstanding in discipline. On one occasion she had told her son to turn off the TV and get busy with homework. He was preoccupied with the program and ignored her edict. Mother finally turned off the tube and looked at her son with all the frustration she felt.

Andy disgustedly said, "Mom, I wish you'd stop yelling at me!" She hadn't uttered a sound, but her emotional intensity was like a scream. They both helped me see that there are different ways of yelling at a child.

Although this episode occurred with an older child, the principle is the same for preschoolers. Who is to know, except the child, when such yelling becomes abuse? Guard your temper. Act before it gets out of control—while you can be firm and clear without striking terror in your child's heart. Remember the three-step formula for anger control.

A primary disciplinary measure for a preschooler is a clear directive about what to do and what not to do. A sentence or two of explanation regarding reasons will help. If this simple step is not accomplishing the needed lesson, use time-out. I recommend a certain spot where a child is alone, must sit still and think about the wrong done, and must decide never to do that again. Equally important is to help the child see what he should do and think about how he'll remember next time. A minute per year of age is usually long enough. I strongly recommend that you use the time-out period to regain your composure and think through the whole event.

Know your most effective method of discipline: speaking sternly, using time-out or physical restraint, or outwaiting the child. The latter is a wonderful option in which you explain to your child that there will be no activities of any sort until she finishes the assigned task. Of course, you must be prepared to follow through. Work on only one or two issues at a time. You may want your child to learn to share toys and take turns at choosing play activities with a friend. Then discuss these ideas with your child, explain exactly what you expect, and then observe the child's play, clearly guiding your child to do what the two of you have discussed.

Try to establish uniformity among everyone who takes care of your child. Your husband, the grandparents, and all baby-sitters need to know the issues you're working on and the methods you're using. Consistency is extremely important.

Encouragement and praise are the best forms of discipline for most people. Just be certain they are honestly deserved, stated simply, and accompanied by a smile and a touch. When your child discovers that what he does has value, he will probably continue doing it.

If negative consequences must be used, be sure your child knows you still love her. Even preschoolers can tell the difference between who they *are* and what they *do* that is wrong.

Finally, when a particular episode is over, don't bring it up again. Many children have been damaged by constant reminders of their past misdeeds. We all need hope for the future more than reminders of the past.

WHAT CAN THEY DO?

What are preschoolers capable of? Most of them can use their big muscles with quite a bit of dexterity. They can run, climb, tumble, and walk. They can do some simple dancing or gymnastics.

Fine motor skills vary a great deal in their development. Their fingers are not nearly as skillful as their arms or legs. They can use large crayons or pencils and are quite creative with them. Building with large blocks and playing with big toys are suitable activities. As you observe the progress in your child's abilities, invite her to do more complex activities, but never push her to the point that she becomes discouraged. Apart from learning basic courtesies and respect, a preschooler needs to be free to grow, explore, and love life.

Toilet training can usually be accomplished with some ease in three-year-olds. The nerves for both holding and releasing the sphincter muscles of the bladder and rectum are well-developed. Just seek your child's willingness to achieve control, and work out your own technique for teaching mastery of this function.

Children's eating should be fairly skillful, and spills are much less frequent as time goes on. I recommend setting your table with unbreakable dishes, small drinking glasses, and silverware that can be handled easily. Never force children to eat certain quantities of foods. Although they need to learn to eat a variety of foods, trying to force that process is more likely to

Perhaps never again will your child be as teachable as she is in these two or three years. More learning occurs through encouragement and praise than from criticism and punishment.

result in vomiting than success. Demonstrate by your eating habits the natural process of eating a serving of everything on the table. A comment about how good the peas taste may prompt your child to try them more readily than forcing them into her mouth. The more you make mealtimes into a battleground, the less cooperative your child will be. There are battles to fight and win, but eating should not be one of them.

Preschoolers often give up daytime sleeping. To ensure adequate sleep each night, allow naps to stop unless your child seems to need them. It is wise, however, to schedule a quiet time for an hour in the afternoon. Reading a story, playing quietly, or just rocking and singing for a while can offer the relaxation and closeness both of you need. If you have to work, plan a short cuddle time when you get home. Talk about the events of your day and his.

In all of your interactions, include your individual faith. Including God as the Source of love, energy, wisdom, and creativity makes life secure. You can do this through a thanksgiving prayer of gratitude for His care at bedtime.

These rituals may be kept very short. They need to be sincere and simple sentences that remind you and your family of that Power beyond your own, a Power who is infinitely wise and kind, always available, and always exactly right!

CHAPTER FOURTEEN

Children from Ages Five to Twelve

The most important challenge for kindergarten and elementary school children is learning an appropriate sense of responsibility. Actually, in your training and discipline practices, you have already begun this process. These are the years for refining and polishing this jewel. Without a reasonable sense of duty and the self-discipline to put it to work, your child will be handicapped later.

Despite whatever preschool experiences your child has known, entering school is a major transition point. Preschool has been at least partly for fun, but this is for real! There are grade cards and measuring tools by which success and failure are judged.

Wendy's mother had tried very hard to explain to her children why she might seem tired or a bit grouchy at times. She often said, "Wendy, I've had a really bad day. I need you to help me this evening. Be nice to your brother, and we'll all get through this." And being an understanding and cooperative child, Wendy helped her mother.

After her first full day in the first grade, Wendy came home tired and grouchy. As she sat down for dinner, she placed her round pink cheek in the palm of her hand. In a forlorn and weary voice, she pleaded, "Please be nice to me this evening, Mommy! I've had a hard day!"

That is typical of how most conscientious children feel after especially difficult times. But only a few are able to express directly how they feel and what they need. Far more of them act out their needs in aggressive behaviors or moody withdrawal. One of your tasks, Mom, is to be alert to any unusual or unpleasant attitudes in your child. Discover what underlies the negative behaviors, and deal with those root causes. Probably the underlying problems are similar to your own, just as Wendy and her mother reflected each other's needs and expressions.

After she starts school (and even in preschool), your child's life becomes immensely more complicated than earlier because she has to deal with academic requirements and peer pressure. Jean had several close friends and adjusted comfortably with most of her classmates. One friend, however, was of grave concern to Jean's mother. For several days in succession, Arlene would be Jean's very best friend. Then, without warning, there would be days when she refused to speak to Jean. In class activities, at playground games, and after school, she would ignore her patient friend. Somehow that friendship survived, but it is an example of peer pressure of a painful sort. Jean had no idea why Arlene was so unpredictable and went through anguished times during their relationship.

The major developmental task of children ages five to twelve is to develop a healthy sense of responsibility.

Jean's mother helped her understand that Arlene's behaviors were related to personal problems, not to any wrongdoing of Jean's. Her mother helped her recognize that her friend needed her to be steadily there for her. And her mother taught her the importance of having several friends so she would not be so alone during Arlene's moods. Girls, by the way, seem to have a difficult time with more than one close friend.

They tend to get into competition with one another and break into little factions or cliques. Do your best to teach your daughter better skills.

Boys, on the contrary, run in packs. They need enough members to play team sports, go on hikes, and build clubhouses. They shy away from girls until the fifth or sixth grade. In my opinion, it is healthy for boys and girls to spend time apart during the grade-school years. Both boys and girls need time with the same-sex friends to establish their individual sexual identity. In today's culture, many of the gender qualities of male and female have become blurred, which may confuse children about how to act, look, and behave.

I do not recommend rigid social rules for boys and girls. It's quite healthy for boys to know how to do household tasks and care for children. It is equally great for girls to participate in sports, learn mechanics, and be able to do household repairs. It is up to each family to teach its own definition of a boy's or girl's unique roles. The school can help if you take an active role in your parent-teacher organization. If you are active in your church or synagogue, you can also use your influence to promote separate youth activities for boys and girls part of the time. There should be some coed activities, too, but provide enough separateness to encourage individuality and some sexual identity.

Peer Pressure

Peer pressure comes in many negative forms and some positives. Look for negative pressure from your child's friends in at least five areas:

1. Language. If your child comes home using four-letter words you do not use, explore where he learned them. Clearly explain why you do not allow such language, yet help your child know that you understand how hard it is to refuse to follow the habits of classmates. Even school-age children can see that the habit of crude language is a mask for feeling insecure and is an attempt to act sophisticated.

2. Antisocial conduct. It is not unusual for grade-school youngsters to defy the authority of their teachers, lie, cheat, steal, and insult one another and the school staff. Your child may be one of these, or she may come to think that such conduct is the way to behave. In an increasingly violent world, you may even let yourself believe that a person has to be tough to survive. If by tough you mean strong and resilient, you are absolutely right. But if you think tough means rude, disrespectful, and violent, you are terribly mistaken.

Do not allow your child to practice the antisocial behaviors that are so prevalent. Teach him to be honest, considerate, kind, and responsible. The way to teach values is to explain them, establish rewards and consequences, enforce them consistently, and above all, model them constantly.

3. Poor attitudes. If your child acts indifferent to good values, uncaring about the needs and feelings of others, or unmoved by your attempts at discipline, think of peer pressure. Perhaps you have become estranged from your child, so examine your relationship with him or her. But very often, callous attitudes are learned from peers. The swagger or strut of a school bully can seem deceptively powerful. And your child could copy the attitudes of a powerful peer. You may be the mother of such a negative person. By all means, in either event, pull such false power away from your child.

Teach the real strength of gentleness. Explain that acting "macho" is false and is unacceptable. Use the teaching steps noted in the previous section, and stick with them until the needed change occurs.

4. Snobbishness. For several years, the advertising media have abused our children and us. Many mothers have mourned the financial cost of and personal vanity associated with the brand-name clothes their children demand. Less affluent children often feel persecuted by the snobbishness of children who flaunt expensive clothes with recognized labels for all to see. To alleviate such pain, many parents have deprived themselves unduly to provide those high-priced clothes.

I urge you not to give in to such pressures—not only from peers, but also from designers and advertisers. Even if you can easily afford those luxuries, please refuse to become part of such exclusivity. If each mother will take this task seriously, we can transform values and eliminate one very destructive pressure.

5. Chemical abuse. In one school I know, there was a high level of destructive peer pressure. Somehow a gang of fifth and sixth graders had evolved. They literally terrorized local merchants by stealing anything they wanted. To belong to this gang, children had to bring drugs, alcohol, or money to the leaders. If they refused to do so, they were beaten or hurt in a variety of ways. Though an extreme example of peer pressure, it is not an unusual one.

I know children who find drugs in their parents' possession. More commonly, they get them from older siblings. And I know it is frighteningly easy to acquire samples from young drug dealers, who are the pawns of professional dealers. These degenerates know that once a habit is formed, they will have customers hooked.

One parent, a drug user herself, said to me, "Yes, I use marijuana. I don't want my son to use it, but I have no intention of stopping." Her son did not hear her words, but he followed her example. He became severely addicted and has wasted irretrievable years, tranquilized to the point of failure in school.

Resist the temptation to put your habits ahead of your child's needs. Your child cannot hear what you say if your actions do not back up your words. If you abuse drugs or alcohol, you become worse than peer pressure, and your child may be the negative pressure on her peers.

If you suspect your child of having or using chemicals, find out if it is true. Your doctor can order laboratory tests that are very accurate. Teach your child the damaging impact of drugs and make it clear that you love her too much to allow her to harm herself. Find out the source of supply and report that to your law enforcement staff. Better still, have your child go with you to make that report. If you cannot get your child to stay away from drugs and drug abusers, a professional counselor may be needed to help you and your child to eliminate this habit.

It is disheartening to consider so many serious, destructive areas of peer pressure. There are also positive pressures. I hope you will master them and teach them to your children.

POSITIVE PEER PRESSURE

1. Being friendly. Teach your child to be friendly to all peers and to school staff. Practice with your child making good eye contact, greeting people, using simple good manners, taking turns, standing up for herself or himself appropriately but avoiding bullying, being helpful but not letting others use him or her.

2. Competing honorably. A healthy child wants to win but can learn to lose graciously. If your child will practice such a balance, she can influence her entire classroom. Team activities are opportunities for your child to learn to compete constructively and to help others do that, too.

3. Showing compassion. Sooner or later, most children go through some form of loss and grief. If your child is one of them, teach him how to cope with loss and get through the anger and pain of such experiences. In turn, when his friends endure grief experiences, teach him how to reach out in understanding and comfort. Your example will be his best teacher, but you can make suggestions and do some role-playing with your child. He will be more capable of helping peers with this kind of guidance from you.

4. Being independent. Reaching independence is the goal of adolescence. But preadolescence is none too early to begin teaching this value. It is far easier for a child to say no to negative peer pressures if she is self-confident and independent. So teach her to think for herself. By offering information and asking thought-provoking questions, you will develop clear thinking and wise decision making in your child. Successful independence will grow in a child who practices these processes.

5. Doing the right thing. Some children choose to behave in rebellious, self-destructive ways, influencing peers to join them. Equally positive peer influence can be exerted. Being a successful mother demands that you protect your child from negative peer pressure and enable your child to exert even stronger positive peer pressure. Help your child know what makes a decision and an action right or wrong.

Let me reiterate these points. Right decisions make one wiser, stronger, healthier, and generally a better person. Right decisions never damage another person or put him in a bad light. If everyone in the entire world made this choice, it would be a better place. Right decisions open broader options instead of limiting one's possibilities. See to it, then, that both you and your child make wise decisions and exert a positive influence on others.

EDUCATION ABOUT DANGER

Although we all would like to have children live in a safe world, we know that wish is not possible today. We are responsible, then, to warn our children about dangers. Whether those dangers are physical, social, intellectual, or spiritual, you are the one to teach about them. Your children's father needs to assist in this task, but don't leave it to him or others. Approach your protective role at once with a plan.

There are too many physical dangers to list them all. A few obvious ones include household protection through plans to use in case of fires or natural disasters; protection from serious illnesses through immunizations; protection from abuse of all kinds by knowing the reliability of all caretakers and by being in control of your angry impulses; safety from dangerous strangers by teaching your child to have nothing to do with a stranger who approaches her, to stay close to others, and to know what to do if anyone seems to be following; and caution in physical activities to avert accidents whenever possible.

Finding yet another balance is essential here. You must protect your child from harm, but you also need to protect him from living in constant fear. You may do this by teaching good judgment and reinforcing the natural intuition. Teach your child to realize that any stranger who approaches a child for any reason is at best thoughtless and at worst dangerous. Smiling at others while with you in a store is friendly, but talking with a stranger who stops a child on her way home from school is bad judgment.

How you teach your child to cope with dangerous people depends on where you live, the child's age, and her resourcefulness. Being alert but minding his own business is the best approach. Riding a bicycle, running fast, and entering a nearby house or store are some examples of self-protection.

Coping with natural disasters demands some knowledge on your part. Protection from thunderstorms means that you must know lightning tends to strike single trees but not groves; that being in a building is the wisest place, if one is accessible, for a child who may be caught outside, as is possible on a hike; that most tornadoes approach from the southwest, so refuge under pillows or a table in the southwest corner of a basement offers the best protection from that danger. Whatever the dangers you face, have a plan of defense, a habit of caution and, ultimately, the courage to face the worst. Such resources provide for you and your child the best answers to life's dangers.

RESPECT

Among all too many schoolchildren, I have observed a major lack of respect for others. When I look into this tendency, I usually discover they have a lack of respect for themselves. True enough, they are brash, which leads one to think they are strong and self-reliant. Actually, they dare not show that they need others because they have been let down too many times when they were vulnerable. In their lives, there is too little protection against fears, so they mask their concerns with bravado, rationalize away their needs, and convince themselves they can manage anything.

You are the key to changing such disrespect. You must treat yourself and your husband with respect, first of all. Then you will be able to show respect for your children, their friends, and their teachers.

Let me explain with an example. Todd grew up utterly spoiled by a doting mother. Somehow, she came to believe that a good mother always served her children. She waited on them as a slave would serve her master. She gave them anything they wanted and never expected any gratitude or service in return. Todd recalled that when he and his brother were teenagers, they often partied until they were drunk. In the early morning hours, when they returned home, they would get their mother up, and she would cook steaks and make a full meal for them.

> *You are not your children's servant. You are their teacher, example, and honest friend. Teach them to respect you as such.*

Todd eventually gave up his drinking, but he took with him into his marriage the well-established expectation that his wife would be like his mother. He lived as he always had, taking all the privileges and offering little in return. His attitude will contribute nothing to building a healthy marriage.

You are *not* the servant of your children. You are their teacher, example, and honest friend. Respect yourself as such, and teach your children to respect you. Do not allow them to be ungrateful, call you names, or insult you so that you can prove you're patient and long-suffering. Teach and require the courtesies you know are essential to successful living.

Respect eventually must be earned, but it also must be learned. Teach it well. And let me add, teach your family to show respect to others who may not deserve it. In working with disrespectful, rude schoolchildren, I have seen teachers, in exhaustion and despair, treat such youngsters with harshness as severe as their rudeness, and I have observed the vicious cycle of cruelty this behavior establishes.

Be certain your child never imitates this pattern of disrespect. Even more important, keep her from reacting to rudeness in others. Even if someone else treats you badly, responding in kind is not permissible. Doing so will eventually make one as rude as the other. So teach the mastery of self-control and insight that will enable your child to be a person of respect in all circumstances.

HEALTHY COMPETITION

Public schools have great value for children. Learning to compete well and fairly is a big lesson to all of us. In academics and sports, school offers many opportunities for healthy competition. By healthy, I mean competition that is energetic but not life-or-death in intensity, that calls forth one's very best in trying to win, that wants teammates also to win and avoids any damage to opponents in the process of the contest.

Healthy competition means one can lose with grace or win with humility.

Healthy competition means one can lose with grace or win with humility. You can be a key factor in teaching this sort of competitiveness to your child. You need to practice these habits. Believe in your child and her ability to win. Tell her what you see in her that makes you confident. Work with your child to practice and master the required skills.

My friend took her son to batting cages every day until he became an excellent hitter. During practice, give positive suggestions and encouragement. Praise success and require continued efforts to redeem failures.

At the point of any contest, avoid all criticism, and give unqualified praise for success in the outcome (if that happens), for efforts, for courage, and for good sportsmanship and courtesy.

During further practice, use observations you have made at a contest, always in a positive, teaching manner, to encourage improvement.

If you and your child cannot work together successfully in such efforts, you may need to seek coaching help from another person—your husband, a friend, or a relative. You may be too critical, have unrealistic expectations, or be caught up in power struggles that defeat your efforts. Try to correct such errors, but meanwhile use whatever help you can find.

EARLY INDEPENDENCE

While your elementary-school-age child must learn responsibility, respect, and good teamwork, he also needs to function independently. You can encourage the development of this quality in several ways.

Require some individual study and practice times. She needs your guidance, discipline, and tutoring at times, but your child also must function without your direct supervision more frequently.

After you assign a practice task, set a timer to remind both you and your child that he must have some accomplishments during the allotted period. Follow through by seeing what he has done. Praise it if it is worthy, or require it to be done correctly if it is not. Don't settle for careless work, but don't demand perfection in practice, either.

Offer your child choices in as many situations as possible. Help her learn to collect information, think about the situation, and make decisions from limited options. Then help her review the outcome. Did the decision work for the good of your child? Or were there risks or even damaging outcomes? Never say, "I told you so!" But help her see the strengths or weaknesses so she can enjoy even better results next time.

Teach cooperation; help your child learn the value of both independence and teamwork. You can teach these values in household work and family play as well as through school activities.

As you teach your child to be independent, practice your own balance in individuality and collaboration. Discuss with your husband or some other person the organization of tasks, the process of decisions about family affairs, and the discipline of completing projects you begin. Your lifestyle, more than your words, teaches your child all of life's lessons.

PEER PRESSURE

Thoughtful parents dread the day when friends' influence carries more weight with their children than they do. Don't panic when you see signs of peer pressure. Form a plan and follow it.

Know your child's classmates and friends. Invite them into your home, and observe their attitudes and interactions. Try to be friendly with them, but remember, you are the mother, not a child.

Point out to your child the qualities you admire or respect in those peers (as well as in him). Avoid unfavorable comparisons with your child.

If your child's friends have doubtful or negative traits, ask her if she has noticed them too. Without being condemning, help her analyze the strong and weak points she observes. If possible, establish some ways you and your child can help those peers.

If the peers' influence on your child is damaging, you may have to stop the relationship. It is best, of course, if you can help your child make such a decision independently. But if she cannot, don't be afraid to take this action yourself. Do so kindly but firmly. Your job description includes protecting your child from harmful influences.

Continue to teach decision-making to your child. The need for a decision about any peer pressure must be focused. Information must be gathered. Possible choices must be clarified. Action must be taken in carrying out the decision made. Your child will not always have the clear thinking or courage to follow this process alone. Don't be afraid to do it with him. In due time, he will see the advisability of your action and benefit from your protection.

A WORD ABOUT EIGHT-YEAR-OLDS

In the developmental scheme of life, there are crucial turning points. One of these is around age seven or eight. By that time, children begin to form opinions about their world and how they fit into it. They take fleeting mental excursions into their future and decide how that future will be for them.

Spend a little extra time with your child at this age. Try to explain your beliefs and values. Express your confidence in your child and her abilities. Help her think very simply about what she could do to make her world a better place. Her world is her school, your home, and perhaps your church or synagogue. Help her know how to act in each setting in a way that benefits everyone.

If your child cannot succeed at such lifestyles alone, guide and require him to do so. Prod him gently but consistently to follow through in positive behaviors. Then by your encouragement, praise, and feedback, help her see that the efforts required are truly worthwhile.

Help your child discover safe spots in an often-dangerous world. Show her your ever-present availability as guide and protector. And help him discover his strength of mind, body, and will that ultimately will be his protection.

Above all, introduce to him the Power beyond his or yours that is constantly with him.

COMMON MISTAKES

"I have to call her at least ten times in the morning before she ever gets up!" wailed the distraught mother of six-year-old Kim. "She should be able to get up when her alarm goes off!"

Kim's mother is one of a large group of moms who make mistakes with their school-age children. Her expectations are unrealistic. Kim's mother didn't realize that a first grader still sleeps soundly; she may not hear an alarm. Furthermore, she needs mother's gentle, loving presence to provide strength to get up and face a long, hard day.

At the other extreme is seven-year-old Della's mother, who gets her up physically, dresses her, collects her school items for her, and often takes her to school instead of putting her safely on the school bus.

Know what your child can do and help him do those tasks as independently as possible. Know each child's strengths and weaknesses.

Six-year-old Cara could make her bed respectably and did so daily. Her eight-year-old brother didn't have the patience to evenly spread the linens on both sides of his bed. He could learn, but it was harder for him. Angrily telling him he was not as good as his younger sister failed to help. He decided not to compete with a "goody-goody" girl.

Children who have weak spots need them strengthened by interpreting why those problems exist and by helping in overcoming them. Knowing your child's strengths will enable you to help him overcome the weaknesses.

Many parents fail to build self-esteem. To create healthy self-esteem, you must have some of it yourself. You also need to define your husband's strengths, since your child is part of both of you. Then you must help your child discover and develop her special abilities.

Regular, positive feedback about her praiseworthy attributes is necessary. And help in living beyond guilt is vital. To eliminate guilt, teach your child to acknowledge errors, correct them, make restitution, and practice forgiveness.

A common complaint of preadolescents relates to the way discipline is carried out. As children stretch toward early adolescence, they resent being treated as if they were still preschoolers. Guard your attitude. Respect your child. Always reach for her help in defining lessons that need learning and methods for teaching that will be effective.

Stop reacting to your child. Focus on goals to be reached, and work as a family team to achieve them.

You may fail to show enough affection. Even the most independent son needs to be hugged or have his back scratched or his feet rubbed. Find private times to exchange affection. And even when a child is moody and does not respond, love her anyway. She may be too proud to acknowledge needs, but believe me, she knows it! Be big enough to reach through childish pouts with unconditional love, gently and sensitively.

Many childhood traumas are insignificant to you who have really serious concerns. But watch your child's face. Read the lines that depict worry, fear, or anger. Help your child verbalize whatever he thinks and feels. Guide her to discover some of her own answers. By asking questions, making comments, and sharing personal experiences, you can teach your child to see that troubling issues have solutions. You don't need to minimize problems to reassure or comfort your child.

> *Every mother makes mistakes. Confess the ones you didn't avoid, and seek your child's forgiveness.*

I was a painfully shy child. When I saw my daughter standing back and failing to enter into activities with others, I ached for the pain I was certain she felt. Actually, she was not shy—only wisely assessing the group to discover what she wanted to do with them. Recognize that your child is an individual, separate from you. Don't assume that he feels like you did because he looks or acts similarly.

Let me tell you a secret: Every mother makes mistakes. Just try to avoid as many as possible. Confess the ones you didn't avoid, and seek forgiveness. Be sure to forgive yourself. And do the best you can, day by day, until the next error. Work it through, in turn, and move on. Your children know you're human, and they'll respect your honesty.

SPECIFIC TECHNIQUES

My youngest child helped me see how much she wanted my presence. In her profound simplicity she said, "Mom, when I walk into this house alone, it's like a big, dark cave. I wish you would always be in the big armchair when I get home from school!" I was there as often as I could be, but I felt the pressure of using my hard-earned medical skills. And all too often the needs of others took precedence over my heart and my children's needs.

Avoid my mistakes if you possibly can. *Be there for your child.* A hundred days may pass without any urgent need of your presence. But the hundred and first day may present a crisis. If you are gone, who will meet it? Your child lives in a stress-filled and often dangerous world. He needs you in that big chair to light the cave!

Healthy families share activities— both work and play.

Have some snacks available, and sit with your child in this nurturing environment. Don't prepare rich desserts that will curb her appetite for dinner, but do have something that your child will enjoy and that will replenish the calories she has burned during the day. A few cookies and milk, vegetable sticks and juice, or an occasional no-caffeine soda are examples.

Talk with your child about your day. A brief vignette of something you experienced or read can open the door for your child to share her day's happenings. Respond to her comments with genuine interest and without being critical. A few well-phrased questions can guide your child to analyze and make good judgments about the events she discussed. Harshness and a condemning attitude are almost certain to cut off communication.

Look over your child's schoolwork. Be quick to point out the successful aspects of papers he brings home. Later, during study time, you may bring up the mistakes in terms of reviewing and mastering materials. Post especially good papers on your bulletin board or refrigerator. Be sure Dad and grandparents know how good the project is.

Let your child tell you about her day. Use your child's narratives about her day to teach little ideas and enhance her understanding of herself and others. Don't lecture or sermonize.

Ask questions: "I wonder why Sally snubbed you today? How does she get along with her parents? Suppose she had a punishment last evening. She could still be upset today." This process can teach insight and compassion.

Remember the crucial comment and the crucial moment. Don't overlook either one, but be there to listen, respond, care, and help solve problems.

Your evening activities should include some work together. After you and your child have relaxed, talked, and eaten, some chores will need to be done. Children must recognize their importance in keeping family affairs moving smoothly. Many mothers seem to believe they must do all the work and children are to be totally carefree. Some moms, on the other hand, seem to think children should automatically pitch in and get work done independently.

Neither extreme is likely. Healthy families, according to an excellent study by Dr. Nick Stinnett, share activities, both work and play. Don't wait for your children to see tasks that need doing and then volunteer. Consider these ideas one mother taught me.

Every Monday, family members meet for a weekly planning session. They list all the activities that must be done daily and decide who will be responsible for each job. They include social events, church and school activities, and family fun times as well as laundry, cleaning, cooking, and yard work. A list is posted for each family member.

In this family, the mother acts as supervisor to be sure the jobs get done. She allows trade-offs of both time and tasks occasionally, but with the basic plan established, everything is done by Saturday evening. Sunday is a free day with no big jobs.

In supervising, this mother makes certain the jobs are done thoroughly. Without raising her voice and only occasionally speaking with extra firmness, she inspects and evaluates. Often it takes only a suggestion to "polish the sink a little better." At times, she may firmly declare, "Gina, this bathroom must be done over. It's not close to your usual good quality of work!"

When tasks are done according to their standards of excellence, Mom makes clear and concise statements about the quality of work, the way that helped her, and how proud of her family she feels. She seems to find a way to give an extra hug or a light touch that communicates her pride.

Once in a while, Mother bakes a batch of the family's favorite cookies. She lets them know these are a sweet way of saying how much she appreciates the children's efforts. Also, now and then, especially during extremely stressful times for the children, she will surprise them by doing a job for them. These rewards make their efforts less onerous.

My friend faithfully schedules time for family fun—a picnic, a game night, or an occasional meal at their favorite restaurant. Don't you wish you had grown up in a family like this?

Both the mother and father work along with their children. I have heard many self-pitying children complain, "I have to do all the work! I never see Dad or Mom working!" Too often Mom and Dad are reading or watching TV while the children do their assigned jobs. The children may not see you doing heroic tasks while they are out playing. I urge you to work together. Your children will observe your skills, you can naturally supervise and reward their efforts, and the teamwork that develops will unite your family in respect and love.

INDIVIDUALITY

Our world, so molded by slick media advertising, doesn't properly value the individual. You are the one to change that. You can teach your children, as you practice it yourself, to respect each one's individuality.

First, *find out who you are and what you believe in.* Read, listen, and think. Then talk about your ideas, values, and the character traits you view as significant. What are your unique skills? Practice them creatively. Even in the way you decorate your home and dress yourself, you can express your individuality.

Next, *allow your husband to be his own person.* There were times when I tried to make my husband conform to my ideas about child rearing, vacation plans, and household management. That wasn't fair, and we struggled hard to establish mutual respect for each other's wishes, ideas, and values.

Finally, *look for individuality in each of your children.* You will find that one is best in sports, another in academic achievement, and another in social charms. Value each one's specific capability, and encourage its development. Then help them discipline themselves to learn to do reasonably well in the other areas of life as well.

The finely tuned balances of life are very difficult to establish in seeking your child's uniqueness. Peers will constantly pressure your child to conform, and a degree of adaptation is essential. Determining how far you allow the conformity to go and where you demand individuality is your challenge. In every instance, these questions provide guidelines:

- Is this activity, clothing, or privilege good for this special child?
- Will it help her develop confidence and enable her to be strong in character?
- Will it teach him solid, lasting values on which he can build his life and prepare to handle your grandchildren?
- Will it open more options to her, or will it limit her in some unhealthy way?
- Can your family financially afford this, or are you trying to keep up with the Joneses?

PHYSICAL NEEDS

Children grow quite slowly from ages five to seven or eight, but then they usually hit a growth spurt. Again between ages ten and twelve, they may grow and develop quite rapidly. During growth spurts, children's appetites increase dramatically. At other times, children seem to live on air and water. Don't worry unless there are signs of depression or illness. If in doubt, ask your doctor or the school nurse or counselor.

Physical dexterity varies a great deal, so encourage your child to play, using the large muscles, and to be creative with arts to develop the fine motor skills. Encourage, don't push! Play and work with your child at times to teach him how to make skill development into fun.

Keep mealtimes and bedtimes reasonably regular. Part of good self-control, so vital in personal growth, demands giving up pleasure for certain scheduled regularity. Only a few children willingly stop TV viewing or play to go to bed. If you give in and allow her to live without some structure, she'll fail to develop self-discipline.

PUBERTY

Watch out for good hygiene habits. I've known moms to let their children go to bed in their school clothes. They may even wear them to school the next day. Instead, they need to shed tight jeans and sweaty, soiled underwear. They will sleep better after a soothing bath, and their teacher and friends will enjoy their fresh, clean smell the next day. Especially as children approach puberty, teach good hygiene habits. Tuck them in bed, and as you kiss them good night, let them know you appreciate their cooperation.

Puberty sex education has become a public issue because parents have neglected it at home. *It is your job to instill in your children healthy attitudes about sex and sexual responsibility.* This teaching demands that you review your attitudes. Have you gradually formed permissive ideas about sexual activity by teenagers, outside marriage, or flirtatiousness among married couples? What do you believe about sexual responsibility? And how do you view healthy, pleasurable sex in marriage? If you aren't sure about what you believe, you cannot teach your children. Sort it out; review your values and their logic. Get comfortable regarding sexuality, and then you will be ready to teach your children.

Observe them for evidences of physical development. The appearance of breast tissue, axillary and pubic hair and the onset of menarche in girls, and wet dreams and male sexual development in boys often occur at eleven or twelve years of age. Help your children understand the hormonal changes that prompt this physical development. Tell them that young people change at very different times and rates. Teach them to be sensitive to peers who develop either earlier or later than they do. And be sure your children know sexual development and functions are not for jokes or ridicule. Enable them to see sexuality as a part of the wholeness of life—normal, healthy, beautiful, and purposeful in marital intimacy and child rearing.

Teach sons and daughters to be responsible for their behavior and beliefs. And help them recognize that they are also responsible for their peers. Before they get caught up in the intensity of sexual feelings, help them know how to prevent premature sexual encounters. They must keep their thoughts on wholesome values, expend their energy in nonsexual activities, and postpone any focus on sexual activity until they are ready for marriage. These values can best be taught by allaying their natural curiosity. If you refuse to listen to their interests and try to stifle their questions, they will be even more curious, and they are then likely to turn to negative sources of information. In most grocery and drugstores masses of magazines tout sexual "freedom" and stimulate sexual interests and even desire. Don't make it necessary for your children to learn from such explicit and amoral sources.

Teach them honestly, clearly, and only as they are ready to understand in a healthy way. Not only in sexual matters but also in all aspects of their lives, teach your children solid values. Two children revealed to me that their parents would buy one newspaper from a public vending machine, but as the coins allowed the door to open, they would take two papers. The parents probably did not know their children understood this act was stealing, or they may not have cared. Don't destroy your children's innocence and basic sense of honesty. Practice and teach being honest.

Encourage compassion for others, which begins by teaching sensitivity to feelings, positive and negative. Convey that it is never acceptable to inflict pain on others and it is not necessary to allow others to hurt them.

So teach your children to be kind and also how to confront unkindness. Role-play how to deal with the neighborhood bully. It may even be wise to teach them self-defense skills. In a world where violence seems relentless, your children should not initiate physical or verbal aggression, but at the same time they should be able to defend themselves or others when they are picked on or attacked.

You and your children will need great courage to become whole, well-integrated individuals. Courage does not develop without fear, so never disparage a child if he is afraid. Help him know that courage faces fear with all the skills and energy one has in the effort to overcome both fear and danger.

Whatever your personal values are, teach them. Talk about those values and how you learned them. Exemplify them. In every aspect of your life, live out those values consistently. And then require that your children live in accordance with them. By rewards and consequences, help them to practice the values in sufficient depth to know whether they will adopt them personally. If you don't get them to try, they can never know how well they work in terms of self-respect, healthy relationships, and successful living.

DISCIPLINE

During the years from five to twelve, children's minds develop exponentially. They become capable of amazing insights and are very perceptive. Using the guidelines described in this book, help your children understand that they must learn to choose what is good and right even when that is difficult.

Just because others cheat and make better grades, or get by with dishonesty, doesn't mean those things are okay. You will find your best teaching tools are logic and love more than punishment and anger. How incongruous it is to a child to have a mother demonstrate abuse and loss of self-control while disciplining him for dishonesty! Do I mean you have to be perfect? Not at all. But you must find a way to practice all of the values you want your child to adopt.

SELF-CONTROL

This rare skill involves recognizing and expressing one's emotions honestly and in a controlled manner. You may choose how intensely you will express excitement, fear, or anger, but never allow powerful emotions to take over the control from you.

Few areas of mastery can build the sense of great inner strength like self-control. The child who achieves this skill will be able to manage most areas of being responsible. The child who acquires self-control can:

- avoid hurting others in any serious manner verbally or physically
- learn self-defense in a safe, effective manner and not retaliate
- accomplish unpleasant and difficult tasks when he would rather play
- avoid impulsive, risky behaviors because she is in charge of her decisions
- recognize the need for help because he will not have to prove how smart he is or become a "know-it-all"

DEMOCRACY IN THE HOME

There are many models for governing families. When I was a child, I recognized that my mother was in charge of certain issues, but my father clearly ruled the clan. He was kind, firm, and clear, and he always knew what was best for us. I, at least, never doubted that he knew. He also cared enough to see to it that each of us did what we were supposed to do.

Much as I loved my father and respected his authority, I suspect there is a better way. In today's permissive society, I like for mothers and fathers to consider teaching and practicing democracy in the home. In this system everyone gets a voice and a vote, but there is eventually a veto power that can prevent disasters. In case there is a tie in the voting, the chairperson may cast the deciding vote.

Here's how this plan can work in your family. When all the family members can get together, hold a council session. Bring your own agenda and add to your list the concerns of everyone else. There are a few basic rules: no yelling, fighting, or insulting. Anyone who breaks these rules is excused for the rest of the meeting.

You, Mother, conduct the meeting. (Or father may be willing to do this, if you prefer.) Take one issue at a time, listen to all sides of it, and ask for a group decision. Whenever possible, give that choice a chance. If your experience makes it clear that the risks are too great, you must veto that action.

Such a family session provides an incomparable teaching opportunity. You can demonstrate how to collect information, balance those facts with people's emotions, point out the possible choices, and predict the likely consequences.

Wise decisions have the greatest possibility of coming from such a process, and imagine how helpful this learned logic will be when your children become adults.

All types of responsibilities and privileges may be determined in these sessions. Misunderstandings can often be removed, empathy for one another's feelings and needs will certainly come through, and a family can grow into a healthy, mutually supportive team.

Family council meetings offer an opportunity for practicing and teaching democracy in your home. Use the parental veto power to prevent disasters.

Once policies are established and responsibilities are assigned, you will need to follow through. With the best intentions in the world, children (and parents, too!) tend to forget their tasks, and hassles develop. Establish rewards and consequences. You are the ultimate boss, and it's up to you to enforce the agreement. That final follow-up eventually gets the job done, the responsibility learned, and the self-esteem established.

Do not do your children's jobs at any cost (except as suggested earlier, as a special treat). They will feel guilty and resent your doing it, but they are lazy enough that they will try to get out of it and want you to do it. These strong, negative feelings are confusing, so don't allow them to get started. Just enforce the family's agreements. Express your appreciation and pride to your family—including yourself—every time you can.

RESPONSIBILITY

Remember that the major task of children ages five to twelve is to develop a healthy sense of responsibility. We have thought about that task in many regards.

Responsibility is gained through increasing opportunities to make wise decisions. Clarify for your child the process for choosing wisely, then offer her chances to practice that skill. The steps to safe choices include collecting information from all sides, listing the possible choices, actually making the choice, and recognizing and coping with the consequences.

Refusing to rescue a child from the natural consequences of poor decisions will bring reality into focus—an excellent teaching-learning device. On the other hand, to avoid defensiveness, do not say, "I told you so!" Simply review the decision-making process and help your child see at which point she erred.

Even more important are *your compliments when the choice was right.* Give your child the credit he deserves. Say, "Your decision to study rather than go bike riding was what helped you do so well on your test!" Not, "I'm so glad you obeyed me by studying last night."

When your child's decisions are negative too often, resulting in failures and pain, you may need to be more the authority and less the teacher temporarily. But as soon as possible, go back to helping your child decide.

THOSE INEVITABLE CONSEQUENCES

No matter how hard you try to be positive, encourage responsibility, and even allow natural consequences to happen, sooner or later you must be prepared with consequences. Before any punishment, however, your child must recognize the misdeed. Children are quick to pass the blame on to others or get you to excuse them by pleading fatigue, not feeling well, or forgetting. Don't accept such excuses.

I recommend clear confrontation and a firm statement: "I see that you did not do your cleaning job. You remember the consequences we agreed on. So, sorry as I am, there'll be no TV for you this evening, since you'll be busy doing that work!"

Here are some useful consequences:

- The child loses a privilege such as playing outside, watching TV, or even reading (my parents' favorite consequence for me since I read to the exclusion of doing my jobs).
- Time-out in a special chair or your child's room makes the point and also allows for cooling off. (It's often helpful to use some time-out for yourself to think more clearly.)
- Total grounding from all pleasure for a period of time is effective for many infractions.
- When the wrongdoing is due to being careless or roughhousing, your child should repair or replace any broken or ruined objects. Apologizing for hurt feelings is a good practice, but only when the rage has died down so he can be sincere.
- Extra chores may be very useful to earn money for restitution or to compensate for careless work.
- Waiting it out with your child may be far more successful than trying to force compliance immediately.

Whatever consequence you choose, enforce it matter-of-factly but firmly. Good discipline is best done in a friendly but no-nonsense manner. The fewer words you use, the better. Above all, don't expect your child to be grateful for your efforts. Discipline can be very painful, but your tough love can take that pain and know that even painful consequences, well-administered, will be superbly effective in your child's healthy development.

For most schoolchildren, spanking creates more rebellion and hate than compliance. Be creative in your consequences—no dinner for you until the pets are fed; no TV until studies are done; no time with the family when you are rude and hit people.

Discipline can be painful, but even painful consequences, well-administered, will be effective in your child's healthy development.

Limit the consequences to the day of the "crime." Very rarely they may extend to a few days. But giving a week's grounding may leave you with no other consequences to use tomorrow. Too much punishment can result in discouragement or angry rebellion.

RESOURCES

Few parents can do it alone. Even if yours is a two-parent family, you can use community resources to help.

Nearly every community has a Scouts organization. If yours doesn't, start one. You can get books and materials by writing to Boy Scouts of America, P.O. Box 152079, Irving, TX 75015, or Girl Scouts of the U.S.A., 420 Fifth Avenue, New York, NY 10018-2798. (Or see the Web sites—Boy Scouts: www.bsa.scouting.org.; Girl Scouts: www.gsusa.org.) The merit badge system teaches all kinds of skills, and children proudly wear the badges and medals they have earned.

All sorts of activities are available at churches and synagogues—Sunday school, youth groups, vacation Bible schools, summer camps, and service opportunities in most communities. These organizations will be encouraged by your children's involvement, and they offer a chance for the children to learn lasting values, make friends, and explore spiritual growth.

Look for a church that promotes family unity. Sometimes churches have so many separate activities that they divide families instead of strengthening them.

Your local YWCA or YMCA usually offers a variety of sports, crafts, and social enrichment classes and activities. Take advantage of them. The fee for joining is a good investment, and membership can open a wide range of healthy, fun-filled adventures for the entire family.

Most communities have several choices of sports teams. Softball, soccer, swimming, and other sports are usually fairly well-coached and teach physical and social skills to children. But don't make so many commitments that your child has too little time to just "be"! And guard with your very life the time it takes to be a really connected family.

Once when I visited my married daughter, she was busily involved with a cluster of neighborhood children. They were sitting under a big tree on old blankets around a huge wicker basket. In it were many scraps of all kinds and materials. I could see that she was having as much fun as they were, making clever craft objects. Later she explained. In their new neighborhood, she had found people to be aloof, but she likes to have lots of friends. She discovered that the way to the hearts of her neighbors was through their children. Never, several told me, had they known anyone like Wendy, who just loved children.

So if your neighborhood lacks community groups, create your own. It will enrich your life as well as your child's. Mothering skills are a scarce commodity. As you develop yours, put them to use.

I hope you will grow gradually into more friendship and a little less parenting role with your child. In the next stage, you will need every possible skill to cope with mothering an adolescent.

CHAPTER FIFTEEN

Adolescents

*I*t was one of those days! Mom and Joyce had struggled through early adolescence with considerable difficulty. There were good and bad times, but Mother had realized a very important fact: Teenagers like to think of themselves as adults. Therefore, she agreed to consider Joyce an adult and vowed to treat her like one.

In the book *Understanding Adolescence,* Dr. Donald Kotesky reviews the historic fact that until the past century, when children reached puberty, they were considered adults. Girls could marry, and boys often had full-time jobs. Many of the problems of adolescents, Dr. Kotesky writes, are due to the no-man's-land modern society has created for them. There is a great deal of truth in his philosophy.

At any rate, Joyce and her mother made their best adjustments when Mom remembered her adult status—until the inevitable day arrived. It was Sunday, and Joyce began the day by complaining about having to attend church. She remained sullen through the delicious Sunday dinner her mom ritually prepared. In the afternoon she insisted on going swimming when she had previously promised to go on an outing with another friend. She knew the family rule that prior commitments must be honored. It wouldn't be fair to abandon one friend when a more exciting event popped up.

Throughout the day, Joyce and Mom skirmished or fought outright battles. Late that Sunday evening, Mom went to Joyce's room to kiss her good night. As she sat on the side of Joyce's bed, she regretfully thought of the lovely day that had been wasted in fighting and anger. She said softly, "Joyce, I'm sorry about this day. I promised never to treat you like a two-year-old, but I realize I've done that very thing all day. I'm sorry!"

To Mom's delight, Joyce grinned and replied, "That's okay, Mom. I know I was acting like one! I'm sorry, too." As they hugged each other, Mom shed a few tears, realizing gratefully that both of them had won another battle, and the bonds of love had been strengthened through honesty and understanding.

ADOLESCENTS' GOAL

Developmental psychologists have clearly defined the major task of adolescents: the establishment of responsible independence. Teenagers make most of their own decisions, wisely or not. Whether parents like it or not, they adjust skirt lengths, apply makeup, and change hairstyles to suit the trends even after they arrive at school. The more intensely you try to make them obey you, the more certainly they will rebel.

Your best chance of preventing such power struggles is to move from an authority role to a wise mentor status. You *must* remain steady and consistent because your teen cannot. As he bounces about in the stormy winds of physical, social, and emotional development, you must remain his anchor, safely set and immovable.

You see, the teen years are partly a replay of those terrific twos. Do you remember the main task of two-year-olds? It is to begin to separate from Mom and Dad and to discover who they are, what they can do, and how far they can push you. How successfully you and your toddler made that separation has much to do with the successful weathering of the storms now.

Both then and now, children are highly ambivalent. They want the security of dependency, and at the same time they crave the excitement of what they see as freedom. This mixture of wishes and feelings is responsible for the confusing behaviors of teens. One day, or even one hour, they are mature and show responsibility. The next, they are throwing childish tantrums and seem beyond control.

> *The major task of adolescence is establishing responsible independence.*

This time, the struggle for independence is real and for the rest of life. Both your two-year-old and you knew there was much more time for the struggle to adulthood. Now, there is very little time, and every day counts with your adolescent.

PHYSICAL ISSUES

If you had a chance to teach your preteen about the immense forces of growth and development at work in the body, it will be easier to communicate with her now. If you missed that opportunity, however, don't despair. You can begin now.

If your adolescent is somewhat naive and innocent, approach this topic simply. First, inform yourself. Check out a library book on human growth and development or borrow your child's biology book. Make yourself so familiar with the basic facts of life that you can be comfortable discussing them.

Be observant. Mothers can be so close to their children that they fail to recognize the tiny, daily increments of change until too much time has elapsed. Suddenly, it seems, your child has grown up. You must school yourself to be aware of the appearance of hair on your son's chin and the change in his voice or to notice your daughter's budding breasts and her generally more contoured body.

As you become aware of these signs of physical maturity, privately comment on them. Find a place and time when neither of you is in a hurry. After describing the changes you see, express pleasure and pride in the person your child is becoming. Explain that these processes of change are natural but often awkward. You may recapture some of your memories of adolescence. Don't be surprised if your child has no questions. He probably is too overwhelmed to know what to ask.

Explain the Creator's genius of setting an individual time clock in everyone. That clock determines how much the body changes, how tall a person will be, and how early and rapidly those changes take place. If your child is very different from her peers, let her know that is okay. This is one more chance for you to teach the value of individuality.

Find some books on human development for your adolescent to read. Some, frankly, are grotesque and designed as caricatures. Many seem to be far too blatant for teens, almost pornographic in their descriptions. But there are a few sound, middle-of-the-road books that will present facts honestly yet tastefully. (See the Suggested Reading at the back of this book.) Your teen needs a wholesome attitude about his body, and today's social climate does not foster such health. It's up to you to provide it. You can begin a wisely planned campaign to mold your teen's beliefs.

- Develop values and beliefs that are responsible, wholesome, and based on facts.
- Work on forming a relationship with your teen based on mutual respect.
- Practice your communications skills with your teen in all phases of life. That means you learn to ask questions, listen honestly, and speak clearly.
- Gradually introduce some of your values to your teen. Use news articles or some ideas you have read as a starting point. Well-known authorities advocate abstinence from sex outside marriage. You may

start by simply asking your teen, "What do your friends believe about sexual involvement?"

- Avoid trying to convince your teen all at once about your beliefs. Just teach her to think in terms of right (healthy, constructive) and wrong (damaging, destructive).

- Remember to weave in your ideas about sexual issues to the whole of your teen's life. Also show an interest in school, recreation, and social activities.

DRUG AND ALCOHOL ABUSE

Statistics reveal that vast percentages of teens abuse drugs and alcohol. While drug use, thankfully, is currently on the decline, alcohol consumption is not. Among both adults and young people, its abuse is frighteningly common.

According to the May 2000 issue of the *Harvard Mental Health Letter*, about 14 million people in the U.S. abuse or are dependent on alcohol. Alcohol accounts for 15 percent of our medical costs, causes 100,000 deaths annually, and is involved in one-third of child abuse cases. This source also states that the average consumption of alcohol is falling, and more people are trying to change their drinking habits.

TV documentaries, however, continue to reveal the excessive use of alcohol on college campuses. Also, the use of drugs to heighten pleasure (e.g., meth and speed) and to subdue girls for use as sex objects by manipulative young men continues to trouble our society.

A good mother does not lurk behind the door when her child comes home from the ball game to smell his breath. She is, however, always aware that any young person can be vulnerable to a drinking problem.

Schools are doing a heroic job of teaching teens the risks of drugs and alcohol. But you dare not leave such a vital task to outsiders. You, too, must educate your teen about addiction. Most people have personal experience with addictive friends or relatives. Without condemning or preaching, inform your teen of the tragedy of their situation.

Be alert to signs of chemical use. A change in attitude or behavior after being out with friends may mean nothing. Or it could be your tip-off that your son is experimenting. When he leaves notes or other writings lying around, the chances are that he wants you to read them. Do so. I even urge you to spot-check his room at times. You may discover drugs or drug paraphernalia. If you do, please confront your child. She will be angry with you for checking, but relieved that you will protect her from dangerous chemicals.

Other signs of drug abuse depend on the type of chemical involved. Unusual talking or behavior that is nervous and excitable, a flushed look to the face, and pupils (the black centers of the eyes) that are dilated even in bright light indicate the use of uppers or speed. A dull, listless, super-relaxed demeanor with drowsiness often means a person has taken downers, such as barbiturates or certain sleeping pills. Once again, look for the balance between believing the best of your teen but also knowing that the worst can befall anyone.

Should you strongly suspect chemical abuse and your teen denies it, I urge you to see your doctor. It is easy to have a laboratory do a drug screen to determine the truth. If there is clear evidence of abuse, do not hesitate to seek a professional family therapist who also can work with drug problems.

Tax-supported public counseling agencies are quite affordable. And a qualified psychologist or psychiatrist can be located through your clergyperson or family physician. Don't let your pride prevent asking for help, and don't assume this is a stage that will pass. That may be true, but waiting may allow even worse addiction to develop. Ask for a professional's opinion to guide you. Love, you must remember, often needs to be tough. Any hint that your child may be addicted to drugs is a signal that it's time for tough love.

High Tide of Emotions

Just as your two-year-old vented strong emotions by temper tantrums or loud wailing, so your teen will express her emotions intensely. Such emotional storms are exhausting and even frightening, but be grateful that your growing child can express those feelings. Your job is to try to wade through them to the genuine, understandable needs and pain that prompt them.

When your adolescent becomes temporarily overwhelmed by her emotions, don't try to counteract them by becoming equally upset. Now is the time for you to remain (or become!) calm, reasonable, and patient.

Tips for Dealing with Your Turbulent Teen

1. Whatever is going on, call time-out. You sit down and think, and ask your teen to go to his room and regain control.

2. When you have a clearer grasp of the situation and some degree of reason has returned to your child, go to him and lay some ground rules for dealing with both the emotions and the situation that caused them.

3. The ground rules may be that there will be no insults or yelling, and both of you will try to stay logical and constructive.

4. Stick with the issue at stake, and consider only what is in the best interest of your teen. Don't get caught in a power struggle.

5. Remember your own adolescence. Issues that seem trivial now would then have caused you absolute anguish. Your teen is now as you were then, so you can understand her while she has no way to see a mother's point of view.

6. Guide your teen to discover her solutions and help her see how she can learn to control her emotional responses rather than allow them to control her.

Emotions are natural reactions to some kind of inner stress. Excitement and joy, fear and anxiety, anger and frustration—all are healthy. It's how a person understands them and their cause and how one expresses them that makes them positive or negative. It's your opportunity, mother, to teach these basic facts and skills to your teen.

Bev is a teen with strong emotions. She had been a sensitive, caring child. She was easy to love and a joy for her mother to hold and comfort after an episode that caused pain. When Bev became a teenager, however, her mother realized that her upsets were becoming too frequent and entirely too dramatic. So she stopped reacting to her daughter's wails of despair when she suffered some small injustice or slight.

One day, Bev had endured an unusually difficult day at school, and when she arrived home, she threw herself on the sofa, crying out her woes. After a short time, her mother went to her and sat quietly beside her, simply squeezing her hand. She waited, trying to think of words that would comfort her growing child without encouraging her overly emotional reaction. Abruptly, Bev regained control, and in a moment of remarkable insight, she said, "You know, Mom, I kind of think I enjoy getting upset!"

Learn from Bev and her mother. Try to find a way to encourage your teen to understand and express feelings without overdramatizing or overreacting. Teach your teen to express the emotions and then to analyze the situation and resolve the problems.

PEER PRESSURE

Peer pressure is difficult for young children to resist. It is even harder for teens to deal with social pressures from their friends and classmates. In fact, an unfortunate phenomenon occurs among teens.

In their search for independence, teenagers commonly rebel against their parents. They refuse to follow the rules and avoid joining the family for meals, activities, or religious observances. Since they are not ready for total independence, they often feel bewildered and lonely. Their pride, of course, prevents their admitting vulnerability, but they have a ready recourse to other adolescents who experience identical feelings and reactions. When these young people find one another, it is easy to see how subculture and even counterculture groups are established.

Far short of the extreme groups who often follow intense musical heroes or cults, there is widespread peer pressure. You can count on your teen, too, getting caught up in this pressure to some degree. Consider it normal, and find ways to help your adolescent through this stage.

Remember your adolescence. How did you feel being very different from your peers? Without lecturing, share with your teen some of your experiences and the lessons you learned from them.

Allow your teen some freedom to explore many areas of life. She must see and experience certain aspects of life to learn to distinguish positive values from negatives.

Always keep the avenues of communication open. You may do this by listening to your child thoughtfully, without harsh judgments or panic.

Define the bottom line. Where are the risks of freedom too great? In giving your teen a chance to learn and grow, do not allow him to be destroyed. Once again, we're talking about balance.

Observe every sign of true individuality and healthy independence in your teen. Without overdoing it, compliment her for being assertive and doing her own thing rather than following a peer leader. And by all means, become a role model in such endeavors. As you make decisions based on logic and love, not on what someone else might say, your family will notice, and your habits will guide others in their decision making.

Teach your teen to feel so good about himself and so secure in your acceptance and approval that he needs very little peer approval. The better your child's self-esteem, the more likely he will be to choose peers of high quality. Your child can quietly become a leader in her peer group, turning peer pressure into a helpful and uplifting entity, not a negative, destructive one.

REASONS FOR REBELLIOUS BEHAVIORS

Gilbert was a teen in serious trouble. His extremely strict but loving parents had never allowed their children to attend movies, believing they would damage the moral values they had so carefully taught. Despite the emphatic rule, Gilbert had seen *Gone with the Wind,* and to his credit, he was honest when his father confronted him.

> *Through his behavior, your teen may be asking, "Are you wise and strong enough—do you care enough to make me do what I do not yet have the strength to do on my own?"*

After some deliberation, Gilbert's father decided his son must be punished. He almost never administered physical punishment, but the infraction, Dad believed, was too much. He felt that his son's spiritual life and his moral values were at stake, so he whipped his stalwart teenage son. Gilbert submitted, but he steadfastly held to his belief that the movie was not harmful. As soon as he could, he left home and for a long period did exactly as he pleased, rebelling in every area of his life.

At one time, there were many parents like Gilbert's. They had established their values, and family rules were based on them. Infractions warranted severe punishments, and all too commonly, the process ended in total rebellion. Such rebellion, in my experience, is extremely rare now because parents are no longer so sure of their beliefs. They are often afraid of losing their relationship with their teens, so they allow too much freedom in many cases.

Behaviors that were once called rebellious are basically breaking the rules. They include truancy from school and refusal to study; the use of tobacco, alcohol, and other drugs; cheating, lying, and stealing; sexual promiscuity; and often, violence in various forms. Unique attire and hairstyles and general disrespect round out the list. There are three basic reasons for such conduct disorders.

1. Testing the limits of authority. Young people, as you know, are at best caught in the dilemma of wanting independence but also needing some boundaries. They want the authority of wise adults at times, but they test out that authority constantly. What they need to know is this: Are you wise enough? Are you strong enough? And do you care enough to make me do what I do not yet have the willpower to do?

When your authority is inconsistent, your teen will test you all the more. You must find the courage to stand by the policies your wisdom creates. Include your teen in forming policies, but at times it's up to you to enforce them.

2. Resisting authority that is too rigid. As in Gilbert's case, too-strict parents stand a good chance of seeing their children rebel in a destructive manner. Let me clarify that being rigid does not always involve religious or moral values. It may mean that you feel yours is the only correct way to function. You may demand a degree of perfectionism and compliance that destroys your teen's individuality. Evaluate your expectations.

Ask a friend if you are too demanding; an objective observer may see dynamics that you miss. If you are holding the reins too tightly, your teen may bolt and run!

3. Avoiding unbearable pain. Teens suffer emotional trauma for many reasons. Often the pain stems from parental strife and/or divorce. It may relate to unfair expectations of parents and teachers. Often trauma comes from parental ways of attempting to motivate or discipline that involve guilt or shame. And very often it relates to a sense of failure with peers or in school activities.

In today's large, impersonal schools, the solid, average teen is a nobody. The gifted students and those with serious problems receive massive amounts of attention, but the vast majority who function in between receive neither praise nor punishment. And perhaps the worst abuse of all is to go unnoticed and to feel unimportant.

It is up to you, Mom, to provide that recognition so needed by every teen.

Establish activities. Involve your teen in small groups that will offer him an opportunity to find a sense of belonging, status, and fulfillment.

Evaluate yourself. Are you too inconsistent, making it necessary for your teen to test the boundaries? Or are you too rigid, preventing the natural growth toward independence that is the main function of adolescence? Or have you allowed or even caused the pain that becomes unbearable to a teen? Wherever you have made mistakes, you can also make corrections. True, you will feel your anguish when you face the fact that you have traumatized the child you love. But only when you admit your errors can you correct them. Be sure of both your mistakes and your plans for change. Then go for it.

- Find a private time to talk to your teen about where your methods and actions or words were wrong.
- Apologize. You needn't grovel or be maudlin. Simply explain your motives and how it happened that your methods erred. Just say, "I'm so sorry!"
- Outline briefly your plans to change, and admit that at your age, change takes place slowly. Habits are deeply ingrained and will not be replaced readily.
- Ask for your teen's help. Believe me, you'll need it. He can tell you many facts that will help you reform your mothering. Listen to him, and incorporate his needs and ideas into your plan for change.
- Follow through. When you slip into old habits, don't give up! Just get up and get going again, always with the help and encouragement of your teen.

Admitting failure does not cause you to lose respect. Your teen knows before you do that you have goofed. She will respect you for admitting it.

I can confidently assure you that following these guidelines will transform your relationship with your adolescent. Once your friendship with him is established, you can comfort the pain he endures. But when you have caused the pain, it is not likely your teen will accept your help or comfort until you admit your mistakes and apologize.

TEENS ARE USUALLY SLOBS

For the hundredth time that day, Kathy's mom reminded her to clean up her room. When she was only four, Kathy had learned to make her bed, put away her toys, and hang up her clothes. Now, at fourteen, she suddenly could do none of those simple tasks.

Trying her best to be patient but firm, Mother said, "Kathy, I've always been proud of your neatness. You're better organized than I am. But lately your room looks like a disaster. I want you to clean it up!"

Kathy looked around her room, so neatly furnished in white. She grinned ever so slightly as she answered, "Yeah, Mom, it's a disaster. But you oughta be glad that's the only way I'm rebelling. If you knew what some of my friends were doing, you'd never say a word about this room!"

She was right, of course. And her mother hugged her tightly as she said, "Okay, Honey! As long as you stay out of really bad trouble, I'll not complain again!" Later, Kathy resumed her neat ways. Her life at fourteen seemed such a disaster that her room simply matched it.

Don't overreact to your teen's temporary carelessness. Help keep the room orderly, and remind him that you can wait until his life returns to a semblance of calm for him to become orderly again. But if you have never taught him to be responsible, you need to remedy that.

Responsibility needed to be learned before adolescence, so it will be harder to teach now. But by all means make the effort. Start by organizing a short family work time each week. Try to make that time fit your teen's schedule so you won't defeat the program by asking for defiance. If Dad and everyone work together, you can get your teen to see how important teamwork is and how much better the family functions when each member is responsible.

In counseling countless families over many years, I have learned that being neat is an asset. The husband who refuses to put his dirty clothes in the laundry and never washes his dishes after a snack grieves his wife. And a woman who watches soap operas, leaving the house cluttered most of the time, can irritate even the best husband. Be sure your teen has a basic knowledge of neatness. In spite of temporary sloppiness, a teen is almost certain to return to better habits when the tensions of adolescence are past.

COMMON MISTAKES

Some mistakes are unique to mothering adolescents. Chances are, you are in the very act of making those mistakes right now. But don't despair! They can be corrected if you know about them.

Overreaction. The very essence of adolescence is intensity. Emotions, activities, and reactions are dramatic in their quality. The temptation is to indulge in panic.

And when you panic, you can't see situations clearly or respond logically. You will, instead, try to overpunish or overprotect your teen. You will believe you have failed as a mother and your teen is a lost cause.

None of the above is probably true. You may need to make some corrections, and you certainly need to believe in your teen's ultimate success.

Take some time to think; observe objectively; check with your husband and a friend. Then react to problem situations with wisdom and strength. You can prevent most serious rebellion if you will do so.

Too much freedom. Marlene's thirteen-year-old face showed precocious lines of anger and hardness. She had done just about all the bad things a young girl could do. She had repeatedly skipped school, shoplifted almost everything she wanted, abused drugs and alcohol, and was extremely rude to her mother and teachers.

To help Marlene change the destructive course of her life, I was trying to find out how such habits had gotten started. Her story revealed the truth.

Her mother had divorced her father when Marlene was still a pre-schooler. Mother had a series of boyfriends with whom she invested a great deal of time and energy. Without intending to, she had sorely neglected her daughter. It seemed easier to let the child do her own thing. At times Mother did yell at Marlene but took no action to change her wild ways.

At last, Marlene's extreme misbehavior brought her to the attention of the local juvenile court. Her mother was required to be with Marlene as she confronted the stern black-robed judge. With tears in her blue eyes, Marlene described the scene. These words are burned into my memory: "I never knew my mom loved me. But in court, she cried and told the judge she wanted me to come back home because she loved me." It had taken grave risks and great heartache for Marlene's mother to rearrange her priorities and discover how to meet her daughter's needs. Sadly enough, some mothers never make this discovery.

> *Gradually increase your adolescent's freedom to choose behaviors and activities. When you see her veering off course, gently prod her back.*

Gradually increase your adolescent's freedom to choose activities and behaviors. When you see her veering too far off course, gently prod her back. If this gentle but strong approach is to work, you must maintain a friendly relationship and clear, open communication.

Lack of adult consistency. Predictability makes a child secure. You may even make mistakes, but if you do so consistently, you may get by with them. Not knowing what to expect creates many teenage problems.

You and your husband must come to some basic agreements about your values and the rules and consequences that support them. Teens, having begun as children, have become master manipulators. They know exactly which parent is more likely to give in to their wishes and whims, and they will always catch that parent to ask permission or tell their plans.

While they enjoy having their way, all but the most callous teens feel some remorse and guilt when you and their father argue about what they have done. Keep disagreements about a child quite private. Settle the issue as quickly as possible, and establish a plan for more unity in the future.

Becoming consistent in dealing with your teen demands logical thinking, good communication, and an affirming attitude. Sit down together, parents and teen. Discuss these issues, and agree on the steps to resolve them:

- *What are the goals your teen needs to establish?* These goals must include little, daily ones as well as big, life-affecting value formation. Being helpful, courteous, sensitive, and responsible are examples I consider to be extremely important in the short- and long-range aspects of life.
- *What are your needs relating to your adolescent?* To avoid worry so I could sleep at night, I needed for my teenage son to let me know where he would be and about when I could expect him home. When I explained this as my need and not as a means of controlling him, he gladly complied. To work, this step must be absolutely honest.
- *What are the decisions your teen may make independently?* In what areas must she discuss choices with you? And what bottom-line verdicts and vetoes do you reserve as parents? You and your husband need to agree on this. If you are divorced, find a way to get your teen's father to join you in this total effort if at all possible.
- *What are the consequences and rewards that will most likely reinforce your efforts and ensure cooperation?* How will you remember to follow your new plan and avoid the old habits of yelling, arguing, and setting up power struggles?

You may need professional guidance to break old habits and make necessary changes. Sometimes the communication gap is too wide and the power struggles too intense. You may be unable to see any answers.

Don't be reluctant to seek a family counselor. Such a person is trained to analyze family problems and help you find answers tailor-made for you.

DON'T TREAT ME LIKE A CHILD!

Adolescents don't always know who they are, and neither do their parents. But there is one fact you can count on: they are not children! And they certainly don't want to be treated as such.

Jim's steel-gray eyes blazed as he talked. He had been referred to me because he was having major difficulty in school. He was known as the class clown—disruptive, unmotivated, and insolent. He had given up any effort to be a responsible, achieving young adult. At fifteen, Jim was well on the way to setting habits of failure and rebellion.

His anger flared in response to my questioning him about his parents' attempts to help him get back on track. I learned that his mother felt sorry for him and made excuses for him. "She treats me like I'm a child!" he yelled. His father, in contrast, lectured him at length in a condescending, know-it-all manner that Jim could not tolerate.

Jim needed the kind of handling that Ray's parents had discovered. They, too, had tried to make him comply, just as they had ten years earlier. They pleaded, set up behavior modification plans, and threatened, in turn. They, too, found excuses when all else failed.

Finally, they faced the facts. They could not make Ray learn. They could not follow him around and see to it that he behaved as they wanted him to do.

So they confronted him clearly with the facts. He was a senior in high school, and if he wanted to graduate with his friends, he could do so. He would, however, have to do it on his own. If he needed help, he would have to ask for it. They loved him and weren't giving up on him, but they realized that they could not earn a high-school diploma for him.

Ray understood what his parents said, but he didn't believe them. Surely, they would rescue him, hire a tutor, or intercede with the principal on his behalf. But the wise, courageous parents held firm. They loved Ray but refrained from rescuing him. Only eight weeks before graduation, Ray became a believer. He paid attention in class, studied regularly, and enrolled in an evening class. To everyone's amazement, Ray made it. He graduated with his class. And he did it on his own.

I hope you will not wait quite as long to help your child grow up. But start now. Believe in your teen and in yourself. Even if Ray had needed to attend summer school or take an additional semester, he had to become a responsible adult. And the extra time and effort he may have spent would have been well worth the lessons learned. Avoid treating your young adult like a child. If you consider him to be capable and he knows it, more than likely he will be.

You Are Not an Adolescent!

Sue was chatting away amiably. Her shiny blonde hair bounced and her eyes sparkled as she described her friends and their many activities. Her mother had asked me to see her because she felt they were growing apart. Sue was only sixteen, and her mother hated to have the two years before college spoiled.

Sue was obviously a vivacious, bright, and well-adjusted young lady. What, then, was the reason for the rift between her and Mother? Sue made it quite clear. "Mom," she stated, "thinks she's a teenager, too. I love her, but I don't like her to talk, dress, and act like my friends. It's embarrassing! Sometimes I think she even flirts with my boyfriend!"

Later, when I talked with Sue's mother, I learned that she had enjoyed her high-school years immensely. She had been popular, did well in school, and felt those were the best years of her life. Without realizing it, Sue's mother was trying to relive her teen years through her daughter.

It is sad to have to give up deep yearnings and wishes. I wished with Sue's mother that she could indeed relive those glorious times. It simply was impossible. Instead, I was able to help her grieve the loss of her youth and accept with dignity her maturity. What a difference her change made to Sue! The two of them became dear friends as well as mother and daughter, once Mother accepted that they could never be peers.

There is a gradual transition from parenthood to friendship with your teen. Don't hurry that process, but also don't try to delay it. In each child's life, there comes the point to relinquish mothering, so look for the right time. Accept the fact that losing a child is painful, but gaining an adult friend more than compensates. Your child can one day join you as an adult, but you can never go back and join her in being an adolescent. So don't try!

THE BIGGEST MISTAKE OF ALL

In the early 1970s our Western society became concerned about the serious deterioration of family life. We heard a great deal about communication gaps. Parents commonly misunderstood what their children were saying, and children certainly were no longer listening to parents. A mentor of mine commented sadly during that era, "I clearly see the biggest communication gap of all is silence!" And so it is.

When rebellion and anger become too painful, the temptation is to withdraw in helplessness. Both parents and children find reasons to spend increasing amounts of time apart. Mother, I plead with you to resist that temptation.

Through painful situations, Ellen began to realize that she and her thirteen-year-old son had drifted into very separate channels. If he said he had no homework, she chose to believe him. She worked all day and had many tasks to do in the evening. Besides, he was often grouchy when he had homework, and Ellen was too tired to cope with her son's irritable attitudes.

Only when his report card revealed failing grades did Ellen understand what had been happening. She also knew what she needed to do. She rearranged her time and the priorities of her tasks. Her son now comes first.

She no longer asks him if he has homework. She goes through each subject with him.

When he isolates himself in his room, she allows him some time alone. But she often goes into his room and sits with him. If he wants to talk, they do so. If he prefers to be quiet, she sits in relaxed, intimate silence with him. If she feels anxious about other duties or longs for time alone, she works thoughtfully through such feelings. Ellen knows her first love is her son. He deserves her best and foremost energy and time. Everything else can wait; growing into, and through, adolescence can't!

The changes in this young man validate Ellen's evaluation and reward her efforts. His grades quickly returned to their original quality. He left off most of his grouchiness and resumed his well-rounded, enthusiastic lifestyle.

Don't give in to the drift toward separation and silence that add up to neglect or a sense of total abandonment. You are the mother, the adult. Look through the unpleasantness and your pain to the needs of your teen. Keep touching!

GROUND RULES

There are ten rules to master if you plan to be a successful mother of an adolescent. Learn them well.

1. *Invite your teen (at about age thirteen) into your adult world.* Gently and clearly teach her how to be a healthy adult.

Your teen is a young adult. Educate yourself and discipline your attitudes and thoughts so that you treat him like an adult friend. Remember to explore this new world with your teen. If you must have expectations, keep them positive. Seek and maintain the delicate balance between freedom and responsibility. Remind your teen that living up to responsibilities earns new freedoms. Help your teen learn to make wise decisions. Teach him to collect information, list the possible options, and risk a final choice. Then allow the natural consequences to show the correctness or error of that decision.

2. *Strive for balances with, and for, your teen.*

- *Social life.* Friends and activities are important but must be balanced with family activities, study, and private time.
- *Achievement.* Success and its motivation must be balanced by the ability to lose without despair and yet try again.
- *Peer pressure.* Your teen needs to feel like one of the crowd, to fit in. Yet he needs the balance of individuality.
- *Involvement.* Adolescents need to try out various interests and activities. Yet busyness must be balanced by quietness if your teen is to learn a sense of *being,* so vital to maturity.

3. *Respect your teen's need for privacy, but like Ellen, invade that space regularly.* As a psychiatrist, I work with seriously troubled adolescents. From almost all of them I have learned that when they withdraw in anger and pain, they yearn for Mom to come to them. They are too independent to admit it or ask for the presence they crave. Give them some time alone, but then visit them with comfort and problem solving.

4. *Though you need to treat your teen like the adult she is becoming, remember that she is very much a child at times.* She needs to be allowed to regress now and then and receive the warmth, protection, and guidance all children need.

5. *Teach your teen all you can learn about sexuality*—its awesome beauty in proper circumstances, the fearful pain when it is abused, and the crucial need to be sexually responsible.

6. *At all times, build and strengthen your teen's self-esteem.* Self-esteem grows out of your esteem of your teen. Maintain both an inner attitude and an outward expression of respect.

7. *Teach values to your teen.* Make her keenly aware of the dangers involved with the wrong crowd and damaging behaviors. Teach the

courage it takes to stand against a crowd when necessary to avoid dangers and cultivate integrity.

8. *Recognize your teen's need for affection.* But don't forget that affection is acceptable mainly in private.

9. *Debate and even argue with your teen at times as you might with a friend.* Disagree agreeably. Avoid name-calling, put-downs, and negative predictions. When you are wrong, be strong enough to admit it and praise your teen for being right. Treat your adolescent at least as well as you do a respected neighbor.

10. *As part of his growing sense of responsibility, encourage compassion, respect, and logic in your teen.* You may best teach these qualities by modeling them.

SUCCESSFUL DISCIPLINE

Ron was horrified to hear the siren blaring and to see the red lights flashing behind him on the freeway! He had a new car, given to him on his sixteenth birthday by his parents. He reveled in its powerful motor and ready response to his touch. On the freeway, late in the evening, he had pushed the sleek car to its limit. The speedometer registered well over one hundred miles an hour, but he had allowed it to slow to a smooth eighty miles per hour. Ron knew he deserved the lecture and ticket the patrolman gave him.

> *Hold your ground on important issues. Your teen will be angry now, but later he will respect you for it.*

It was confusing, then, to hear his father saying that Ron should not have been ticketed. In fact, Dad decided to have his attorney "fix" the ticket in court. And fix it he did. Ron was both amazed and pleased at the ease with which he got off.

You can see the mistakes this true example reveals. Yet many of you have done the same thing. It is intuitive to want to protect your child and avoid the costly consequences of his wrongdoing. By giving in to such impulses, however, you are teaching irresponsibility and silently giving permission to do wrong again.

Ralph was fourteen, a husky young man who loved sports, was curious about girls, but hated to study. His mother believed he might have a learning disability and understandably felt sorry for him. Somehow, she believed that if only she and his father were good enough to him, he would be so grateful that he would apply himself and earn decent grades.

Mother bought for her son all the status apparel he wanted. She saw to it that he had a TV and computer games in abundance. She spared no luxuries for her son. When his grade card revealed even lower grades, Mother became desperate. Perhaps if they bought him a motorcycle, he would realize how much they loved him and wanted him to succeed.

Once again, you can see the fallacy in this mother's thinking. But have you, perhaps, made similar mistakes?

Let's look at some disciplinary guidelines:

- *Schedule regular family meetings to review basic needs, rules, and communications.* Keep these meetings informal and positive, but use the time to see to it that you and your teen are in tune with each other.
- *Rules are meaningless without consequences.* Ron failed to learn to observe speed limits by his parent's rescue. If you ask for their input, many teens will establish harsh consequences that will be effective in making good changes occur. If your teen has no ideas regarding consequences for wrongdoing, you need to come up with some. Be certain they are fair, time limited, and related to the misdeeds.
- *Follow through in enforcing established consequences.* Ron should have worked to pay his fine for speeding. Broken items should be mended or replaced by the teen who damaged them. Poor grades need to be improved through a loss of TV time and telephone privileges. Rudeness deserves an apology.

- *When your teen does disastrous acts, stand by her.* Guide and support her in corrective measures, but don't imply that her misdeeds were acceptable.
- *Avoid making your adolescent's problems yours.* Those hassles affect you, but I've known too many moms who worry and work at their kids' problems far more intensely than the teens do. Your teen cannot learn for himself if you act for him. Guide him, but don't solve problems for him.

APPROPRIATE CONSEQUENCES

Many mothers don't know what consequences to levy when a teen goofs. Most teens say the following actions are useful:

- Grounding, the time-honored act of keeping a teen at home. No pleasures away from home and few at home are allowed until corrective action is taken.
- Loss of specific privileges—no driving, no TV, no allowance, and no telephone use until responsible living is achieved.
- Assignment of extra duties when a teen has sloughed off on jobs. This offers a practice effect when the teen's performance is demonstrably under par.
- Getting a teen out of bed at night or early in the morning to do an assigned task that was forgotten may teach a valuable lesson. It worked for me when I was a kid!
- If you have had a strong and loving relationship, a loss of your trust and approval is indeed powerful! But you must be extremely careful not to use your relationship to coerce or manipulate your teen. If your relationship is poor, mend it.
- Avoid physical punishment. I have heard of cases where spanking a spoiled adolescent seemed to be corrective. My experience, however, is that most teens who are spanked become overtly rebellious.
- Always maintain unconditional love. You can clearly express disapproval for a wrong act and, with equal clarity, unswerving love for and

commitment to your child. As long as your teen knows you love him or her, you can get by with all sorts of mistakes.

PHYSICAL FACTORS

We have already discussed physical development of preadolescents. If you have been fortunate enough to begin educating your child earlier, it will be easier to build on that foundation now. If you are starting a bit late, however, don't let that deter you.

Check your adolescent's current fund of knowledge about physical development. Find an opportunity to casually discuss some event on the news or in your reading. If you will be open and listen to your teen, you will learn what she already knows and how much of the information is erroneous.

Think carefully about how to teach the basic facts of life to an adolescent. Make certain you have accurate information by reading and having a talk with your physician. Then plan on a slow, gradual process of teaching.

Don't say to your son, "Burt, you are absolutely wrong about the time of ovulation when girls can get pregnant." Instead say, "Burt, do you remember our talk about girls and their monthly cycles? I found an article you may want to read."

The most significant aspect of an adolescent's physical development is sexual maturation. Growth in height and weight and changes in voice are all relatively insignificant compared with sexual development. The powerful chemistry of those hormones must not be underestimated! This fact becomes even more relevant in a society that is permissive regarding seductiveness and sexual behavior. Casual sex has become the norm for altogether too many young people, and the consequences in terms of diseases, pregnancy, and loss of values and meaning are heartbreaking.

Teach your teen to understand her body, and help her respect herself and others. Help her recognize the stress she creates for her boyfriend when she dresses and acts seductively! Teach him how to see sexuality as part of his whole being, not as an end in itself. And teach him to be responsible and respectful with a girl.

Teens need to turn their energies to creative projects, sports, and mastery of their skills. Sexuality becomes a part of them that will wait for marriage. They need not become preoccupied with sexual thoughts or actions.

If your teen has become overly involved in sexual actions, don't threaten and lecture, but don't ignore it, either. Have a talk with her. Is your teen searching for love, acceptance, and a sense of importance through such activity? Perhaps you have not been as available as your teen needs you to be.

A teen has an intense sort of pride. If he feels you don't have time for him, he will decide he doesn't need you. The result is a drifting apart that carries with it vague feelings of loss and sadness, commonly expressed in anger.

Your teen may, in fact, not need you for days on end in any specific way. But he needs your presence, interest, and availability every day. When those special moments arrive, when you are desperately needed, what if you are not there? To whom, then, can he turn? Mothering a teen is no easy task. So be patient, be loving, and be available!

DIFFERENT TIMING IN DEVELOPMENT

A heartache for teens comes from their sense of being different from their peers. Boys or girls who see classmates developing physically much earlier and faster than they can feel devastated. They often worry secretly that something is terribly wrong with them. They may fear that they will be freaks of sorts. At least, they feel inferior to others and may be truly depressed.

One teenager mourned, "Mother, I'm fat and flat in all the wrong places! No boy will ever look at me!"

If your teen is a late bloomer, you can honestly reassure her. Help your teen understand there is a long time to be an adult. Show him how to enjoy each day for itself, by doing tasks thoroughly and feeling satisfaction from achievement. Help him have fun by practicing a sense of humor and playing together. Tell her about your youth and how you felt, yet remind her that you lived through those trying times and so will she!

On the other end of that developmental spectrum are the teens who develop early. Young women commonly flaunt their physical curves, and young men strut about in their new manliness. Sadly enough, these young people add to the misery of their slower peers, and they often acquire a false set of values.

Once again, show your teen the values of compassion, responsibility, and genuineness.

GRIEF OVER DIFFERENCES

You have certain dreams and hopes for your children even before they are born. Sometimes those dreams don't materialize, and you are likely to experience a sense of loss and grief. I suspect that some of the struggles between mothers and children relate to that very fact. Unconsciously, you may resent your child's failure to fulfill those desires.

If such painful emotions are familiar to you, you can identify with your teen. She, too, has dreams and basic needs. When those dreams do not happen, a sense of real sadness will touch her. If she also senses your disappointment, think of the impact on her life. Most girls dream of being beautiful, capable, and popular. In addition, boys and girls dream of being sports heroes, drama stars, or outstanding musicians. Young people have endless numbers of dreams, but few ever realize the fulfillment of all those bright wishes. No wonder so many teens go through times of depression.

To help your teen through these sad times, put away your own disappointment. *Learn to accept your teen unconditionally.* Daily review all of his good points and let him know you value them.

When she mourns her real or imagined defects or deficiencies, don't belittle her grief. Encourage her to talk out all of the feelings tucked away inside. Don't try so hard to comfort that you fail to listen until she has talked out all her feelings.

Once the negative emotions are expressed, offer hope. Explain the differences in physical development, appearance, and capabilities. Some of your teen's hopes may come about later, but if not, the grief will pass. And then his energy can be focused on accepting and developing his qualities.

Express pride in your teen's abilities and physical traits. Help her make the most of her good qualities through grooming and appropriate styles in clothing.

Be prepared for repetitions of emotional storms. Your teen may go along for days seeming happy, and just as you begin to relax, thinking this stage is over, there will be even worse times to endure. Try to be patient, expect the best, but be prepared for some difficult days.

Wish with your child. When he wishes he could be six feet tall and a gifted athlete, let him know you'd like that, too. And then tell him how well he does in soccer or remind him that few young men have as great a smile as he does. Tell him of your pride in his honesty and sensitivity to others. In even the most difficult teen, there are redeeming qualities to be seen and mirrored back.

MEDICAL SUPERVISION

A teen's physical changes create a great deal of stress in the body, so consult your physician regularly. Your doctor can become a friend to your teen and an ally to you. He or she can offer reassurance and explanations to your teen that will bring comfort. The information may be similar to the facts you have discussed, but hearing from another person that everything is fine means more. Your teen often thinks you are only trying to make her feel better. She is more likely to believe an impartial source.

Ask your doctor or nurse to discuss such controversial issues as diet, exercise, skin care, and sexual development and expression with your teen.

Unless you specify the issues that you know are of concern to your teen, they may go unaddressed. I recommend that you allow your child to go into the examination room without you. Some teens may prefer a mother's presence during a physical, but at least offer the option of this step toward independence.

Request that your doctor explain the hormone cycles of menstruation to your daughter. She needs to understand the scientific basis for what we now call PMS—premenstrual syndrome. Once she knows what causes the physical and emotional stress of those days, she will cope much more successfully. Furthermore, some hormonal and other medical prescriptions can alleviate much of the distress of those days.

Be sure your son understands the changes in his body and the powerful effect of male hormones. Wet dreams will occur, and your son needs to know that is nature's plan for preparing him for sexual activity later. He also needs to understand some of the physiology of young women. An understanding of the opposite sex as well as one's own can transform dating and friendship relationships.

Above all, teach emphatically a sense of responsibility. Each bodily function is for a purpose and must be understood and respected. Be certain your teen knows how to take care of every part of the body. Avoiding excess in all areas of physical function is vital. Diet, exercise, rest, and play must all be done with common sense and control.

I make an urgent plea that you stress the importance of refraining from sexual activity until marriage. The statistics are startlingly revealing. According to a 1999 survey by the Centers for Disease Control, one-half of all high-school students had been sexually active. Also, the same survey revealed that 66 percent of male students in the twelfth grade had had intercourse, compared to 33 percent of female students and 45 percent of male students in the ninth grade.

You *can* make a difference, and you must discuss these issues with your teen. It's not a teen's right to practice adult living. Youth have an extreme need to learn self-control, responsibility, and the willingness to postpone present pleasure for future good. Teach your teen to enjoy the present rather than borrowing from the future. Abstinence from sex until marriage is not old-fashioned; it is good sense.

CONTROVERSY

A difficult part of mothering a teenager is learning how to deal with controversy. In some homes there seems to be constant arguing with anger, hurts, and increasing withdrawal from each other. Some disagreements are right and normal. You must make a stand on some issues and should win when your child's welfare is at stake.

However, many disagreements between you and your teen are unnecessary. You are likely to overreact to a variety of situations and will almost certainly misinterpret others. Your teen's sometimes-sassy talk is really her attempt to assert herself and establish some independence. So instead of reprimanding and punishing her, try this.

> *Your teenager's sometimes-sassy talk is an attempt to assert herself and establish some independence.*

Interpret to her, the next time she sounds rude, what you believe is going on, and ask if she will calm down and discuss the issue. Then talk adult-to-adult with her. Listen carefully and honestly—not so you can out-debate her but so you will truly hear her emotions, requests, and needs. Surprisingly often, the thing a teen asks for isn't what she really wants anyway. All you need to do is help her discover that fact by asking thought-provoking questions and giving her time.

Once in a while, a teen may discover ways to make a wish come true. And that wish could be a legitimate one. Your teen must become independent, so allow him as much freedom to practice that art as is safe. Help him collect necessary information, separate his feelings and wishes from the facts, and guide his decision making as wisely as possible.

Avoid rescuing him from any consequences of bad choices. Don't say,

"I told you so!" but help him discover the mistakes and correct them. Next time, he'll be wiser.

When you have to put down your foot and enforce some limits, do so courageously. Be prepared for the fact that no self-respecting teen likes to give in, and she will certainly be angry. She may yell or withdraw in pouty silence. You will be tempted to give in just to avoid the scene. But don't allow such behavior to win out. Smiles and surface happiness are not worth your teen's growing habit of manipulating. Learning to get her way in such a fashion will create problems in other relationships.

Hold your ground when an issue is clear and important. Your teen will be angry now, but he'll respect you for holding steady and sometime he'll be grateful for your efforts.

SPIRITUALITY

Most mothers have concerns about adolescents' spirituality. They don't know how to cope with the changes that so often occur in this period.

Whether Jewish, Catholic, or Protestant, most teens go through a time of rebellion and rejection of their spiritual lives and their religious practices. You may become worried and nag her to attend services and practice the rituals of your faith. Or you may see this as a normal function of his search for independence.

Remember that true rebellion occurs when you hold the reins too tightly. On the other hand, wild behavior will occur if you give too much freedom. You certainly will need divine guidance to find the comfortable, correct path to take.

Again and again, I have asked adolescents to define for me their concept of God. I find that most of them define God in terms similar to how they describe their fathers. Certainly, God is not like Dad or Mom, but most teens project onto Him the qualities of their human parents.

Because of this projection, you must deal with two facts. First, you must be the best parent you can be so your teen will at least want to know the heavenly Father. Second, you need to talk comfortably about God at home. Through the healthy concepts you teach about God, your teen will have some solid beliefs to consider.

It is normal for teens to question their earlier beliefs and practices. Out of the questions will emerge in an adult frame either strong affirmation or rejection of those beliefs. How you handle this aspect of life will make a difference.

By finding the balance between strictness and freedom, you can prevent much of the rebellion most teens experience.

As you sense your teen's resistance to religious observations and beliefs, avoid panic. Allow some freedom from every area of the family's religious observances. Let her choose those activities that are most meaningful to her, and occasionally, allow her to miss other functions. It is far better for him to gain some meaning from his involvement in a few areas than to reject everything while attending most activities.

> *It is normal for teens to question earlier beliefs and practices. Out of all the questions will emerge either strong affirmation or rejection of those beliefs.*

Budget your time so you can pray for your teen daily. I'm not sure how prayer works, but I'm sure it does. Practice your own faith in a Power beyond your own.

Avoid lectures, tears, and any implication that your teen is "bad." When you imply negative qualities, your teen will see herself in such terms. Keep your expectations positive as you help your teen explore her way through these days.

The Jewish ceremony of bar mitzvah or bat mitzvah is a wonderful tradition. After months of study and preparation by the young person, a lovely service and a feast are held in the synagogue. The significance of this occasion is the transition of a thirteen-year-old from child to adult in the observance of Jewish religion. It seems to me that this comprises a stately, well-defined gateway into adulthood.

You may not be Jewish, but I urge you to personalize a similar ritual for your teen. All the family will know in this manner (and so may you!) that this person has now become an adult. I believe the tradition will help you remember to see your teen in a new, more positive light.

In our increasingly pagan world, I feel grave concern over a growing trend for youth to be involved in cults. Many teens dabble in the evil practices of witchcraft (Wicca) or even Satan worship. Those who will discuss their beliefs reveal great fear. Knowing too little of God's power, they believe in Satan's deceptive strength. By professing allegiance to him, they believe he will not hurt them.

The practices of these ultimate evils are horrifying. Make it your business to learn about them. Look for strange symbols, the typical upside-down cross, and other evidence of strange beliefs and practices. Your local bookstore and library will have a large section of books about cults. It's your responsibility to inform yourself so you can teach your teen the fallacies of such beliefs.

As you exemplify and discuss your beliefs in the God of love and real power, your teen is likely to return to your faith and his. If, however, you discover that your child has come to really believe in cults or demonic forces, seek help. Both counseling and help from clergy are clearly needed in such a case!

COMMUNITY RESOURCES

Your teen's school will be a major source of involvement. Get to know the teachers and even explore the textbooks used. If values being taught are contrary to yours, discuss them with your teen. Stay intellectual and avoid emotional harangues so your teen will listen with respect. The fact is, your children will confront false values and wrong information every day. You must be prepared to counteract these, and you can do that best by teaching the truth.

Teaching a teen is different from teaching a younger child. A teen must be led carefully to think for himself. Your best approach is to discuss with him the ideas and ideals that are eternal truth. Ask questions and respect his ideas even when you disagree. A question you will find useful many times is this: "I hear what you say, but have you ever considered a different aspect of this issue?" Natural curiosity will help him explore various angles until he discovers the truth.

Be involved with your teen's sports, pep club, interest groups, and other school activities. Troubled young people often reveal that their parents do not seem to care about their activities. You must care, and you need to be there.

Your church or synagogue is another source of support. If the one you attend doesn't offer enough activities or teach the values you want your child to know, look around. Meanwhile, put some energy into making your current church a better place for people of all ages.

Encourage your teen to spend time with relatives and close friends of yours. Your teen needs to know that extended family well enough to go to them for help or advice. Many times another adult can reach your teen when you can't.

Try to keep your teen involved in community sports activities. Softball teams are available almost everywhere, as are swim teams and many other wholesome activities. Practice with your teen and encourage her to take part in team activities. Through them, she can develop skills and friendships that are good for a lifetime.

Finally, *make your home an appealing gathering place for your teen's friends.* When our children were young, we made our basement as presentable as possible. We purchased some game tables and recreational equipment. I had high grocery bills for years, but we kept snacks available. Our home became headquarters for our teens' friends.

I recommend such an environment. You will know your teen's friends and can even affect their lives. You will also know where your teen is and what he is doing most of the time. What could be better for all of you?

CHAPTER SIXTEEN

Adult Children and Parents

ADULT CHILDREN

After his junior year in college, my son returned home for the summer and said, "Mom, I didn't get you a gift for Mother's Day because I have a surprise for you!" His surprise was to work until he had enough money to take me on a trip. He had been on the crewing team at the university, and one trip had taken him to some unusual sights in Wisconsin. He wanted me to enjoy those experiences with him.

True to his word, about mid-July he made all of the arrangements, and we flew to the area of some architectural and natural wonders. From the moment we left our home until we were safely back, he carefully planned and managed every detail.

It was a unique experience to share with this young man so many warm and awe-inspiring moments. We talked of profound values, laughed together, and were silent together. Near the end of the trip, I realized its actual value. My son had become my friend, a source from whom I could draw richly in enjoying life.

Sadly, some parents cannot enjoy such experiences with adult children. One mother shared with me an opposite set of circumstances. She sat in my office with tears washing the mascara away from her lovely but aging eyes.

Her son was in prison. From early on, he had been a demanding and aggressive child. She had tried to discipline him and teach him right from wrong. His father was away so much of the time that he hardly knew the boy.

In his early teen years the young man began to drink and abuse drugs. No attempts to help him curb those addictions made a dent in his habits. His father rescued him repeatedly from courtroom scenes. But now, at some thirty years of age, his habits had become crimes that could no longer be ignored. His abuse and dealing of drugs resulted in a lengthy prison sentence.

Even now the mother wanted to help her son, but the help for which he cried out was money. With a long list of lame excuses, he pleaded for money. For snacks, the small TV set prisoners were allowed, and the few extra items of clothing permitted, he demanded sizable sums of money every month. And the mother had been giving those sums to her "boy."

As we talked together, it became clear that this child-man was using his mom to continue the very habit that had imprisoned him. Finding the courage to practice tough love on this spoiled son was not easy. But to her credit, the mother was finally able to say, "No more, Son!"

It's a new challenge to mother adult children. There is an entirely new balance to be established in your attitudes, communication, and the activities you share. This balance must be established carefully with logic rather than with emotion.

RELINQUISHMENT

My son made it easier for me to relinquish mothering because he offered me information about his adulthood. Nevertheless, I found it painful to let go, and to be absolutely honest, I can't completely let go of my children. Nor, I think, can any parent who is committed to the family.

When my adult children have difficulties, I ache with some of their pain. When they are successful, I share their joy. When they have legitimate needs, I try to meet them in appropriate ways.

In finding the new balances between mothering and being a friend, you can benefit from four guidelines.

1. *Release the controls.* After two decades of parenting, you will be tempted to try to manage your adult child's life. Don't do that! You must release the controls to your child. The more you try to dictate what should be done, the more difficulty there will be. Either she will submit to your control and grow dependent and immature, or she will refuse to hear you at all and make foolish mistakes from rebelling. Power struggles are always destructive. You can prevent such struggles by focusing on what is best, not who is right.

2. *Avoid giving too much to your children, and beware of needing them too much.* In the hearts of most mothers, there is great pain in cutting the emotional umbilical cord. To avoid that pain, you may be tempted to stay attached to your adult children.

Lillian called me one day, distraught. She was getting ready for a short vacation and was facing a major time shortage. Her mother had called her during the night to demand that Lillian take her to the emergency room. She was certain she was having a heart attack. Such urgent calls were habitual, and Lillian recognized them as her mother's way of seeking attention. Over time, Lillian's resentment had grown, and what attention she could give her mother was spoiled by it. Yet she could never be quite sure. Perhaps she really was having a heart attack.

Don't do this to your adult children. You must find your own life apart from them. So don't besiege your children with unnecessary demands. And if you must give them material gifts or services, do so with no strings attached.

3. *Be available for advice, but wait to be asked for it.* Unless you see a truly dangerous situation arising, unsought advice is useless. And when it is rejected, you are likely to be hurt.

Charlene knew her daughter was becoming involved with a man who seemed most unsuitable for her. She surveyed the potential for disaster and panicked. She wanted to shout to her beautiful adult child to get her to pay careful attention to what she was doing. She yearned to draw her daughter into her lap and protect her from making a horrible mistake.

She was wise, however, and waited to talk with a friend. As she poured out her fears, she discovered that her instincts to interfere probably would defeat her goal. If she tried to force her daughter away from the relationship, the strong-willed daughter likely would become all the more committed to it. Charlene decided to deal gently and cautiously with the situation. Her wisdom and control, fortunately, saved her daughter from impulsively making a serious mistake.

4. *Sometimes you have to practice tough love.*

Lorraine was facing the end of her marriage. With four young children, she couldn't imagine how she would manage on her own. When she called her retired mother to ask for help with child care while she searched for a job and established her independence, she was horrified at her mother's response.

Her mother said, "Lorraine, I've raised four children. I'm not willing to raise yours." At first, Lorraine believed she had not heard her mother correctly. But that was just what she said. It was one more rejection for a traumatized young mother. But she determined not to beg for help and discovered that she could manage on her own.

There are many ways in which adult children need help—financial, child care, advice, and physical help. My opinion is that family members must stand by one another without becoming overly dependent. When one of my adult children moves into a different apartment or house, I am there to be excited about it and help clean, paint, and fix it up. Then I leave it in her or his hands.

They, in turn, are in my home to help when I need that. When I can offer care and companionship to my grandchildren, I do so. If I truly cannot, I say so.

You can set limits on what you can offer your adult children, and you must do so. But don't cut off your help entirely, except when doing so is necessary to make them become mature and independent.

Stand ready to offer help, but don't try to control your adult child. Don't manage your adult son's or daughter's career, finances, personal or family lives.

No matter how painful or lonely you may feel, don't allow yourself to be too attached to your adult child. Through too-ready availability, too many offers of financial aid, or too many needs of him, you can intrude. Don't do that.

When she asks, offer the best, most objective advice you can. But avoid telling her, either aggressively or tactfully, what she should do! Be ready to help your "child" when he asks and you are able, but don't offer too much. Establish some basic guidelines about where you will or cannot help. For example, I mentioned that I always help my adult children relocate.

As long as they use school or professional training to improve their lives and careers, I am prepared to pay the tuition and costs of equipment. I would not do this, however, if they used advanced schooling to avoid getting a job and supporting themselves. I would allow my adult son or daughter to return home for a limited time if stress of some sort made that necessary. But he or she could not stay beyond a pre-agreed-upon time.

You may set quite different limits and standards. You certainly are the one to do so. Just be certain both you and your child understand those limits, respect them, and follow them consistently.

BE A REFUGE

A natural function of parents is providing a refuge—a place to which their children can return when life's storms seem too harsh to survive. The sight of my mother's silver hair, smiling face, and the wave of her arthritis-gnarled hand is engraved in my memory. As we would arrive home or leave after a visit, she was always there for as long as she could see us.

My father, walking with a slow pace but with proud, erect posture, greeted us from the yard as he and the collie approached our car. The buildings grew older and the trees we planted as kids grew taller, but home was always there—a never-failing reminder of what love, commitment, and doing the very best job we could do were all about.

In today's frantically mobile society, you may not have had a permanent residence for your children to return to. If that is the case, you, as a mother, can be symbolic of the refuge. You must write, phone, and visit your children whenever you can. Try not to invade their space, and try to invite them to your home. But do keep the fact of your existence as their safe place in the forefront of their minds.

One day, sooner than you want to think, you will need your children to care for you. Be sure they know and love you as you do them. The transition zones of life are difficult to traverse at best. You can be the one, by what you do and who you are now, who makes possible getting through those times successfully.

YOUR PARENTS

On May 15, 2000, *Larry King Live* did a segment on the problems of aging. This program revealed that by the year 2030, there will be 75 million people in America over sixty-five years old, and about one million over 100 years of age. The care of children coupled with the multitudinous concerns of the aging catch the middle generation broadside.

Middle-aged mothers ease away from struggling to raise children and meet some of their young adult needs only to find themselves sprung into the sorrowful awareness of the deterioration of their parents. They wonder, *When is it going to be my turn?* If you are experiencing this bind, you are in a large company of mothers.

And I will agree, it isn't fair! But as you so often must have reminded your children, life just isn't fair. However, you are not as powerless as you may feel. You can cope successfully with mothering your parents.

UNDERSTAND, FORGIVE, AND LOVE YOUR PARENTS

The most tragic situations I have encountered professionally are those in which grave misunderstandings exist. It is extremely common for women to feel their parents have not treated them well.

Mothers tell me sad stories of critical and even abusive parents. Somehow they have survived those insecure years of childhood and often have mercifully blocked those experiences from memory. But now, in mid-life, facing the needs of those abusive parents, the old memories return, and with them comes a flood of hurt, bitterness, and a desire for revenge.

If you are one of these abused people, try to find out how your parents grew up. Chances are they, too, were abused as kids. They practiced the only parenting skills they knew. Remember the mothering imprint concept in the Introduction? Knowing your parents' childhoods will give you great insights that will enable you to forgive them.

It is from their backgrounds that your parents learned to raise you. If you are to forgive your parents, this information will help you do so. And unless you are willing to forgive them, you cannot realistically meet their needs successfully.

I recommend that you review your childhood experiences in the light of your parents' childhoods. When you understand how they had to live, you will find it possible to be forgiving and compassionate, and you will be able to help supply their needs, even though they may not have always met yours.

For decades, Alice tried to get along with her critical mother-in-law, Amy. Her children avoided her as much as possible, and yet the entire family realized that Amy had worked hard, even sacrificially, for them.

The inevitable time came. Amy would no longer be able to live alone in her home. The maintenance and even daily living were simply too much. Where would she go, and who would take care of her? Alice knew that she would very likely be asked to provide a home for her mother-in-law. For several reasons, her home seemed adequate to supply the needs of the aging woman.

But Alice resisted the idea of adding a new responsibility to her already busy life. Why should she be the one to lose her privacy and gain a critical, increasingly dependent family member? Fortunately, Alice kept the negative thoughts to herself. She felt guilty for not wanting to offer the support Amy needed, but she could not imagine how she would cope with such a burden.

Alice knew that God often provides answers that people fail to consider, so she prayed. God's solutions come in a variety of forms, and Alice's arrived in the form of a story.

Amy frequently visited in Alice's home, and she loved to linger after dinner to talk. Alice, of course, would have preferred to clear the table and then relax for the rest of the evening. As she deferred to her mother-in-law, she was thinking, *If she comes to live with us, how can I stand giving in to her wishes and demands? Is there no hope of some freedom for myself?*

Her self-pitying reverie was interrupted by the amazing story Amy was telling. For the first time in her eighty-six years, the matriarch was revealing some significant events from long ago. Her mother had died after the birth of Amy's baby brother, and both Amy and the baby had gone to live with relatives. They grew to be healthy, active children. By the time the baby boy was five, their father had remarried. Since the father had a large ranch, the boy would become a valuable asset, so he returned to live with four older brothers.

Amy decided after his returning home that soon it would be her turn to rejoin the big, happy family. There was a baby sister, and Amy loved to play with her when she visited the ranch. One day, knowing her father planned to visit her, Amy decided that was the day she would return home with him.

Excitedly, and without a word to the aunt who cared for her, she packed all of her belongings in a big valise. Finally, her father arrived. It bothered her a bit that he was riding his big black horse instead of riding in the surrey. But to her seven-year-old mind, anything was possible for Daddy. She would hold the valise on her lap behind him.

After a short visit, Daddy rose to leave. "Wait a minute, Daddy," Amy called out excitedly. "I'll get my bag. It's all packed."

There was a brief pause. Then her father asked, "What bag, Amy? What are you talking about?"

Sudden fear froze her words for a moment, but Amy explained, "Daddy, Freddie got to go home with you to live, and I want to go, too. I'm lonely here, and I want to be with you." Her eyes were wistful, and tears blurred her vision.

Daddy was a firm, even rough, man, a rancher who had to be tough and decisive. In a no-nonsense voice, he settled the issue abruptly. There was no wavering, no negotiation. "Amy, you know Aunt Olive wants you to live with her. She has no children, and you've lived with her for six years. That's how it is!"

Amy described to Alice how she cried. Her heart was broken, and she found neither hope nor comfort. She did not give up easily, however. She begged and pleaded with her father to take her home. He never relented and finally strode from the house and mounted his horse.

"I was deathly afraid of horses," Amy recalled, "but I followed my father and clung to the foreleg of his horse, begging him to take me home." At last, he flicked her tender flesh with his riding crop until she released her grip. He rode away.

Amy went to her room, where she wept again at the sight of her bag packed so hopefully only a few hours ago. At last there were no more tears. And Amy made a fateful decision. Tears did no good; wishes and hopes didn't come true; she would never cry again. Amy tried to adapt to the life allotted to her, but she had to become callous and realistic to survive. In her effort to make things right, she learned to be critical.

> *If you were mistreated or neglected, you were not the cause. Your parents simply lacked the tools they needed to raise you.*

For the first time in all those years, Amy wept. And Alice, moved to tears, went to her mother-in-law, put her arms around the frail body, and comforted her. The information Alice learned that evening made the difference. She could gladly welcome Amy into her home!

It is not difficult to understand, forgive, and love with the proper information available. But perhaps you don't have the information Alice was able to obtain. And many women tell me they have no way to get their older parents to talk about themselves. In that case, ask another relative, search old photo albums, or keep trying to get your parents to reminisce.

If all of these methods fail, simply try to imagine your parents as children. Are they happy, playful, and creative? Or is it easier to see them lonely, neglected, and abused? By their attitudes now, you can be quite accurate in your evaluation. Knowing that they, like Amy, may have suffered as children can enable you to forgive their mistakes with you.

If you were mistreated or neglected, you can count on one vital fact: you were not the cause. You were not a burden or a bad child. Because your parents were not mothered adequately, they simply lacked the tools they needed to raise you.

It takes a strong will to do it, but you can release all of the old hurts and anger. And you can feel the compassion and tenderness that will enable you to reach out and mother your aging parents.

ASSESS THEIR NEEDS

To offer the best help to your parents, you must know their capabilities and weaknesses. Having always seen them in their parent role is a handicap in assessing their current status. Think of them as if they were neighbors you want to become acquainted with for the very first time. Try to see yourself as a professional counselor to aging people.

You'll need information to do your counseling job well. Set about collecting it methodically. First, observe for yourself. In what condition is their home? Does it show signs of neglect, and is it in need of repair? Is the kitchen covered with soot from burning foods?

Are your parents physically healthy? Do they show signs of poor hygiene and a need for care of their clothing?

Next, ask their family physician about their health. Tell him or her that you want to provide the best care and planning possible for your parents. Their doctor can be of great help in deciding how long it will be safe for your parents to manage to live alone. Some elderly people will be able to recognize and face their growing limitations better than others. If your parents are unable to deal with the facts, it is much more painful, but you may have to decide for them. When you were two and didn't always realize the dangers around you, they had to protect you. It's time now for you to return the favor.

If your parents oppose you, your task will be harder. Your parents may require legal advice. The elderly are notoriously victims of con artists. Furthermore, their mental functioning may deteriorate so that they can no longer keep an accurate bank balance. Their material welfare becomes gravely at risk.

If you try to do some financial management for them, they may accuse you of interfering. They may feel you are insulting them or, even worse, that you are trying to take advantage of them and rob them.

To avoid some of these unpleasant circumstances, I suggest you consult an attorney. Try to get your parents to choose one and to see the value in this sort of advice. They may need to write a will or update the one they have. You may need the attorney to take legal action to protect your parents' assets and tell you how to manage their business affairs with them or, when that time comes, for them. Financial management may be the most difficult facet of your parents' aging. It is equally one of the most important, because the cost of proper care for them has become exorbitant.

Include all of your brothers and sisters in these procedures. In most families, the major responsibility for parent care falls on one person. If you are that one, avoid feeling sorry for yourself and angry with other family members. Instead, do everything you can to share the providing of care with them.

Arrange a family conference, perhaps by phone, and discuss your parents' physical and business status. Have a list of their emerging needs, and ask for volunteers to help with specific areas. If there are none, assign them. If you must be the boss, act like one, and in a businesslike manner, get every area of need delegated. Then with some regularity let your siblings know how their parents are and how much you value their help.

No, I'm not naive! I know many families will not cooperate with the "assigned" caretaker of their elderly parents. But the positive approach is the one most likely to work. You may have to give up on some family members because they just will not help. These very ones will probably condemn you and your efforts. Try to see that such people are not bad or mean but generally are unable to give. For various reasons, they are emotionally so poor that they cannot give assistance. You will find it tempting to be angry with them, but that will only make you bitter and drain your energy. Instead, feel sorry that they are so impoverished, stop expecting their help, and let their criticisms bounce off you.

Just as you think you have your parents' needs assessed and know exactly what to do for them, conditions will change. Not long ago a friend told me about her parents. Both have been quite ill and are managing to maintain their home only with immense effort. But with some visiting and a little housekeeping help, their lives seemed stable.

On a nightly trek to the bathroom, her mother fell. You know the result: a broken hip. The entire dynamic equilibrium was suddenly upset. My friend's mother will be in the hospital for weeks and then probably will require nursing home care. To complicate matters, her strong-willed father believes he can care for his injured wife by himself at home.

You, too, will find both gradual and sudden changes occurring. You will face anxiety, frustration, and grief. By knowing this, you can be prepared to weather the emotional storms, fulfill your responsibilities, and face the end with equanimity.

Some time ago a young woman faced the long illness and untimely death of her husband. I tried to offer comfort to her in this tragic loss, but she taught me a piece of great wisdom. The grieving wife and mother stated, "Dr. Grace, I can deal with this because I have no regrets." May you feel this same comfort after your parents are gone!

Look in your local telephone directory. You are likely to find several agencies or individuals listed who can help you evaluate your parents' capabilities.

As a general rule, older people are more comfortable and confident in their familiar environment. As long as they can be safely provided for in their home, they need to stay there. Giving them some of your time or hiring help if necessary provides the very best for the needs of deteriorating elderly individuals. Besides that, it is significantly less expensive. Later on, care may be extremely expensive as disabilities increase.

Of course, you must balance your parents' need to be in their own place with their safety. If they are seriously forgetful, there is danger of water damage, electrical overuse, and even fire. Don't wait for a disaster before you arrange for proper help for your parents.

Just as it was difficult for you to see clearly your children's needs when you mothered them, so it is hard to see your parents' needs precisely. Ask your doctor, clergyperson, attorney, friends, and relatives for help. And don't forget to ask your parents themselves. Even as they grow infirm and incapable of the wisest decisions, you will catch times when they recognize that they need to make a change in their living arrangements.

MAKE THE DECISION

Take as much time as you can to collect information. Your collection must be ongoing as your parents' condition varies. Then hold a family conference, and include as many of the appropriate people as you can. Together, compile lists of your parents' needs and resources, and then help them decide what must be done to make them safe and comfortable. If they cannot decide, you may need to do that for them. Make this important decision with their welfare far ahead of your convenience or any other factor. Categorically, there are not many choices:

1. Remain in their home. This choice is best as long as it is safe and not worrisome to them to keep up.

2. Move into a sheltered environment in their own quarters. Many retirement centers are available around larger cities. They vary from one-room to luxury apartments and condominiums. Your parents' familiar furnishings can make such a setting quite lovely.

3. Move into a life-care center where they may live in an apartment, a single room later, or a nursing-care room if needed. Familiar surroundings and staff make transitions easier, and elderly citizens can feel attached and sense a caring environment.

4. Move into a nursing-care center directly. If your parents suffer a disabling accident or illness, such care may be absolutely necessary. But you may be able to locate home nursing care that will be much less costly and much more comfortable for your parents.

5. Last, but not least, consider having your aging parents live with you. A number of years ago, I traveled briefly in the Orient. One aspect of their culture that most vividly caught my attention was their attitude toward the elderly. There were, then, no retirement homes. It is clearly

the defined duty of the eldest son to care for the parents until their deaths.

It is not easy or convenient (does that sound familiar?) to mother your parents. And in many families it is totally impossible to bring aging parents into your home. But when it is, it can profoundly bless your children as well as you. The intimate knowledge transmitted from generation to generation has a major impact on children and grandchildren. The role model to your children of your providing such care can establish the values you have taught. And the knowledge that you need have no regrets about your love and care for your parents is the best legacy you can be given.

In finalizing your decision, then, let me summarize the steps you must take:

- Collect all the information you need.
- Consider the many options possible.
- Eliminate, one by one, those that are impossible or impractical.
- Convene appropriate family members, and together with your parents (when that is possible) make the final decision.
- Keep your options open. As circumstances change, you may reverse your last decision.
- Finally, discipline yourself to live with the decision that is made. We are all tempted to use hindsight, and in retrospect, a different course may have worked better. But don't allow yourself to be so judgmental. You must be fair to yourself. If you made a mistake, try to correct it, and if you were right, be grateful.

SEEK HELP

Almost no one can adequately care for children, grandchildren, and elderly parents at the same time. You must take care of yourself if you are to offer any help to those who need you. We have already listed people who can participate in assessing your parents' needs when you are no longer sure of your own judgment. In addition, many services are available in most communities to help you care for your parents.

The Visiting Nurse Association. A great many communities are served by the well-respected VNA. An experienced registered nurse from this agency will visit any home in the area. She is capable of checking on and administering medication; she can check the vital signs so helpful to a doctor in evaluating patients; she can change dressings and apply bandages; and usually she will administer the tender, loving care older people crave.

County or city public health nurses. These nurses may run a free or low-cost clinic, which may even provide transportation. Sometimes they make home visits, and the fees are extremely low. In fact, they are usually tax-supported and may cost nothing.

State and county welfare agencies. Most of the staff are overworked and underpaid, but they are caring, often heroic people who may help you in various ways. Do not hesitate to call and clearly state your problems, asking guidance and specific assistance.

Senior citizens' centers. Many communities have organized a program for themselves. Centers are located in places convenient to retired people. There they may congregate during the day to talk, play games, do crafts, or organize activities and projects. Rather than allow your parents to give up life and sit with TV, day after day, try to get them into such centers. Once they get involved in the center's routine, I've discovered that many seniors regain an interest in life that is exciting to see.

Older adults' transportation services. Government grants may make it possible for a community to have a special bus service for the elderly. These vehicles are equipped for people with handicapping conditions and are low in cost to the riders. Funds for such services come and go, but you may be instrumental in helping acquire this service in your area.

Meals on Wheels. In many communities, nutritious hot meals are prepared and delivered to the homes of subscribers. Many elderly people have been enabled to stay in their homes for much longer than one would expect through this service. An elderly couple told me how delicious their meals were. And, they confided, there usually was enough left over to supply a small second meal. What a bargain!

Veterans' organizations. Sometimes people who have served in the armed forces of this country forget that service entitles them to some benefits. Contact your nearest government office for veterans and ask what benefits your parents may be entitled to.

Voluntary private agencies. Frequently, I hear radio announcements about counseling and information services for the elderly. Experienced and knowledgeable people can help you discover resources to meet a range of needs in wonderful ways. Check your telephone directory for these agencies in your vicinity.

Let me remind you of an extremely important fact. Everyone needs physical touching of a tender, loving type. You may not have thought about it, but older people often lack such expressions of affection. Remember to stroke your parents' heads, gently massage their necks and shoulders, and hug them often.

Speak to them gently. They may have difficulty hearing, which can be irritating to them. They'd rather hear perfectly, so speak loudly but without sounding angry.

They can't walk as energetically as they once did. It is tempting to leave them at home, but they love to be in their world. Budget your time and patience to take them shopping now and then. Let them decide how long to stay and never push them too much. Going out to eat and to see young people and children can give them joy for days to come.

Personal hygiene can be a problem for older people. They often spill food or drink on their clothing. Kindly help them with shampoos and baths. And see to it that their clothing is clean and attractive.

Everyone is better for laughter. Try to see humor in life that your parents can enjoy. Tell them jokes; reminisce with them about happy events from the past. Don't look at them with much pity, and avoid anger. Keep your face, voice, and demeanor pleasant.

Someday You Will Be Old

As you consider all the aspects of mothering your mother and father, think of your own old age. When you discover solutions to problems, jot them down. Someday your children can draw on your experiences to your benefit.

You will be troubled over mistakes and trying habits of your parents. Make a mental note to prevent similar, or worse, habits in your life.

Anticipating your latter years, you may make positive plans for them now. Saving money, simplifying your life, and decreasing the clutter of many possessions will help you both now and later.

While your mind is still clear, decide what living arrangements will likely be your preference later. Discuss your ideas with your family, or write them in a letter that can be sent when the time is right. Try to practice common sense, and be aware of the best solutions for everyone not only yourself.

Practice the humbling art of facing your personal needs. Find ways to ask for those needs clearly, without apology, and with genuine gratitude. Learn to behave in endearing ways that will make it easy for your children to love and care for you when you need that.

I suspect that God makes it difficult to mother your parents so it will be easier to give them up when He calls them. You must recall that your teens' often-ugly behavior enabled you to launch them from home with less pain than if they were angels. If your parents get grouchy and demanding, just remember they will not always be there. I hope you will find in this thought both patience for now and the capacity to relinquish them later without regrets.

SECTION EIGHT

Balance

CHAPTER SEVENTEEN

The Roles of a Mother

Several years ago I sat around a table with eight mothers. While we ate lunch, we discussed our work as people helpers and mothers. Most of us are also wives, active in a church, children's schools and other activities, and various groups. I was, by far, the oldest, and the others looked to me for some answers that I had discovered through the years. Despite some progress over time, I had to admit that I still search for the balances that make life bearable. As we shared and thought together, we arrived at some conclusions I'll convey to you.

- *To begin to balance our loads, we had to find and believe in our individual worth.* Most of us had tried (and some are still trying) to prove we were good women by the many good deeds we accomplished. That is an endless cycle because it just doesn't work. So start with discovering who you are inside and your capabilities that want to be expressed.
- *We had to stop worrying about what others thought of us.* Several of us were slaves to our children's, husbands', or parents' constant approval. It became clear that when children discover that mothers need their

approval, they capitalize on that. They learn very quickly how to make moms feel guilty and gain a variety of benefits from that guilt.

A central function of stopping the search for others' constant approval is learning to say no. Out of habit, if nothing else, we all agreed that saying no is most difficult at first, but it does get easier. On the other hand, as we grow in the knowledge of ourselves and discover new interests and abilities, there are many more things clamoring at us. So the art of saying no becomes quite complex and difficult.

- *We had to manage our time.* Accomplishing all that must be done along with all we want to do demands organization. By keeping a flexible daily calendar, we found we accomplished more, forgot less, and could even work in some leisure time now and then.

- *Delegating responsibilities also helped.* We agreed that children not only must not lay guilt trips on us, but they can feel important and needed when we ask for their help. That is not to make excuses for abandoning your children. Children and mothers need plenty of time together, but kids can sometimes become selfish and demanding, and out of feeling guilty, mothers can spoil and pamper them. Children need not become tyrants.

- *Most of us knew that children can sense and need to understand why moms are working.* A child's worst fear is that of abandonment: "What if Mom doesn't love me and wants to get away from me? Maybe I'm a terrible burden to her." We could all think of a rare mother who acted as if her children were burdens. But most of the moms we knew had to work to help overburdened husbands.

- *A few loved their children genuinely but were so depressed or bored with housework that they were irritable, grouchy mothers.* We decided that children could understand that feeling and could be proud of their mothers' abilities and services. Many times, I have been asked to thank my children for relinquishing me for an evening's event. I have tried to always communicate the appreciation of others for whatever help I could be to them. I believe my children know that I could not have been effective in my work had I felt guilty of neglecting them. The other side of that was that I did limit my time away and I adored them every hour I was with them (well, almost!).

- *Teamwork with husbands was our last big discussion.* When Mom is gone now and then while Dad is home, children require his attention. If Mother is there, children are drawn to her by sheer habit, allowing Dad to slide into the role of sleeping stranger. Most of these mothers had to work a few evening hours, and they learned that their husbands really became fathers while they were gone. Most of them learned to love putting children to bed, reading stories, or even tutoring homework. They had the family under control when the moms arrived home tired.

I realize that not all men are so cooperative, but it was reassuring to learn that they can be. Perhaps both moms and dads will learn, in these economically difficult times, to become a supportive, loving team. For some months I have kept a list of the many roles mothers fill in their families. I have been amazed at its length, and you may have more activities to add.

DIETITIAN

From the time they are conceived, it is your responsibility to nourish your children. Through their likes and dislikes, growth spurts and lags, the diet fads and fashions of teens, consider your challenges in planning and preparing meals.

And do you have the trouble I had getting them all to the table? The balance to find in this role is that of noticing the children's special likes and dislikes of certain foods, then serving mainly those healthy foods they need and do like with an occasional offering of something they hate.

Children often eat in the homes of friends and relatives, and it is rude for them to refuse a dish the hostess has worked to prepare. Teach them to eat just a little bit of everything. Rarely do children hate all healthy foods unless eating has become a battleground. Keep serving balanced meals, expect them to eat enough, and don't fight over it. Our bodies have an amazing capability of creating an appetite for the food elements they need, over time.

Make mealtimes pleasant, friendly, and happy. Save good and funny topics for mealtime, and reserve reprimands or discipline to a private time later.

NURSE

I've already described what a wonderful nurse my mother was. When children are small, sickness can be a frightening and exhausting experience. Choose a pediatrician in whom you have great confidence, and find a friend who will help you when you reach the end of your strength. A mother or sister can be a wonderful ally during such times.

As children reach age two or three, they become quite independent, and you may miss the cuddling you loved when they were babies. When they are sick, most children love to be held and rocked, read to, and entertained. Enjoy doing all of those things because most childhood illnesses don't last long. With effective medicines and a few days' time, sick children bounce back to wellness.

A few chronic illnesses, however, will challenge you to the maximum. A friend faced a long period of bed rest for her seven-year-old son. He had a disease of his hip joint that was not too painful, but it was essential that he lie with that leg and hip straight. He was an extremely active boy, used to running and climbing, and the enforced bed rest was totally unacceptable to him. He was eventually demanding and even refused to stay quiet.

Darlene learned a unique balance as his nurse. She had to be firm and require his cooperation. And she had to find activities that he could do to make life bearable. Her tough love did the former, and her creativity enabled her to do the latter. Her excellent nursing brought her son through the trying episode.

PLAYMATE

When I work with a child who doesn't know how to play with other children, I've learned to ask, "Mom, did you play with this child when she was a toddler?" Many times mothers don't know how to (or even that they should) play with young children. They buy toys for them and may show them how to use them, but then they go about their other duties. And sometimes that's okay.

Babies really don't need to be entertained all of the time. But you need to play with them enough to teach them healthy interaction.

Roll a ball with a one-year-old, teach building with blocks to a two-year-old, and play "let's imagine" with a three- or four-year-old. Run with them; play hide-and-seek or any game you can create. Doing such activities will be a happy way of saying, "I love to play with you!" And your children will learn to play harmoniously with others. They will become the best playmates in the neighborhood. And by teaching these wholesome games, you will find the neighborhood children less likely to get into undesirable activities.

I suggest you also play with your preschool child's friends. Some of them will not be blessed with mothers who have taught them what you are teaching your child. Being near them or interacting with them can be a wonderful influence on them, and you can be sure no aggressive or sexual activities harm them.

With school-age children, I suggest you be around them, but usually they will not want you to play with them. Offer a snack or a drink now and then, and quietly help settle the arguments children will have. They may need you to play Monopoly or Clue, and if you can, I think that's wonderful.

Adolescents are all too often totally unsupervised, so you will travel troubled waters with your teens. Due to the degree of freedom many teens are allowed, yours are likely to feel angry and embarrassed if you restrict them.

But they will also feel safe and protected. So once again, balance their quest for independence with enough restrictions to keep them out of danger. Once in a while, they will enjoy having fun with you. Keep recreational events pleasant, and don't use them to lecture or vent frustrations. There are times for doing that, but don't mix that with playing together.

PROTECTOR

Infants and toddlers would never survive without constant protection. One psychologist said that up to one year, no child should be out of sight of the mother except when asleep. And up to two years, the mother should be within hearing distance at all times. I tend to agree with him, but the balance in this role lies in the fact that you do not need to touch a child all the time.

Development of a healthy child demands enough freedom to explore within the limits of the child's physical coordination. Teach your child how to manage stairs, but be beside him until you are certain of the ability to avoid falls.

And be sure the stairs are enclosed on both sides to prevent a tumble off the edge. Allow your child to climb where it is safe, but make any area for which she is not ready off-limits. Your ability to establish and maintain those limits is an absolute necessity in protecting your child.

Encourage your children to learn to swim, skate, ski, climb, hike, bicycle, and take part in sports. Every skill they can master adds to their confidence, broadens their social options, and can keep them from the boredom of idleness. Be involved and cheer them on in their pursuits.

The worst periods of my life were my children's first weeks of driving alone. I wanted to go with them, and I wanted to keep them at home.

I dreaded their exposure to the traffic of the city. They all survived with only a rare fender bender, and so did I. I could no longer be there to personally protect them.

Nor could I go away to college with them and tell them how to live and select friends. I couldn't choose their spouses or dictate their lives. Letting go meant quitting my role as protector.

My adult daughter is a school psychologist, and occasionally, she had to visit the homes of students. Many times she told me of interrupting family fights by her visit or finding parents high on drugs. How I wanted her to come home and not be exposed to such dangers! During these times, my faith comes into focus most comfortingly. I know I will not restrict my adult children's careers or limit their choices. But I know the Father who loves them so much more than I ever can will care for them.

Even if harm comes, I know He will see us all through any eventuality. The ultimate protection lies in His hands.

TEACHER

Recently I met with a middle-aged woman who is going through a divorce, has endured the slowly emptying nest, and is immeasurably sad. As we probed carefully into her tender areas, some interesting facts surfaced. She had grown up in a family where it was taught that everyone had to be happy.

Ever-so-gentle but extremely painful words were rooted in this woman's very heart: "Now, Pam, you're not really angry with your sweet little sister! Tell her you're sorry you yelled at her. You know Jesus wouldn't like that!" Under the threat of her mother's disapproval and that of Jesus Christ Himself, Pam was powerless. She learned to deny her real and understandable feelings and to pretend a surface set of proper emotions, as defined by her mother.

Don't repeat this sort of mistake. Instead teach deep-down honesty and a solution-finding philosophy. Help your children learn how to be real so that the way they look, the way they talk, and the way they feel will all be congruent. They will match up.

Good discipline always explores a child's possibilities, expects the best he can do within his limits, and offers appreciation for the child's efforts.

The way you act becomes the blueprint. Your genuineness gives the basic permission to be honest to your family. And how kindly you can express your honesty makes it bearable and useful in their lives, another example of the importance of balance.

As described earlier, your role as teacher involves lessons on each child's individuality, the environment in which they move, and the others whom they will encounter in their world. Help them find the balances in having self-esteem but not being ego-centered; being exuberant over their world but assuming responsibility for taking care of it; exhibiting friendliness to others but using caution regarding those who cannot be trusted.

DISCIPLINARIAN

A disciplinarian teaches right from wrong and some guidelines for discerning what makes any given act or thought right. To be effective, discipline must include establishing healthy controls, not denial as Pam above experienced but recognizing and staying in charge of one's feelings and impulses. Ultimately, each child must internalize the practices we have discussed as effective discipline.

Making such a process one's very own, believing and doing it, requires four techniques: (1) teaching and modeling clearly and consistently; (2) requiring compliance for a period of time; (3) relinquishing your authority gradually, and allowing children to explore on their own how to do it;

and (4) monitoring and giving positive feedback on how they're doing with correction as needed.

Good discipline always explores a child's possibilities, expects the best she can do within her limits, and offers praise and appreciation for her efforts. It never condemns, labels, or destroys a child's self-respect or dignity. You don't need to do negative things to offer effective discipline. Give your child blessing, not cursing.

TAXI DRIVER

From the loftiness of philosophy, let's move to the practical functions you must perform. Taking children where they need to go makes you feel, many times, as if you're running a taxi service. From school in the morning through music lessons after school, and finally to and from Scouts at night, you are constantly on the move. Fighting traffic and meeting deadlines can wreck your peace of mind. Among all the scheduled activities there are the unexpected trips to the grocery store, library, and church.

Let me tell you a true story. My last child was involved in many activities, and her older brother was rarely around to help, so once again, I was a frequent taxi driver. She made our trips a great pleasure by deliberately using them as our sharing time. She would tell me many thoughts, feelings, and experiences, yet it seemed I could never hear enough. And she asked me to share some of my life with her. She never betrayed a confidence, and we became intimate friends on those many excursions.

Set limits on how many trips you will make each day. Balance your desire to provide for your child's needs with the reality of teaching her to plan ahead.

When she turned sixteen, she was ready to obtain her driver's license, but she really never was pushy about it and even delayed getting it for a day or two. One day she stated, "Mom, I kind of wish I didn't have to drive myself now. I'm gonna really miss our times for talking in the car." That comment made it all worthwhile.

You can make the choice. You can take your children where they need to go but be resentful and grouchy; they'll grow up hardly able to wait to drive so they can get free of you. Or you can turn those times into the private joy of sharing with each other.

You can set some limits on how many trips you will make each day. It's easy to try too hard to please your child. By doing so, you can make a tyrant of him—one who controls your life and also tries to boss teachers and friends in ways that are downright obnoxious. Schedule with your child enough activities to enrich his life but not so many that both of you are overburdened. Balance your desire to provide for your child's needs with the reality of teaching her to think ahead and plan for items needed in school or for other aspects of life. Once in a while going without that new tablet or pencil for a day can teach a lesson in organizing and planning ahead.

If your children forget lunch or homework on a regular basis, you really need to avoid becoming a delivery woman. Children who know Mom will always come to the rescue never need to grow up and become responsible for themselves. Think ahead. You can save a significant number of trips for your "taxi," and you can teach your children responsibility as well.

COMFORT AND GRIEF EXPERT

Not long ago I had lunch with a church staff member who was trained as a religious educator for children. She was gracious and intelligent, but one extremely important facet of childhood had eluded her attention. She had never thought about the many losses and grief experiences of children. She wanted to keep children stimulated, growing, learning, and happy. And all of these are vital concerns for children, yet many adults forget children's recurrent disappointments and hurts.

When I lost my mother's approval as a child, I would find comfort in one of two places with my soft, gentle collie or on that amazingly soft cover folded at the foot of Grandmother's bed. There, alone, I could cry, talk, or just be quiet. Grandma's coverlet was called a comforter, and so indeed it was.

Every mother needs to be like that comforter during children's pain—always available, soft, absorbent of tears, and usually quiet. While children are in acute pain, they need no lectures, no distractions, no reassurances of how great tomorrow will be. They need to be able to talk and be heard, to cry and find soft absorbency, to even yell or hit something and find a resilient shock absorber. It takes great strength to be that comforter.

After the acuteness of the grief is over, you may well offer a few words of caring and tell of a time when you, too, experienced pain and some ideas about ways to get out the strong emotions of grief.

Some losses children endure are small, but many are huge. All offer a significant opportunity to teach your child how to survive them and cope with grief. The most common losses are toys that break or are lost; friends who move away; less parental attention due to the arrival of a new brother or sister; the loss of certain freedoms and dependency when they are replaced by responsibilities (not a fair trade!); grandparents who die; the loss of a familiar environment when the family moves; the loss of a loved teacher when a child is promoted; the loss of friendship through a fight or misunderstanding; the loss of a child's whole world through a divorce; the loss of self-esteem through failure or excessive punishments; the loss of wishes and dreams when a young person can't make the groups for which he or she competes. In each case, the responses are the same, and the reassurance needed does not change.

Master those stages of grief—denial, anger, blame, pain and preoccupation, guilt and remorse. And when all of them are expressed, comfort is received, and healing is complete, joy can return. Your presence, caring, comfort, and quiet optimism will help your child survive the most tragic loss and find hope and courage for the next day and beyond.

Your comfort must also be balanced. Too much can teach your child to almost enjoy a dramatic grief episode. Too little can allow her to feel insignificant and abandoned. Look for the center of the road—warm, caring availability, suggestions for help, and enough privacy so your child can learn to cope on his own in due time.

MEDIATOR

I have a dear friend who is a negotiator in labor-management disputes. He is good because he stays clearheaded and impartial and listens extremely well.

Many times a week, you need to fill this role. Your children will argue or even fight with one another. They will have squabbles with their playmates, and very often, they will disagree with you.

Years ago, the noted psychologist Haim Ginnott (author of many books on adult-child communications) lectured in my community. His philosophies were so wise I have used them many times. Sorry to say, his books are now out of print and difficult to find. One of his techniques applied to school-age children who were at odds. He suggested separating them and giving each a paper and pencil.

Each was to pretend to be a lawyer and write out the case in point. Mother served as judge and staged a hearing, listening wisely and impartially to both arguments.

Usually, each child became tired of writing, decided the fight was not too important, and happily resumed playing. If the cause was really important, he would insist on staying with the task and completing the hearing. Mother could often tell by her child's attitude, therefore, who was really at fault.

At any rate, the process gives both mother and children time to clarify and present issues and determine guilt and consequences.

Much more essential than determining guilt is having the opportunity to interpret the needs and feelings underlying various actions. When an older child can see, for example, that his little sister is bothering him because she craves his attention, he can feel complimented. If he fails to have Mom point this out, however, he may see his sister only as a bother who wants specifically to annoy him.

The balance in helping children settle disputes is crucial in avoiding sibling rivalry. Your approach can make it seem that you love everyone equally or that you favor one over the other. Be careful that both your love and your approval are equal for each child. Work to gain that deep understanding of every child's underlying needs and modes of expression.

Then you can be like my friend Bob, the negotiator, restoring harmony in your home.

FASHION EXPERT AND SEAMSTRESS

When my older daughter went off to college, she and her roommate visited a campus clothing outfitter. They asked the manager for help, and he wisely focused their shopping with one question: "Which group do you belong to?" Being freshmen, they really didn't know about groups, and the man advised, "Wait till you look over the campus. Some dress one way, and others wouldn't be seen dead in such outfits. When you decide where you fit, come back. I'll have just the clothes for you!" I never saw that man, but I loved him for saving us money.

Not only do children's fashions need to fit somewhat with those of their friends, but they also need to fit their physical makeup. The height, weight, and coloring of a young person have everything to do with styles and colors that are attractive and comfortable on them.

My older daughter is five feet one and tiny. My younger one is five seven and has very different proportions. When they were younger, Wendy wanted to copy the styles that were just right for her older sister. On her, they appeared grotesque. We both learned quickly what would be attractive on her, not just on the racks in stores.

Teaching children what colors go well with their eyes and hair, what styles suit them, and what colors can be mixed and matched is a challenge, and it can also be fun. It is easier, of course, if you start when they are young and trust your judgment. They will learn to like things that fit comfortably and accent their best features. They are more likely to receive compliments from friends, and when those reaffirm yours (and hopefully they will), you look all the wiser in your children's eyes.

If your child is older and resists your advice on a shopping trip, you can put your foot down and demand your choice or no new clothes at all, a technique that almost certainly will build resentment and create rebellion. You can suggest looking or thinking further, and hope for a wise salesperson's help. Or you can allow what you consider a bad choice. Sometimes moms are mistaken, and the item may work out. If you were right, your child's friends will make that apparent by their comments. In such an instance you must avoid rescuing your child from her bad decision. Let the consequences teach her. Sympathize with her genuinely, suggest something she could do to salvage some use for it, but do not buy a replacement.

Expensive clothing has become a status symbol for young people, and I deplore that! Several years ago I went shopping with my twelve-year-old grandson. The name-brand sports shoes he really wanted cost $125. Even the ordinary ones were $75 to $100, and at most, he could only wear them for several months.

One answer my husband and I discovered early on was to give each child a fixed clothing budget. It was as fair as we could make it and clearly defined.

We began this in the early teen years, so they could shop, compare prices, and decide for themselves what they could afford. The plan saved countless arguments and taught them good economics.

All three of our children decided they could have more clothes if we made some of them, so I had the fun of helping design some really attractive garments. When he was in his mid-thirties, my son was still wearing a wardrobe of down-filled jackets and vests that I made when he was a teenager. I took pride in doing them, he saved a great deal of money, and the process was my way of saying, "Son, you are important to me, and I want to show you how much I love you by sewing this jacket for you." I might add, that was a lot of love because those projects were very complex.

My grandmother would darn socks with holes, restore torn blouses to nearly new, replace buttons from her stack of infinite types, and neatly mend ripped seams. So did my mother, and so did I! I hope my children will pass on these skills and the love they demonstrate to their children.

The balance for me has not been easy to achieve. I love to sew and design, while my children do not share that interest. It is easier for me to do those tasks than for them to master the skills. I hope you will do better than I. Teach your sons and your daughters the basic sewing and mending skills by not doing so much for them.

SOCIAL COORDINATOR

From your first child's first birthday party to your golden wedding celebration, one of your jobs is to plan parties. Balance in this area is indeed vital. It can be tempting to overlook certain events due to fatigue or lack of knowing how to organize and complete such an event. Or you may make even the smallest celebration so elaborate that it wears you out. Find your best balance by keeping entertaining simple but enjoyable.

For that first birthday, the fun lies in the photographs of a child smeared with frosting and a cake with finger holes poked throughout. Invite a few relatives and friends without too many other children, take the photos, and send everybody home so you can clean up the mess! Later on, by age three or four and thereafter, a few of your child's good friends and their mothers can create a memory and make a birthday tradition to last.

By age seven or eight, a child may invite a friend to spend the night. I recommend that you help your child plan these events. Screen the friends carefully. Before bedtime, I had to return more than one frightened, homesick child who was not ready to be away from parents. Plan the snacks and food so your home will not get beyond repair, and be prepared to supervise games and work out arguments.

Even nine- or ten-year-old children tend to sneak friends of the opposite sex into slumber parties, and I strongly recommend you do not allow that. Girls need time with one another to giggle, talk, and play. And boys seem to relish group events with just fellows. They need to fully identify with their own sex before they're ready for too many activities with the opposite sex. I resent the kids' organizations that have moved to coed status in early elementary school. There is much confusion at that time regarding sexual role definition. Having many social activities geared to just boys or just girls can clarify some of that uncertainty.

If you don't teach your child social responsibility, who will?

Special holidays are made to be fun social events. If you have friends of another religion, invite them to share your religious holidays. If they return that hospitality, take advantage of that. I have been profoundly inspired in lovely ways by sharing Passover with Jewish friends.

Balance parties with special family events, going out to eat with preparing special meals at home, and having large groups with inviting only a few close friends. Allow your children to attend parties elsewhere, but be certain you know where they are and how they will be conducted. I consider many teenage events unwise and even seriously risky. Large "keg" parties where alcoholic beverages are available are all too common. Parents with the best of intentions can be outnumbered and lose control of these events. And some parents won't even stay on the premises.

Several years ago, a teenage patient of mine told me this: "On Mondays, I ask my friends what they did for fun over the weekend. It makes me sad when they tell me they were too drunk or stoned to even remember. I want to have good memories of these years!" What a wise young woman!

I urge you to unite with other parents. Many share the concern of keeping teen activities wholesome and harmless. Before the teens are lost forever, organize parties with fun games and a safe environment. Be creative, energetic, and positive. Many young people are ready to learn how to enjoy healthy fun, but they need someone to show them how.

Teach social skills to your child. Playing tennis, swimming, skating, and skiing are examples of physical skills that can offer activity sharing with friends in a structured and safe setting. But balance the need for friends with the value of family time and opportunities to be alone and discover oneself. In the exciting developments of the teen years, your child may become too adult too soon. Once he enters into adult activities, it is difficult or impossible to return to the world of adolescence.

A divorced couple wanted to give their son a memorable sixteenth birthday party. He had not been doing well in school and was on the verge of serious rebellion. But they believed he would appreciate the occasion and really would "straighten out" after he turned sixteen. The parents rented some rooms in a hotel with access to the pool and recreational facilities. Both food and alcoholic beverages were unlimited because the parents were there to chaperone.

At midnight, the father left to return in an elegant convertible. Ceremoniously, he gave the keys to his son. What an exciting and enviable event! But the following week, the son and a convertible full of his friends skipped school. He received a ticket for speeding and narrowly escaped an accident. His father wondered why.

If you don't teach social responsibility to your kids, who will? Will it be the police, a judge, or our justice system? Please, let it be you!

VOLUNTEER COORDINATOR

On my bedroom mantel is a framed piece of white velvet. On that velvet, my daughter carefully pinned my medals. There are several nice ones, but I cherish most those I earned by serving as Scout den mother and Camp Fire leader. I also taught Sunday school classes for many years, and I even worked one hectic week as a counselor at a youth camp.

I chose those volunteer activities because I believed in the values those organizations stood for and because of the opportunities I found to be with my children and their friends. We did many activities that were fun, learned some meaningful rituals, and cemented some lifelong friendships. I wish I could have served even more time, but over fifteen years probably were enough.

Countless needs in every community are best served by volunteers—people who care enough to give themselves and demonstrate a special definition of love. Children often have too little quality time with an adult, so I hope you will find some avenue through which to give to them. Teach them about heroes, about values, about nature, and about giving themselves.

Include your children, and they, too, will learn the value of giving. When one is blessed, she has an attendant responsibility to bless others.

Volunteer work can, in its own right, become too demanding, leaving you drained of time and energy for yourself and your family. Keep the balance. Give only what you can afford to give; take care of yourself and your family because no one else will do that. Then give as freely as you like of whatever is left over. Living within balances is a comfortable lifestyle.

STUDY HALL SUPERVISOR

I have already written about the importance of learning. You have a vital part in communicating that value to your children. Review the establishment of a studious environment. Remove distractions, make lighting convenient, have supplies available, and above all, be there and be free to help. Most children need encouragement. Almost all of them need you to give spelling words, drill them with metric flash cards, and quiz them on history and science.

Keep your mind active and growing. As you discuss new concepts or ideas you have discovered through reading or thinking, you will inevitably enhance your child's interest and motivation to learn.

Above all, never ask your child if she has homework. You are the one who knows she does. He can never learn all he needs to know in any class time. Instill the love of learning in your child, and he will learn all of his life.

Ask your young teens thought-provoking questions gleaned from the news or your own reading. Share a new thought you have discovered and ask his/her opinion about it. Plan a family vacation to some historic spot and learn together some facts about it. As your own curiosity and interests come into focus, share them with your child, always asking his opinions about them. Be sure to show respect for teens' ideas.

VALUES CLARIFIER

In today's society, no one is doing much teaching of values. Schools fear trying to do so because of the vast differences in families' beliefs. Many children never attend church, and most parents seem to have forgotten that they need to teach values.

A young woman came to me in tears. She had made plans for a fun activity with a friend. She needed a break from her child and house and was eagerly anticipating an outing. On the morning of the event, her friend called and blithely canceled their plans. She preferred to do something else that had just occurred to her. My friend felt rejected; she was hurt and angry. She knew her friend would call her the next time she needed a favor, but she was insensitive to the needs of another.

When my children were small, I passed along the value of fairness and integrity. When you make a plan with a friend, that plan comes first. No matter what opportunity knocks later, the first commitment stands. That policy prevented a lot of trouble and hurt feelings.

Seeing the far-reaching impact of policies and the values they teach can help you lay good foundations. But begin today if you missed the earlier opportunity. First, think about the values you hold most dear. Honesty, kindness, tolerance, compassion, humor, generosity, adventure, spirituality, excellence in work, relaxation, beauty—these are just a beginning.

Next, look at yourself. Do you live these values? Which ones would come first if you prioritized them? How can you demonstrate them even more convincingly in your life? And how can you teach them to your children? During the years of the depression, there were many homeless people. Men would leave home to look for jobs and would walk the country roads, hoping a farmer might need their help. They were dirty, desperate, defeated men. Often they came by our house and asked for food. They found the right house because my mother could always provide them with a plateful. She would give them a washbasin to wash their hands and faces, good food, and a prayer for their needs. Her example taught me compassion, generosity, kindness, respect for the down-and-out, and spiritual values.

Talk about your values only when your lifestyle demonstrates them. Tolerance for people of other faiths became real to me when Mother invited the Jewish apple peddler, who regularly visited our home, to dinner. We understood he didn't eat pork and respected his preference.

COMPTROLLER

Families vary in their task assignments, and few issues are as controversial as money management in regard to who assumes responsibility.

Frankly, it seems to me that money is everybody's business. Unless you have an unlimited supply, you need to understand how to handle money, and you need to teach this skill to your children.

The basic philosophy about taking care of the economics of your family is simple. The demands must not exceed the supply. How do you achieve such a simple balance? *Be very clear about your total income.* Never assume that a raise will be coming or that you will get an income tax refund. When those good fortunes happen, you can easily cope with them.

Be equally clear about all of your regular expenses. The biggest mistake in this category is forgetting the large bills that come due once a year, such as house and car insurance. Be certain you know them all.

Allow some flexibility for unexpected costs. Replacing an appliance or repairing a leaking roof can be costly.

Avoid using credit cards when at all possible. The interest you pay on them could startle you. The only way they are useful to you is when you can pay them completely every month so interest does not accumulate.

Now match your regular expenditures with your income. I hope that you have enough to save some, spend a bit on fun and foolishness, or expand an area of your budget that is too cramped.

You may need to reduce your lifestyle at times. As extra expenses arise that you must meet, you can often curtail a clothing budget, give up eating out for a while, and cut down your food budget a bit. The poverty-level families in our communities may go without meat for a while and rarely enjoy the luxuries many of us consider necessary. Be prepared to live now and then as if you, too, were on a poverty-income level.

Recently I met with a friend and his pastor. They were concerned over a growing number of parishioners who had suddenly lost jobs and income.

The blow to the pride of these men, in an affluent community, could not be measured. And the constricted budgets created problems for not only the families but also the entire church.

I urge you to *prepare for an economic emergency* such as these families are enduring. Rather than spend the extra money from a raise or a bonus, save it. Make yourself regularly put even small amounts of money into a secure spot.

Learn different skills. If you or your husband should lose a job, do you have a basis for finding a new one in a different occupation? Read about the job market and where there may be an emerging possibility for your skills to be put to work.

Learn to sew and garden. Raising some of your own vegetables can be fun, offers a project for your family to share, and really helps your food budget.

I believe in giving children allowances. Our country has enjoyed unusual prosperity for five or six decades with fairly minor setbacks. Most children have grown up receiving the majority of the things they ask for and many things they haven't even thought about asking for. Because such prosperity is unlikely to last forever, children need to learn money management just as adults do. An allowance is a made-to-order tool for teaching kids.

Start with a five-year-old, perhaps, with fifty cents a week. Teach him to give 10 percent to church—only a nickel, but it's his very own. Next I recommend that she put 10 percent in a piggy bank. She will need a pencil or tablet for school. The tablet will take several weeks' allowance, but she could buy her own pencil. She may want some sugarless gum, so her own money may buy that. You see, you are teaching your children generosity, saving, responsibility, and enjoyment. He will keep track of his pencil if he pays for it out of his own pocket, too.

As a child grows and evidences the ability to be responsible with money, you can enlarge the allowance. But with that, you must remember to also enlarge the areas in which he is to be responsible for spending it. Allowances are not all for pleasure. They are for learning that original principle of supply and demand. If your child overspends, don't rescue him. If she spends all of it the first day, she must wait for the next "pay-day." Don't let them start borrowing unless you want to teach them about bankruptcy. And don't be late in giving the allowance.

An allowance, in its best function, is not pay for helping the family. Family members help one another out of love and respect. There are times, however, when a child may need to earn extra money. He may want an item that is okay to have but beyond the limits of his allowance. If you can, I recommend you keep a list of extra-tough jobs he may do to earn money. Be sure you do not overpay or underpay. Make certain the job gets done well, and add your commendation to the pay when it's done. Someday, your child's spouse will love you for teaching the way to balance a budget.

THE "BOSS"

Many children reach school without ever dealing effectively with author-ity. They wheedle or bully their way with their parents and try the same tac-tics with teachers. You are doing everyone a huge favor by teaching your child you are in charge. There is no license for a mother to be a dictator, controlling or dominating her child. But when a child is out of control, unable to choose wisely or exert sufficient willpower to learn responsibility, your job is to help him or her do that. Refer to the section on discipline for methods, but just know how essential your authority is. Your child will respect and love you all the more when you master the skill of requiring compliance. You will feel confident, and your family will be enjoyable.

ANIMAL TRAINER

Growing up on a farm, I knew the value of pets. Not only was my dog my comforter, but a pet chicken, a lamb, and even a calf became fun for my sisters and me. Many parents obtain pets in the erroneous belief that they will teach their kids to be responsible. Nothing could be further from the truth! You are the one responsible for pets, like it or not. Once that truth is established, I will agree that pets can teach children many things, especially love and loyalty.

> *If you want your child to become responsible for a pet's care, avoid reminding him. Establish a plan with consequences.*

Last week a family who are friends of mine came nearly to blows about the cat and the dog who make messes regularly in their house. Each is waiting on the other to "do something about it." You must train your pet, delegate the job, or live in a smelly, ugly house. Animals were created to live outside, to hunt and forage for food, to scratch and cover their feces, and to fend for themselves. If you expect them to live in a house, you must go against all of their natural instincts and train them in what you want them to do. In training a pet, you can also learn some basic principles about training children. These include consistency, rewards and consequences, love and follow-through.

After your pet is trained, you can train your children to care for it. Children can provide food and water as well as exercise. They can stroke and hug the pet and even groom it if they are taught. If you want your child to become responsible for a pet's care, you must avoid reminding him. Instead, establish a plan with consequences: Unless the dog is fed, you do not have dinner. If you failed to clean the litter box, you must clean up the mess on the floor. And your child's activities stop until those jobs are done. Reminding becomes nagging, and nagging creates resistance, not cooperation.

Enjoy your pet, but remember that it will often be a nuisance and a problem. If you can cope with that fact with some equanimity, you are a great mom! In all of your roles and responsibilities, you have burdens and opportunities, challenges and privileges. As you understand what these are, you can shoulder them effectively. But always look for both extremes—too much, too little; too early, too late; too angry, too patient; expecting too much or too little; being too strict or too lenient. To find the balance, you must explore those extremes, and in doing so you will make many mistakes. That's okay. As long as you are in love with your children, they will know you are doing your best, and they will gladly forgive your mistakes.

Emotions

CHAPTER EIGHTEEN

Healthy Emotional Expression

A big difference between most women and men is the great comfort zone women experience with emotions. Almost universally in my family counseling I see men attacking problems intellectually while women are painfully working through the feelings woven into those issues. Often husbands believe that wives do not appreciate their help, and wives are convinced that their husbands will never understand. Both are right and wrong.

One evening my husband and I were preparing to attend a function, and we needed to be on time. I had had an unusually long day at work and was running late, so I went by a fast-food restaurant to get hamburgers for the children. When I took out my wallet to pay for them, I had no cash, and the restaurant had an unbendable policy against taking checks or credit cards. I had to get a check cashed elsewhere, go back and pick up my order, and by then was very late indeed. I was frustrated, worried, and afraid of the inconvenience to others because of my lateness. I couldn't have prevented any of the problems since I did not know about the cash-only policy.

As I explained the situation to my husband, who was also hurried and late, he responded, "Gracie, you should have known a fast-food store wouldn't bother with a check. Why were you so low on cash?" I wish I could see the face of every woman who reads this story because I'm sure you, too, have participated in similar dialogues. What you want in such times must be just what I needed then—his giving me a quick hug and saying, "Honey, I can see how frustrating that manager must have been. You're so great to work all day, take care of our kids, and still go out with me tonight! I'm sorry, but we'll make it!" You can take some actions that will help such a transformation occur.

This section will describe some of a mother's major emotions and what you can do to make all of them work positively.

ANGER

Since anger is so universally difficult to take and to express, let's address it first. Anger, you may recall, is present in newborn babies, and it is expressed when they feel pain. As you respond to the pain, the anger subsides and trust develops. At birth, the pain is physical hunger, cold, wetness, earaches, and the like. Later, the pain is more likely to be emotional loneliness, fear, or embarrassment.

The Creator gave us anger to set in motion certain physiological functions that can be lifesaving. It stimulates adrenaline and other hormones that act on the heart and circulation to increase blood flow, on the lungs to enhance the oxygen intake, and on the muscles to prepare to run or fight to protect oneself. The trouble is, you can't run from or fight your children or other family members.

So what can you do? The first step must be to *gain understanding and control*. Problems arise when emotions control you rather than your controlling them. Learn to think clearly even in the midst of your emotions, and you will be on your way to that vital control.

Make a habit of identifying your emotions and putting them into words.

Taking this step as soon as possible after that emotion starts makes it much easier.

Ask yourself why this emotion has occurred. What event prompted it? Is that event alone enough to account for your anger?

Anger almost always covers up a very different emotion, such as fear, hurt, or shame. Make yourself look for and face these so-called weaker feelings.

Make yourself sit down, or at least become quiet enough mentally, to *create a plan for dealing with the problem and the feeling.*

Feelings and needs go together like Siamese twins. When you feel angry but discover you're really afraid of rejection, what do you need? Reassurance, comfort, and a trustworthy friend to support you usually will take care of your need.

Whatever your degree of anger or its cause, you can learn to express it verbally. You don't need to yell, hit, or break things! You can decide how to correct that cause and even who can help you in doing so. Perhaps you can even teach that intellectualizing husband to understand your feelings first and then help you solve the problem, if you need such help.

FEAR AND WORRY

April was a dimpled, smiling child with pink cheeks and brown curls. Darrell rarely smiled, and his brown eyes communicated mixed feelings of anger and sadness. He spoke very little.

While their parents and I talked, I watched his fine, sensitive face and also the parents' expressions. It soon became evident that all family members were worried about Darrell. They feared that his anger would cause him to do serious violence. He hit his little sister at times until she cried. As Darrell heard and saw his parents' anxiety, his expression became even sadder, and tears filled his eyes. Clearly, Darrell didn't want to hurt his sister or worry his parents. He was, however, in so much pain that he had to let it out. Wanting to be a strong boy, he felt anger was better than tears.

The typical story of a child whose sibling was more pleasant, in some areas more successful, and seemed more acceptable than he came tumbling out. The parents could see how their worry made Darrell feel that he was a truly bad boy. And he began to understand how much his parents loved him and not just his sister.

He finally believed that their worry was a measure not of his badness but of their love. All of these discoveries and the healing they made possible occurred over time, but I want you to see how your anxious, fearful emotions are often perceived by your children.

To avoid a situation like Darrell's, you might first look at yourself in a mirror to see the worry lines that leave their telltale messages for your child to read. Listen to your tone of voice, and think about the things you say to her. Above all, observe your child's face. Does it look increasingly sad and, at times, angry? If so, you can be certain that there are too many negative messages and too few positive ones flowing.

To dispel fear and worry, clearly define the problem. Be certain that you have accurate facts and that there really is a problem. Equally carefully, list the strengths that can correct the problem—include the people who can best assist you. Put the plan into action, and stick with it until the problem is solved. Enjoy the solution, your child, and the wisdom you've learned.

Concerns and even worry assail all of us. The exciting truth is that they do not need to consume us or become habitual emotions. Implement your plan, and overcome your worry and fear.

SHAME

When I made mistakes with my children, I experienced intense remorse and shame. I would give anything if I could erase the pain of those mistakes in mothering. Although I can't undo those early acts that were so misguided, I have found some things to do that promote healing in my children and myself.

The first step was to admit my errors. For a long time I tried to justify myself and make it look as if I had done the right thing.

Next, I tried to determine why I had done the act that was so wrong. There was great hope in this step. My motives were to help my children become honest, responsible, and loving adults. Surely there was nothing wrong in my motives.

Then I tried to think about what I should have done instead. What lesson did I learn from my wrongdoing?

When I fully understood my mistakes, I discussed the entire situation with my children, who were then young adults. I asked their forgiveness, tried to help them profit from the lessons I'd learned, and then let go. I find no value in continuing to punish myself for past mistakes. I had to forgive myself, accept their understanding, and believe in God's forgiveness.

You need not let shame over past events cripple your present. One family I worked with had great difficulty in training and disciplining their children. They were quite clear that the problem related to their shame over their own imperfections: "How can we expect Sam to be perfect when we know how much we used to drink and carry on?" Don't allow such erroneous thinking to damage your good mothering. Let go of your past and start today!

GUILT

This crippling emotion is closely akin to shame and is a part of many problems in mothering. Shame, by connotation, involves the uncovering of misdeeds, or the fear of discovery, by other people. We are ashamed of our mistakes before our children or others.

Guilt, on the other hand, is a sense of serious wrongdoing on our part, as judged by another. A judge and a jury have the power to determine a person's guilt and assign a penalty. Many parents are critical judges, teaching children to become their own worst enemies.

Does this scenario sound familiar? You spend an entire Saturday cleaning your house. Just as you put away the last dust cloth and are reveling in your sparkling, freshly waxed kitchen floor, four (or more) muddy feet tramp across it. You yell a series of unpleasant comments to the children about those dirty feet and their careless, thoughtless, selfish ways.

That night when they are scrubbed and tucked into bed, you look at their precious angelic faces, and the guilt hits you. They are, after all, only children, and it's the nature of children to get dirty. And where should they go if not into their own kitchen? Guilty! What do you do with this verdict?

In this case you are guilty. You hurt your children by taking out your fatigue and frustration on them.

But they, too, are guilty. They failed to remove their dirty shoes at the back door, and they caused you unnecessary extra work.

Deal with real, definable guilt by (1) admitting and clearly explaining the misdeed, (2) apologizing and asking forgiveness, (3) devising a plan to prevent repeating that error (for example, tape a sign on the door saying "Knock" or lock the door), *and (4) dropping the matter.* Don't torment yourself or your children by bringing up old issues.

Real guilt is easier to define and, therefore, to eliminate than false guilt. By its very name, you can tell there is deception in the emotion. False guilt causes most of a mother's difficulty. You accomplish one task, such as housecleaning, only to realize that you should have been spending time with your three-year-old or helping your six-year-old with her flash cards. No one can do everything at once, but that's what so many supermoms attempt. And then they feel guilty about their self-imposed verdict of guilty! Most false guilt comes from mothers' spending time away from their children; rarely is that truly wrong.

Furthermore, children have their own way of laying on guilt. A friend told me that when her youngest child was five and in school for half days, she began to work now and then as a substitute teacher. She saw to it that her son went to an excellent sitter, and she knew he was well cared for. One day, when he was a bit miffed at her, he said to his sitter, "You know,

Madge, I don't have a mommy anymore, and I don't even have my own house!" His mother felt so guilty, she refused to work anymore until he was quite a bit older.

Actually, five-year-olds can handle being cared for by someone other than Mom. Mother needed the stimulation of her work and the opportunity to return to full-time teaching that could have come with her job as a substitute. Had she taken a little clearer look at her son, she might have discovered a touch of manipulation in his somewhat self-pitying remarks.

So what can you do about false guilt? *Look carefully at your plans—* whether they relate to daily tasks at home, volunteer work, or a career. Have you sorted out needs from wishes? Have you been honest about them? Do you have your values and priorities clear? To the best of your ability, have you included everyone's needs and feelings in your considerations? Is your thinking straight? Be sure your facts are accurate and that you are not setting impossible, unrealistic expectations for yourself. Sound information will help dispel false guilt.

Share your planned activities with your family. They don't need every detail, but in general they will be more secure knowing where you'll be and what to expect.

Let each family member know what you need from him or her. Children don't like being bossed around, but they need to feel important, wanted, and productive. Whether you are a stay-at-home or a working mom, your children need to be needed. You must not feel guilty that they have to help you. It's good for them.

If you must return to work, share events you experience there with your family. Let them become a part of your life. Help them understand why you need to work and be away sometimes.

Help your children feel they are part of your success by being useful at home. Teamwork is so important in families.

Reward them appropriately. You get paid for your job, and with considerable extra responsibility, children need a tangible paycheck, too. It need not be money, however. A family game, a special treat now and then, or an outing can be much better than money for children. Mostly, make sure they know how much you need them and how their efforts help.

Find the energy to enjoy your children. Take five or ten minutes to relax at the end of your workday (at home or on a job), and during that brief time, consider how much you love each other and what you might do to express that love the rest of the evening. It's easy to focus on one's own fatigue and the unfinished tasks; doing so can turn even the best mother into a real grouch.

You may have such an ingrained habit of feeling guilty that you may not be able to conquer it alone. If you do, I recommend you see two types of people—first, your clergyperson, for help in distinguishing real from false guilt and learning about forgiving; second, a counselor who can help you get free from unconscious problems that keep you stuck.

Don't forget your will. By exerting that power to choose and to do the right things, you can overcome the false guilt habit.

LOVE AND JOY

You might not think it necessary to discuss expressing such happy emotions, but let me share a story. Arlene was the mother of three children. She was depressed and unable to function as lovingly as she wanted to do.

As we explored the reasons for her depression, one by one she uncovered the taproots. The one that was unique focused on her memory of a radio broadcast of a Saturday afternoon high school ball game. As her school inched ahead in the close competition, she became excited. She yelled for her team, even from a long distance.

Her father, reading his paper in the next room, harshly lectured her about her ridiculous behavior. He told her how silly it was to get so "worked up" over a ball game. He told her to stop acting excited around him.

That day, out of sadness and fear, Arlene decided never to show her enthusiasm again. She had so schooled herself to be demure that she could not show her exuberance to her own children. It took a long time, but Arlene rediscovered her joy and can now be enthused about all sorts of events in her life and in the lives of her children.

Once again, the concept of balance comes into focus. If you are too loud or boisterous in expressing your joy, it could become embarrassing. And if you are too restrained and "proper," it is difficult for anyone else to share with you.

How do you express your love? There are so many ways. Some people say, "I love you!" by doing acts of kindness. Other examples include earning a living, keeping a neat house and fixing nourishing meals, attending children's events, and trying to teach them what they need to know.

Other people express love by hugs, kisses, touches, and playfulness. Physical contact is more comfortable for some people than others, but children need it always. Some family members have problems with knowing appropriate from inappropriate touch or may have a compulsion to touch children in sexually stimulating ways. What starts as genuine love can turn into sexual exploitation. Studies show that men are more likely to be involved in unhealthy sexual advances than women, but occasionally mothers are tempted to sexually abuse their children.

If you suspect that your child is being sexually abused, try to verify your facts. Reporting abuse falsely does great harm. Observe your child carefully. Are there any signs of irritation, bruising, or pain in genital areas? Be sure these did not occur from rough play or clothing. Is your child tense and nervous around a specific person? Or is she unduly attracted to that person? Is there a change in eating, sleeping, or toilet habits? Is your child preoccupied with his genitals or others' genital areas? Sexual abuse is difficult to establish unless the child decides to tell.

Knowing that the perpetrator could go to jail or that she might hurt the child if the truth comes out makes it extremely hard for a child to reveal the truth. On the other hand, in my work with children and families, an older child has occasionally concocted an accusation against a parent or relative he is angry with.

Lest you overreact or are neglectful, always be aware that sexual abuse can occur, and anyone can do it. Be familiar with the physical signs as well as the behavioral indications just listed. Don't leave your child unprotected.

Tell your child, without accusing anyone, what is inappropriate touch. Let him know he doesn't need to be afraid to let you know if anyone tries to practice such touch on him. If your child does tell you, have a qualified physician check her and tell you what to do. If you have evidence of any abuse, call your local or state child abuse hot line. It will be listed in your telephone directory as such, and trained experts will investigate and guide you in protecting your child.

Such investigations often involve hasty and frightening procedures that can result in a relative's being sentenced to prison. Frankly, I'm convinced that help in a mental hospital would be infinitely more useful. Perhaps someday our society will become knowledgeable about preventing sexual abuse and really treating offenders. But until then, we must protect our children.

By the way, you can protect your children by monitoring their TV watching and their reading materials. The sexually explicit scenes available to children rob them of their carefree, innocent childhood in far too many cases.

Love, you see, must have three expressions: tenderness, toughness, and protection. Tender, loving touches enrich our lives and provide tangible evidence of love. Toughness that cares enough to see to it that children live within proper limits helps them develop self-control and willpower. And the protective love that prevents risks and needless danger enables children to survive. What a marvelous experience is a mother's total love!

Make friends with your feelings—all of them. Cultivate them, control them, and communicate them clearly. They will provide the seasoning that makes life palatable and delightful.

Mistakes

CHAPTER NINETEEN

Minimizing Mistakes

*A*ll of us mothers make our fair share of mistakes. We never planned to make them; we tried very hard, often too hard, to avoid them. Looking at some common errors can help you realize that you are not alone in the "blooper" club as a mother. Even more important, you may discover mistakes you had no idea you were making and how you can stop them.

OVERMOTHERING

One young man I know well tells me his mother "mommies" him. He is quite capable of being independent, and he needs to practice making his own decisions and carrying them out. Sometimes his mother encourages that self-reliance, but she usually finds ways of taking over. He struggles with resentment toward her and yet finds it easier to let her take care of him.

Such overmothering usually starts in infancy. It often accompanies a serious illness or a handicapping condition. When an older child has suffered serious injury, illness, or death, a younger child is almost certain to be overprotected. A mother who craves intimacy may experience that with a dependent child and then unconsciously keep the child in need of her so that she can continue that closeness. On the other extreme, an overburdened mother or one who feels incompetent may resent her child or fear she's not doing a good job. She overfunctions for fear of harming a child in some way.

Your most important task as a mother is to enable your child to gradually become independent. Anything you do to retard or damage that growth will eventually hurt both you and your child. Observe other children who are close to your child's age and capabilities. If your child's development is very far behind, explore the possibility that you are keeping her too close to you and too dependent on you. Think about the causes of overmothering. Do any of them seem to apply to you? If so, you may be able to catch yourself in the habit and change it.

> *Your most important task as a mother is to enable your child to gradually become independent.*

Another expression of overfunctioning comes from the habit of nagging. I have to admit I developed that habit with my daydreaming, creative son. He would get so involved in a variety of projects that he would forget his duties.

I began nagging by simply reminding him. But he was so caught up in building endless wonderful models or mechanical gadgets, he persisted in forgetting. Before I knew it, my reminders moved into nagging, and my mild irritation became intense frustration at times.

Of course, the more a mother reminds a dreamer child, the more he relies on her and the less on himself. So we moms end up defeating ourselves and blaming our children! Furthermore, those resentments hurt our children and estrange us from each other.

My son and I finally found a way to solve our problems. First, I had to realize that I was focusing on the negatives and unwittingly failing to comment on the many positives. I had to change my attitude. Admitting my mistake was painful because I had to face the fact that I had hurt my only son, whom I loved dearly. It was also a relief because facing the problem ensured my changing for the better.

Next, we outlined a plan that listed his duties and the consequences of neglecting them. He would get to choose a time by which he would have the jobs done. My duty was to avoid any reminders. If he missed the school bus, he walked to school. If he forgot to feed the dog, he had no dinner until he did. If his food was cold because he came late to the dinner table, I would not reheat it.

Our habits didn't change overnight, but no one was angry anymore. My tongue was shortened by my biting it off, centimeter by centimeter, but a shorter tongue may be good for lots of mothers! The only other problem was remembering to follow through with the consequences.

Overmothering may also be demonstrated by being overly critical, screaming, or punishing too severely. According to David A. Wolfe's book *Child Abuse* (Sage Publishers, 1999), reports of abuse and neglect rose 9 percent from 1993 to 1997. In 1998 more than one million cases of child abuse or neglect were confirmed.

Most mothers who overpunish are intensely anxious that their children do well and behave properly. They want them to be perfect. Yet they fear their own weaknesses and imperfections in mothering will not create model children. To compensate, they overreact, are overly critical, and punish too harshly and too angrily. It is easy to slip over the line from overpunishing to outright abuse and not even realize it.

If you ever find bruises or red marks that you inflicted on your child, or if you realize your child is becoming afraid of you, ask for help. The best place to find that practical help is through a group called Parents Anonymous. This national organization has headquarters at 675 W. Foothill Blvd., Suite 220, Claremont, CA 91711. To find the nearest local chapter, see their Web site at www.parentsanonymous-natl.org, or check your telephone directory. A phone call or letter could be your best investment in your child's welfare and your own peace of mind.

Some mothers overprotect a new baby at the cost of an older child's feeling rejected. A friend who has suffered severe depression for years recalls feeling extremely hurt when, at seven, she wanted to play with the new baby in his crib. Her mother screamed at her to get away, and she was not allowed to touch him. The mother had probably known of an older child who harmed a baby, and naturally she would want to prevent that. How much different the story would have been if the mother had supervised this child, teaching her to have fun and be careful at the same time.

Too much or too little responsibility can be equally damaging to a child.

Some mothers overfunction because that's what they consider being an ideal mom. Karla came to see me for help with Sarah, her fourteen-year-old. Sarah, an eighth grader, was failing three of her five subjects. I knew Sarah was bright enough to pass easily, so I explored with Karla the sense of responsibility her daughter demonstrated.

"What are Sarah's jobs at home?" I asked.

Karla's gentle eyes looked surprised. "Jobs? Should she have jobs? I've never asked her to even pick up her pajamas in the morning!" she replied. She went on to define for me the top-of-the-line mother. She was not employed outside the home, and she saw her job description clearly. It was to clean the house daily to picture perfection. Her meals were always gourmet, and the dishes after meals and snacks should be sanitarily clean. Her children just couldn't do that properly.

As we talked, Karla recognized that her efforts to be a perfect mom had cost her daughter the development of any sense of duty. Sarah had no idea how to organize a task, do it well, and finish it. Her schoolwork was simply a continuation of her irresponsibility at home. She had learned that a child's job description was to have fun and be carefree. Fortunately, Karla and Sarah were able to change that philosophy, and Sarah eventually became a successful mother and career woman.

Perhaps you, too, believe you must do it all. Your mother may have taught you such habits. On the other extreme, you may have carried too heavy a load of responsibility as a child. If so, you probably are determined that your child not be as burdened as you were, and without realizing it, you've gone too far.

Once again, remember the need for balance—too much or too little responsibility can be equally damaging. Try to get a perspective of your child's attitude toward life and how she functions. If she can relax, have fun, and yet take her job assignments seriously, you probably have found that near-perfect balance. If not, make some adjustments!

CRITICIZING YOUR CHILDREN'S FATHER

We've already explored the importance of love and support between mothers and fathers. Let me repeat here that being critical of your children's father can hurt their feelings about you as much as about him. Most children love both parents. Furthermore, they are so vulnerable that they tend to side with people who may seem to be fallible and as vulnerable as they are. They may become afraid of you, thinking you will reject them as you have their father. I have known many children in a divorce, for example, to fear that their mother may abandon them as she has left their father.

Certainly, parents often disagree; that's both normal and healthy. But keep those disagreements as calm as possible, rational, and to the point. Don't attack each other to win a power struggle. And if the disagreement even starts to become an attack, stop the discussion until you can become calm and reasonable. Children who develop healthy self-esteem have parents who respect each other.

Let me review why a woman may become so critical of her husband. She chooses a man to marry who is similar in some ways to one parent, but she perceives the similarities only vaguely. When she eventually finds a negative quality in her spouse-to-be, she blithely convinces herself it will change after marriage, after they have a child, or after sometime! When that change doesn't occur, the wife feels deceived and cheated. She tries to force the changes she wants to see and becomes so intense that fights occur. When too many battles are lost (and such battles are almost always lost by both parties), estrangement inevitably occurs, and from the ever-widening distance between spouses emerges the likelihood of affairs and finally divorce.

I hope you can see, then, why you must work at building a strong, healthy marriage. Keep a clear focus on your husband's endearing and strong qualities. Don't get caught in power struggles, and learn good communication skills.

Here is a word of caution I cannot emphasize strongly enough! *Don't criticize your husband to others.* I can recall countless events, when I was a young wife, of getting together socially with other wives. One would describe how furious she felt because her husband failed to pick up his dirty socks to put in the clothes hamper just inches away from where he dropped them. Her description was funny, so another wife, only wanting to enlarge on the humor, described how her husband would reach out to place his coffee cup on the kitchen counter when he was standing right in front of the dishwasher. Before I knew it, I was recounting how my husband would stumble on the front steps because he had not replaced a burned-out lightbulb! It takes only a session or two like that to turn anyone's husband into a foolish slob. Once planted, those seeds of resentment grow until their foliage obscures all the man's good traits. No wonder studies reveal that a positive, affirming attitude makes a marriage and family strong.

GROUPING YOUR CHILDREN

If you have several children, you may make a little mistake and not think of it at all. There were seven children in my family, and my mother often referred to us as "the girls" and "the boys." In her case, we knew pretty well who we were as individuals, but some children don't have that privilege. Certainly, there are times to address children as a group, but doing that excessively can reduce each child's value as an individual.

A unique example of failing to individualize children comes from the birth of twins or other multiple births. Beth had struggled through eighteen months with twin daughters. Finally, they were sleeping through the night and beginning to feed themselves, and Beth could feel almost human at times! However, she faced a new challenge. Whenever she took one child on an errand, leaving the other with her husband, the child at home would scream intensely. She knew he was not abusing the child, but she tried leaving one twin with other caretakers while she had some individual time with the other.

The results invariably were the same. The twins could not tolerate separation from each other. Since learning of Beth's predicament, I have studied other twins and found that it is not unusual for them to become so close to each other, they literally panic when separated. If you are aware of a similar problem, work to correct it. Take turns removing one twin from the other for only a minute or two and promptly return him or her.

Steadily but slowly extend their times apart as they tolerate it. When they are ready, put them in separate beds and separate rooms when that is possible. Dress them differently, and place them in separate classrooms when they go to school. Train yourself to think of them and treat them as separate, whole individuals.

In a world where individuals count too little, where robots and computers control more than a little of our environment, we must be extra cautious about raising children to be themselves. Somehow we must find the time to discover in them the beauty of soul and the capabilities of mind and body that identify them as unique. Discover and develop your own individuality, and it will be easier to practice such techniques with your children. Let me list a few of the methods for cultivating individuality.

Choices. Choose the styles, colors, and ideas that fit you regarding your home, your clothes, and your activities. With some guidance, offer similar choices to your children.

Environment. As far as possible, let each child decorate her or his own room. If two must share a room, each can take charge of a section of the room. Planting a garden can also express each child's preferences. Even a potted plant can serve the purpose.

Creativity. Children need to be exposed to a variety of art, music, and literature. They should be encouraged to create their own projects in clay, crayons, or paints. Performing or even writing music is open to every child who can sing or play an instrument. Encourage your child to create, and do so yourself.

Crafts and play. Children need to be given opportunities for play as well as artistic development. Provide a variety of materials for your children to play with. A child's eventual career may have its roots in the interests developed early on. It is wise to use inexpensive materials.

One young mother saves cardboard milk cartons for creative play. After carefully washing them, she pushes the top in so that both ends are flat. By covering them with bright self-adhesive wrap, she has stacks of building blocks she and her toddler can use to build all kinds of edifices. These and other food containers make excellent indoor gardens where children can watch seeds sprout and where you can start your spring garden instead of buying expensive hothouse plants.

Your creativity and excitement over various activities transform learning and even work into play and fun. Each child has a chance to express uniqueness with your help.

Friends. Who we are is reflected in the people we choose as friends. Help your children choose good friends. When they are young, supervise their activities, and teach them to interact appropriately. Many mothers take for granted that children will automatically learn how to work and play in positive and constructive ways. That idea is wrong! You must observe and correct repeatedly if your young children are to behave in a manner that will win and keep good friends. You must "be there" for your children.

If your children are older, you will find it best to guide their choice of friends instead of choosing for them. But guide carefully. If you are too critical of an adolescent's choices, he is likely to rebel. So once again, observe and comment without insulting your child's choice or his friend's personality. Base your comments on observations, and ask your child if he has noticed certain specific traits and how he feels about them. Try to help your child's friends in tactful ways. You may be the key person in their lives to guide them to become better people.

Help your children feel so good about themselves individually that they will not be interested in gangs or excessive groupness. And in guiding them, keep your awareness and value of their uniqueness high.

NEGLECTING YOUR CHILDREN

We worry a great deal these days about child abuse, and rightly so! Abuse leaves ugly scars on children's bodies and souls. But I believe that even worse than abuse are the subtle ways in which parents neglect children. Social workers in inner cities and affluent suburbs alike tell me of instances of tragic neglect.

It is not uncommon to learn of children as young as six or seven left in an apartment with one or more younger siblings for an entire weekend. Sometimes they have woefully inadequate food and no help with a baby's dirty diapers. For each case of this sort that is discovered, we assume that several go unnoticed.

This extreme failure of a mother's love to be deeply imprinted in a baby's life makes me fear for the generation to come. (Remember the studies of Dr. Harlow noted in the Introduction.) Overburdened mothers who love their children may need them to grow up too soon to alleviate the load of responsibility they carry. They allow privileges and encourage responsibilities that rob youngsters of their childhood. Too many young people work nearly full-time while still in high school, living at home like a boarder, receiving few restrictions, and even less guidance.

In affluent areas, this philosophy has become widely accepted since the 1970s: get all the pleasure you can, and avoid as much pain as you can. Parents who subscribe to this belief frequently go on trips for extended times, leaving teenagers to their own devices. They presume those teens are safe and reliable. They even make a variety of provisions for their care. But they reckon naively without considering the peer pressure of a drug-addictive, hedonistic society. They somehow deny reality and rationalize that things will be as they hope rather than face the facts that teens will push their limits as far as possible.

As more and more teens live relatively unguided and even unrestricted lives, young people with values have a difficult time. Cheryl had been trained well. Her values were clearly taught, and she wanted to become a productive student. Her future plans were mapped out. Her friends, however, moved ever more rapidly onto the fast track. All-night parties complete with beer and wine, marijuana, and sexual exploits became increasingly their focus. Cheryl tried to keep her values, but she just couldn't seem to avoid joining her peers. Her parents caught her several times doing sneaky things that were far more risky than she wanted to believe.

Against her bitterly cynical protests, they finally grounded her, refused to allow her to be with certain friends, and supervised her closely. She was angry for a few days but soon realized the direction she had been headed was a spiral into trouble. Watchful, protective mothering can save most children from disaster.

Finally, the confusion over methods of child rearing makes it most difficult for mothers. They really do their best, but they just don't know! In trying to be fair, they become manipulated by energetic kids who want their way. In wanting their children to have advantages similar to their peers, they spoil them, giving them too many things and privileges and too little guidance and discipline. In wanting to believe the best of their children, they overlook signs of serious trouble. In short, these mothers operate by the "if you don't know what to do, do nothing" principle. That is not safe!

Stephanie couldn't believe what she heard her son saying to her. She had simply told him to go to his room and do his homework, and he retorted with intolerable language and rudeness. At first she yelled at him, trying to correct him and gain control. A young adolescent, however, can yell more loudly than Mom!

After a period of shouting at each other, both mother and son broke into tears and hugged each other. Stephanie began to really hear her son as he poured out his feelings. How could he study when he was so upset about a long list of adolescent problems? As she pondered the issues at stake, she realized that she, unwittingly, was on the list. She had been too busy.

Several weeks later, I chatted with Stephanie, and she excitedly told about the dramatic turnaround in her son's life. His grades were up, sports were again going well, friends were abundant, and his attitude was transformed.

"How," I asked, "did these great changes occur?" There was a brief pause, and Stephanie's gray eyes glistened with unshed tears. "I think," she stated simply, "his mother finally got her priorities straightened out!" She found the will to put her son ahead of all other interests and activities in her life. And it paid off.

Keep your eyes open, your suspicion level high enough to detect early warning signs, and your protective, tough love ready to set limits. Like Cheryl's parents, catch problems when they can't be denied, but before they reach cataclysmic proportions. And like Stephanie, put your child high on your list of priorities.

SHOWING PREFERENCES

We've already discussed sibling rivalry and the fact that parents showing a preference for one child over another may cause it. There is another, subtler type of partiality: neglecting your husband to be with your children. Parents never set out intending to make mistakes. Being separated by their children is the last thing they imagine could happen. Most parents, in fact, believe a baby should be a wonderful bond, holding a marriage together.

Earlier, I used the example of a couple who separated in midlife. But the beginning of their separation was the birth of their child. As Mother devoted herself more and more to the baby, Dad felt left out and used only for his paycheck. He didn't want to resent his son, so he lost himself in his work, leaving his wife to resort even more to enjoying the child. The cycle was long, but it was strong and eventually broke the marriage.

Both spouses were responsible. Your children need both parents, together, loving and respecting each other, so don't be partial to your children.

YOU'RE A MOTHER, NOT A SISTER

Leigh Ann had grown up with a doting but strict and controlling mother. Her mother believed she was always right, and Leigh Ann had allowed her to continue to control her life too much. When her own children arrived, she determined to be a different sort of mom. She played with them, took them out to dinner, and shared with them her makeup and costume jewelry. Without realizing it, Leigh Ann became much more a big sister than a mother.

Leigh Ann's mom's parenting had been strict, and she had high expectations for obedience. Overall, however, her relationship with her child emerged in adolescence as one power struggle after another. Leigh Ann's mother had usually won the battles between them for control. Leigh Ann's unconscious habit was to disagree down deep but to give in on the surface. Her energetic, strong-willed child easily slipped into this tug-of-war with her, just as she had done with her mother, only this time the child won—but lost!

Occasionally, a mother relives her life through her teenage children. Mom might have had a deprived youth, so she enjoys giving her children opportunities she never experienced. She tries, however, to enter into those activities as if she were a teenager again. Or she might have had a rich and wonderful adolescence, and she wants to relive it through the children. She sits with her teenage child's friends, enters into their every conversation, dresses and talks as they do, and even flirts with the young men.

From either extreme, a role aberration may develop that is damaging to the teenagers and the mother's relationship with them. Remember that teenagers need to become independent. To do so, they must separate from you as a parent, and that individuation process is interrupted by your attempt to join them.

The perfect solution is for you to gradually relinquish your mother role and slowly develop a friendship with your teen. In this transition, you will serve as adviser, confidante, supporter, and, occasionally, protective or tough-loving parent. You won't always hit the perfect balance, but your children will know you're trying.

PLAYING THE PLEASE-ME GAME

I can vividly recall my childhood struggles with my mother. The hurts we gave and resentments we felt with each other were frequent and severe for long periods of time. Remembering all that, I worked overtime to please my children and keep our relationships as pleasant as possible. I didn't always succeed, you must understand! But even trying to do so created problems and was a mistake as serious as my mother's excessive expectations.

I became too permissive at times. I went to extremes to make their lives happy. Even when it meant heroic sacrifice, I would take them where they wanted to go.

> *When you work to gain children's approval, you set them up to be the bosses, and you become the servant. Remember, your children aren't God!*

When you work to gain children's approval (which is really what you do when you try to please them), you set them up to be the bosses, and you become the servant. It's one thing to become a servant for God—that's biblical.

But your children aren't God! And allowing them to treat you as a servant, laying on you excessive demands in a rude and imperious manner, makes them lose respect for you.

At seventeen, Clint dropped out of school, refused to look for a job, treated his mother like a servant, and demanded money and the family car whenever he wanted either. Mother became convinced of a fallacious concept: if only she could give him enough and do everything he wanted, he would be so grateful and so convinced of her love, he would be motivated to give in return. She thought that if she just tried harder to please Clint, he would finally want to please her by going back to school.

Instead, Clint felt more and more guilty. If he just pushed Mom far enough, surely she would finally stop being so nice, and would establish discipline and restrictions. He lacked the willpower to stop himself in his search for ease and pleasure. Vaguely, he understood what he needed, but he resisted Mother's feeble, occasional attempts to change and could always manipulate her to give in. Basically, no one was really pleased, but on the surface he would seem happy, so Mom continued to give in.

Most child experts agree that pampering and indulging children are sure ways to ruin them. When you try to keep a baby happy by always giving in to him, you will gain a two-year-old tyrant who can abuse you. Trying to please your children so they will always love you or be happy or oblige you by being "nice" in return doesn't work. Take my word for it! It's extremely hard to reverse the spoiling process. You will suffer great heartache if your child becomes like Clint in adolescence.

Refusing to indulge and spoil your children, however, needs to be balanced by finding pleasure in their joy. If you love anyone, you will get to know that person's likes, dislikes, interests, and skills. Because you love that person, you are interested in his preferences and activities. You concern yourself with her hurts and worries. And so it is with a good mother. You will prepare the meals, for example, not only to be healthy but also to appeal to your child's likes and dislikes within reason. On appropriate occasions, you will select gifts that you know she will enjoy and value. You will, in short, show your goodwill by doing loving and thoughtful acts, and you'll find great pleasure in doing so.

The crucial point is this: you do those things not to get your child to like you or give back anything to you; you do those things that you love to do and that are good for your child. This may sound like a subtle difference, but believe me, it's a powerful one! You will often need to refuse a privilege or an item your child wants. When you know it is not good for her, you can easily say no. And if she gets angry, you can take that and even help her learn to control such anger. Your challenge is to discover what is in your child's best interest, and that becomes the best expression of your love.

BEING A MARTYR

Some mothers, I think, try to control their children through being hurt. Nothing bothers a child like seeing his mother in tears except knowing that he drove her to those tears. Since such martyrish behavior often brings children into compliance, mothers get fixed in the habit.

Natalie grew up with a martyrish mother. As an adult, Natalie experienced crippling depression. She could hardly force a smile on her somber face and couldn't recall when she had last really laughed.

We looked at her habits and those early events that had molded them. Nat quickly recalled a recurring interaction that involved her mother. When Natalie would do anything that displeased her mom, she knew this sequence would invariably take place: First, her mother sent her to her room, where she sat dreading the next segment. At some point, Mother would come to her room, sit sedately on her bed, and begin to lecture. Her eyes would fill with tears of disappointment over her daughter's imperfections. Shortly, the lecture would increase in intensity and usually would include how God Himself must feel over her misdemeanor.

> *When your child is at fault, you need to be kind enough to help him admit his fault but tough enough to help him learn a lesson from the experience.*

The most difficult event in the progression of Nat's "correction" was the last segment. After the tears, Nat could expect an extended period of silence from her mother. For at least a day, and often several days, her mother would not talk, moped around the house, looked sad, and often shed silent tears. Much as she hated the lectures, the silent treatment was far more unbearable to Natalie. As an adolescent, she finally began to ignore her mother's actions. The soggy weapon of her tears no longer served its purpose and became a source of disrespect and resentment. Yet the guilt, fear, and anger generated by the countless times her mother inflicted this pain led to much of Natalie's adult depression.

Sooner or later, children get tired of the tears. They may even believe that you deliberately turn them on to manipulate them, and perhaps you have! Learn to control your tears. Certainly, when you are in a time of real grief, you will cry. But save your tears for real sadness, and don't use them to influence your children to feel sorry for you or give in to you.

The best way to get over martyrish behavior is to use the steps listed for coping with anger. Think about how you are feeling—tired, helpless, even abused. What do you need to take care of those feelings—a little rest, a willingness to take control, a friend to support and encourage you? Think about how you can see to it that those needs are met. You have a great deal more power than you may believe. Use it to make wise decisions, take positive action, and select good feelings.

FINDING NO FAULTS

I sat in a school administrator's office with an angry teen and his parents. He had a long history of fighting with peers and had made some frightening threats against certain teachers. After a period of doing well, he had back-slidden badly, and everyone was concerned—except his parents.

Again and again, they deflected their son's serious problems to the school, to his friends, to society in general. But they refused to see that his problem behavior was really his own.

> *When your child is telling the truth or has been unfairly treated, you need to be his ally.*

They certainly loved him and really wanted him to do right. However, their efforts to deny his responsibility, and even theirs, resulted in the young man's belief that he could do no wrong. Until he learned to be honest with himself, he would have no reason to master the difficult tasks of gaining self-control and honesty and becoming productive. It was almost impossible for him to possess the quality of honesty until his parents confronted him directly and stopped blaming others.

The opposite extreme is equally damaging. Parents sometimes believe the worst about a child and are ready to punish severely or simply to write her off. When a child has no ally, she will find one, and all too often the ones she finds are in equally dire straits.

A boy with whom I have worked for some time found an ally in his father. He adjusted as a borderline boy—sometimes doing well but occasionally misbehaving. One day he was caught in school with a large hunting knife, a serious offense. His story was that a classmate brought it to school and was showing it off. When my young friend's turn came to admire and hold it, the classmate called it to the attention of the teacher. What a predicament! His past reputation made it possible that he was not the owner of the knife but also possible that he denied ownership to get out of trouble.

Finally, the principal called the boy's father. He carefully examined first his son and then the knife. He knew the knife was not his or his son's, and he knew his son well enough to know that this time he was telling the truth. The father had the opportunity to help his son turn a corner, and for the first time in years the two were drawn together.

When your child is telling the truth or has been unfairly treated, you need to be an ally, a champion. When she is at fault, however, you need to be kind enough to help her admit her fault but tough enough to help her learn the necessary lesson.

LISTENING TO TOO MANY ADVISERS

I asked a friend what she believed to be her biggest mistakes as a mother. After extensive thinking, she stated that she asked too many people for advice and then tried to follow all of it.

One of her children had a prolonged period of bed-wetting. Denise had expected the children to wet their beds up to the age of three or four, but by age six, she knew that the majority of children could stay dry most nights.

Several friends had no answers for Denise, or their children had finally outgrown that annoying habit. At last a friend told her to try spanking her daughter whenever she wet the bed. The secret, her friend told her, was being consistent. The friend advised her to spank her child every time she wet the bed.

Though she hated spanking her child, Denise was desperate. At least spanking was a specific action she could take. She felt she would be doing something to correct the problem. So night after night, Denise spanked her bedraggled, sleepy child, only to find the problem growing worse. At last, Denise gave up the spankings. She admitted to her child that she had been wrong and assured her she would not spank her again. When the child was ready to stop wetting her bed, she was to let Mother know, and together they would devise a plan that could work. And that was just what they did.

It's always fine to ask advice from others, but carefully sift it through your values and common sense. If you believe a certain idea is workable, won't damage you or your child, and may solve a problem, try it. But avoid impulsive actions used out of desperation that could actually be abusive.

IF YOU'RE GOING TO DO IT, DON'T DO IT HERE!

Marty decided he was going to smoke. He felt too small in comparison to his classmates and ached at their nicknames of Shrimpie and Peewee. If he could learn to curse a little, swagger as he walked, and smoke at the bus stop, he figured his "friends" would respect him.

His mother found the cigarettes and smelled the telltale odor on his breath and clothes. She chided him and asked him to stop before the habit became too difficult to break. Marty, soon to be thirteen, however, had found that his suppositions were correct. He saw a new sense of respect and even awe as his peers noticed his growing toughness.

The more his mother pleaded with him to stop smoking, the more determined he became. He was enjoying his macho image, and giving in to his mother would be risking what he thought he needed.

In desperation, Marty's mother shouted one day, "Son, if you're going to smoke, for goodness' sake, don't do it here in my house!" Understandable as her feeling of helplessness was, it gave Marty just the out he needed. He wouldn't smoke at home, but it must be okay to smoke elsewhere. So he saved the habit to be practiced with his peers, and he spent more and more of his time with them.

Good parents with the best of intentions may say, "Don't let me see you do that again!" or "Don't let me hear you say such bad words around here!" Do you see, however, what any clever child will quickly decide? "Okay, Mom, not around here, but in my own places I will."

Watch your edicts. State carefully, "Son, I love you too much to let you risk your health! We're going to figure out why you think smoking [or swearing or drinking] is good for you. And together we'll find a better way to meet your needs." Love will find a way—perhaps with professional help, but relentlessly, it will search and win.

DO AS I SAY, NOT AS I DO!

Twelve-year-old Dale and his parents were in my office every week. They struggled to learn why he was hitting classmates and swearing at his teacher. The parents were courteous, and they had tried to teach Dale and his brother good manners and proper behaviors.

One eventful day, Dale seemed unusually fidgety. He had endured another suspension from school and the inevitable lecture and grounding from his father. He was so frustrated that he had used some bad language the neighbors had overheard.

As his father angrily confronted his son, I saw Dale's courage mounting. Finally, he blurted out, "But, Dad, those are the words you use all the time when you're working in the basement and something goes wrong!

If you can say 'em, why can't I?" Dad became embarrassed and flustered, and his gaze focused carefully on the floor.

Then, to my amazement, this basically good man became defensive and angry: "Son, I'm not a kid anymore, and I can do as I please. You'd better learn to do as I say and not care what I do. That's my business!"

If life were that simple, children could grow up being good little robots. But it just won't work. Children know the truth of what a well-known philosopher wrote: "Your actions speak so loudly, I cannot hear what you say!" Don't make the mistake of believing that you can practice bad health habits, lose your temper, or show dishonesty while you expect the opposite from your children. You can't fool them, and they will copy your practices, not hearing what you say.

Make your life congruent so that your language, your behavior, and your feelings all say the same thing. And please, let your messages be positive!

"YES, BUT . . ."

Callie's mother was tactful. She always acknowledged her daughter's efforts, but somehow, Callie knew, they weren't good enough. For weeks, she had tried to set the dinner table perfectly but without success. The knife wasn't straight enough, or the spoon somehow got between the knife and the plate rather than outside. The napkins should be folded just right and laid under the fork, not on the plates. And the glass must go just at the tip of the knife, not on either side.

One evening, with infinite care, Callie made certain every item was exactly right. *At last,* she thought, *Mom will be so proud of me!* She could hardly believe, then, what she heard as she proudly showed her table to her mother. "Well, finally, Callie! Why couldn't you have done this sort of job before?" Callie decided then that she would never experience her mother's simple, honest pride in her work.

I hear many parents say, "That's pretty good, Son, but . . . ," and some critical comment follows that neutralizes the praise. Praise needs to be earned, but it needs to be separate from criticism. And praise is essential to all children's well-being.

If you are bent on teaching your child standards of excellence, I commend you. Doing outstanding work teaches confidence and self-esteem. Just remember to encourage and work with your child until you are satisfied that he has done the best he can do. Then, and only then, applaud him. Give him your unqualified compliments, uncontaminated with "buts"!

DON'T CRY; IT WON'T HURT!

Mothers make many mistakes regarding medical aspects of child care. One of the worst is a sort of dishonesty. All children require shots, unpleasant procedures to diagnose illnesses, and horrible medicines to cure them. Present-day scientific medicine is inevitably going to cause pain. Even when I was a child, a common belief was that any medicine worth its price had to taste terrible. In fact, the worse it tasted, the more effective it surely must be.

> *Praise and encouragement are essential to children's well-being.*

True or not, I'm glad my mother didn't lie to me about the doctor's treatments. She would straightforwardly tell me the procedure would hurt, the medicine would taste awful, and I would feel lousy for a while. All of her statements were true. And I found some degree of courage to cope because I was prepared for them.

Many times, when I practiced pediatrics, I overheard well-intentioned moms saying, "Don't cry, June! The shot is just a little pinprick. It won't hurt!" So when it did hurt (badly!), the child cried doubly hard for the pain and again for the deception! Don't underestimate your children. They can deal with more than you may think they can. But don't mislead them by minimizing the trauma. Don't make yourself look foolish by telling a child crying over a sprained ankle or a scraped knee, "Now, Johnny, stop crying! It can't hurt that bad!" That comment will prompt Johnny to cry even harder to prove how very much it does hurt.

It will work far better to say, "Johnny, I know that scrape hurts terribly. But I also know you are a very brave boy. So if you will use your breath to blow on it while I clean and dress it for you, it will feel better faster."

Let me add that you must avoid too much pity. If you show grave concern and sympathize too much, your child can learn to exaggerate pain to gain attention. Once more, look for the balance—be truthful about the pain, understand the tears and dread,

> *Be honest with your child. If he has to have a shot, don't tell him it won't hurt. If she has to take medicine that tastes awful, don't tell her that it tastes good. Your child needs to be able to trust what you say.*

but predict the best. Describe your child's courage, and let her know you will stand by to reinforce that and help her through difficulties. Honesty is, indeed, the best policy.

FAILING TO LET GO

Marna's brown curls were generously sprinkled with gray, and her sparkling eyes were full of confusion as we talked. "Is it wrong," she asked, "for my children to still live at home?" That simple question, I guessed, had a long history attached, so I settled my thoughts to focus on her family matters.

Her older daughter's marriage had been troubled. Both she and her husband had spent time in drug and alcohol rehabilitation, and their son, now age three, was living proof of the scars their addiction had inflicted. Both Marna's daughter and son-in-law were finally employed at minimally paying jobs. Perhaps they could now become successful adults.

An older son also lived with these middle-aged parents. He worked, but had never married and seemed content to be with his parents. He contributed to the family expenses and seemed to feel that made him independent.

As the story of Marna's family unfolded, almost like a home movie of significant events, I learned some answers to her original question. Yes, Marna, it is wrong for your grown children to take advantage of you and your husband, Marvin.

Your children can become healthy adults only when you nudge them out of the safety and comfort of the nest.

Your daughter realized that you felt guilty for working during her early years. She even took advantage of that guilt to manipulate you into being too easy on her, giving her too many privileges that she hadn't really earned. She chose an equally irresponsible husband who found it easy, even if a bit embarrassing, to live on your generosity.

Your son, Marna, also feels safe at home. Although he makes a modest contribution to the family finances, he enjoys being waited on and loves your catering to his likes in meals and laundry service. He doesn't have to take risks, make many commitments, or assume much adult responsibility.

Furthermore, Marvin has little of your time or attention. He has always supported your dedication to the children, but silently and wistfully, he has yearned for the time when the two of you could enjoy each other. He'd like some privacy, and he's earned the right to the morning newspaper and the TV channel he prefers for the evening news.

All these facts and feelings I sifted from our conversation, and as I handed them back to Marna, I tried to help her see them as the gems of wisdom they are. It was painful for her to receive them, and I may never know if she actually used them to rectify her family problems, but I hope so.

It is often necessary and useful to be that safe harbor for adult children for short times. But allowing them to stay for indefinite periods is more damaging than helpful. As life expectancy lengthens, the time for marriages to be full of the richness of years together is extended. Both Marna and Marvin deserve to rediscover their honeymoon spirit and enjoy their own pursuits and some quietness.

Grown children can never explore and realize their full potential until they experience complete independence. And their being away and returning enhances the enjoyment of grandchildren. Your children can become healthy adults only when you nudge them out of the safety and comfort of the nest.

Yes, Marna, it is wrong for your adult children to still live at home. It is a mistake to allow it. So, find the courage to ease out your child "boarders." Take your time, and do it your way, but do it! Once the pain of separation is over, you will be able to enjoy each other in new ways you wouldn't have thought possible.

HEALING THE HURTS

You've made mistakes. Your children might have run away, used drugs, acted out sexually, or tried to skip school. You feel terribly guilty and helpless. You may believe there is no hope of any healthy change, ever.

Let me tell you that is not true! There is plenty of hope if you are willing to assume some of the fault and make restitution. If this process is not entirely dependent on prayer, it is largely so. I trust that your spiritual life is enough in tune to enable you to seek God's guidance and power to see you through the process of change required to mend your mistakes.

Face the need for change. (You have probably already taken this step.) Seek the permission to change. Most of us rely on the habits we learned from our parents. Unconsciously, we still believe our old ways are right and we must do things that way. But you *can* be different from someone as powerful to you as your parents once were.

Establish a plan for change. Most major changes demand breaking old habits and establishing new ones. That task demands careful planning.

Seek an ally. Just as your child needs a champion, so will you. Choose a friend, a trusted relative, or perhaps a professional counselor who can coach and encourage you when you think this new plan will never work. God will be your very best resource if you let Him.

Stick with the plan. Many people quit too soon, and that is certainly tempting. No matter how you feel, stick with the plan.

We have already worked on the cure for guilt and the power of forgiving. Let me repeat, you must forgive yourself, your husband, your children, and probably your parents if you are to be free to find reconciliation. And you will need to seek forgiveness from them. Don't be afraid to admit your mistakes. Your children know them better than you do, and they will respect you even more for confessing them.

Tell your children about your childhood, both the good and the not-so-good events. Knowing your mistakes can help them avoid repeating those and will enable them to see you as a real human being. Tell them as much as you can about their grandparents. In doing so, you may remember events that will help you understand and forgive their mistakes.

When you can do so honestly, tell your children good things about themselves. Let them know the cute, funny events of their infancy. Remind them of their first day in school, the spring track meets in which they took part, or the school play in which they did well. Even if their events were not great successes, comment on their efforts and your pride. Build for them a set of positive memories that will repair the weak areas of their self-esteem and give them hope for the future.

If your children are grown, tell them positive things about their spouses, and let them know how great their children are. Avoid pointing out their faults, but encourage their strengths in a credible way. Seek their advice at times, but don't become an undue burden on them. As long as possible, plan to stay independent, and make plans far in advance for the months or years when you may not be able to care for yourself.

Constantly build a loving relationship with your family; take daily inventory of the statements you make and the actions you live. I have a philosophy of trying to be at peace with everyone I know before I retire at night. If I owe an apology, I write a letter, make a phone call, or set a time for a personal visit. I try to understand the mistakes that others or I have made that day and forgive them and myself, as well as ask God's blessing.

Ultimately, you may not be able to mend all the mistakes of your past. Sometimes others choose to stay unforgiving and angry. If you have done everything you know how to do, just as I did so long ago in my childhood, you can place both your efforts and your failures in God's hands. He can do what you may never be able to do. Count on that, and rest in Him!

Conclusion

I hope you have gained insights into yourself and your mothering from reading this book. I trust you will recapture some of your childhood experiences and use the memories to reduce the mistakes and hurts for your children, but most of all, I hope you will know the healing power of love and forgiving.

As you learn to love and accept yourself unconditionally, you will more readily accept your children, your husband, and all the significant people in your world. Surely, the more you love, the easier it will be to develop successful patterns of mothering. In all ages and stages of life, you can become a key to unlock the potential for good in the lives you touch. That is my prayer for you!

Suggested Reading

Books for Adolescents

Ages 6 to 8

Where Do Babies Come From? (rev. edition) Ruth S. Hummel. St. Louis: Concordia Publishing House, 1998.

Ages 9 to 14

How You Are Changing, Jane Graver, Book 3, Learning About Sex Series. St. Louis: Concordia Publishing House, 1998. (This book speaks with understanding about changes encountered in adolescence. A delicate explanation of the physiological aspects of sexuality with a positive Christian perspective to help children develop a healthy, responsible view of God's gift.)

My Body, My Self for Boys: A "What's Happening to My Body?" Quiz Book and Journal, Second Edition, Lynda Madaras. New York: New Market Press, 2000.

My Body, My Self for Girls: A "What's Happening to My Body?" Quiz Book and Journal, Second Edition, Lynda Madaras. New York: Newmarket Press, 2000.

Sex and the New You, Rich Bimler, Book 4, Learning About Sex Series. St. Louis: Concordia Publishing House, 1998. (A sound explanation of the basic facts of sexuality: becoming a woman, becoming a man, sexual intercourse, conception, and birth. Also answers questions about pornography, sexual experimentation, venereal disease, unmarried and pregnant, homosexuality.)

The Care and Keeping of You: The Body Book for Girls, Valorie Lee Schaefer, Middleton, Wisconsin: Pleasant Company Publications, 1998.

The What's Happening to My Body? Book for Boys: A Growing Up Guide for Parents and Sons, Third Edition, Lynda Madaras. New York: Newmarket Press, 2000.

The What's Happening to My Body? Book for Girls: A Growing Up Guide for Parents and Daughters, Third Edition, Lynda Madaras. New York: Newmarket Press, 2000.

Ages 15 to 19

Changing Bodies, Changing Lives: A Book for Teens on Sex and Relationships, Third Edition, Ruth Bell. New York: Times Books, 1998.

Love, Sex, and God, Bill Ameiss and Jane Graver, Book 5, Learning About Sex Series. St. Louis: Concordia Publishing House, 1998. (The authors confront cruel myths that often mislead teens regarding drugs, alcohol, and venereal diseases; includes biblical guides.)

Preparing for Adolescence, Updated Edition, James C. Dobson. Ventura, California: Regal Books, 1999. (Speaks to adolescents about such topics as drug abuse, sex, family conflict, friendship, love and conformity.)

PARENTS' GUIDES

How to Talk Confidently with Your Child About Sex, Lenore Buth, Book 6, Learning About Sex Series. St. Louis: Concordia Publishing House, 1998. (Helps parents to be confident in their own sexuality and to lay a solid foundation for their children.)

Sex Respect: The Option of True Sexual Freedom, Coleen Kelly Mast. Bradley, Illinois.: Respect, Inc., 1986. (This curriculum was developed under a grant by the U.S. Department of Health and Human Services. Manuals available for students, teachers, and parents. Topics for the classroom include: sexual freedom vs. sexual impulsiveness, aspects of human sexuality, consequences of teenage sexual activity, dating guidelines, how to say no, secondary virginity, and mature love. The course features ample material for ten hours of classroom time. For more information, contact: Respect Inc., P.O. Box 349, Bradley, IL 60915-0349, Phone: 815-932-8389; Web site: www.sexrespect.com.)

Sexuality, Commitment, and Family, developed by Teen-Aid, Inc., under the direction of Steve Potter and Nancy Roach. (Curriculum explores these topics: friendship and dating, experiencing love, reproduction, marriage, fetal development and childbirth, parenting, the family unit, consequences of adolescent sexual activity, advantages of abstinence, the media, peer pressure, and communication skills. Requires 13 to 15 periods of classroom time and features a take-home paper to encourage discussion between parents and teens. For more information, contact: Teen-Aid, Inc., 723 E. Jackson, Spokane, WA 99207, Phone: 509-482-2868; Web site: www.teen-aid.org.)

BOOKS FOR PARENTS

The Five Love Languages of Children, Gary D. Chapman and Ross Campbell, M.D. Northfield Publications, 1997. (According to the authors, each child expresses and receives love through one of five communication styles. With the help of this book, parents can discover their child's primary "love language" and learn what they can do to communicate with their child in the language he or she best understands.)

The Five Love Languages of Teenagers, Gary D. Chapman, Northfield Publications, 2000. (Practical guidance on how to discover your teen's primary love language—the way he or she will best receive love—and how to express it to him or her. A tangible resource for stemming the tide of violence, immorality, and despair engulfing many teens today.)

How to Really Love Your Teenager, Ross Campbell, M.D. Chariot Victor Books, 1993. (Practical suggestions for parenting based on sound biblical teaching. Includes chapters on parental self-control and dealing with teenage anger.)

Index